All-in-One
Student Workbook
Version A

Prentice Hall

Accelerated Grade 7
MATHEMATICS
Common Core

Taken from
Prentice Hall Mathematics, Course 2
All-in-One Student Workbook Version A, Common Core Edition
and
Prentice Hall Mathematics, Course 3
All-in-One Student Workbook Version A, Common Core Edition

PEARSON

Cover Art: Courtesy of Pearson Education, Inc.

Taken from:

Prentice Hall Mathematics Course 2: ALL-IN-ONE Student Workbook Version A and *Course 3: ALL-IN-ONE Student Workbook Version A*, Global Edition

Published by Prentice Hall
Upper Saddle River, New Jersey 07458

Pearson Learning Solutions, 501 Boylston Street, Suite 900, Boston, MA 02116
A Pearson Education Company
www.pearsoned.com

Printed in the United States of America

7 8 9 10 VOZN 18 17 16 15 14

000200010271778978

JK

ISBN 10: 1-269-42833-0
ISBN 13: 978-1-269-42833-0

Daily Notetaking Guide

Practice, Guided Problem Solving, Vocabulary

Chapter 1: Integers and Rational Numbers

Chapter 2: Exponents

Chapter 3: Equations

Chapter 4: Inequalities

Chapter 5: Ratios, Rates, and Proportions

Chapter 6: Percents

Chapter 7: Introduction to Functions

Chapter 8: Analyzing Data

Chapter 9: Probability

Chapter 10: Geometry and Area

Chapter 11: Geometry Continued

Chapter 12: Surface Area and Volume

Chapter 13: Transformations

Appendix: The Pythagorean Theorem

Daily Notetaking Guide

A Note to the Student:

This section of your workbook contains notetaking pages for each lesson in your student edition. They are structured to help you take effective notes in class. They will also serve as a study guide as you prepare for tests and quizzes.

Name ______________________ Class ______________ Date ______________

Lesson 1-1

Comparing and Ordering Integers

Lesson Objective	Common Core Standard
To compare and order integers and to find and add opposites	The Number System: 7.NS.1.b

Vocabulary

Integers are ____

____

____

Two numbers are opposites if ____

____

____

Example

1 Finding an Opposite Find the opposite of 2.

The opposite of 2 is ☐, because 2 and ☐ are each ☐ units from ☐, but in ☐ directions.

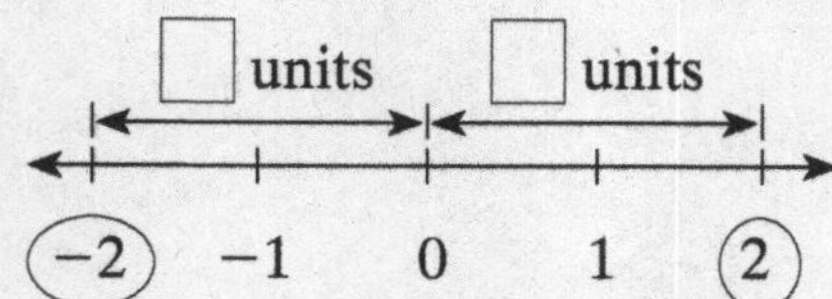

Quick Check

1. Find the opposite of each number.

a. −8 **b.** 13 **c.** −22

Name ______________________ Class ______________ Date ______________

Examples

❷ Adding Opposites What is the sum of −5 plus 5?

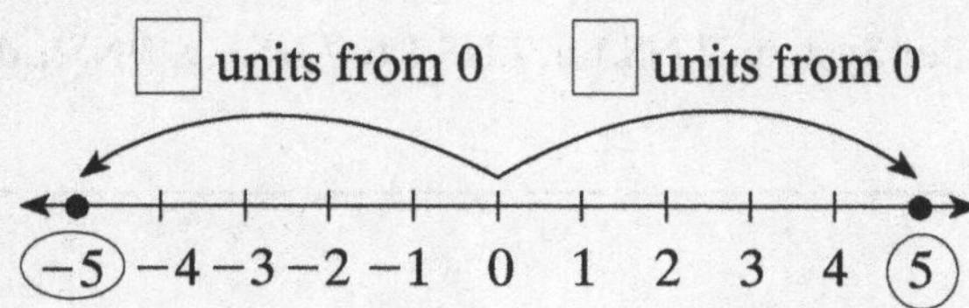

−5 and ☐ are ☐, so they are additive inverses.

The sum of additive inverses is always ☐.

−5 + 5 = ☐

❸ Comparing Integers Compare 3 and −8 using <, =, or >.

−8 is ☐ units to the left of 0. 3 is ☐ units to the right of 0.

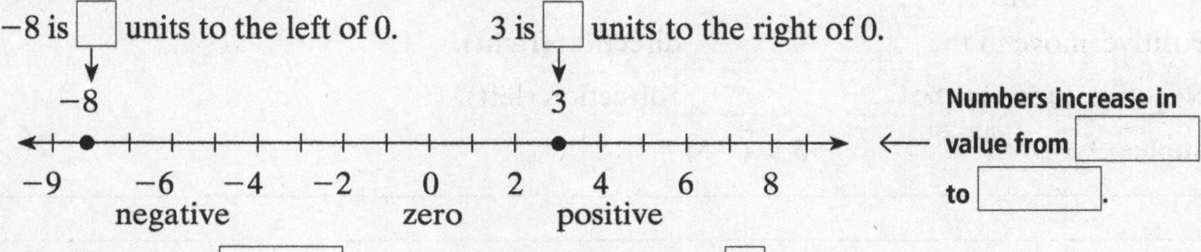

Since 3 is to the ☐ of −8 on the number line, 3 ☐ −8.

Quick Check

2. Find the sum.

a. 8 + −8 ☐

b. 3 + 3 ☐

c. −5 + 5 ☐

3. Compare −8 and −2 using <, =, or >.

☐

Name ____________________ Class ____________ Date ____________

Lesson 1-2

Adding and Subtracting Integers

Lesson Objective	Common Core Standards
To add and subtract integers and to solve problems involving integers	The Number System: 7.NS.1.a, 7.NS.1.b, 7.NS.1.c, 7.NS.1.d

Vocabulary and Key Concepts

Adding Integers

Start at zero. Move to the first integer. Find the ______ of the second integer and move that distance.

If the second integer is

- Positive: move in the ______ direction (right).
- Negative: move in the ______ direction (left).

Examples $3 + 5 =$ ______ $-3 + (-5) =$ ______

Subtracting Integers

To subtract an integer, add its ______.

Examples $3 - 5 = 3 + ($ ______ $) =$ ______ $-3 - 5 = -3 + ($ ______ $) =$ ______

Two numbers are additive inverses if ____

____

Example

1 Adding Integers With a Number Line Use a number line to find the sum $-4 + (-2)$.

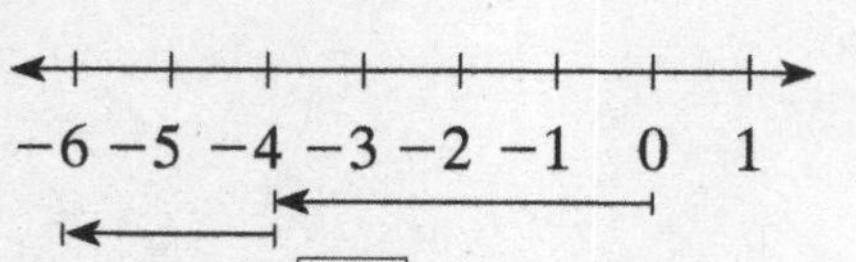

Start at ______**. Move 4 units** ______**.**

Then move another 2 units ______**.**

The sum is ______.

Quick Check

1. Use a number line to find each sum.

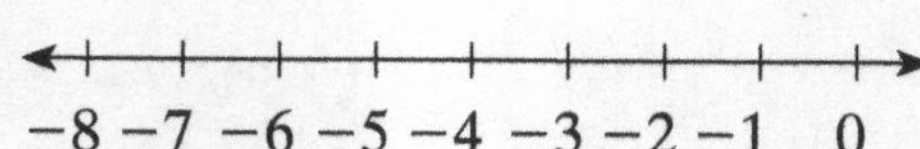

a. $-8 + 1$ ______

b. $-1 + (-7)$ ______

c. $-6 + 6$ ______

Name ____________ Class ____________ Date ____________

Examples

2 Adding Integers Find $24 + (-6)$.

$|24| =$ ☐ and $|-6| =$ ☐ ← **Find the absolute value of each integer.**

$24 -$ ☐ $=$ ☐ ← **Subtract ☐ from 24 because $|-6|$ ☐ $|24|$.**

$24 + (-6) =$ ☐ ← **The sum has the same sign as ☐.**

3 Subtracting Integers Find $-7 - 2$.

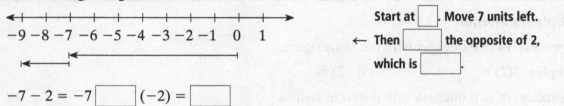

−9 −8 −7 −6 −5 −4 −3 −2 −1 0 1

Start at ☐. Move 7 units left.

← **Then ☐ the opposite of 2, which is ☐.**

$-7 - 2 = -7$ ☐ $(-2) =$ ☐

4 Application: Weather Recorded temperatures at Amundsen-Scott Station in Antarctica have ranged from a low of -89°F to a high of -13°F. Find the difference in temperatures.

Subtract to find the difference.

$-13 - (-89) = -13 +$ ☐ ← **Add the ☐ of −89, which is ☐.**

$=$ ☐ ← **Simplify.**

The difference in temperatures is ☐.

Quick Check

2. Find each sum.

a. $-97 + (-65)$ **b.** $21 + (-39)$ **c.** $22 + (-22)$

3. Find $-6 - 1$.

4. During the biggest drop of the Mean Streak roller coaster in Ohio, your altitude changes by -155 ft. The Texas Giant™ in Texas has a -137 ft change. How much farther do you drop on the Mean Streak?

Name ____________________ Class ____________ Date ____________

Lesson 1-3

Multiplying and Dividing Integers

Lesson Objective	Common Core Standards
To multiply and divide integers and to solve problems involving integers	The Number System: 7.NS.2, 7.NS.2.a, 7.NS.2.b

Key Concepts

Multiplying Integers

The product of two integers with the same sign is ____.

Examples $3(2) =$ ____ $\qquad -3(-2) =$ ____

The product of two integers with different signs is ____.

Examples $-3(2) =$ ____ $\qquad -3(-2) =$ ____

Dividing Integers

The quotient of two integers with the same sign is ____.

Examples $10 \div 2 =$ ____ $\qquad -10 \div (-2) =$ ____

The quotient of two integers with different signs is ____.

Examples $-10 \div 2 =$ ____ $\qquad -10 \div (-2) =$ ____

Example

1 Multiplying Integers Find each product.

a. $3(7) =$ ____ ← ____ **signs;** ____ **product.** → **b.** $-3(-7) =$ ____

c. $3(-7) =$ ____ ← ____ **signs;** ____ **product.** → **d.** $-3(7) =$ ____

Quick Check

1. Simplify the expression $-4(-7)$.

____

Name ______________________ Class ______________ Date ______________

Example

2 Dividing Integers You are riding your bicycle at a speed of 12 ft/s. Four seconds later, you come to a complete stop. Find the acceleration of your bicycle.

$$\text{acceleration} = \frac{\text{final velocity} - \text{initial velocity}}{\text{time}}$$

$$= \frac{\square - \square}{\square}$$ ← **Substitute ☐ for final velocity, ☐ for initial velocity, and ☐ for time.**

$$= \frac{\square}{\square} = \square$$ ← **Simplify. The ☐ sign means the bicycle is slowing.**

The bicycle's acceleration is ☐ ft/s per second.

Quick Check

2. Find the vertical speed of a climber who goes from an elevation of 8,120 feet to an elevation of 6,548 feet in three hours.

Name ____________________ Class ____________________ Date ____________________

Lesson 1-4

Fractions and Decimals

Lesson Objective	Common Core Standards
To convert between fractions and decimals	The Number System: 7.NS.2.d, 8.NS.1 Expressions and Equations: 7.EE.3

Vocabulary

A terminating decimal is ______________________________

____

A repeating decimal is ______________________________

____

Examples

1 Writing a Terminating Decimal The total amount of rainfall yesterday was reported as $\frac{1}{4}$ in. Write this fraction as a decimal.

$\frac{1}{4}$ or $1 \div 4 = 4\overline{)1.00}$ ← **quotient** [ ]

$-$[ ]

20

-20

0 ← **The remainder is 0.**

So $\frac{1}{4}$ = [ ]. The total amount of rainfall as a decimal is [ ] in.

2 Writing a Repeating Decimal Write $\frac{7}{15}$ as a decimal.

Method 1: Paper and Pencil

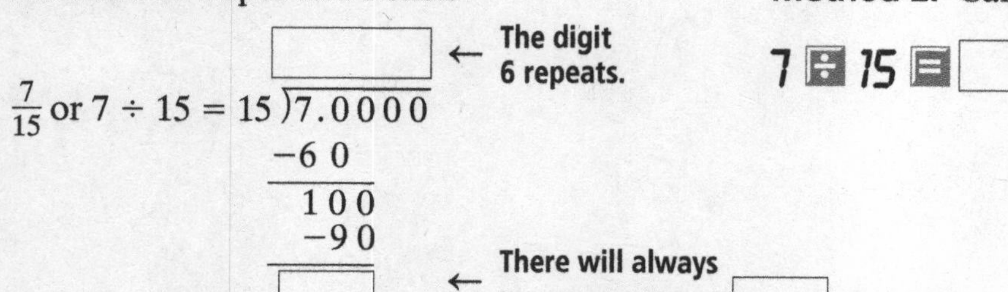

The digit 6 repeats.
$\frac{7}{15}$ or $7 \div 15 = 15\overline{)7.0000}$
-60
100
-90
There will always be a remainder of [ ].

Method 2: Calculator

7 ÷ 15 = [ ]

So $\frac{7}{15}$ = [ ].

Name ______________________ Class ______________ Date ______________

❸ Writing a Decimal as a Fraction Write 4.105 as a fraction in simplest form

Since $0.105 = \frac{105}{1000}$, $4.105 = \square\frac{\square}{\square}$.

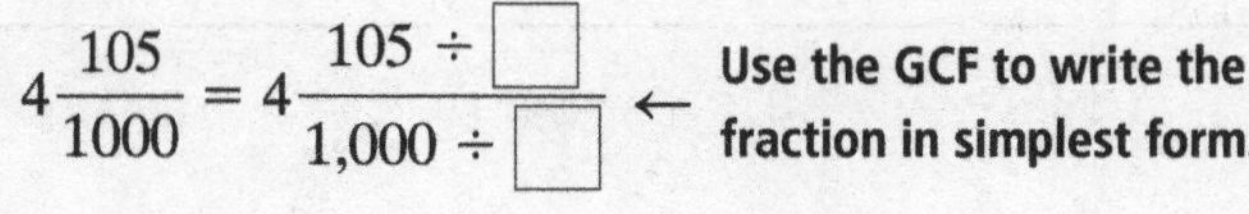

$4\frac{105}{1000} = 4\frac{105 \div \square}{1{,}000 \div \square}$ ← **Use the GCF to write the fraction in simplest form.**

$= \square\frac{\square}{\square}$

❹ Ordering Fractions and Decimals: Surveys In a survey of next year's seventh-grade students, 0.25 said they will come to school by bus, $\frac{5}{24}$ said they will walk, 0.375 said they will come in a car, and $\frac{1}{16}$ said they will ride their bicycles. Order the means of transportation from most used to least used.

walk $\frac{5}{24} = \square$

bicycles $\frac{1}{16} = \square$

← **Rewrite the fractions as decimals.**

Since 0.375 $\square$ 0.25 $\square$ 0.208 $\square$ 0.0625, the means of transportation are ______, ______, ______, and ______.

Quick Check

1. The fraction of nitrogen in a chemical sample is $\frac{5}{8}$. Write the fraction as a decimal.

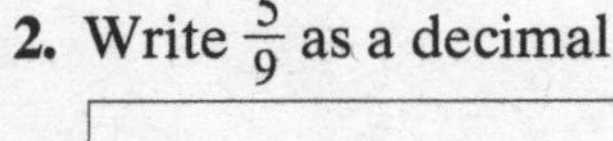

2. Write $\frac{5}{9}$ as a decimal.

3. Write each decimal as a mixed number in simplest form.

a. 1.364 **b.** 2.48 **c.** 3.6

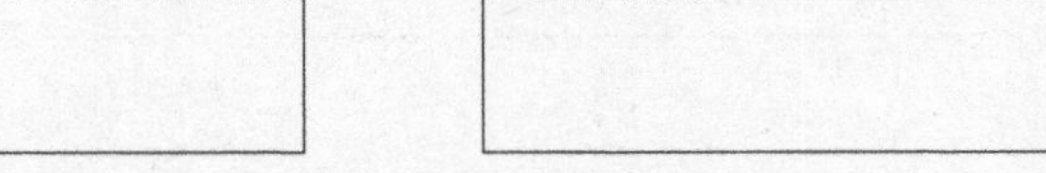

4. In a survey about pets, $\frac{2}{5}$ of the students prefer cats, 0.33 prefer dogs, $\frac{3}{25}$ prefer birds, and 0.15 prefer fish. List the choices in order of preference.

Name ______________________ Class ______________ Date ______________

Lesson 1-5

Rational Numbers

Lesson Objective	**Common Core Standards**
To compare and order rational numbers	The Number System 7.NS.2.b, 7.NS.2.d, 8.NS.1

Vocabulary

A rational number is ____

____

Example

1 Comparing Rational Numbers Compare $-\frac{1}{4}$ and $-\frac{3}{8}$.

Method 1

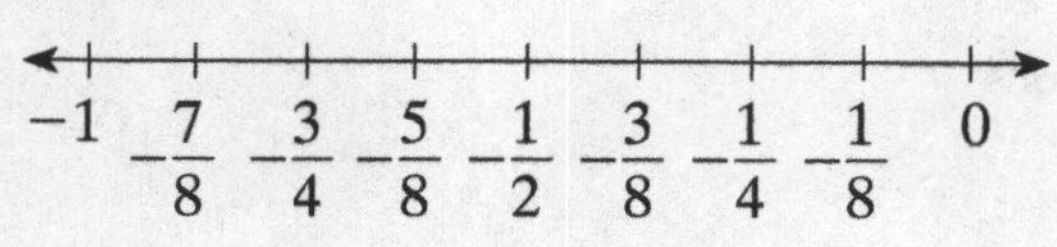

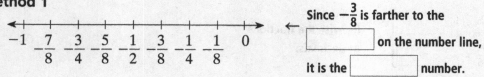

← **Since $-\frac{3}{8}$ is farther to the ☐ on the number line, it is the ☐ number.**

So, $-\frac{1}{4}$ ☐ $-\frac{3}{8}$.

Method 2

$-\frac{1}{4} = \frac{-1}{4}$ ← **Rewrite $-\frac{1}{4}$ with -1 in the numerator.**

$= \frac{-1 \times \square}{4 \times \square}$ ← **The LCD is ☐. Write an equivalent fraction.**

$= \frac{-2}{8} = -\frac{2}{8}$ ← **The fraction $\frac{-2}{8}$ is equivalent to $-\frac{2}{8}$.**

Since $-\frac{2}{8}$ ☐ $-\frac{3}{8}$, $-\frac{1}{4}$ ☐ $-\frac{3}{8}$.

Quick Check

1. Compare $-\frac{2}{3}$ and $-\frac{1}{6}$. Use <, = or >.

Name ______________________ Class ______________ Date ______________

Examples

❷ Comparing Decimals Compare. Use $<$, $=$, or $>$.

a. 8.7 and 8.1

8.7 ☐ 8.1 ← **Both numbers are positive. Compare the digits.**

b. −8.7 and 8.1

−8.7 ☐ 8.1 ← **Any negative number is less than a positive number.**

c. −8.7 and −8.1

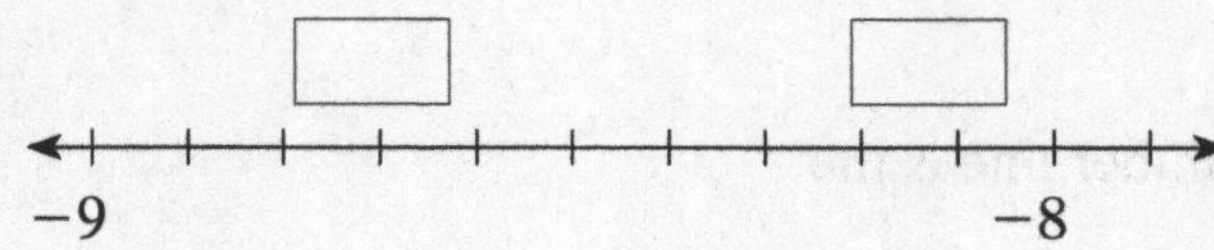

← **Place the decimals on a number line and compare their locations.**

−8.7 ☐ 8.1

❸ Ordering Rational Numbers Which list shows the numbers $-\frac{3}{5}$, 0.625, $\frac{2}{3}$, and −0.5 listed in order from least to greatest?

A. $-\frac{3}{5}, -0.5, 0.625, \frac{2}{3}$ **B.** $-0.5, -\frac{3}{5}, 0.625, \frac{2}{3}$ **C.** $-0.5, \frac{2}{3}, -\frac{3}{5}, 0.625$ **D.** $-\frac{3}{5}, \frac{2}{3}, 0.625, -0.5$

$-\frac{3}{5} = -3 \div 5 = -0.6$ ← **Write as a decimal.**

$\frac{2}{3} = 2 \div 3 = 0.66666\ldots = 0.\overline{6}$ ← **Write as a repeating decimal.**

−0.6 ☐ −0.5 ☐ 0.625 ☐ $0.\overline{6}$ ← **Compare the decimals.**

From least to greatest, the numbers are

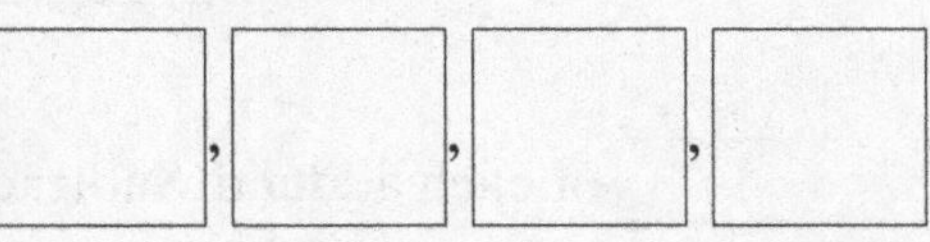

The correct answer is choice ☐.

Quick Check

2. Compare −4.2 and −4.9. Use $<$, $=$, or $>$.

3. The following temperatures were recorded during a science project: $12\frac{1}{2}$°C, −4°C, 6.55°C, and $-6\frac{1}{4}$°C. Order the temperatures from least to greatest.

Name ____________________ Class ____________________ Date ____________________

Lesson 1-6

Adding and Subtracting Rational Numbers

Lesson Objective	Common Core Standards
To add and subtract rational numbers	The Number System: 7.NS.1, 7.NS.1.b, 7.NS.1.c, 7.NS.1.d, 7.NS.3

Key Concepts

Distance on a Number Line

The distance between two numbers on a number line is the ____________________.

Example

1 Adding Rational Numbers

Same Sign

The sum of two positive rational numbers is ______.

The sum of two negative rational numbers is ______.

$1\frac{1}{2} + 2\frac{1}{4}$ ← **Both numbers are ______, so the sum is ______**

$-2.2 + (-1.5)$ ← **Both numbers are ______, so the sum is ______**

Different Sign

Find the ______ of each addend. Subtract the ______ from the ______ absolute value. The sum has the sign of the addend with the ______ absolute value.

$-2.07 + 6.56$ ← **$|-2.07|$ = ______; $|6.56|$ = ______**

______ > ______, so the sum is $6.56 - 2.07 =$ ______.

Quick Check

1. Find each sum.

a. $-6.25 + (-8.55)$

b. $4\frac{3}{5} + \left(-3\frac{2}{5}\right)$

c. $-5.35 + 1.25$

Name ______________________ Class ______________ Date ____________

Example

❷ **Subtracting Rational Numbers** To subtract a rational number, add its opposite.

a. Find $5\frac{5}{6} - \left(-2\frac{1}{6}\right)$.

$5\frac{5}{6} + \left(2\frac{1}{6}\right)$ ← **Add the opposite of** ____

So the difference is ____

b. Find $-1.65 - (-4.22)$.

$-1.65 + 4.22$ ← **Add the opposite of** ____

So the difference is ____

Quick Check

2. Find each difference.

a. $-3\frac{2}{5} - \left(-2\frac{4}{5}\right)$ **b.** $4.35 - (-8.27)$ **c.** $-13.45 - 12.25$

Example

❸ **Application: Temperature** The temperature was −5.5°F at 2:00 A.M. and −8.0°F at 4:00 A.M. Find the change in temperature.

$-5.5 - (-8.0)$ ← ____ **to find the difference.**

$-5.5 + 8.0$ ← **Add the** ____.

The difference is ____ °F.

Quick Check

3. What is the temperature difference between −2.5°F and −6°F?

Name ______________________ Class ______________ Date ______________

Lesson 1-7

Multiplying Rational Numbers

Lesson Objective	Common Core Standards
To use number lines and properties to understand multiplication of rational numbers and to multiply rational numbers	The Number System: 7.NS.2, 7.NS.2.a, 7.NS.2.c, 7.NS.3

Key Concepts

Multiplying Rational Numbers

You can use the ______ to multiply rational numbers.

$$\left(2\tfrac{1}{4}\right)\cdot\left(1\tfrac{1}{2}\right) = 2\left(1\tfrac{1}{2}\right) + \tfrac{1}{4}\left(1\tfrac{1}{2}\right) = \square + \square = \square$$

Example

1 Multiplying Positive Rational Numbers When both factors are positive, the product is positive

$3\frac{1}{3} \times 1\frac{1}{2} = \left(\square \times 1\frac{1}{2}\right)$ ← **Write $3\frac{1}{3}$ as a ______.**

$= \left(\square \times 1\frac{1}{2}\right) + \left(\square \times 1\frac{1}{2}\right)$ ← **Use the Distributive Property.**

$= \square + \square$ ← **Multiply.**

$= 5$ ← ______.

Quick Check

1. Find the product. Write your answer in simplest form.

a. $4.75 \cdot 2.2$ **b.** $\left(8\frac{2}{5}\right)\left(\frac{15}{24}\right)$ **c.** $3.7 \cdot 5.1$

Example

2 Multiplying Negative Rational Numbers When both factors are negative, the product is positive.

$(-2.2)(-10.4) = (-1 \cdot 2.2)(-1 \cdot 10.4)$ ← **Write the negative factors as products.**

$= -1 \cdot (2.2 \cdot -1) \cdot 10.4$ ← **Use the ______ Property of Multiplication**

$= -1 \cdot (-1 \cdot 2.2) \cdot 10.4$ ← **Use the ______ Property of Multiplication**

$= (-1 \cdot -1) \cdot (2.2 \cdot 10.4)$ ← **Use the ______ Property of Multiplication**

$= (1)(2.2 \cdot 10.4) = \square$ ← **Multiply.**

Name ______________________ Class ______________ Date ____________

Quick Check

2. Find the product. Write your answer in simplest form.

a. $\left(-2\frac{2}{3}\right)\left(-2\frac{1}{4}\right)$ b. $-7.5 \cdot (-3.1)$ c. $\left(-2\frac{2}{5}\right)\left(-1\frac{1}{3}\right)$

Example

❸ Multiplying with Different Signs When both factors have different signs, the product is negative.

Find $(-5.1)(1.5)$.

$(-5.1)(1.5) = (-1 \cdot 5.1)(1.5)$ ← **Write the ______ factor as a product.**

$= (-1)(5.1 \cdot 1.5)$ ← **Use the ______________.**

$=$ ______ ← **Multiply.**

Quick Check

3. Find the product. Write your answer in simplest form.

a. $\left(-\frac{3}{5}\right)\left(4\frac{1}{6}\right)$ b. $-8.5 \cdot (1.2)$ c. $\left(-1\frac{11}{16}\right)\left(\frac{8}{9}\right)$

Example

❹ Application: Freediving If Sofia freedives and descends $\frac{7}{8}$ ft per second below sea level, how far can she descend in 16 seconds?

$\left(-\frac{7}{8}\right)(16) = \left(-\frac{7}{8}\right)\left(\frac{16}{1}\right)$ ← **Use multiplication to write an expression for the amount.**

$=$ ______ ← **Multiply to find the distance below sea level.**

Sofia descends ______.

Quick Check

4. Marta is conducting a science experiment. She changes the temperature of a chemical solution by $-\frac{3}{4}$°F each minute. What is the total change in the temperature of the chemical solution after 11 minutes?

Name ____________________ Class ______________ Date ______________

Lesson 1-8

Dividing Rational Numbers

Lesson Objective	Common Core Standards
To use the rules for dividing integers to divide rational numbers and to solve problems by dividing rational numbers	The Number System: 7.NS.2, 7.NS.2.b, 7.NS.2.c, 7.NS.3

Key Concepts

Dividing Rational Numbers

When you divide two numbers that have ______ signs, the quotient is ______.

When you divide two numbers that have ______ signs, the quotient is ______.

Example

❶ Dividing Rational Numbers: Same Sign

a. Find 7.055 ÷ 0.85.

$0.85\overline{)7.055} \rightarrow 85\overline{)705.5}$ with quotient 8.3

680
255
255
0

Multiply the divisor and the dividend by ______ to make the divisor a whole number.

Place the decimal point in the quotient above the decimal point in the dividend.

b. Find $\left(\frac{-2}{3}\right) \div \left(\frac{-1}{2}\right)$.

$\left(-\frac{2}{3}\right) \div \left(-\frac{1}{2}\right) = \frac{-2}{3} \times \frac{-2}{1}$ ← **Multiply by the ______ of the divisor.**

$= (-1)\left(\frac{2}{3}\right)(-1)\left(\frac{2}{1}\right)$ ← **Write −1 as a factor.**

$= (-1)(-1)\left(\frac{2}{3}\right)\left(\frac{2}{1}\right)$ ← **Use the ______ Property to rearrange.**

$= \square\left(\frac{2}{3}\right)\left(\frac{2}{1}\right)$ ← **Multiply.**

$= \square$ or $1\frac{1}{3}$ ← **Simplify if you are asked to.**

Quick Check

1. Find each quotient.

a. −16.9 ÷ −1.3

______

b. $-\frac{2}{3} \div \frac{1}{6}$

______

Name ______________________ Class ______________ Date ______________

Example

❷ Dividing Rational Numbers: Different Sign

Find $-5\frac{1}{4} \div 2\frac{1}{2}$.

$-5\frac{1}{4} \div 2\frac{1}{2} = \square \div \square$ ← Write both mixed numbers as fractions.

$= \left(-1 \cdot \frac{21}{4}\right) \div \frac{5}{2}$ ← Write the negative number as a product with −1.

$= \left(-1 \cdot \frac{21}{4}\right) \times \frac{2}{5}$ ← ________ by the ________ of the divisor.

$= (-1)\left(\frac{21}{4} \times \frac{2}{5}\right)$ ← Use the ________ Property.

$= (-1)\left(\frac{21}{10}\right)$ ← Multiply.

$= -\frac{21}{10}$ or ________ ← Simplify if you are asked to.

Quick Check

2. Find each quotient.

a. $-\frac{3}{4} \div \frac{1}{8}$ ________

b. $5\frac{4}{9} \div -\frac{7}{10}$ ________

c. $-43.68 \div 5.6$ ________

Example

❸ Application: Paying Bills

Kendra has \$159.25 left to pay on a repair bill. She will finish paying the bill in $6\frac{1}{2}$ months. How much is her monthly payment?

$159.25 \div 6\frac{1}{2} = 159.25 \div \square$ ← Express both numbers as decimals.

$= \square$ ← Divide.

Kendra will pay ________ each month. The last payment will be ________.

Check

$6.5 \times 24.50 = (\square \times 24.50) + (\square \times 24.50)$ ← Use the Distributive Property.

$= \square + \square$ ← Multiply.

$= \square$ ← Simplify.

Quick Check

3. Solve.

a. Lucy owes \$125.40 for repairs on her laptop. She agrees to pay this back in $5\frac{1}{2}$ weeks. By what amount will her checking account change each week to do this?

____

b. Randy borrows \$315.25 from his mother to buy a tablet computer. He promises to pay her back in $6\frac{1}{2}$ months. If he does this, what will his last payment be?

____

Name ______________________ Class ______________ Date ______________

Lesson 1-9

Irrational Numbers and Square Roots

Lesson Objective	**Common Core Standards**
To find and estimate square roots and to classify numbers as rational or irrational	The Number System: 8.NS.1, 8.NS.2 Expressions and Equations: 8.EE.2

Vocabulary

A perfect square is ____________________

The square root of a number is ____________________

____

Irrational numbers are ____________________

____

The real numbers are ____________________

Examples

1 Finding Square Roots of Perfect Squares Find the two square roots of each number.

a. 81

$\square \cdot \square = 81$ and $\square \cdot \square = 81$

The two square roots of 81 are $\square$ and $\square$.

b. $\frac{1}{36}$

$\square \cdot \square = \frac{1}{36}$ and $\square \cdot \square = \frac{1}{36}$

The two square roots of $\frac{1}{36}$ are $\square$ and $\square$.

2 Estimating a Square Root Estimate the value of $-\sqrt{70}$ to the nearest integer and to the nearest tenth.

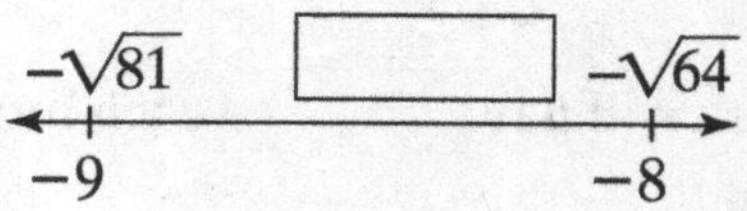

Since 70 is closer to 64 than it is to 81, $-\sqrt{70} \approx \square$.

Since 70 is closer to 70.56 than to 68.89, $-\sqrt{70} \approx \square$.

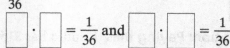

Quick Check

1. Find the square roots of each number.

a. 36 $\square$

b. 1 $\square$

c. $\frac{1}{16}$ $\square$

2. Estimate the value of $\sqrt{38}$ to the nearest integer and to the nearest tenth. $\square$

Name ______________________ Class ______________ Date ______________

Examples

❸ Comparing Square Roots Which is greater, $\sqrt{28}$ or 5.1?

First, estimate the value of the square root to the nearest tenth. $\sqrt{28} \approx$ ☐

Since ☐ ☐ 5.1, $\sqrt{28}$ ☐ 5.1.

❹ Surface Area of a Sphere The formula S.A. $= 13r^2$ gives the approximate surface area S.A. in square units of a sphere with radius r. Find the radius of a sphere with surface area 650 square units.

S.A. $= 13r^2$ ← **Use the formula for the surface area of a sphere.**

☐ $= 13r^2$ ← **Substitute ☐ for S.A.**

$\frac{650}{13} = r^2$ ← **Divide each side by ☐ to isolate r.**

☐ $\approx r^2$ ← **Simplify.**

$\sqrt{50} \approx \sqrt{r^2}$ ← **Find the positive square root of each side. Use a calculator.**

☐ $\approx r$ ← **Round to the nearest tenth.**

The radius of a sphere with surface area 650 square units is about ☐ units.

❺ Classifying Real Numbers Is each number *rational or irrational*? Explain.

a. $-9333.\overline{3}$ ☐; the decimal repeats.

b. $4\frac{7}{9}$ ☐; the number can be written as the ratio ☐.

c. $\sqrt{90}$ ☐; 90 is not a ☐ square.

d. 6.363663666 . . . ☐; the decimal does not terminate or repeat.

Quick Check

3. Which is greater $\sqrt{20}$ or 4.7?

☐

4. Use the formula S.A. $= 13r^2$ to find the radius of a sphere with a surface area of 520 square units. Round to the nearest tenth of a unit.

☐

5. Is $0.\overline{6}$ *rational* or *irrational*? Explain.

☐

Name ____________________ Class ______________ Date ______________

Lesson 1-10

Cube Roots

Lesson Objective	**Common Core Standard**
To find cube roots and to solve cube root equations	Expressions and Equations: 8.EE.2

Vocabulary

A perfect cube is a ______________________________

A cube root is a ______________________________

____

Example

1 Finding Cube Roots of Perfect Cubes Find the cube roots of each number.

a. 27

$\square \cdot \square \cdot \square = 27$

So, the cube root of 27 is $\square$.

b. -343

$\square \cdot \square \cdot \square = -343$

So, the cube root of -343 is $\square$.

c $\frac{1}{512}$

$\square \cdot \square \cdot \square = \frac{1}{512}$

So, the cube root of $\frac{1}{512}$ is $\square$.

Quick Check

1. Find the cube root of each number.

a. 216

b. -1

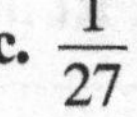

c. $\frac{1}{27}$

Name ______________________ Class ______________ Date ______________

Example

2 Finding the Side Length of a Cube A cube-shaped storage container has a volume of 1,728 cubic inches. What is the side length of the container?

$V = s^3$ ← **Volume formula**

$\square = s^3$ ← **Substitute** $\square$ **for** ***V.***

$\square = \sqrt[3]{s^3}$ ← **Find the cube root of each side.**

$\square = s$

The side length of the storage container is $\square$.

Quick Check

2. A different cube-shaped packing box has a volume of 125 cubic feet. What is the side length of the box? $\square$

Example

3 Solving a Cube Root Equation Solve $x^3 = \frac{343}{729}$.

$x^3 = \frac{343}{729}$

$\sqrt[3]{x^3} = \sqrt[3]{\frac{343}{729}}$ ← **Find the cube root of each side.**

$x = \frac{\sqrt[3]{343}}{\sqrt[3]{729}}$ ← **Find the cube root of the** $\square$.
← **Find the cube root of the** $\square$.

$x = \square$ ← **Simplify.** ***Think:*** **343 =** $\square$ **and 729 =** $\square$.

Quick Check

3. Solve $x^3 = \frac{27}{216}$.

$\square$

Name ______________________ Class ______________ Date ______________

Lesson 2-1

Scientific Notation

Lesson Objective	Common Core Standard
To write numbers in both standard form and scientific notation	Expressions and Equations: 8.EE.3

Key Concepts

Scientific Notation

A number is in scientific notation if ____

____

Examples 1×10^8 1.54×10^7 9.99×10^4

Example

❶ **Writing in Standard Form** At one point, the distance from the Earth to the moon is 1.513431×10^{10} in. Write this number in standard form.

$1.513431 \times 10^{10} = 1.5134310000.$ ← **Move the decimal point** ☐ **places to the right. Insert zeros as necessary.**

= ☐

At one point, the distance from the Earth to the moon is ☐ in.

Quick Check

1. Write 7.66×10^6 km^2, the area of Australia, in standard form.

☐

Name ______________________ Class ______________ Date ______________

Examples

❷ **Writing in Scientific Notation** The diameter of the planet Jupiter is about 142,800 km. Write this number in scientific notation.

142,800 = 1.42,800. ← **Move the decimal point ☐ places to the left.**

= ☐ × $10^{☐}$ ← **Use ☐ as the exponent of 10.**

The diameter of the planet Jupiter is about ☐ km.

❸ **Scientific Notation With Negative Exponents** A typical width of a human hair is about 8.0×10^{-5} m. Write this number in standard form.

8.0×10^{-5} = 0.00008.0 ← **Move the decimal point ☐ places to the ☐ to make 8 less than 1.**

A typical width of a human hair is ☐ meters wide.

❹ **Numbers Less Than 1** Write the quantity 0.000089 in scientific notation.

0.000089 = 0.00008.9 ← **Move the decimal point ☐ places to the ☐.**

= ☐ × $10^{☐}$ ← **Use ☐ as the exponent of 10.**

Quick Check

2. Write 3,476,000 m, the moon's diameter, in scientific notation.

3. Write 2.5×10^{-4} inch, the diameter of a cell, in standard form.

4. Write 0.0000035 in scientific notation.

Name ______________________ Class ______________________ Date ______________________

Lesson 2-2

Exponents and Multiplication

Lesson Objective	Common Core Standard
To multiply powers with the same base	Expressions and Equations: 8.EE.1

Key Concepts

Multiplying Powers With the Same Base

To multiply numbers or variables with the same base, ______ the exponents.

Arithmetic	Algebra
$3^2 \cdot 3^7 = 3^{(2+7)} = 3^9$	$a^m \cdot a^n = a^{(m+n)}$

Examples

1 Multiplying Powers Write the expression $(-3)^2 \cdot (-3)^4$ using a single exponent.

$(-3)^2 \cdot (-3)^4 = (-3)^{(\square + \square)}$ ← **Add the exponents.**

$= (-3)^{(\square)}$ ← **Simplify the exponent.**

2 Application: Geometry Find the area of the square.

x^5 cm

A. x^{10} cm^2 **B.** x^{25} cm^2 **C.** $2x^{10}$ cm^2 **D.** $2x^{25}$ cm^2

$A = s \cdot s$ ← **Write the area formula.**

$A = x^5 \cdot x^5$ ← **Substitute** ______ **for** ***s*****.**

$A = x^{(\square + \square)}$ ← **Add the exponents.**

$A = x^{\square}$ ← **Simplify.**

The area of the square is $x^{\square}$ cm^2. The correct answer choice is A.

❸ Using the Commutative Property Simplify the expression $-6x^5 \cdot 3x^4$.

$-6x^5 \cdot 3x^4 = \square \cdot \square \cdot x^5 \cdot x^4$ ← **Use the Commutative Property of Multiplication.**

$= \square\, x^{(\square + \square)}$ ← $\square$ **the exponents of powers with the same base.**

$= -18x^{\square}$ ← **Simplify.**

Quick Check

1. Write each expression using a single exponent.

a. $6^2 \cdot 6^3$ **b.** $(-4) \cdot (-4)^7$ **c.** $3 \cdot 3^2 \cdot 3^3$

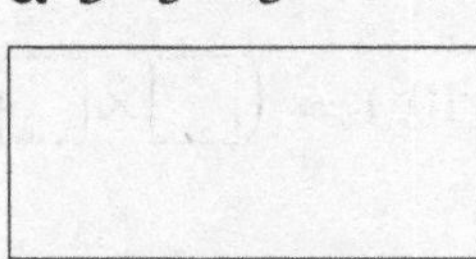

2. A square has a side length of n^3. Find the area of the square.

3. Simplify each expression.

a. $2a^2 \cdot 3a$ **b.** $x^{10} \cdot x^3$ **c.** $-4y^5 \cdot -3y^5$

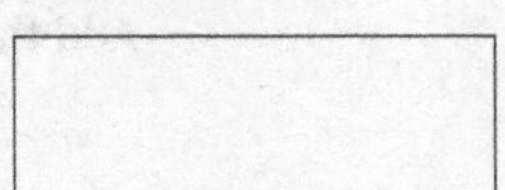

Name ________________ Class ________________ Date ________________

Lesson 2-3

Multiplying with Scientific Notation

Lesson Objective	**Common Core Standard**
To multiply numbers written in scientific notation and choose appropriate units of measure	Expressions and Equations: 8.EE.4

Example

1 Multiplying With Scientific Notation Multiply $(3 \times 10^3)(7 \times 10^5)$. Write the product in scientific notation.

$(3 \times 10^3)(7 \times 10^5) = (\square \times \square) \times (10^{\square} \times 10^{\square})$ ← **Use the** ☐ **and** ☐ **properties.**

$= \square \times (10^{\square} \times 10^{\square})$ ← **Multiply** ☐ **and** ☐.

$= \square \times 10^{\square}$ ← **Add the exponents for the powers of 10.**

$= \square \times 10^{\square} \times 10^{\square}$ ← **Write** ☐ **in scientific notation.**

$= \square \times 10^{\square}$ ← **Add the exponents.**

Quick Check

1. Multiply. Write each product in scientific notation.

a. $(2 \times 10^6)(4 \times 10^3)$ **b.** $(3 \times 10^5)(2 \times 10^8)$ **c.** $12(8 \times 10^{20})$

Name ______________________ Class ______________ Date ______________

Examples

2 Multiple choice A light-year is about 5.9×10^{12} miles. A mile is about 1.609×10^3 meters. How many meters are in a light-year? Write your answer in scientific notation.

A. 9.5×10^{15} **B.** 9.5×10^{16} **C.** 9.5×10^{36} **D.** 9.5×10^{37}

$(5.9 \times 10^{12})(1.609 \times 10^3)$ ← **Multiply by conversion factor.**

$= (\square \times \square) \times (10^{\square} \times 10^{\square})$ ← **Use the ______ and ______ properties.**

$\approx \square \times (10^{\square} \times 10^{\square})$ ← **Multiply ______ and ______. Round to the nearest tenth.**

$= \square \times 10^{\square}$ ← **Add the exponents.**

There are about ______ meters in a light-year. The correct answer is choice ______.

3 Choosing Units with Scientific Notation Choose the most reasonable unit to describe the quantity. Then use scientific notation to describe the quantity using the other unit.

a. The length of a school bus is 9 ______. (m, km)

$9 \square \times \dfrac{\square \text{ km}}{1 \text{ m}} = 9 \times \square \text{ km}$ ← **Multiply by a conversion factor.**

b. The mass of a horse is about 500 ______. (g, kg)

$500 \square \times \dfrac{\square \text{ g}}{1 \text{ kg}} = 500 \times 10^3 \text{ g}$ ← **Multiply by a conversion factor.**

$= 5 \times \square \text{ g}$ ← **Simplify.**

Quick Check

2. Astronomy The speed of light is about 3.0×10^5 kilometers/second. Use the formula $d = r \cdot t$ to find the distance light travels in an hour, which is 3.6×10^3 seconds.

3. Choose the most reasonable unit to describe the quantity. Then use scientific notation to describe the quantity using the other unit.

A pencil is 7 ______ long. (cm, m)

Name ______________________ Class ______________ Date ______________

Lesson 2-4

Exponents and Division

Lesson Objective	Common Core Standard
To divide powers with the same base and to simplify expressions with negative exponents	Expressions and Equations: 8.EE.1

Key Concepts

Dividing Powers With the Same Base

To divide nonzero numbers or variables with the same nonzero base, ☐ the exponents.

Arithmetic

$\frac{8^5}{8^3} = 8^{(5 \square 3)} = 8^{\square}$

Algebra

$\frac{a^m}{a^n} = a^{(m \square n)}$, where $a \neq 0$.

Zero as an Exponent

For any nonzero number a, $a^0 = \square$.

Example $9^0 = \square$

Negative Exponents

For any nonzero number a and integers n, $a^{-n} = \frac{1}{\square}$.

Example $8^{\square} = \frac{1}{8^5}$.

Examples

1 Dividing Powers Write $\frac{x^{14}}{x^9}$ using a single exponent.

$\frac{x^{14}}{x^9} = x^{(14 \square 9)}$ ← ☐ **exponents with the same base.**

$= x^{\square}$ ← **Simplify.**

2 Expression With a Zero Exponent Simplify each expression.

a. $(-5)^0$

$(-5)^0 = \square$ ← **Simplify.**

b. $2y^0$, $y \neq 0$

$2y^0 = \square$ ← **Simplify.**

Name ______________________ Class ______________ Date ______________

❸ **Expressions With Negative Exponents** Simplify each expression.

a. 2^{-3}

$2^{-3} = \frac{\square}{2^{\square}}$ ← **Use a** ______ **exponent.**

$= \frac{\square}{\square}$ ← **Simplify.**

b. $(p)^{-8}$

→ $= \frac{\square}{p^{\square}}$

Quick Check

1. Write $\frac{w^8}{w^5}$ using a single exponent.

2. Simplify each expression.

a. $(-9)^0$ **b.** $(2r)^0$ **c.** $2r^0$

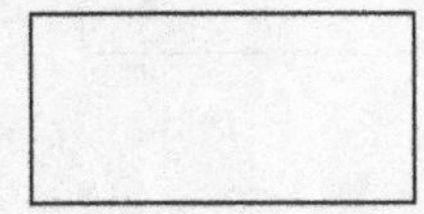 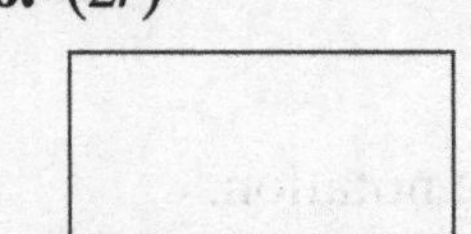 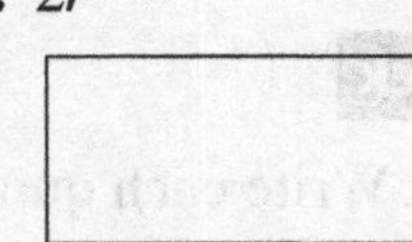

3. Simplify each expression.

a. 3^{-1} **b.** w^{-4} **c.** $(-2)^{-3}$

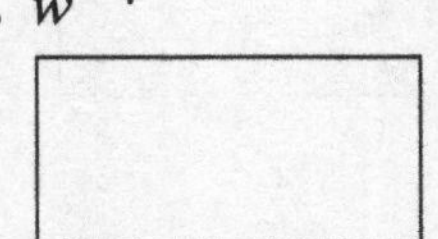 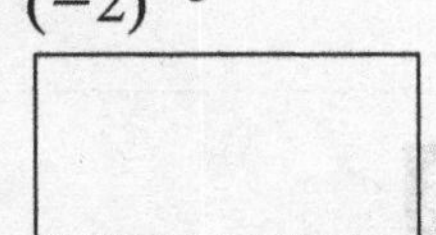

Name ______________________ Class ______________ Date ______________

Lesson 2-5

Dividing with Scientific Notation

Lesson Objective	**Common Core Standards**
To divide and compare numbers written in scientific notation	Expressions and Equations: 8.EE.3, 8.EE.4

Example

1 Dividing Numbers in Scientific Notation Simplify $(5.4 \times 10^5) \div (9.1 \times 10^2)$. Write the quotient in scientific notation.

$(5.4 \times 10^5) \div (9.1 \times 10^2) = \frac{5.4 \times 10^5}{9.1 \times 10^2}$ ← **Write a fraction.**

$= \frac{\square}{\square} \times \frac{10^5}{10^2}$ ← **Separate the coefficients and the powers of ten.**

$\approx 0.59 \times \frac{10^{\square}}{10^{\square}}$ ← **Divide the coefficients.**

$\approx 0.59 \times 10^{\square}$ ← **Subtract the exponents.**

$\approx \square \times 10^{\square} \times 10^3$ ← **Write 0.59 in scientific notation.**

$\approx 5.9 \times 10^{\square}$ ← **Add the exponents.**

Quick Check

1. Simplify. Write each quotient in scientific notation.

a. $\frac{7.9 \times 10^5}{2.3 \times 10^3}$

b. $\frac{4.8 \times 10^4}{2.95 \times 10^6}$

c. $\frac{3.7 \times 10^7}{5.2 \times 10^2}$

Examples

2 Application: Astronomy The average distance between the sun and Jupiter is about 4.8×10^8 miles. Light travels about 1.1×10^7 miles per minute. Estimate how long sunlight takes to reach Jupiter. Write your answer in standard form and round to the nearest whole number.

$\text{time} = \frac{\text{distance}}{\text{speed}}$ ← **Use the formula for time.**

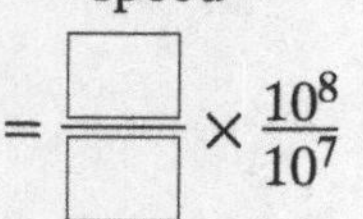

$= \frac{\square}{\square} \times \frac{10^8}{10^7}$ ← **Substitute. Write as a product of quotients.**

$= \frac{4.8}{1.1} \times 10^{8 \square 7}$ ← ______ **the exponents.**

$\approx 4.4 \times 10^1$ ← **Divide and simplify.**

Sunlight takes about 4.4×10^1 minutes, or ______ minutes to reach Jupiter.

Name ____________ Class ____________ Date ____________

3 Dividing by Numbers in Standard Form Divide. Write each quotient in scientific notation.

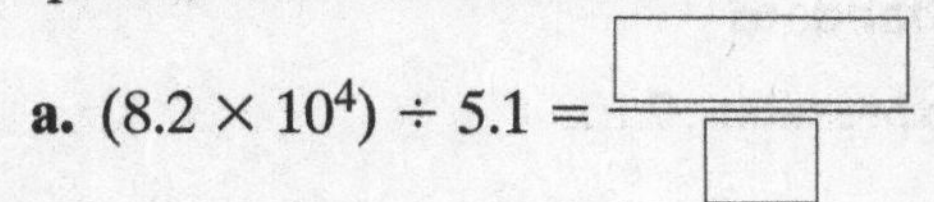

a. $(8.2 \times 10^4) \div 5.1 = \frac{\square}{\square}$ ← **Write a fraction.**

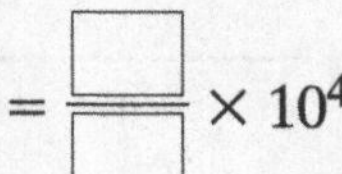

$= \frac{\square}{\square} \times 10^4$ ← **Separate the coefficients and the powers of ten.**

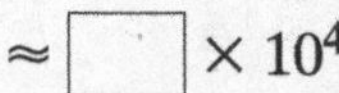

$\approx \square \times 10^4$ ← **Divide the coefficients.**

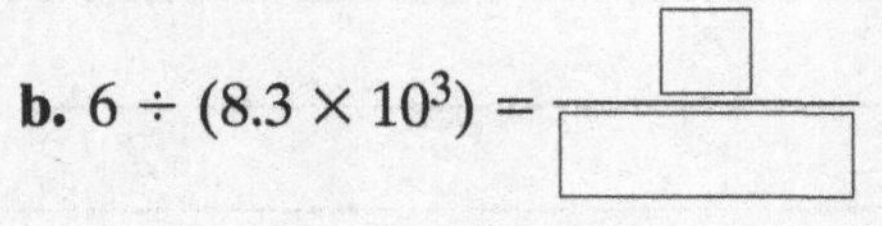

b. $6 \div (8.3 \times 10^3) = \frac{\square}{\square}$ ← **Write a fraction.**

$= \frac{6}{8.3} \times 10^{\square}$ ← **Separate the coefficients and power of ten.**

$\approx \square \times 10^{-3}$ ← **Divide the coefficients and divide the powers of ten.**

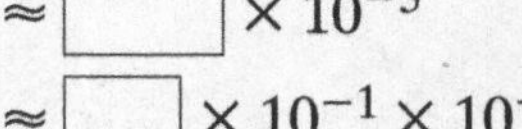

$\approx \square \times 10^{-1} \times 10^{-3}$ ← **Write 0.72 in scientific notation.**

$\approx \square \times 10^{\square}$ ← **Add the exponents.**

4 Ordering Numbers Order $6.5 \times 10^3, 6.4 \times 10^{-3}, 5.8 \times 10^3$, and 8.9×10^2 from least to greatest.

$\square$, 8.9×10^2, $\square$, 5.8×10^3 ← **Sort the numbers using the powers of ten, least to greatest.**

$6.4 \times 10^{-3}, 8.9 \times 10^2$, $\square$, $\square$ ← **Sort the numbers with the same power of ten, using the first factor.**

Quick Check

2. The distance between the sun and Earth is about 9.3×10^7 miles. Light travels about 1.1×10^7 miles per minute. Estimate how long sunlight takes to reach Earth. Write your answer in standard form and round to the nearest tenth.

3. Divide. Write each quotient in scientific notation.

a. $\frac{6.2 \times 10^6}{4.1}$ **b.** $\frac{-3.5 \times 10^3}{5}$ **c.** $\frac{17}{1.4 \times 10^8}$

4. Order the numbers from least to greatest.
$3 \times 10^6, 3.11 \times 10^5, 3 \times 10^{-6}, 3.8 \times 10^{-5}$

Name ____________________ Class ____________ Date ____________

Lesson 3-1

Evaluating and Writing Algebraic Expressions

Lesson Objective	Common Core Standard
To write and evaluate algebraic expressions	Equations and Expressions: 7.EE.4

Vocabulary

A variable is ______________________________

____

An algebraic expression is ______________________________

____

Examples

1 Writing Algebraic Expressions Write an algebraic expression for each word phrase.

a. 6 less than *d* dollars [ ]

b. the sum of *s* students and 9 students [ ]

c. 12 times *b* boxes [ ]

d. 20 hours of work divided equally among *w* workers [ ]

2 Art Supplies The cost of a package of markers is *d* dollars. Write an algebraic expression for the total cost in dollars of 7 packages of markers.

Words — number of packages | times | cost per package

Let d = cost per package.

Expression — [ ] · [ ]

An algebraic expression for the total cost in dollars is [ ].

3 Writing Word Phrases Write three different word phrases for $2y$.

____

____

____

4 Evaluating Algebraic Expressions Evaluate each expression. Use the values $r = 8, s = 1$, and $t = 3$.

a. $6(t - 1)$

$6(t - 1) = 6(\square - 1)$ ← **Substitute**

$= 6(\square)$ ← **Subtract.**

$= \square$ ← **Multiply.**

b. $\frac{r}{s + t}$

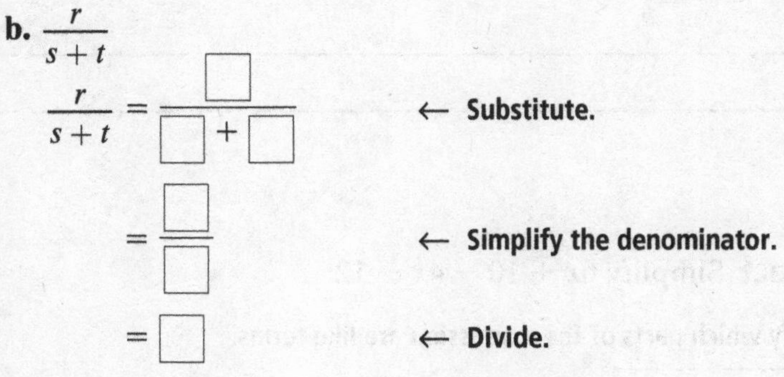

$\frac{r}{s+t} = \frac{\square}{\square + \square}$ ← **Substitute.**

$= \frac{\square}{\square}$ ← **Simplify the denominator.**

$= \square$ ← **Divide.**

Quick Check

1. Write an algebraic expression for a price p decreased by 16.

2. Nine students will hang t posters each. Write an algebraic expression for the total number of posters the students will hang.

3. Write three different word phrases for $c - 50$.

4. Use the values $n = 3, t = 5$, and $y = 7$ to evaluate $(n + t) \cdot y$.

Name ______________________ Class ______________ Date ______________

Lesson 3-2

Simplifying Expressions

Lesson Objective	**Common Core Standard**
To simplify algebraic expressions using properties of operations	Expressions and Equations: 7.EE.1

Vocabulary

Like terms are ____.

A coefficient is ____.

Examples

❶ Using Properties to Add and Subtract Simplify $6x + 10 - 4x - 12$.

$\square + 10 \square - 12$ ← **Identify which parts of the expression are like terms.**

$= 6x - 4x + 10 - 12$ ← $\square$ **Property of Addition**

$= (6 - 4)x + 10 - 12$ ← $\square$ **Property**

$= \square + 10 - 12$ ← **Simplify the coefficient.**

$= \square - \square$ ← **Simplify.**

The simplified expression is $\square$.

❷ Expanding Expressions Simplify $\frac{1}{2}(6x - 8) + 11$.

$\frac{1}{2}(6x + 8) - 11.$

$= (3x + 4) - 11$ ← $\square$ **Property**

$= 3x + (\square - 11)$ ← **Associative Property of Addition**

$= 3x - \square$ ← **Simplify**

The simplified expression is $\square$.

Name ______________________ Class ______________ Date ______________

❸ Factoring Expressions Factor $21x + 35$.

GCF of 21 and 35 is $\square$. ← **Identify the GCF.**

$21x + 35 = 7 \cdot \square + 7 \cdot \square$. ← **Factor each term by the GCF.**

$= 7(\square + \square)$ ← **Distributive Property**

The factored expression is $\square$.

Quick Check

1. Simplify each expression.

a. $2x + 8 + 4x - 5$ $\square$

b. $6 + 7.2y - 4.2y + 1$ $\square$

c. $10r - 5 + 3 + r$ $\square$

2. Simplify each expression.

a. $6(2x + 3) - 4$ $\square$

b. $\frac{1}{2}(2 - 8v) + 5$ $\square$

c. $9 - 4(3z + 2)$ $\square$

3. Factor each expression completely.

a. $9x + 15$ $\square$

b. $36 + 24t$ $\square$

c. $8c - 20$ $\square$

Name ______________________ Class ______________ Date ____________

Lesson 3-3

Solving One-Step Equations

Lesson Objective	**Common Core Standard**
To solve equations by adding, subtracting, multiplying, or dividing	Expressions and Equations: 7.EE.4

Vocabulary and Key Concepts

Properties of Equality

Addition Property of Equality

If you ☐ the same value to each side of an equation, the two sides remain ☐.

Subtraction Property of Equality

If you ☐ the same value from each side of an equation, the two sides remain ☐.

Division Property of Equality

If you ☐ each side of an equation by the same nonzero number, the two sides remain ☐.

Multiplication Property of Equality

If you ☐ each side of an equation by the same number, the two sides remain ☐.

Inverse operations are ______________________________

Example

1 Solving Equations by Adding Solve $t - 58 = 71$. Check your solution.

$t - 58 = 71$

$t - 58 + ☐ = 71 + 58$ ← ☐ **Property of Equality: Add** ☐ **to each side.**

$t + ☐ = 129$ ← **The numbers 58 and −58 are** ☐.

$t = 129$ ← ☐ **Property**

Check ☐ ← **Check the solution in the original equation.**

☐ $- 58 \stackrel{?}{=} 71$ ← **Substitute 129 for** ***t*****.**

☐ $= 71$ ← **Subtract.**

Name ______________________ Class ______________ Date ______________

Examples

❷ Solving Equations by Subtracting Your friend purchased a DVD and a CD. The DVD cost \$6 more than the CD. The DVD cost \$22. How much did the CD cost?

Words ______ is \$6 more than ______.

Let c = the cost of the CD.

Equation ______ = 6 + ______

$22 = 6 + c$

$22 - \square = 6 - \square + c$ ← **Subtract ______ from each side.**

$\square = c$ ← **Simplify.**

The CD cost ______.

❸ Solving Equations by Multiplying Solve $-\frac{m}{3} = 27$.

$-\frac{m}{3} = 27$ ← **Notice that m is ______ by −3.**

$\square \cdot -\frac{m}{3} = \square \cdot 27$ ← ______ **each side by ______.**

$m = -81$ ← **Simplify.**

❹ Solving Equations by Dividing Solve $-3j = 44.7$.

$-3j = 44.7$ ← **Notice j is being ______ by −3.**

$\frac{-3j}{\square} = \frac{44.7}{\square}$ ← ______ **each side by ______ to get j alone.**

$j = \square$ ← **Simplify.**

Quick Check

1. Solve the equation $x - 104 = 64$.

2. A hardcover book costs \$19 more than its paperback edition. The hardcover book costs \$26.95. How much does the paperback cost?

3. Solve the equation $\frac{w}{26} = -15$. Check your answer.

4. Solve each equation. Check your answer.
   - **a.** $3x = -21.6$
   - **b.** $-12y = -108$
   - **c.** $104x = 312$

Name ______________________ Class ______________ Date ______________

Lesson 3-4

Exploring Two-Step Equations

Lesson Objective	**Common Core Standard**
To write and evaluate expressions with two operations and to solve two-step equations using number sense	Expressions and Equations: 7.EE.4.a

Examples

1 Writing Expressions Define a variable and write an algebraic expression for the phrase "four times the length of a rope in inches, increased by eight inches."

Let ☐ = length of rope in inches. ← **Define the variable.**

☐ · ☐ + ☐ ← **Write an algebraic expression.**

☐ + 8 ← **Rewrite 4 · *l* as ☐.**

2 Evaluating Expressions Evaluate the expression if the length of a rope is 9 inches.

$4\ell + 8$

4 · ☐ + 8 ← **Evaluate the expression for a rope length of ☐.**

☐ + 8 ← **Multiply.**

☐ ← **Simplify.**

3 Using Number Sense Solve $3n - 4 = 14$ by using number sense.

$3n - 4 = 14$

■ $- 4 = 14$ ← **Cover 3*n*. *Think:* What number minus 4 is 14?**
Answer: ☐.

$3n =$ ☐ ← **So ■, or 3*n*, must equal ☐.**

3 · ■ = ☐ ← **Now cover *n*. *Think:* What number times 3 is ☐?**
Answer: ☐.

$n =$ ☐ ← **So ■, or *n*, must equal ☐.**

Check

$3n - 4 = 14$ ← **Check your solution in the original equation.**

$3(6) - 4 \stackrel{?}{=} 14$ ← **Substitute 6 for *n*.**

$18 - 4 \stackrel{?}{=} 14$ ← **Simplify.**

$14 = 14$ ← **The solution checks.**

Name ______________________ Class ____________ Date ____________

4 **Shopping** The Healy family wants to buy a TV that costs \$200. They already have \$80 saved toward the cost. How much will they have to save per month for the next six months in order to have the whole cost saved?

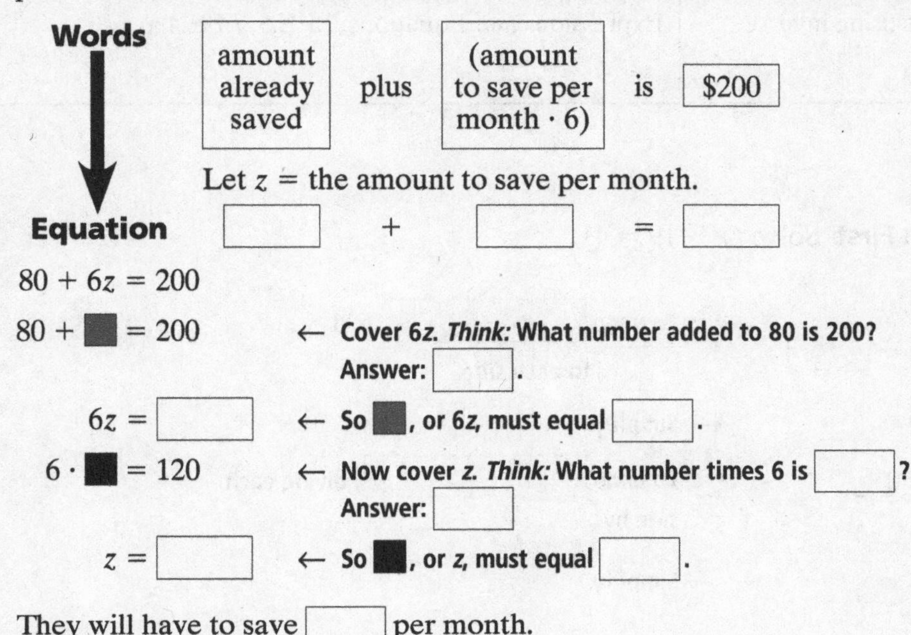

$80 + 6z = 200$

$80 + \blacksquare = 200$ ← **Cover 6*z*. *Think:* What number added to 80 is 200?**
Answer: ____.

$6z =$ ____ ← **So ■, or 6*z*, must equal ____.**

$6 \cdot \blacksquare = 120$ ← **Now cover *z*. *Think:* What number times 6 is ____?**
Answer: ____

$z =$ ____ ← **So ■, or *z*, must equal ____.**

They will have to save ____ per month.

Quick Check

1. Define a variable and write an algebraic expression for "a man is two years younger than three times his son's age."

2. Evaluate the expression to find the man's age if his son is 13.

3. Solve each equation using number sense.

a. $3m + 9 = 21$

b. $8d + 5 = 45$

c. $4y - 11 = 33$

4. **Basketball** During the first half of a game you scored 8 points. In the second half you made only 3-point baskets. You finished the game with 23 points. Write and solve an equation to find how many 3-point baskets you made.

Name ____________________ Class ____________ Date ____________

Lesson 3-5

Solving Two-Step Equations

Lesson Objective	Common Core Standards
To solve two-step equations using inverse operations	Expressions and Equations: 7.EE.3, 7.EE.4.a

Examples

1 Undoing Subtraction First Solve $6r - 19 = 41$.

$6r - 19 = 41$

$6r - 19 + \square = 41 + \square$ ← **To undo ______, add ______ to each side.**

$6r = 60$ ← **Simplify.**

$\frac{6r}{\square} = \frac{60}{\square}$ ← **To undo ______, divide each side by ______.**

$r = \square$ ← **Simplify.**

Check $6r - 19 = 41$ ← **Check your solution in the original equation.**

$6(\square) - 19 \stackrel{?}{=} 41$ ← **Substitute ______ for *r*.**

$\square - 19 \stackrel{?}{=} 41$ ← **Simplify.**

$\square = 41$ ✓ ← **The solution checks.**

2 Undoing Addition First Solve $\frac{a}{5} + 4 = 10$.

$\frac{a}{5} + 4 = 10$

$\frac{a}{5} + 4 \square 4 = 10 \square 4$ ← **To undo addition, ______ 4 from each side.**

$\frac{a}{5} = 6$ ← **Simplify.**

$(\square)\left(\frac{a}{5}\right) = (\square)(6)$ ← **To undo division, multiply each side by ______.**

$a = \square$ ← **Simplify.**

Name ______________________ Class ______________ Date ______________

❸ Solving Two-Step Equations An amusement park charges $15.00 for admission and $.50 for each ride. You spend $27.00 total. How many rides did you go on?

A. 54 **B.** 43 **C.** 24 **D.** 6

Words ☐ times the number of rides plus ☐ is 27.

Let n = number of rides you went on.

Equation ☐ $\cdot$ n + ☐ = 27

☐ $\cdot n +$ ☐ $= 27$

☐ $\cdot n +$ ☐ $- 15 = 27 - 15$ ← **Subtract 15 from each side.**

☐ $\cdot n = 12$ ← **Simplify.**

$\frac{0.50n}{0.50} = \frac{12}{0.50}$ ← **Divide each side by** ☐.

$n =$ ☐ ← **Simplify.**

You went on ☐ rides. The correct answer is choice ☐.

Quick Check

1. Solve the equation $-8y - 28 = -36$. Check your answer.

2. Solve the equation $\frac{x}{5} + 35 = 75$. Check your answer.

3. Solomon decides to make posters for the student council election. He bought markers that cost $.79 each and a poster board that cost $1.25. The total cost was $7.57. Write and solve an equation to find the number of markers that Solomon bought.

Name ______________________ Class ______________ Date ____________

Lesson 3-6

Solving Multi-Step Equations

Lesson Objective	**Common Core State Standards**
To write and solve multi-step equations	Expressions and Equations: 7.EE.4, 8.EE.7, 8.EE.7.b

Example

❶ Simplifying Before Solving an Equation Solve $2c + 2 + 3c = 12$.

$2c + 2 + 3c = 12$

$2c + 3c + 2 = 12$ ← ☐ **Property of Addition**

$\square + 2 = 12$ ← **Combine like terms.**

$\square + 2 - \square = 12 - \square$ ← **Subtract ☐ from each side.**

$5c = \square$ ← **Simplify.**

$\frac{5c}{\square} = \frac{\square}{\square}$ ← **Divide each side by ☐.**

$c = \square$ ← **Simplify.**

Check $2c + 2 + 3c = 12$

$2(\square) + 2 + 3(\square) \stackrel{?}{=} 12$ ← **Substitute ☐ for *c*.**

$\square = 12$ ✓ ← **The solution checks.**

Quick Check

1. Solve $-15 = 5b + 12 - 2b + 6$. Check the solution.

Name ______________________ Class ______________ Date ______________

Example

2 Using the Distributive Property Eight cheerleaders set a goal of selling 424 boxes of cards to raise money. After two weeks, each cheerleader has sold 28 boxes. How many more boxes must each cheerleader sell?

A. 15 boxes **B.** 25 boxes **C.** 50 boxes **D.** 53 boxes

Words [8 cheerleaders] · ([28 boxes per cheerleader] + [additional boxes per cheerleader]) = [424 boxes]

Let x = the number of additional boxes per cheerleader.

Equation [ ] · ([ ] + [ ]) = [ ]

$8(28 + x) = 424$

[ ] $+ 8x = 424$ ← [ ] **Property**

[ ] − [ ] $+ 8x = 424 -$ [ ] ← **Subtract** [ ] **from each side.**

$8x = 200$ ← **Simplify.**

$\frac{8x}{[\ ]} = \frac{200}{[\ ]}$ ← **Divide each side by** [ ].

$x =$ [ ] ← **Simplify.**

Each cheerleader must sell [ ] more boxes. The correct answer is choice [ ].

Quick Check

2. Class Trips Your class goes to an amusement park. Admission is $10 for each student and $15 for each chaperone. The total cost is $380. There are 12 girls in your class and 6 chaperones on the trip. How many boys are in your class?

[ ]

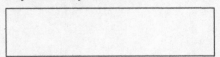

Name ______________________ Class ______________ Date ____________

Lesson 3-7

Solving Equations With Variables on Both Sides

Lesson Objective	Common Core State Standards
To write and solve equations with variables on both sides	Expressions and Equations: 8.EE.7, 8.EE.7.b

Example

1 Variables on Both Sides Solve $9 + 2p = -3 - 4p$.

$9 + 2p = -3 - 4p$

$9 + 2p + \square = -3 - 4p + \square$ ← **Add $\square$ to each side.**

$9 + \square = -3$ ← **Combine like terms.**

$9 - \square + 6p = -3 - \square$ ← **Subtract $\square$ from each side.**

$6p = \square$ ← **Simplify.**

$\frac{6p}{\square} = \frac{\square}{\square}$ ← **Divide each side by $\square$.**

$p = \square$ ← **Simplify.**

Check $9 + 2p = -3 - 4p$

$9 + 2(\square) \stackrel{?}{=} -3 - 4(\square)$ ← **Substitute $\square$ for p.**

$\square = 5✓$ ← **The solution checks.**

Quick Check

1. Solve $7b - 2 = b + 10$. Check the solution.

Name ______________________ Class ______________ Date ____________

Example

❷ Using the Distributive Property The chess club decides to sell shirts and hats for fundraising. The total cost of a shirt and a hat is \$21. Paula purchased 4 hats for the same price as 3 shirts. What is the cost of one shirt?

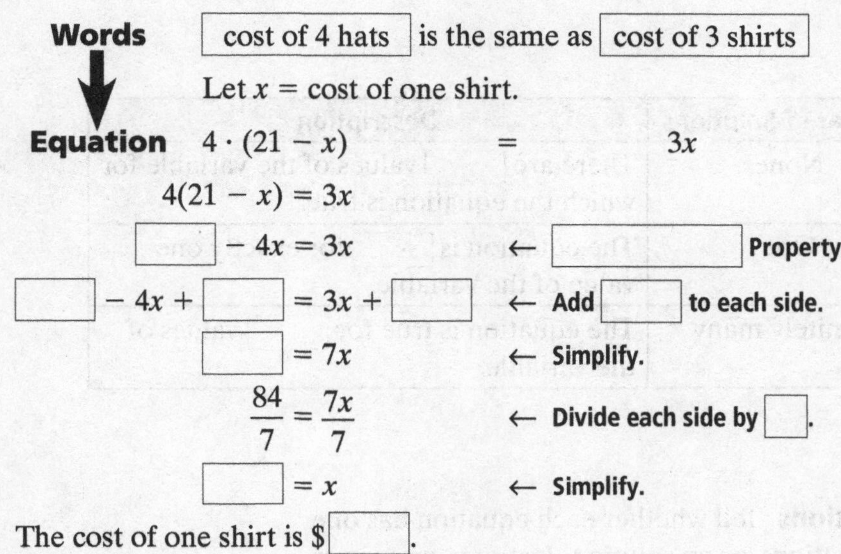

The cost of one shirt is \$$\square$.

Quick Check

2. One cell phone plan costs \$29.94 per month plus \$.10 for each text message sent. Another plan costs \$32.99 per month plus \$.05 for each text message sent. For what number of text messages will the monthly bill for both plans be the same?

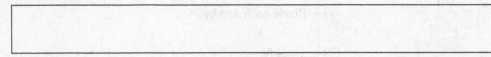

Name ______________________ Class ______________ Date ______________

Lesson 3-8

Types of Solutions of Linear Equations

Lesson Objective	Common Core State Standards
To identify whether a linear equation in one variable has one, infinitely many, or no solutions	Expressions and Equations: 8.EE.7, 8.EE.7.a, 8.EE.7.b

Key Concepts

Algebraic Form	Number of Solutions	Description
$a = b$	None	There are ☐ values of the variable for which the equation is true.
$x = a$	One	The equation is ☐ for exactly one value of the variable.
$a = a$	Infinitely many	The equation is true for ☐ values of the variable.

Examples

1 Identifying Types of Solutions Tell whether each equation has one solution, infinitely many solutions, or no solution. Justify your answer.

a. $6w + 3 = 4w - 1$

$6w - \square + 3 = 4w - \square - 1$ ← **Subtract ☐ from each side.**

$\square + 3 = -1$ ← **Simplify.**

$2w + 3 - \square = -1 - \square$ ← **Subtract ☐ from each side.**

$2w = -4$ ← **Simplify.**

$\frac{2w}{\square} = \frac{-4}{\square}$ ← **Divide each side by ☐.**

$w = \square$ ← **Simplify.**

The result is an equation of the form ☐ = ☐. So, the equation has ☐ solution(s).

b. $6w + 3 = 6(w + 0.5)$

$6w + 3 = \square + \square$ ← **Use the Distributive Property.**

$6w - \square + 3 = 6w - \square + 3$ ← **Subtract ☐ from each side.**

$3 = \square$ ← **Simplify.**

The result is an equation of the form ☐ = ☐. So, the equation has ☐ solution(s).

c. $6w + 3 = 6(w - 4)$

$6w + 3 = \square - \square$ ← **Use the Distributive Property.**

$6w - \square + 3 = 6w - \square - 24$ ← **Subtract $\square$ from each side.**

$3 = \square$ ← **Simplify.**

The result is an equation of the form $\square = \square$. So, the equation has $\square$ solution(s).

Quick Check

1. Tell whether each equation has one solution, infinitely many solutions, or no solution. Justify your answer.

a. $5x + 8 = 5(x + 3)$ **b.** $9x = 8 + 5x$ **c.** $6x + 12 = 6(x + 2)$ **d.** $7x - 11 = 11 - 7x$

Example

2 Comparing Costs A movie club card costs \$10. Cardholders pay the member's cost for a movie ticket. A person without a club card pays \$2 more for a ticket. A friend tells you that the cost of 5 tickets is the same for both members and nonmembers. Is this true? Justify your answer.

Words $\square + 5 \cdot \square = 5 \cdot (\square + \$2)$

Let t = cost of one member's ticket in dollars.

Equation $\square + 5t = 5(t + 2)$ ← **Substitute 10 for cost of card in dollars.**

$10 + 5t = \square + \square$ ← **Use the Distributive Property.**

$10 + 5t - \square = 5t - \square + 10$ ← **Subtract $\square$ from each side.**

$10 = 10$ ← **Simplify.**

The result is an equation of the form $\square = \square$. So, the equation has $\square$ solution(s), and the statement is $\square$.

Quick Check

2. Admission to the museum is \$8 for students and \$16 for adults. Yesterday, twice as many students as adults came to the museum. The total admissions paid by students and the total admissions paid by adults were equal. How many adults came to the museum yesterday? Justify your answer.

Name ______________________ Class ______________ Date ______________

Lesson 4-1

Graphing and Writing Inequalities

Lesson Objective	Common Core Standard
To graph and write algebraic inequalities	Expressions and Equations: 7.EE.4.b

Vocabulary

An inequality is ______________________

____

A solution of an inequality is ______________________

____

Examples

1 Identifying Solutions of an Inequality Find whether each number is a solution of $k > -6$; $-8, -6, 0, 3, 7$.

Test each value by replacing the variable and evaluating the sentence.

$-8 > -6$ ← **-8 is greater than -6; false.**

$-6 > -6$ ← **-6 is greater than -6; ______.**

$0 > -6$ ← **0 is greater than -6; ______.**

$3 > -6$ ← **3 is ______ than -6; ______.**

$7 > -6$ ← **7 is ______ than -6; ______.**

The numbers ____, ____, and ____ are solutions of $k > -6$.

The numbers ____ and ____ are not solutions of $k > -6$.

2 Graphing Inequalities Graph the solution of each inequality on a number line.

a. $r \leq 2$

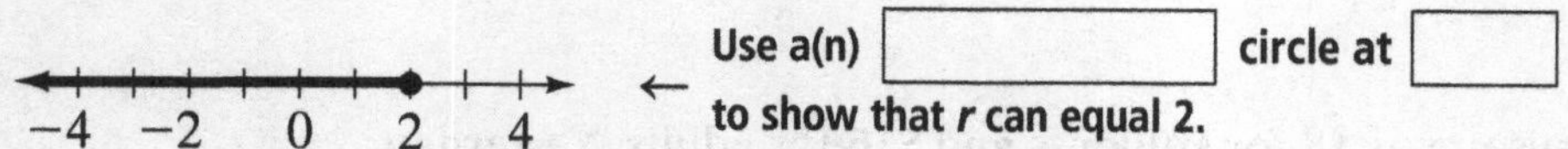

← **Use a(n) ______ circle at ______ to show that r can equal 2.**

b. $m > -5$

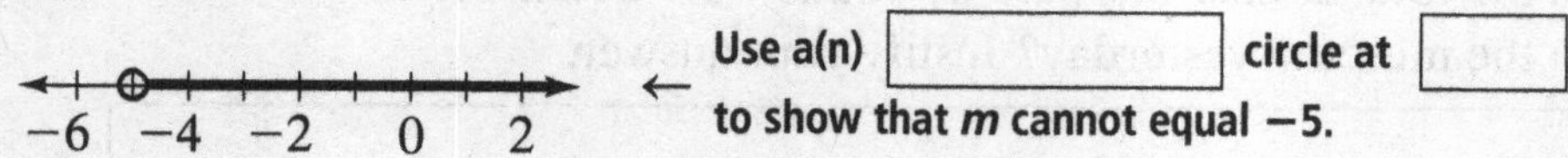

← **Use a(n) ______ circle at ______ to show that m cannot equal -5.**

3 Writing Inequalities Write an inequality for the graph.

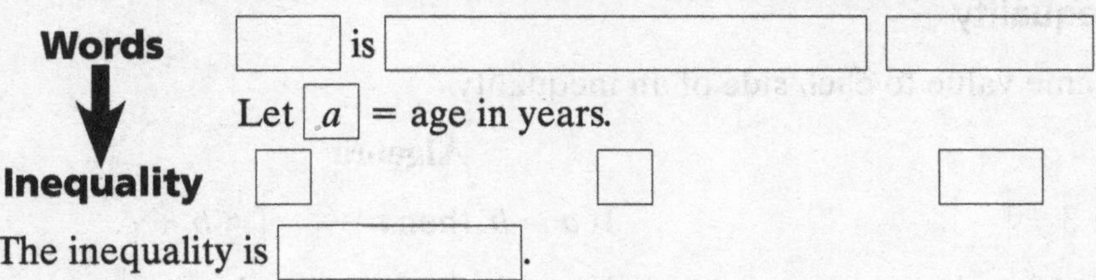

−4
−2
0
2
4
Since the circle at 1 is closed,
1 ☐ a solution.
y ☐ 1 ← Since the graph shows values ☐ or ☐ 1, use ☐.

4 Social Studies You must be at least 18 years of age to vote in a presidential election in the United States. Write an inequality for this requirement.

Words ☐ is ☐ ☐

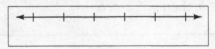

Let a = age in years.

Inequality ☐ ☐ ☐

The inequality is ☐.

Quick Check

1. Which numbers are solutions of the inequality $m \geq -3$; $-8, -2, 1.4$?

2. Graph the solution of the inequality $w < -3$.

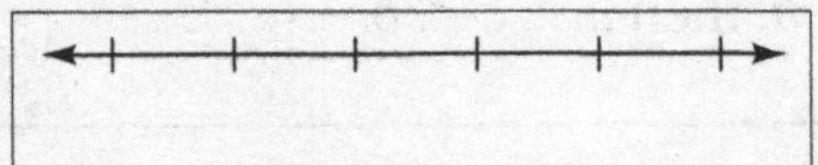

3. Write an inequality for the graph.

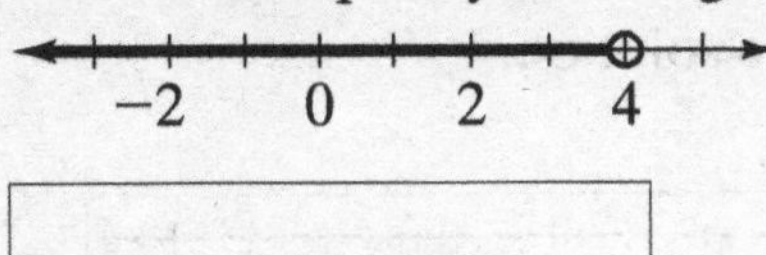

4. Write an inequality for "To qualify for the race, your time can be at most 62 seconds."

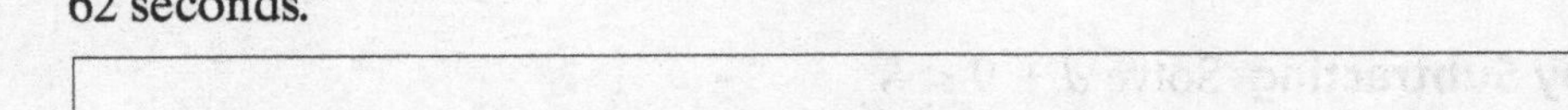

Name ______________________ Class ______________ Date ______________

Lesson 4-2

Solving Inequalities by Adding or Subtracting

Lesson Objective	Common Core Standard
To solve inequalities by adding or subtracting	Expressions and Equations: 7.EE.4.b

Key Concepts

Addition Property of Inequality

You can ☐ the same value to each side of an inequality.

Arithmetic	Algebra
Since $7 > 3, 7 + 4 > 3 + \square$.	If $a > b$, then $a + \square > b + c$.
Since $1 < 3, 1 + \square < 3 + 4$.	If $a < b$, then $a + c < b + \square$.

Subtraction Property of Inequality

You can ☐ the same value from each side of an inequality.

Arithmetic	Algebra
Since $9 > 6, 9 - 3 > 6 - \square$.	If $a > b$, then $a - \square > b - c$.
Since $15 < 20, 15 - \square < 20 - 4$.	If $a < b$, then $a - c < b - \square$.

Examples

❶ **Solving Inequalities by Adding** Solve $q - 2 \geq -6$. Graph the solution.

$q - 2 \geq -6$

$q - 2 + \square \geq -6 + \square$ ← **Add ☐ to each side.**

$q \geq \square$ ← **Simplify.**

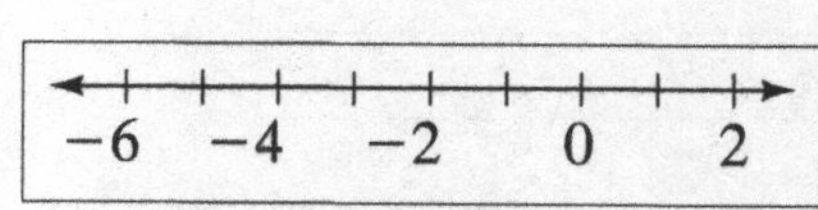

❷ **Solving Inequalities by Subtracting** Solve $d + 9 < 8$.
Graph the solution.

$d + 9 < 8$

$d + 9 - \square < 8 - \square$ ← **Subtract ☐ from each side.**

$q < \square$ ← **Simplify.**

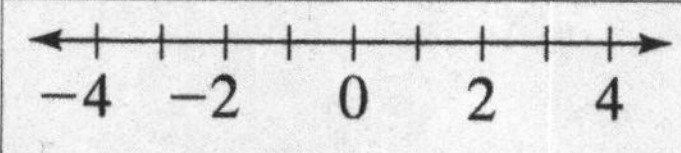

Name ______________ Class ______________ Date ______________

Example

3 **Budget** The Drama Club can spend no more than \$120 for costumes. They already spent \$79. How much more can they spend for costumes?

Words amount spent already | plus | amount spent on costumes | is at most | \$120.

Let c = amount the Drama Club can spend on costumes.

Inequality ___ + ___ ___ ___

$79 + c \leq 120$

$79 - \_\_\_ + c \leq 120 - \_\_\_$ ← **Subtract** ___ **from each side.**

$c \leq \_\_\_$ ← **Simplify.**

They can spend at most ___.

Quick Check

1. Solve $y - 3 < 4$. Graph the solution.

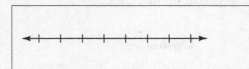

2. Solve each inequality. Graph the solution.

a. $x + 9 > 5$

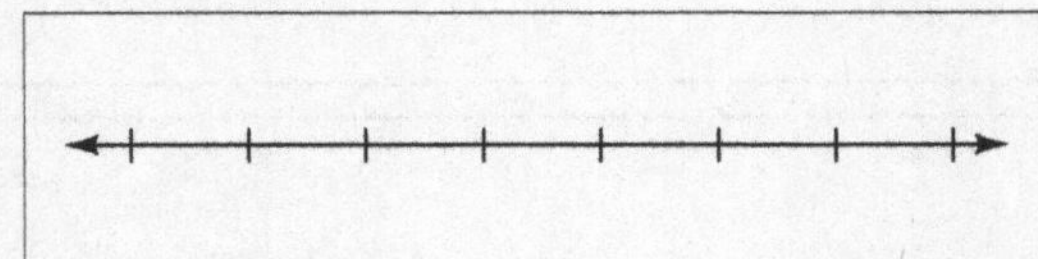

b. $y + 3 < 4$

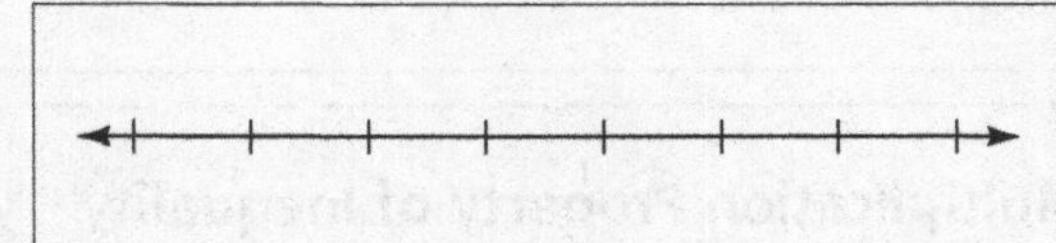

c. $w + 4 \leq -5$

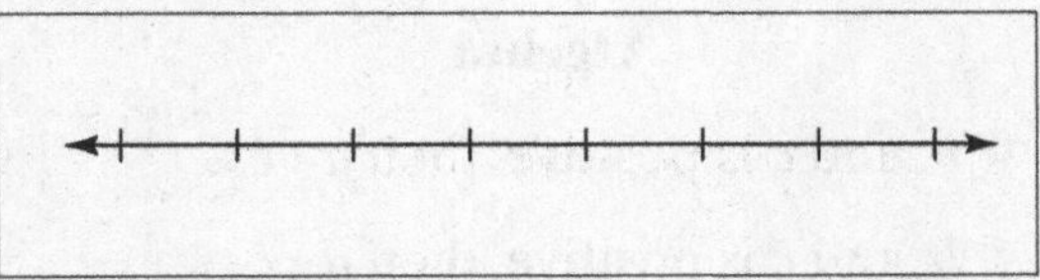

3. To get an A, you need more than 200 points on a two-part test. You score 109 points on the first part. How many more points do you need?

Name _______________________ Class _______________ Date _______________

Lesson 4-3

Solving Inequalities by Multiplying or Dividing

Lesson Objective	Common Core Standard
To solve inequalities by multiplying or dividing	Expressions and Equations: 7.EE.4.b

Key Concepts

Division Property of Inequality

If you _______ each side of an inequality by the same positive number, the direction of the inequality symbol remains unchanged.

Arithmetic

$9 > 6$, so $\frac{9}{3}$ ☐ $\frac{6}{3}$

$15 < 20$, so $\frac{15}{5}$ ☐ $\frac{☐}{☐}$

Algebra

If $a > b$, and c is positive, then $\frac{a}{c}$ ☐ $\frac{b}{c}$.

If $a < b$, and c is positive, then $\frac{a}{c}$ ☐ $\frac{☐}{☐}$.

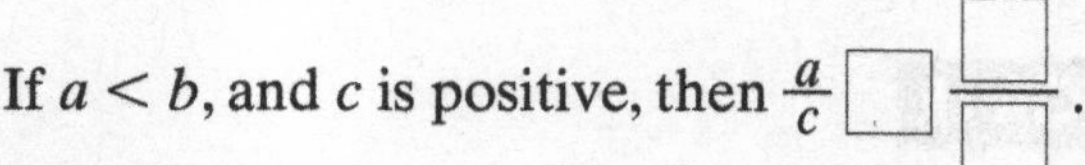

If you _______ each side of an inequality by the same negative number, the direction of the inequality symbol is reversed.

Arithmetic

$16 > 12$, so $-\frac{16}{4}$ ☐ $-\frac{12}{4}$

$10 < 18$, so $-\frac{10}{2}$ ☐ $\frac{☐}{☐}$

Algebra

If $a > b$, and c is negative, then $\frac{a}{c}$ ☐ $\frac{b}{c}$.

If $a < b$, and c is negative, then $\frac{a}{c}$ ☐ $\frac{☐}{☐}$.

Multiplication Property of Inequality

If you _______ each side of an inequality by the same positive number, the direction of the inequality symbol remains unchanged.

Arithmetic

$12 > 8$, so $12 \cdot 2$ ☐ ☐ $\cdot 2$

$3 < 6$, so $3 \cdot 4$ ☐ ☐ $\cdot 4$

Algebra

If $a > b$, and c is positive, then $a \cdot c$ ☐ ☐ $\cdot c$.

If $a < b$, and c is positive, then $a \cdot c$ ☐ ☐ $\cdot c$.

If you _______ each side of an inequality by the same negative number, the direction of the inequality symbol is reversed.

Arithmetic

$6 > 2$, so $6(-3)$ ☐ ☐ (-3)

$3 < 5$, so $3(-2)$ ☐ ☐ (-2)

Algebra

If $a > b$, and c is negative, then $a \cdot c$ ☐ ☐ $\cdot c$.

If $a < b$, and c is negative, then $a \cdot c$ ☐ ☐ $\cdot c$.

Name ______________________ Class ______________ Date ______________

Examples

1 **Business** A woodworker makes a profit of $30 on each picture frame that is sold. Write an inequality to describe the number of frames the woodworker must sell to make a profit of at least $500.

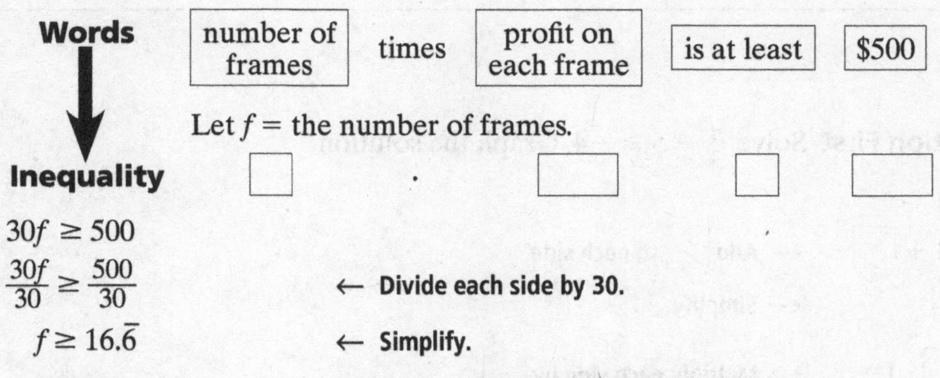

$30f \geq 500$

$\frac{30f}{30} \geq \frac{500}{30}$ ← **Divide each side by 30.**

$f \geq 16.\overline{6}$ ← **Simplify.**

$f \geq 17$ ← **Round up to the nearest whole number.**

The woodworker must sell at least ☐ frames.

2 **Solving Inequalities by Multiplying** Solve $\frac{b}{-3} < -12$.

$\frac{b}{-3} < -12$

☐ $\cdot -\frac{b}{3}$ ☐ ☐ $\cdot -12$ ← **Multiply each side by ☐. Reverse the direction of the symbol.**

b ☐ ☐ ← **Simplify.**

Quick Check

1. A long-distance telephone company is offering a special rate of $.06 per minute. Your budget for long-distance telephone calls is $25 for the month. At most how many minutes of long distance can you use for the month?

2. Solve $-\frac{k}{5} < -4$. Graph the solution.

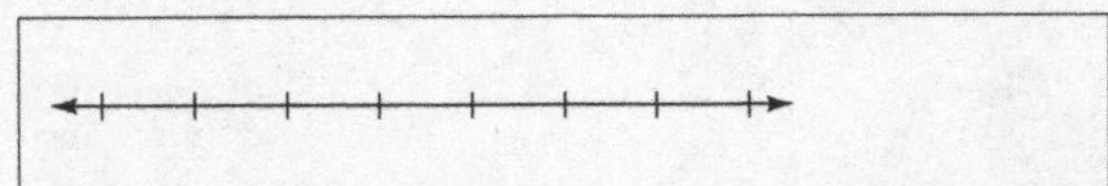

Name ____________ Class ____________ Date ____________

Lesson 4-4

Solving Two-Step Inequalities

Lesson Objective	**Common Core Standard**
To solve two-step inequalities using inverse operations	Expressions and Equations: 7.EE.4.b

Examples

1 Undoing Subtraction First Solve $\frac{n}{3} - 5 \geq -4$. Graph the solution.

$$\frac{n}{3} - 5 \geq -4$$

$$\frac{n}{3} - 5 + \square \geq -4 + \square \quad \leftarrow \textbf{Add } \square \textbf{ to each side.}$$

$$\frac{n}{3} \geq \square \quad \leftarrow \textbf{Simplify.}$$

$$\square \cdot \frac{n}{3} \geq \square \cdot 1 \quad \leftarrow \textbf{Multiply each side by } \square.$$

$$n \geq \square \quad \leftarrow \textbf{Simplify.}$$

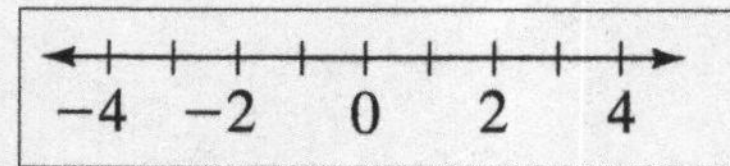

2 Undoing Addition First Solve $-4.4x + 2 > 8.6$. Graph the solution.

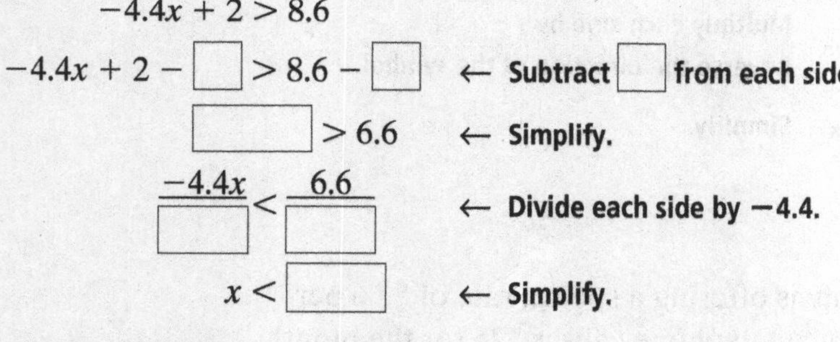

$$-4.4x + 2 > 8.6$$

$$-4.4x + 2 - \square > 8.6 - \square \quad \leftarrow \textbf{Subtract } \square \textbf{ from each side.}$$

$$\square > 6.6 \quad \leftarrow \textbf{Simplify.}$$

$$\frac{-4.4x}{\square} < \frac{6.6}{\square} \quad \leftarrow \textbf{Divide each side by } -4.4.$$

$$x < \square \quad \leftarrow \textbf{Simplify.}$$

−6 −4 −2 0 2

Name ______________________ Class ______________ Date ______________

❸ **Archery** An archery range charges $50 for membership plus $5 per round. Vivian wants to join the range and shoot as many rounds as possible, but she has only $75. What is the greatest number of rounds she can shoot?

Words | cost per round | times | number of rounds | plus | membership fee | is at most | total cost |

Let r = the number of rounds

Expression 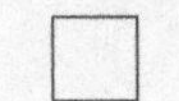 $\cdot$  + ☐ = ☐

$5r + 50 \leq 75$

$5r + 50 - 50 \leq 75 - 50$ ← **Subtract** ☐ **from each side.**

$5r \leq$ ☐ ← **Simplify.**

$\frac{5r}{☐} \leq \frac{25}{☐}$ ← **Divide each side by** ☐.

$r \leq$ ☐ ← **Simplify.**

Quick Check

1. Solve the inequality $-5 + \frac{c}{3} > -1$. Graph the solution.

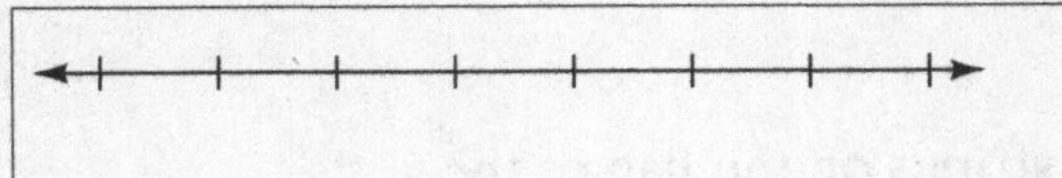

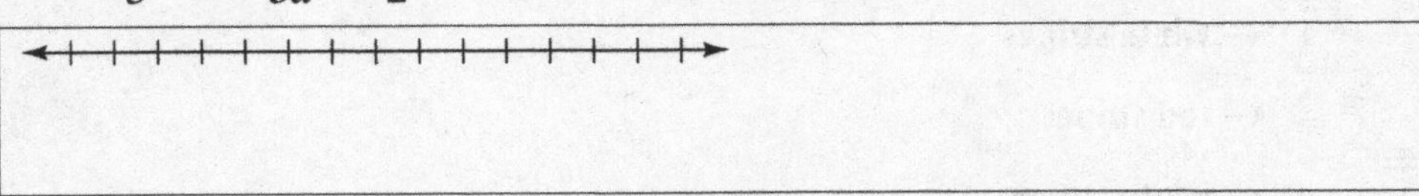

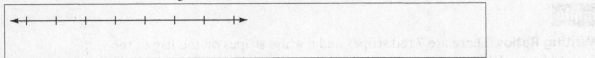

2. Solve $\frac{1}{5} \geq -\frac{1}{3a} + \frac{1}{2}$. Graph the solution on a number line.

3. A phone plan charges $.20 per text message plus a monthly fee of $42.50. Lin can spend at most $50. Write an inequality for the number of text messages Lin can send. Describe the solution.

Name ____________________ Class ____________ Date ____________

Lesson 5-1

Ratios

Lesson Objective	**Common Core Standard**
To write ratios and use them to compare quantities	Ratios and Proportional Relationships: Prepares for 7.RP.1

Vocabulary and Key Concepts

Ratio

A ratio is ____________________

You can write a ratio in three ways.

	Arithmetic			**Algebra**	
5 to 7	☐	☐/☐	☐	$a : b$	☐/☐, where $b \neq 0$

Equivalent ratios are ____________________

Example

1 Writing Ratios There are 7 red stripes and 6 white stripes on the flag of the United States. Write the ratio of red stripes to white stripes in three ways.

red stripes → ☐ ← white stripes

red stripes → ☐ ← white stripes

☐ ← red stripes
—
☐ ← white stripes

Quick Check

1. Write each ratio in three ways. Use the pattern of piano keys shown at the right.

   a. white keys to all keys

   ☐

   b. white keys to black keys

   ☐

Name ______________________ Class ______________ Date ______________

Examples

② Writing Equivalent Ratios Find a ratio equivalent to $\frac{14}{4}$.

$\frac{14 \div \square}{4 \div \square} = \frac{\square}{\square}$ ← **Divide the numerator and denominator by 2.**

③ Writing Equivalent Ratios Write the ratio 2 lb to 56 oz as a fraction in simplest form.

$\frac{2 \text{ lb}}{56 \text{ oz}} = \frac{2 \times 16 \text{ oz}}{56 \text{ oz}}$ ← **There are 16 oz in each pound.**

$= \frac{\square \text{ oz}}{56 \text{ oz}}$ ← **Multiply.**

$= \frac{\square \div \square \text{ oz}}{56 \div \square \text{ oz}}$ ← **Divide by the GCF, $\square$ oz.**

$= \frac{\square}{\square}$ ← **Simplify.**

④ Comparing Ratios The ratio of girls to boys enrolled at King Middle School is 15 : 16. There are 195 girls and 208 boys in Grade 8. Is the ratio of girls to boys in Grade 8 equivalent to the ratio of girls to boys in the entire school?

Entire School				Grade 8
$\square$	←	**girls**	→	$\square$
$\square$	←	**boys**	→	$\square$

$\frac{\square}{\square} = \square$ ← **Write as a decimal.** → $\frac{\square}{\square} = \square$

Since the two decimals are $\square$, the ratio of girls to boys in Grade 8 is $\square$ to the ratio of girls to boys in the entire school.

Quick Check

2. Find a ratio equivalent to $\frac{7}{9}$.

$\square$

3. Write the ratio 3 gal to 10 qt as a fraction in simplest form.

$\square$

4. Tell whether the ratios below are *equivalent* or *not equivalent*.

a. 7 : 3, 128 : 54

$\square$

b. $\frac{180}{240}, \frac{25}{34}$

$\square$

c. 6.1 to 7, 30.5 to 35

$\square$

Name ______________________ Class ______________ Date ____________

Lesson 5-2

Unit Rates and Proportional Reasoning

Lesson Objective	**Common Core Standard**
To find unit rates and unit costs using proportional reasoning	Ratios and Proportional Relationships: 7.RP.1

Vocabulary

A rate is ____

____

A unit rate is ____

A unit cost is ____

Examples

1 Finding a Unit Rate Using Whole Numbers You earn $33 for 4 hours of work. Find the unit rate of dollars per hour.

dollars → $\frac{33}{4} = \square$ ← **Divide the first quantity by**
hours → **the second quantity.**

The unit rate is $\frac{\square}{\square}$, or $\square$ per hour.

2 Finding a Unit Rate Using Fractions Ely walks $\frac{7}{8}$ mile in $\frac{1}{3}$ hour. What is his speed in miles per hour?

miles to hours $= \frac{7}{8}$ to $\frac{1}{3}$ → **Write the ratio.**

miles $\square$ hours $= \frac{7}{8} \div \frac{\square}{\square}$ → **Divide the first quantity by the second quantity.**

$= \frac{\square}{\square}$ → **Simplify.**

$= \square\frac{\square}{\square}$ → **Write as a mixed number.**

Ely walks $\square\frac{\square}{\square}$ miles $\square$ $\square$.

Name ______________________ Class ______________ Date ______________

Quick Check

1. Find the unit rate for 210 heartbeats in 3 minutes.

[ ]

2. Find the unit rate for $\frac{3}{10}$ mile in $\frac{3}{4}$ hour.

[ ]

Example

❸ **Using Unit Cost to Compare** Find each unit cost. Which is the better buy?

3 lb of potatoes for $.89
5 lb of potatoes for $1.59

Divide to find the unit cost of each size.

cost → / size → $\frac{\$.89}{3 \text{ lb}} \approx$ [ ]

cost → / size → $\frac{\$1.59}{5 \text{ lb}} \approx$ [ ]

Since [ ] < [ ], [ ] for [ ] is the better buy.

Quick Check

3. Which bottle of apple juice is the better buy: 48 fl oz of fruit juice for $3.05 or 64 fl oz for $3.59?

[ ]

Name ______________________ Class ______________ Date ______________

Lesson 5-3

Proportions

Lesson Objective	Common Core Standards
To test whether ratios form a proportion by using equivalent ratios and cross products	Ratios and Proportional Relationships: 7.RP.2, 7.RP.2.a

Key Concepts

Proportion

A proportion is ____

Arithmetic $\frac{1}{2} = \frac{2}{4}$

Algebra $\frac{a}{b} = \frac{c}{d}, b \neq 0, d \neq 0$

Cross Products Property

Cross products are ____

____

If two ratios form a proportion, the cross products are equal. If two ratios have equal cross products, they form a proportion.

Arithmetic

$\frac{6}{8} = \frac{9}{12}$

$6 \cdot 12 = 8 \cdot 9$

Algebra

$\frac{a}{b} = \frac{c}{d}$

$ad = bc$, where $b \neq 0$, and $d \neq 0$

Example

1 Writing Ratios in Simplest Form Do the ratios $\frac{42}{56}$ and $\frac{56}{64}$ form a proportion?

$\frac{42}{56} = \frac{42 \div \square}{56 \div \square} = \frac{\square}{\square}$ ← **Divide the numerator and denominator by the GCF.** → $\frac{56}{64} = \frac{56 \div \square}{64 \div \square} = \frac{\square}{\square}$

The ratios in simplest form are not equivalent. They ______ form a proportion.

Quick Check

1. Do $\frac{10}{12}$ and $\frac{40}{56}$ form a proportion?

Name ______________________ Class ______________ Date ____________

Example

2 Using Cross Products Do the ratios in each pair form a proportion?

a. $\frac{4}{10}, \frac{6}{15}$ **b.** $\frac{8}{6}, \frac{9}{7}$

$\frac{4}{10} \stackrel{?}{=} \frac{6}{15}$ ← **Test each pair of ratios.** → $\frac{8}{6} \stackrel{?}{=} \frac{9}{7}$

$4 \cdot \square \stackrel{?}{=} 10 \cdot \square$ ← **Write cross products.** → $8 \cdot \square \stackrel{?}{=} 6 \cdot \square$

$\square\ \square\ 60$ ← **Simplify.** → $\square\ \square\ 54$

$\square$, $\frac{4}{10}$ and $\frac{6}{15}$ $\square$, $\frac{8}{6}$ and $\frac{9}{7}$

$\square$ a proportion. $\square$ a proportion.

Quick Check

2. Determine whether the ratios form a proportion.

a. $\frac{3}{8}, \frac{6}{16}$ **b.** $\frac{6}{9}, \frac{4}{6}$ **c.** $\frac{4}{8}, \frac{5}{9}$

Name ______________________ Class ______________ Date ______________

Lesson 5-4

Solving Proportions

Lesson Objective	**Common Core Standards**
To solve proportions using unit rates, mental math, and cross products	Ratios and Proportional Relationships: 7.RP.1, 7.RP.2

Examples

1 Using Unit Rates The cost of 4 lightbulbs is $3. Use the information to find the cost of 10 lightbulbs.

Step 1 Find the unit price.

$\frac{3 \text{ dollars}}{4 \text{ lightbulbs}} = \$3 \div 4$ lightbulbs ← **Divide to find the unit price.**

$\frac{\square}{\text{lightbulb}}$

Step 2 You know the cost of one lightbulb. Multiply to find the cost of 10 lightbulbs.

$\square \cdot \square = \square$ ← **Multiply the unit rate by the number of lightbulbs.**

The cost of 10 lightbulbs is $\square$.

2 Solving Using Mental Math Solve each proportion using mental math.

a. $\frac{5}{c} = \frac{30}{42}$

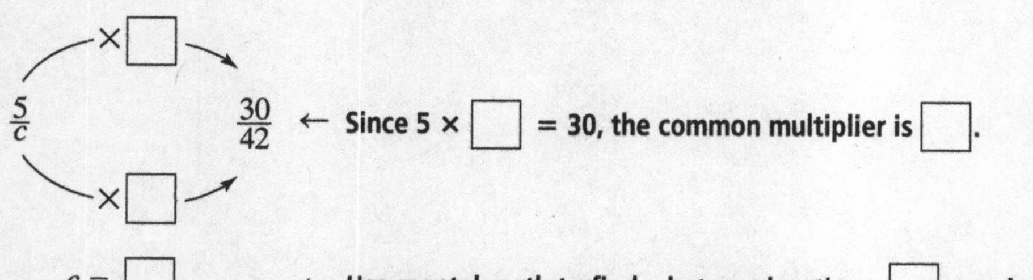

← **Since 5 × $\square$ = 30, the common multiplier is $\square$.**

$c = \square$ ← **Use mental math to find what number times $\square$ equals 42.**

b. $\frac{9}{4} = \frac{72}{t}$

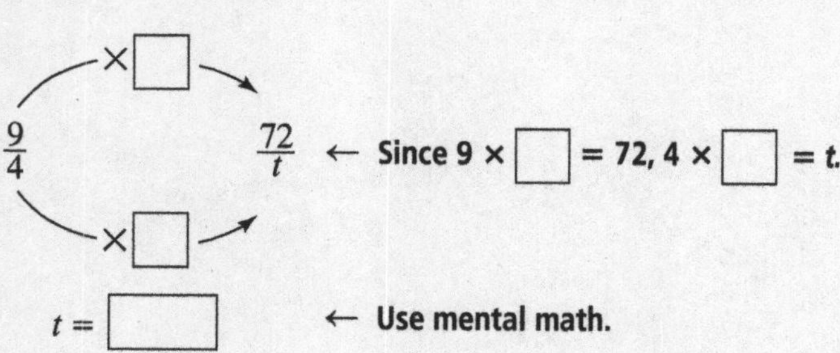

← **Since 9 × $\square$ = 72, 4 × $\square$ = t.**

$t = \square$ ← **Use mental math.**

Name ______________________ Class ______________ Date ______________

3 Solving Using Cross Products Solve $\frac{6}{8} = \frac{9}{a}$ using cross products.

$\frac{6}{8} = \frac{9}{a}$

$6a = 8(9)$ ← **Write the cross products.**

$6a = \square$ ← **Simplify.**

$\frac{6a}{\square} = \frac{\square}{\square}$ ← **Divide each side by $\square$.**

$a = \square$ ← **Simplify.**

Quick Check

1. a. Postcards cost \$2.45 for 5 cards. How much will 13 cards cost?

b. Swimming goggles cost \$84.36 for 12. At this rate, how much will new goggles for 17 members of a swim team cost?

2. Solve each proportion using mental math.

a. $\frac{3}{8} = \frac{b}{24}$ **b.** $\frac{m}{5} = \frac{16}{40}$ **c.** $\frac{15}{30} = \frac{5}{p}$

3. Solve each proportion using cross products.

a. $\frac{12}{15} = \frac{x}{21}$ **b.** $\frac{16}{30} = \frac{d}{51}$ **c.** $\frac{20}{35} = \frac{110}{m}$

Lesson 5-5

Similar Figures

Lesson Objective	**Common Core Standards**
To use proportions to find missing lengths in similar figures	Ratios and Proportional Relationships: 7.RP.1, 7.RP.2 Geometry: 7.G.1

Vocabulary and Key Concepts

Similar Polygons

Two polygons are similar if

- corresponding angles ________________
- the lengths of corresponding sides ________________

A polygon is ________________

Indirect measurement is ________________

Example

1 Finding a Missing Measure $\triangle ABC$ and $\triangle DEF$ are similar. Find the value of c.

$\frac{AB}{DE} = \frac{AC}{DF}$ ← **Write a proportion.**

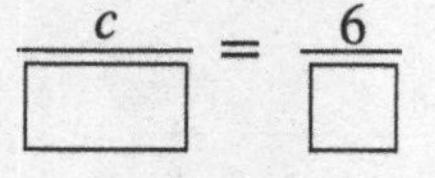

← **Substitute.**

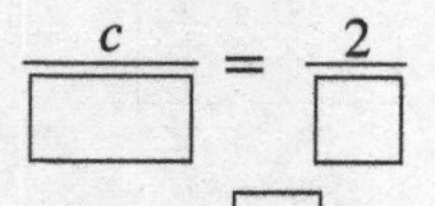

← **Write $\frac{6}{\square}$ in simplest form.**

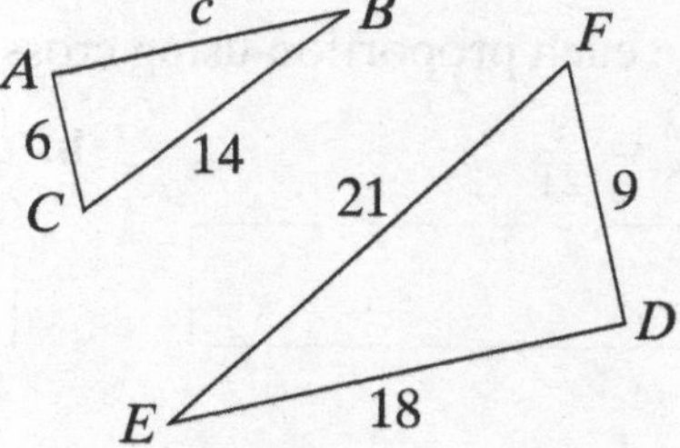

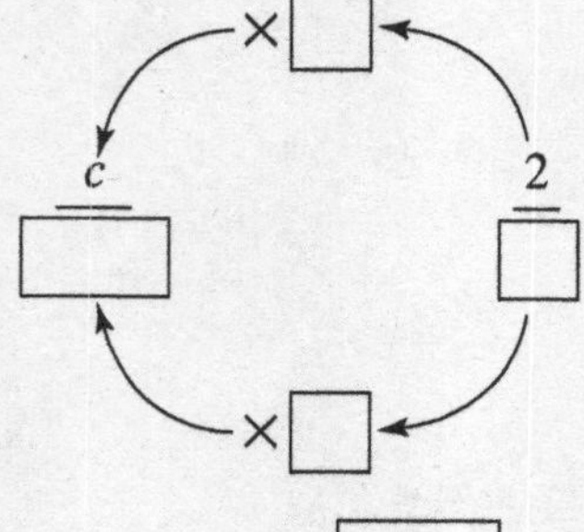

← **Find the common multiplier.**

$c = \square$ ← **Use mental math.**

Name ________________________ Class ____________ Date ____________

❷ **Multiple Choice** A 5-ft person standing near a tree has a shadow 12 ft long. At the same time, the tree has a shadow 42 ft long. What is the height of the tree?

A. 17.5 ft **B.** 35 ft **C.** 49 ft **D.** 100.8 ft

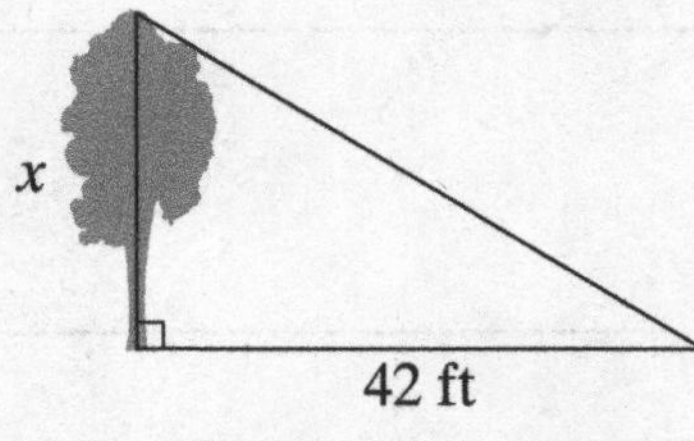

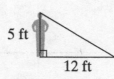

Draw a picture and let x represent the height of the tree.

$\frac{x}{\square} = \frac{42}{\square}$ ← **Write a proportion.**

$\square x = \square \cdot 42$ ← **Write the cross products.**

$\frac{12x}{12} = \frac{5 \cdot 42}{12}$ ← **Divide each side by 12.**

$x = \square$ ← **Simplify.**

The height of the tree is ☐ ft. The correct answer is choice ☐.

Quick Check

1. The trapezoids below are similar. Find x.

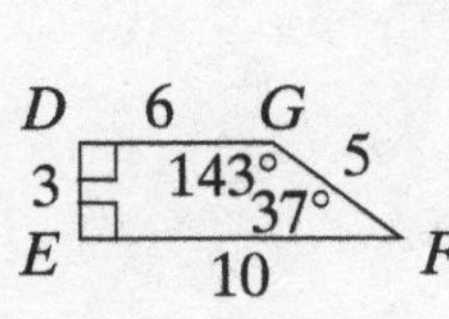

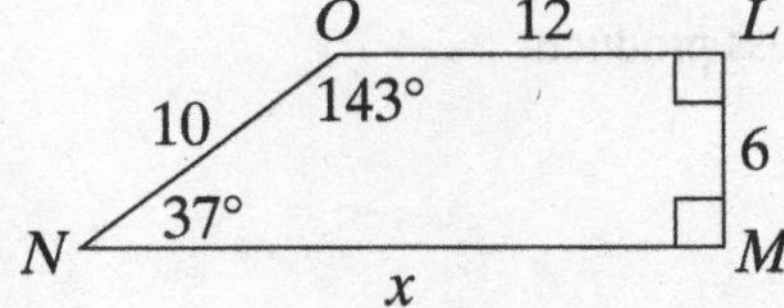

2. A 6-ft person has a shadow 5 ft long. A nearby tree has a shadow 30 ft long. What is the height of the tree?

Name ______________________ Class ______________ Date ______________

Lesson 5-6

Maps and Scale Drawings

Lesson Objective	Common Core Standards
To use proportions to solve problems involving scale	Ratios and Proportional Relationships: 7.RP.1 Geometry: 7.G.1

Vocabulary

A scale drawing is ____

A scale is ____

Example

1 **Using a Scale Drawing** The scale of a drawing is 1 in. : 6 ft. The length of a wall is 4.5 in. on the drawing. Find the actual length of the wall.

You can write the scale of the drawing as $\frac{1 \text{ in.}}{6 \text{ ft}}$. Then write a proportion.

Let n represent the actual length.

drawing (in.) → $\frac{1}{6} = \frac{\square}{n}$ **← drawing (in.)**
actual (ft) → **← actual (ft)**

$\square n = \square(4.5)$ **← Write the cross products.**

$n = \square$ **← Simplify.**

The actual length is $\square$ ft.

Quick Check

1. The chimney of a house is 4 cm tall on the drawing. How tall is the chimney of the actual house?

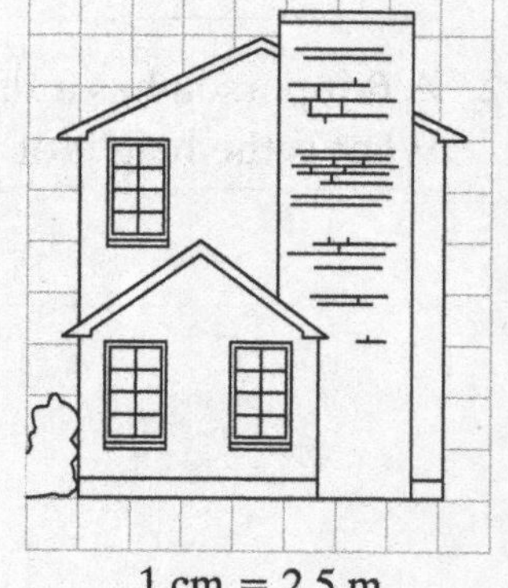

1 cm = 2.5 m

Name ________________ Class ________________ Date ________________

Examples

❷ Finding the Scale of a Model The actual length of the wheelbase of a mountain bike is 260 cm. The length of the wheelbase in a scale drawing is 4 cm. Find the scale of the drawing.

scale length → / **actual length →** $\frac{4}{260} = \frac{4 \div \square}{260 \div \square} = \frac{\square}{\square}$ **← Write the ratio in simplest form.**

The scale is ☐ cm : ☐ cm.

❸ Multiple Choice You want to make a scale model of a house that is 72 feet long and 24 feet tall. You plan to make the model 12 inches long. Which equation can you use to find x, the height of the model?

A. $\frac{24}{72} = \frac{x}{12}$ **B.** $\frac{12}{72} = \frac{x}{24}$ **C.** $\frac{12}{24} = \frac{x}{72}$ **D.** $\frac{x}{24} = \frac{72}{12}$

model (in.) → / **actual (ft) →** $\frac{\square}{\square} = \frac{?}{?}$ **← model (in.)** / **← actual (ft)** **← Write a proportion.**

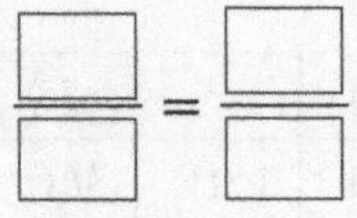

← Fill in the information you know. Use *x* for the information you don't know.

The correct answer is ☐.

Quick Check

2. The length of a room in an architectural drawing is 10 in. Its actual length is 160 in. What is the scale of the drawing?

3. You want to make a scale model of a sailboat that is 51 ft long and 15 ft wide. You plan to make the sailboat 17 in. long. How wide should the model be?

Name ______________________ Class ______________ Date ____________

Lesson 5-7

Proportional Relationships

Lesson Objective	**Common Core Standards**
To identify proportional relationships and find constants of proportionality	Ratios and Proportions: 7.RP.2.a, 7.RP.2.b, 7.RP.2.c, 7.RP.2.d

Vocabulary

A constant of proportionality is ____

____

Examples

1 Using a Table to Determine a Proportional Relationship The table below shows the number of times Linda skipped rope in minutes during a fundraiser. Is there a proportional relationship between time and skips?

Compare the ratios of time and rope skips.

Minutes	0	5	12	15	17
Skips	0	150	360	450	510

rope skips → / time → $\frac{150}{5} = \frac{\square}{12} = \frac{450}{\square} = \frac{\square}{\square}$

The ratios are ____, so there is a ____ relationship between time and ____.

2 Using a Graph to Find a Unit Rate The graph below displays the data given in Example 1. What is Linda's speed in skips per minute?

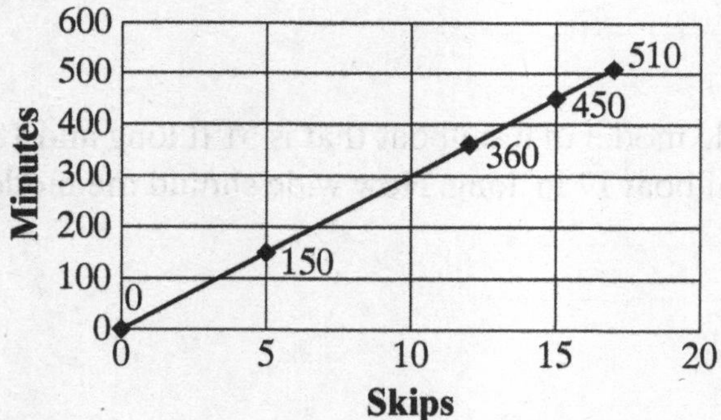

Linda's speed is a unit rate. Find the value of r in the ordered pair $(1, r)$.

The graph of this relationship passes through (0, 0) and $(\square, 150)$. So, it must also pass through $(1, \square)$. Since $r = \square$, the unit rate is ____ ____ per ____.

Linda's speed is ____ ____ per ____.

Name ______________________ Class ______________ Date ______________

❸ Using a Ratio to Identify a Unit Rate The table below shows a proportional relationship between the number of songs downloaded on a music site and the amount the customer pays. Identify the constant of proportionality.

Songs Downloaded, s	Price, p (dollars)
20	$10
40	$20
100	$50
120	$60

Step 1 Use one data point to find the constant of proportionality c.

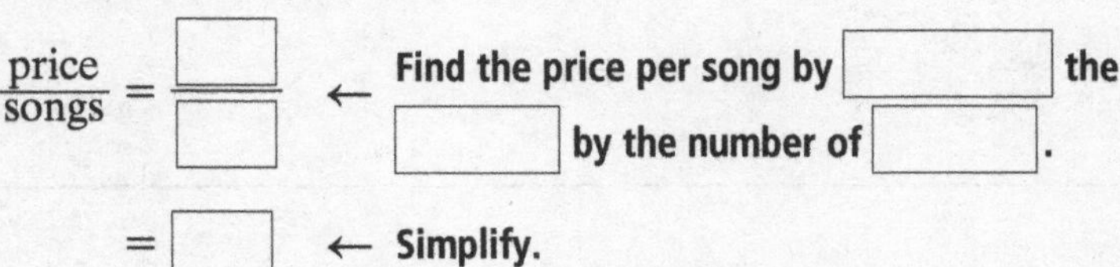

$\frac{\text{price}}{\text{songs}} = \frac{\square}{\square}$ ← **Find the price per song by ____ the ____ by the number of ____.**

$= \square$ ← **Simplify.**

Step 2 Check by multiplying c times the first quantity.

$20 \times \square = \square$ $40 \times \square = \square$

$100 \times \square = \square$ $120 \times \square = \square$

The constant of proportionality is ____. This unit rate represents a payment of ____ per song.

Quick Check

1. The table at the right shows the distances Dave rode in a bike-a-thon. Is there a proportional relationship? Explain.

Dave

Hours	0	3	6	8	9
Miles	0	18.6	35.2	49.6	56.8

____

____

2. Use the graph at the right. What is Damon's reading speed in pages per day?

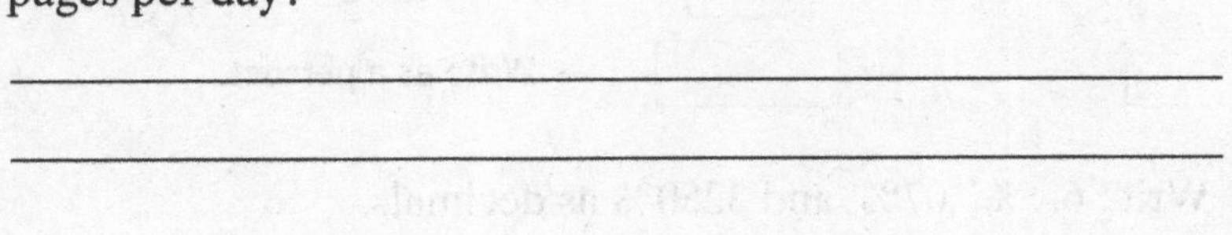

____

____

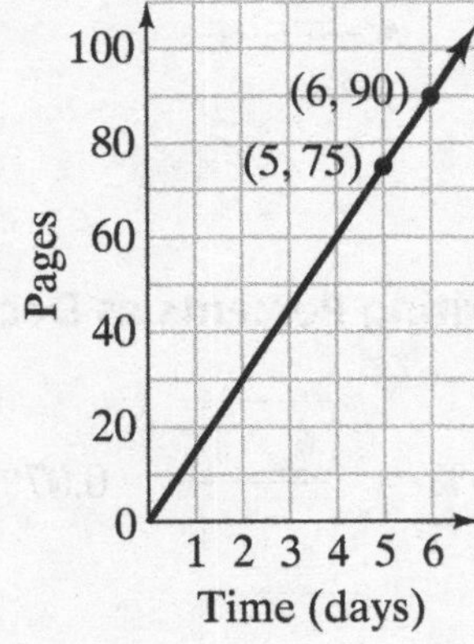

3. Find the constant of proportionality for each table of values.

a. yards of cloth per blanket

Yards(y)	16	32	40
Blankets (b)	8	16	20

____

b. pay per hour

Hours(h)	2	10	16
Pay (p)	$11	$55	$88

____

Name ______________________ Class ______________________ Date ______________________

Lesson 6-1

Percents, Fractions, and Decimals

Lesson Objective	Common Core Standard
To convert between fractions, decimals, and percents	Expressions and Equations: 7.EE.3

Key Concepts

Fractions, Decimals, and Percents

You can write 21 out of 100 as a fraction, a decimal, or a percent.

Fraction	Decimal	Percent
$\frac{\square}{\square}$	$\square$	$\square$

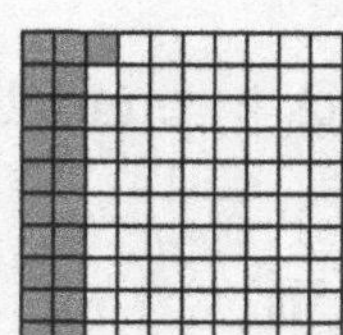

Examples

1 Writing Decimals as Percents Write 0.101, .008, and 2.012 as percents.

$0.101 = \frac{101}{\square}$ $\quad 0.008 = \frac{8}{\square}$ $\quad 2.012 = \frac{2,012}{\square}$ ← **Write as a fraction.**

$= \frac{\square}{\square}$ $\quad = \frac{\square}{\square}$ $\quad = \frac{\square}{\square}$ ← **Write an equivalent fraction with $\square$ in the denominator.**

$= \square$ $\quad = \square$ $\quad = \square$ ← **Write as a percent.**

2 Writing Percents as Decimals Write 6.4%, .07%, and 3250% as decimals.

$6.4\% = \frac{\square}{\square}$ $\quad 0.07\% = \frac{\square}{\square}$ $\quad 3250\% = \frac{\square}{\square}$ ← **Write the percent as a fraction.**

$= \square$ $\quad = \square$ $\quad = \square$ ← **Divide.**

Quick Check

1. Write 0.607, 0.005, and 9.283 as percents.

$\square$ $\quad \square$ $\quad \square$

2. Write each percent as a decimal.

a. 3500% $\square$ **b.** 12.5% $\square$ **c.** 0.78% $\square$

Name ______________________ Class ______________ Date ______________

Examples

3 Writing Percents as Fractions Write each percent as a fraction in simplest form.

a. 12% **b.** 45%

$12\% = \dfrac{12}{\square}$ ← Write as a fraction with a denominator of $\square$. → $45\% = \dfrac{45}{\square}$

$= \dfrac{12 \div \square}{100 \div \square}$ ← Divide the numerator and the denominator by the GCF. → $= \dfrac{45 \div \square}{100 \div \square}$

$= \dfrac{\square}{\square}$ ← Simplify the fraction. → $= \dfrac{\square}{\square}$

4 Ordering Rational Numbers Order $\frac{3}{5}$, $\frac{2}{10}$, 0.645, and 13% from least to greatest. Write all numbers as decimals. Then graph each number on a number line.

$\frac{3}{5} = \square$ ← Divide the $\square$ by the $\square$.

$\frac{2}{10} = \square$ ← Divide the $\square$ by the $\square$.

0.645 ← This number is already in decimal form.

$13\% = \square$ ← Move the decimal point $\square$ places to the $\square$.

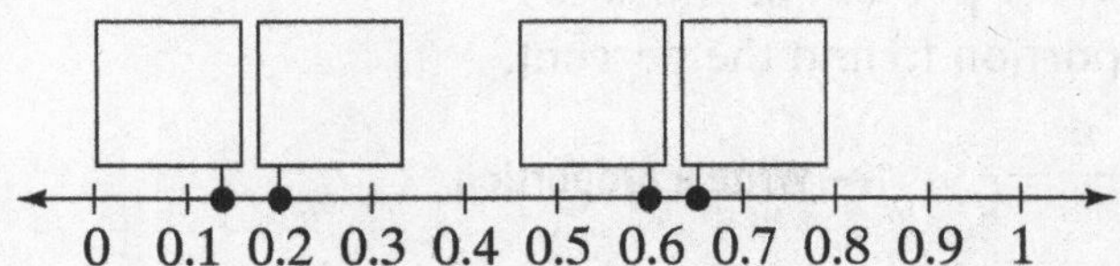

Quick Check

3. An elephant eats about 6% of its body weight in vegetation every day. Write this as a fraction in simplest form.

4. Order from least to greatest.

a. $\frac{3}{10}$, 0.74, 29%, $\frac{11}{25}$

b. 15%, $\frac{7}{20}$, 0.08, 500%

Name ____________________ Class ____________ Date ____________

Lesson 6-2

Solving Percent Problems Using Proportions

Lesson Objective	**Common Core Standard**
To use proportions to solve problems involving percent	Ratios and Proportions: 7.RP.3

Key Concepts

Percents and Proportions

Finding a Percent

What percent of 25 is 5?

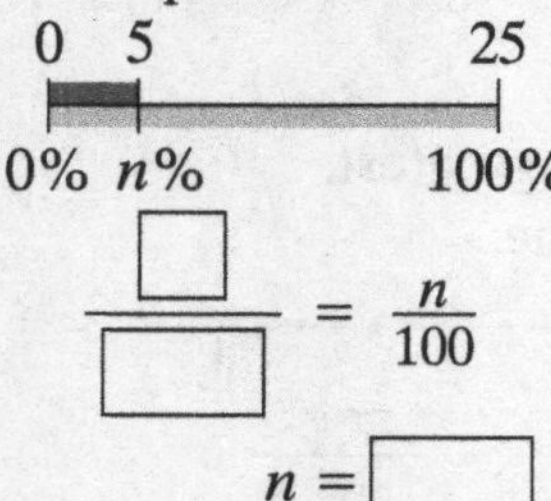

$\frac{\square}{\square} = \frac{n}{100}$

$n = \square$

Finding a Part

What is 20% of 25?

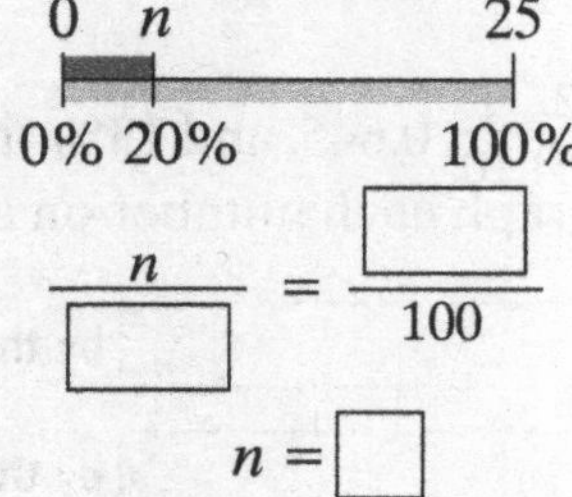

$\frac{n}{\square} = \frac{\square}{100}$

$n = \square$

Finding a Whole

20% of what is 5?

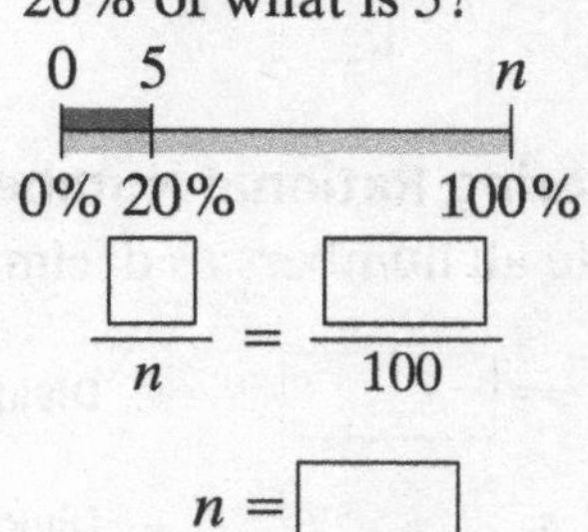

$\frac{\square}{n} = \frac{\square}{100}$

$n = \square$

Example

1 Finding a Percent What percent of 150 is 45?

You can write a proportion to find the percent.

$\frac{45}{\square} = \frac{n}{\square}$ ← **Write a proportion.**

$\square n = 45(\square)$ ← **Write the cross products.**

$\frac{150n}{\square} = \frac{45(100)}{\square}$ ← **Divide each side by** ____.

$n = \square$ ← **Simplify.**

45 is ____ % of 150.

Quick Check

1. What percent of 92 is 23?

Name ______________________ Class __________ Date __________

Examples

2 Finding a Part 24% of 25 is what number?

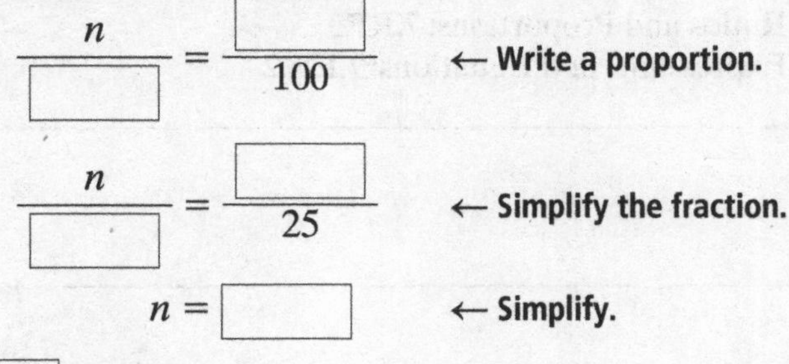

☐ is 24% of 25.

3 Finding the Whole Use a proportion to answer the question: 117 is 45% of what number?

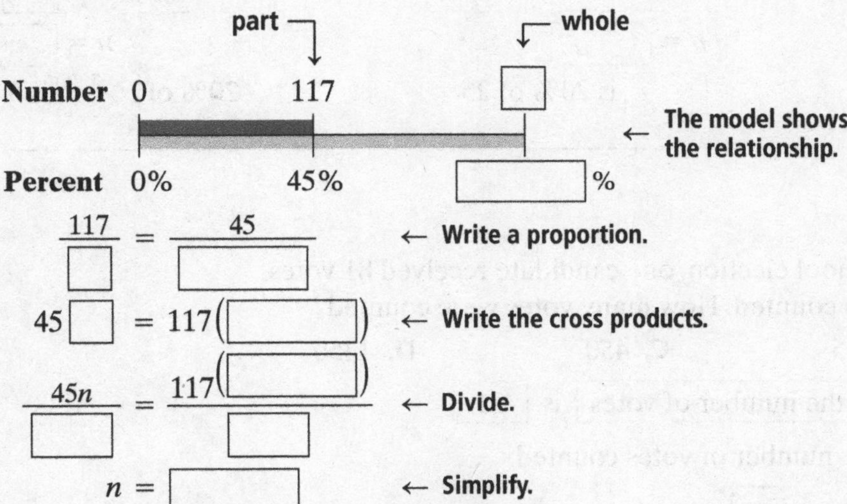

Quick Check

2. 85% of 20 is what number?

3. Your math teacher assigns 25 problems for homework. You have done 60% of them. How many problems have you done?

Name ______________________ Class ______________ Date ____________

Lesson 6-3

Solving Percent Problems Using Equations

Lesson Objective	**Common Core Standard**
To use equations to solve problems involving percent	Ratios and Proportions: 7.RP.3 Expressions and Equations: 7.EE.2

Key Concepts

Percents and Proportions

Finding a Percent	**Finding a Part**	**Finding a Whole**
What percent of 25 is 5?	What is 20% of 25?	20% of what is 5?
$n \cdot$ ☐ = ☐	$n =$ ☐ · ☐	☐ $\cdot n =$ ☐
$n =$ ☐	$n =$ ☐	$n =$ ☐
5 is ☐ of 25.	☐ is 20% of 25.	20% of ☐ is 5.

Examples

1 Finding a Whole In a school election, one candidate received 81 votes. This was 18% of the votes counted. How many votes were counted?

A. 45 **B.** 145 **C.** 450 **D.** 1450

Words 18% of the number of votes is 81.

Let n = the number of votes counted.

Equation ☐ · ☐ = ☐

☐ · ☐ = ☐ ← **Write the equation.**

$$\frac{0.18n}{\square} = \frac{81}{\square}$$ ← **Divide each side by** ☐.

$n =$ ☐ ← **Simplify.**

☐ votes were counted. The correct choice answer is ☐.

2 Finding a Part What number is 32% of 40?

Words A number is 32% of 40.

Let ☐ = the number.

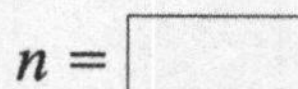

Equation ☐ = ☐ · ☐

= ☐ ← **Simplify.**

Name ______________________ Class ______________ Date ______________

Example

❸ **Finding a Percent** Of the 257 sandwiches sold at a delicatessen one day, 45 were turkey sandwiches. What percent of the sandwiches were turkey?

Estimate About 50 of 250 sandwiches were turkey.

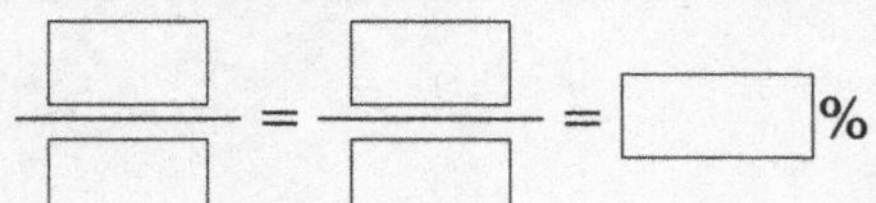

$\frac{\square}{\square} = \frac{\square}{\square} = \square\%$

$\square \cdot \square = \square$ ← **Write an equation. Let p = the percent of sandwiches that are turkey.**

$\frac{257p}{\square} = \frac{45}{\square}$ ← **Divide each side by** $\square$.

$p \approx \square$ ← **Use a calculator.**

$p \approx \square\%$ ← **Write the decimal as a percent.**

Check for Reasonableness $\square$% is close to the estimate $\square$%.

Quick Check

1. A plane flies with 54% of its seats empty. If 81 seats are empty, what is the total number of seats on the plane?

2. 27% of 60 is what number?

3. It rained 75 days last year. About what percent of the year was rainy?

Name ________________________ Class ________________ Date ________________

Lesson 6-4

Applications of Percent

Lesson Objective	Common Core Standard
To find and estimate solutions to application problems involving percent and to use different ways to represent a situation	Ratios and Proportions: 7.RP.3 Expressions and Equations: 7.EE.2

Examples

❶ **Finding Sales Tax** A video game costs $34.98. The sales tax rate is 5.5%. How much will you pay for the video game?

☐ · 34.98 ≈ ☐ ← **Find the sales tax. Round to the nearest cent.**

34.98 + ☐ = ☐ ← **Add the sales tax to the purchase price.**

You will pay ☐ for the video game.

❷ **Estimating a Tip** Use estimation to calculate a 15% tip for $34.50.

34.50 ≈ ☐ ← **Round to the nearest dollar.**

0.1 · ☐ = ☐ ← **Find 10% of the bill.**

$\frac{1}{2}$ · ☐ = ☐ ← **Find 5% of the bill. 5% is $\frac{1}{2}$ of the 10% amount.**

☐ + ☐ = ☐ ← **Add 10% amount and 5% amount to get ☐.**

A 15% tip for $34.50 is about ☐.

❸ **Finding a Commission** Find the commission on a $300 sale, with a commission rate of 8.5%.

☐ · ☐ = ☐ ← **Write 8.5% as ☐ and multiply.**

The commission on the sale is ☐.

Quick Check

1. Find the total cost for a purchase of $185 if the sales tax rate is 5.5%.

☐

2. Estimate a 15% tip for each amount.

   a. $58.20 ☐ **b.** $61.80 ☐ **c.** $49.75 ☐

3. Find the commission on a $3,200 sale, with a commission rate of 6%.

☐

Name ______________________ Class ______________ Date ______________

Examples

4 Finding a Commission Find the total earnings for a salesperson with a salary of $550 plus 4% commission on sales of $1,485.

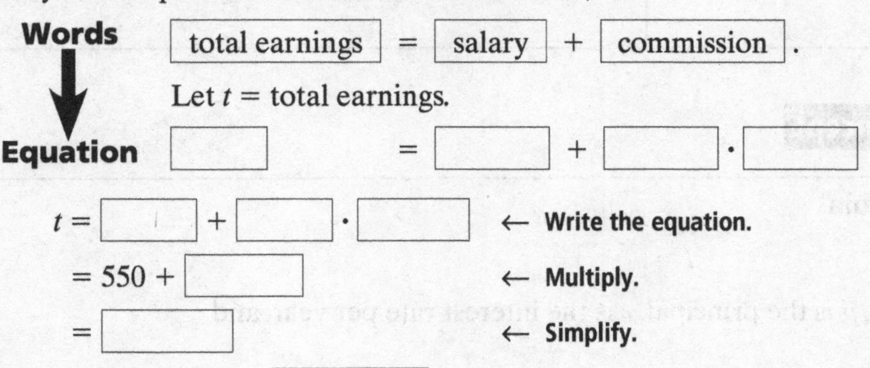

t = ____ + ____ · ____ ← **Write the equation.**

= 550 + ____ ← **Multiply.**

= ____ ← **Simplify.**

The salesperson earns ____.

5 Application: Percent Error in Manufacturing

A 625-g mass measures 625.18 g. What is the percent error?

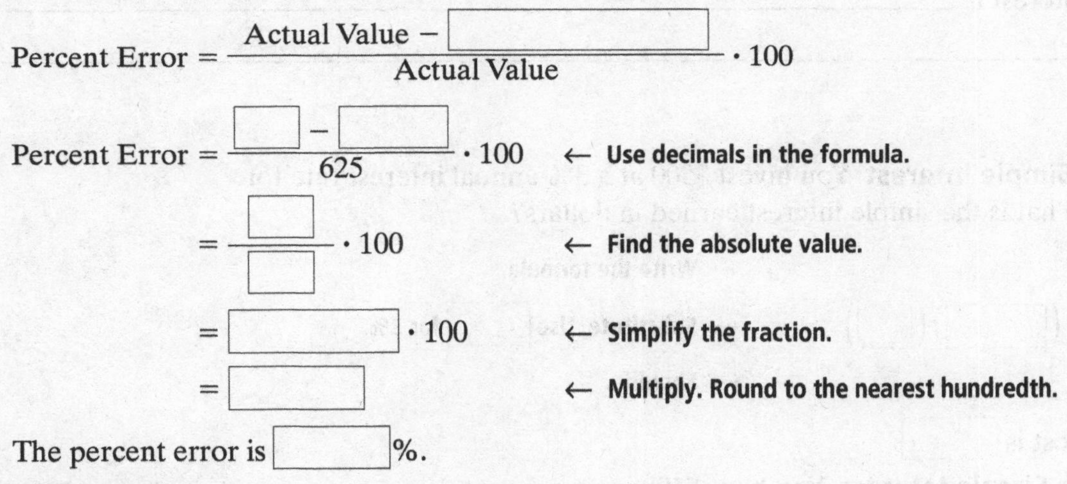

Percent Error = (Actual Value − ____) / Actual Value · 100
Percent Error = (____ − ____) / 625 · 100 ← Use decimals in the formula.
= ____ / ____ · 100 ← Find the absolute value.
= ____ · 100 ← Simplify the fraction.
= ____ ← Multiply. Round to the nearest hundredth.

The percent error is ____%.

Quick Check

4. Suppose you earn a weekly salary of $800 plus a commission of 3.5% on all sales. Find your earnings for a week with total sales of $1,400.

5. At a sporting goods factory, a quality control technician checking the weights of baseball bats measures a bat that should weigh 26 oz at $26\frac{1}{4}$ oz. If a bat is not within 0.6% of its specified weight, it is rejected. Why does this bat pass or fail this test?

Name ______________________ Class ______________ Date ____________

Lesson 6-5

Simple Interest

Lesson Objective	Common Core Standard
To find simple interest	Ratios and Proportions: 7.RP.3

Vocabulary and Key Concept

Simple Interest Formula

$I = \square$

I is the interest earned, *p* is the principal, *r* is the interest rate per year, and *t* is the time in years.

Principal is ____

____

Simple interest is ____

____

Examples

❶ **Finding Simple Interest** You invest $500 at a 3% annual interest rate for 4 years. What is the simple interest earned in dollars?

$I = prt$ ← **Write the formula.**

$I = (500)(\square)(\square)$ ← **Substitute. Use** $\square$ **for 3%.**

$= \square$ ← **Simplify.**

The interest is $\square$.

❷ **Graphing Simple Interest** You have $500 in an account that earns an annual rate of 3%. At the end of each year, you withdraw the interest you have earned. Graph the total interest you earn after 1, 2, 3, and 4 years.

Step 1 Make a table.

Time (yr)	Interest ($)
1	15
2	
3	
4	

Step 2 Draw a graph.

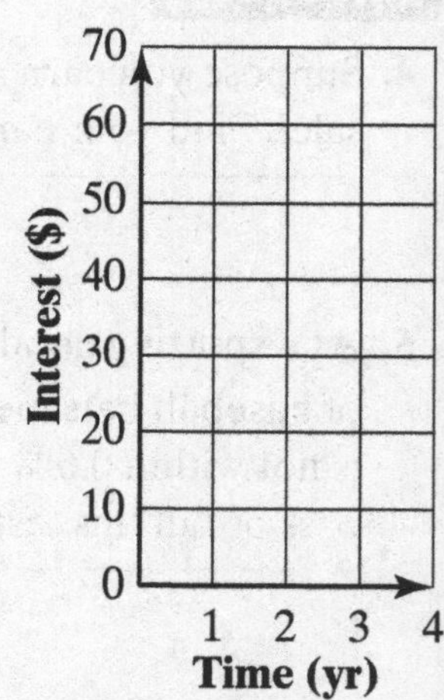

Name ______________________ Class ______________ Date ______________

Example

3 Comparing Loans You need to borrow \$2,000. There is a 4-year loan with a 6% simple interest and a 2-year loan with a 11% simple interest. Which loan will cost more?

4 Year Loan	2 Year Loan	
$I = prt$	$I = prt$	← **Write the formula.**
$I = 2{,}000 \cdot$ ☐ $\cdot$ ☐	$I = 2{,}000 \cdot$ ☐ $\cdot$ ☐	← **Substitute.**
$I =$ ☐	$I =$ ☐	← **Simplify.**
☐ > ☐		← **Compare.**

The ☐ -year loan will cost more.

Quick Check

1. Find the simple interest you pay on a \$220 loan at a 5% annual interest rate for 4 years.

2. Graph the simple interest earned on \$950 at an annual rate of 4.2%.

3. Barbara wants to borrow \$2000. She can get a loan of \$2000 at 7% simple interest for 3 years or at 11% simple interest for 2 years. Which loan will cost her more?

Name ______________________ Class ______________ Date ______________

Lesson 6-6

Finding Percent of Change

Lesson Objective	Common Core Standards
To find percents of increase and percents of decrease	Ratios and Proportions: 7.RP.3 Expressions and Equations: 7.EE.2

Vocabulary

The percent of change is ______________________

____

A markup is ______________________

____

A discount is ______________________

____

Example

1 Finding a Percent of Increase Last year, a school had 632 students. This year the school has 670 students. Find the percent of increase in the number of students.

$670 - 632 = \square$ ← **Find the amount of change.**

$\frac{38}{\square} = \frac{n}{\square}$ ← **Write a proportion. Let n = percent of change.**

$100 \cdot \frac{38}{\square} = \frac{n}{\square} \cdot 100$ ← **Multiply each side by 100.**

$\frac{3800}{\square} = n$ ← **Simplify.**

$n \approx \square$ ← **Divide.**

The number of students increased by about $\square$.

Quick Check

1. In 2010, Georgia went from 13 to 14 representatives. Find the percent of increase in the number of representatives.

Name ______________________ Class ______________ Date ______________

Examples

❷ Finding a Percent of Markup Find the percent of markup for a car that a dealer buys for $10,590 and sells for $13,775.

$13{,}775 - 10{,}590 = \square$ ← **Find the amount of markup.**

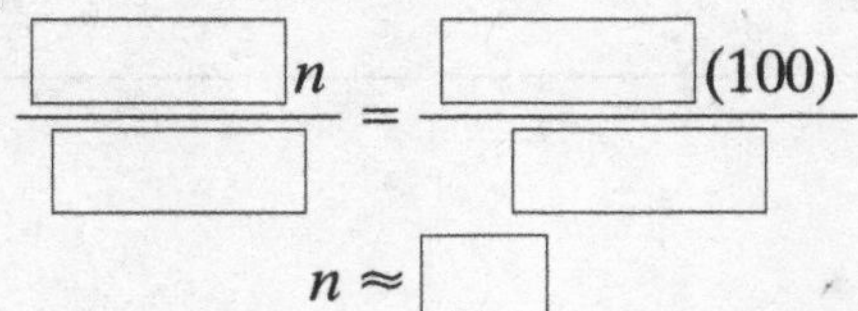

$\frac{3{,}185}{\square} = \frac{n}{\square}$ ← **Write a proportion. Let *n* be the percent of markup.**

$\square n = \square(100)$ ← **Write cross products.**

$\frac{\square n}{\square} = \frac{\square(100)}{\square}$ ← **Divide each side by** $\square$.

$n \approx \square$ ← **Simplify.**

The percent of markup is about $\square$.

❸ Finding a Percent of Discount Find the percent of discount for a $74.99 tent that is discounted to $48.75.

$74.99 - 48.75 = \square$ ← **Find the amount of the discount.**

$\frac{26.24}{\square} = \frac{n}{\square}$ ← **Write a proportion. Let *n* be the percent of discount.**

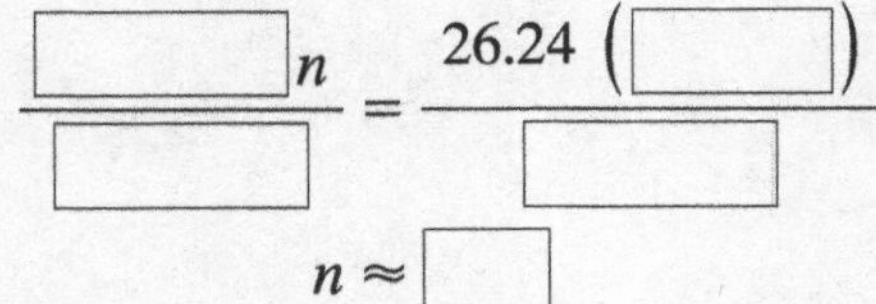

$\square n = 26.24(\square)$ ← **Write cross products.**

$\frac{\square n}{\square} = \frac{26.24(\square)}{\square}$ ← **Divide each side by** $\square$.

$n \approx \square$ ← **Simplify.**

The percent of discount for the tent is about $\square$.

Quick Check

2. Find the percent of markup for a $17.95 headset marked up to $35.79.

3. Find the percent of discount of a $24.95 novel on sale for $14.97.

Name ______________________ Class ______________ Date ____________

Lesson 7-1

Relating Graphs to Events

Lesson Objective	**Common Core Standard**
To interpret and sketch graphs that represent real-world situations	Expressions and Equations: Prepares for 8.EE.5

Vocabulary

Change in data is linear if ______________________

Change in data is not linear if ______________________

Example

1 Interpreting a Graph The graph shows the altitude of a helicopter during a flight.

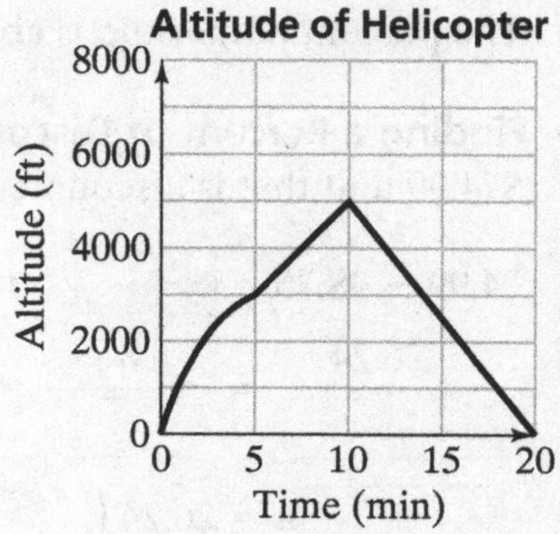

Altitude of Helicopter

Altitude (ft): 0, 2000, 4000, 6000, 8000

Time (min): 0, 5, 10, 15, 20

a. Is the helicopter's altitude increasing or decreasing during each of the following times?

0 to 2 min [ ]

7 to 8 min [ ]

12 to 16 min [ ]

b. Is the helicopter's altitude linear or nonlinear during each of the following times?

3 to 4 min [ ]

9 to 10 min [ ]

15 to 18 min [ ]

Quick Check

1. Between which two times did the speed increase the most?

[ ]

Name _______________ Class _______________ Date _______________

Example

❷ Sketching a Graph An athlete jogs for 30 min, sprints for 5 min, and walks for 10 min. Sketch and label a graph showing his speed.

As the athlete starts jogging, the speed increases and then becomes constant for about 30 minutes. Then the speed increases again for the sprint and becomes constant for about 5 minutes. Then the speed decreases when the athlete slows to a walk for 10 minutes.

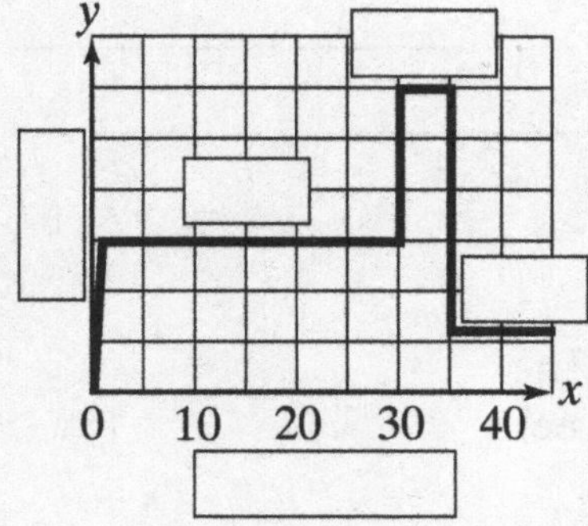

Quick Check

2. You walk to your friend's house. For the first 10 min, you walk from home to a park. For the next 5 min, you watch a ball game in the park. For the last 5 min, you run to your friend's house. Sketch and label a graph showing your distance from home during your trip.

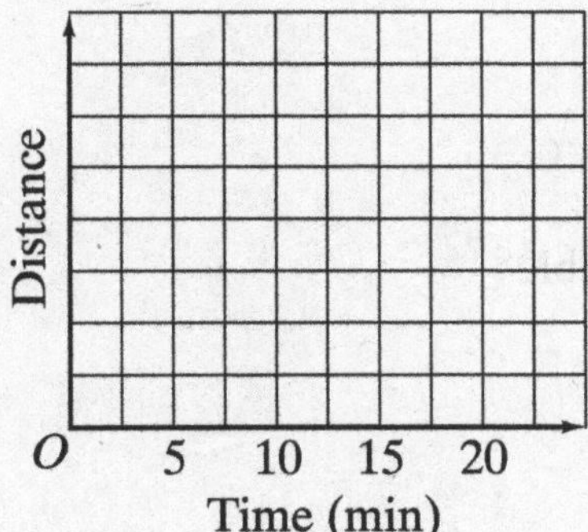

Name ____________________ Class ____________ Date ____________

Lesson 7-2

Functions

Lesson Objective	Common Core Standard
To evaluate functions and complete input-output tables	Expressions and Equations: Prepares for 8.EE.5

Vocabulary

A function is ______________________________

A function rule is ______________________________

Examples

1 Evaluating Functions Julia deposited \$40 in a savings account. The function $s = 5w + 40$ gives the total savings s in dollars after w weeks that Julia has been saving. Find the output s for the input $w = 12$.

$s = 5w + 40$ ← **Write the function.**

$s = 5 \cdot \square + 40$ ← **Substitute the input value for** ***w*****.**

$s = \square + 40$ ← **Simplify.**

$s = \square$

The output s for the input $w = \square$ is $\square$. So, after depositing \$40, Julia's total savings is $\square$.

2 Input-Output Tables The function $t = 2h + 15$ gives the outdoor temperature t in degrees Fahrenheit h hours before, at, and after sunrise on a cold winter day. Use the function to complete the table for $h = -4, -2, 0, 2, 4$.

Input *h*	Output *t*	
−4		← $2(\square) + 15 = \square$
−2		← $2(\square) + 15 = \square$
0		← $2(\square) + 15 = \square$
2		← $2(\square) + 15 = \square$
4		← $2(\square) + 15 = \square$

Name ______________________ Class ______________ Date ______________

3 Input-Output Table Application Complete the table of input-output values for the function rule $t = 4c$, where c represents the number of cars and t represents the number of tires.

Input c (number of cars)	Output t (number of tires)	
3		$\leftarrow 4 \cdot$ ☐ = ☐
6		$\leftarrow 4 \cdot$ ☐ = ☐
9		$\leftarrow 4 \cdot$ ☐ = ☐

Quick Check

1. The function $F = \frac{9}{5}C + 32$ converts temperatures in degrees Celsius, C, to degrees Fahrenheit, F. Evaluate the function for $C = 20$.

2. Use the function $m = \frac{1}{3}n + 1$ to make an input-output table for $n = -1, 0, 1$, and 2.

Input n	Output m
−1	
0	
1	
2	

3. The deposit on a drink container is \$.10 in the state of Michigan. Use the function rule $d = 0.1c$. Make a table of input-output pairs to show the total deposits on 5, 10, and 15 containers.

Input c	Output d

Name ______________________ Class ______________ Date ______________

Lesson 7-3

Proportional Relationships

Lesson Objective	Common Core Standard
To determine if relationships are proportional	Expressions and Equations: 8.EE.5

Vocabulary

A proportional relationship is ____

____

Examples

❶ Proportional Relationships in Tables: Distance-Time Relationships

Determine if the relationship is proportional.

Jason's Hiking Trip	
Time t (days)	Distance d (mi)
1	12
2	24
3	36
4	48

Write the ratio of each input to its corresponding output. Then simplify.

$\frac{1}{\square}$

$\frac{2}{\square} = \square$

$\frac{\square}{\square} = \square$

$\frac{\square}{\square} = \square$

The ratios are ______________, so the relationship is ______________.

❷ Proportional Relationships in Tables: Comparison Shopping

Determine if the relationship is proportional.

Polo Shirts
2 for $16
4 for $32
5 for $40
7 for $49

Write the ratio of each input (number of shirts) to its corresponding output (cost). Then simplify.

$\frac{2}{\square} = \square$

$\frac{4}{\square} = \square$

$\frac{\square}{\square} = \square$

$\frac{\square}{\square} = \square$

The ratios are ______________, so the relationship is ______________.

Name ______________________ Class ______________ Date ______________

3 Input-Output Tables and Graphs Sarah makes and sells quilted tablet covers for $18 each. She uses the function $s = 18c$, where s represents sales in dollars and c represents number of covers sold. Complete the input-output table and graph your results. Does the function have a proportional relationship? Explain.

Tablet Cover Sales	
Number of Covers c	Sales s (in dollars)
0	0
1	18
2	36
3	54

Write the ratio of each input to its corresponding output. Simplify.

$\frac{0}{0}$ **undefined**

$\frac{1}{\square}$

$\frac{\square}{\square} = \square$

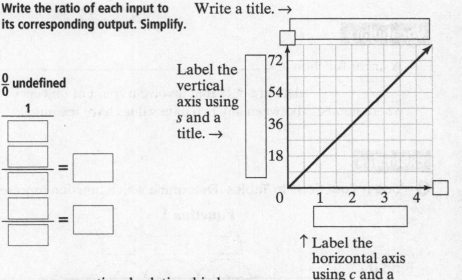

$\frac{\square}{\square} = \square$

Write a title. →

Label the vertical axis using s and a title. →

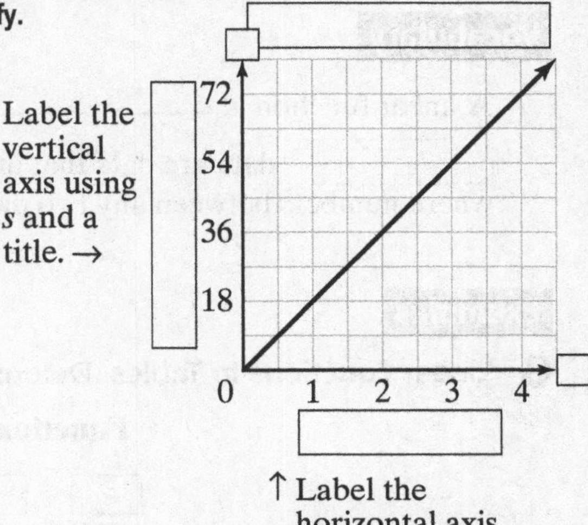

↑ Label the horizontal axis using c and a title.

The function ______________ a proportional relationship because ______________

____

Quick Check

1. The ratios of all the inputs to the outputs in a table are $\frac{1}{4}$. Is the relationship proportional?

2. Pizza slices are selling as follows: 1 for $2, 2 for $3, or 4 for $5. Is this relationship proportional? Explain.

3. The function $t = 4m$ gives the temperature t in degrees Celsius after m minutes of a liquid during a science experiment. Determine if the function has a proportional relationship.

Name ____________________ Class ____________________ Date ____________________

Lesson 7-4

Linear Functions

Lesson Objective	Common Core Standard
To recognize linear functions and use tables and equations to graph them	Expressions and Equations: Prepares for 8.EE.6

Vocabulary

A linear function is ____________________

[ ] data are data that involve a count of objects. [ ] data are data where numbers between any two data values have meaning.

Examples

1 Linear Functions in Tables Determine which function represented by a table is linear.

Find the changes in variables.

Function 1

x	−2	0	2	4
y	4	7	10	16

Ratios in changes between variables:

________, ________, ________

The ratios are ________, so

the function ________ linear.

Function 2

x	3	5	9	15
y	10	6	−2	−18

Ratios in changes between variables:

________, ________, ________

The ratios are ________, so

the function ________ linear.

2 Graphing Discrete Data It costs $9.50 to download a book to an e-reader. The total cost of downloading books is a function of the price of one book. Make a table and graph the function. Determine whether the data are discrete or continuous.

You ________ buy part of a book, so the data are ________.

Complete the table.

Number of Books	Total Cost (dollars)
0	
1	
2	
3	

Connect data points with a dashed line.

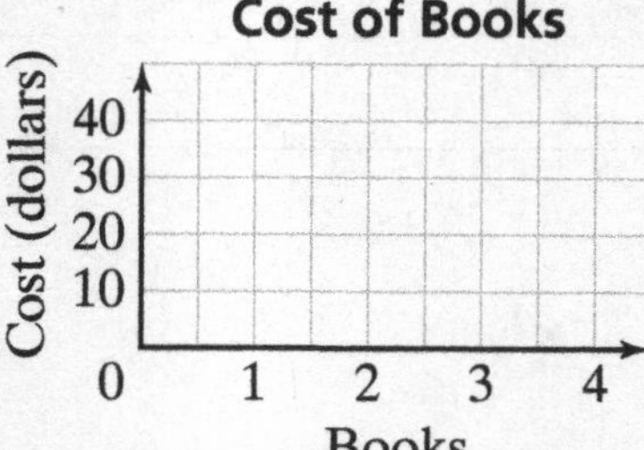

Name ______________________ Class ______________ Date ______________

3 Graphing Continuous Data A shopper buys some grapes that cost $2.19 per pound and a watermelon that costs $4.00. The function $c = 2.19p + 4$ gives the total the shopper spent on produce where c represents total cost and p represents number of pounds of grapes. Use the equation to make a table and graph the function.

Determine whether the data are discrete or continuous.

You ____________ buy part of a pound of grapes, so the data are ____________.

Complete the table.

Pounds of Grapes	Total Cost (dollars)
0	
1	
2	
3	

Connect data points with a solid line.

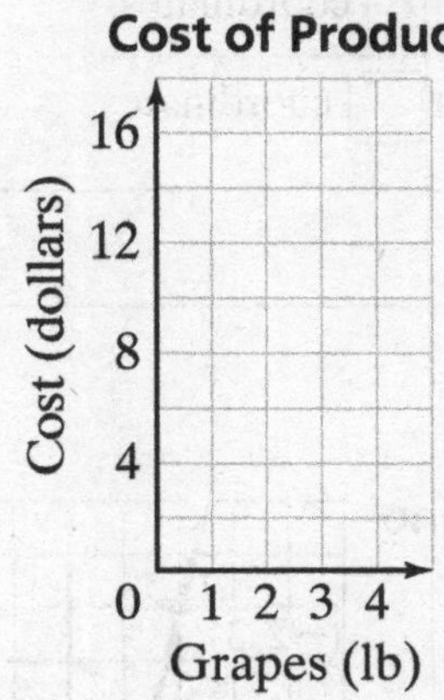

Quick Check

1. Determine if the function represented in the table is linear. Explain.

x	5	9	17	21
y	−12	−13	−15	−16

2. **Tickets** The function $c = 15t$ represents the cost (in dollars) of t adult tickets to a museum. Make a table and graph the function.

3. **Flying** The function $a = 4{,}000 - 600m$ gives the altitude a of a plane in feet after m minutes. Make a table and graph the function.

Name ______________________ Class ______________ Date ______________

Lesson 7-5

Understanding Slope

Lesson Objective	**Common Core Standards**
To find the slope of a line from a graph or table	Expressions and Equations: 8.EE.6

Vocabulary and Key Concepts

Slope of a Line

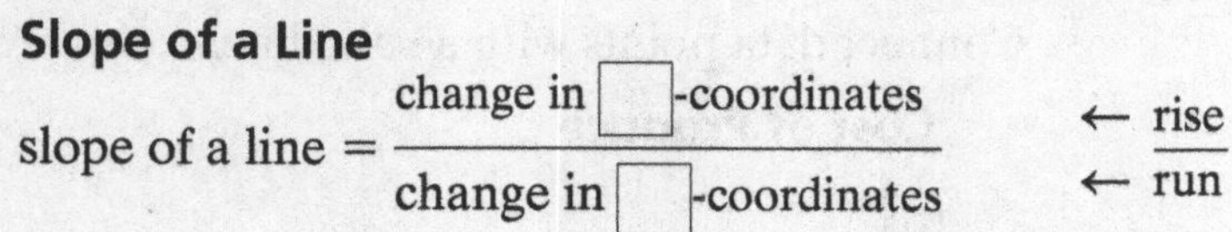

Slope is ____

Examples

1 Finding the Slope of a Line Using coordinates, find the slope of the line between $P(-2, 3)$ and $Q(-1, -1)$.

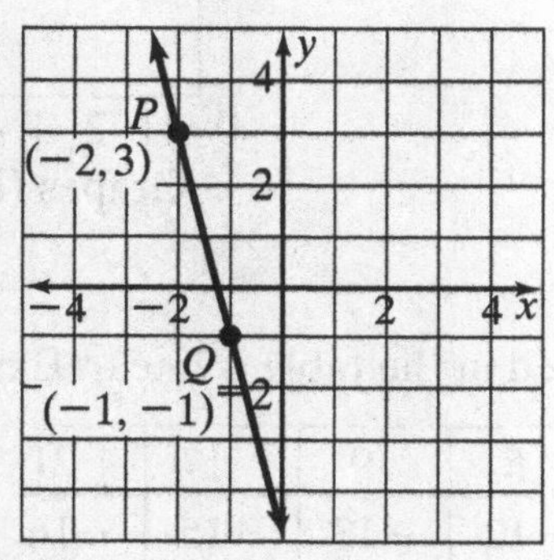

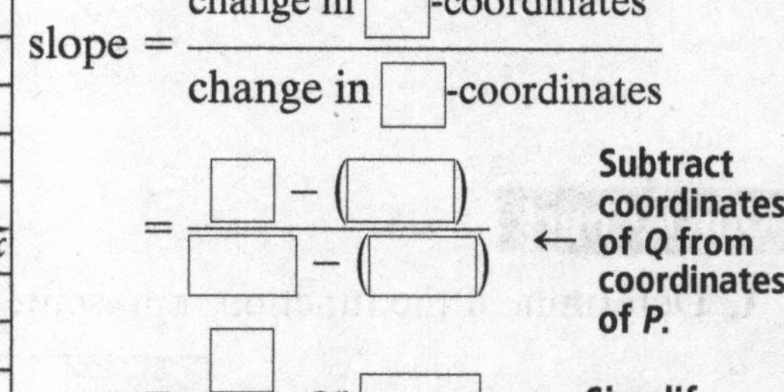

2 Slopes of Horizontal and Vertical Lines Find the slope of each line. State whether the slope is zero or undefined.

a. line k

slope = $\dfrac{1 - (\square)}{\square - 2} = \dfrac{\square}{\square}$

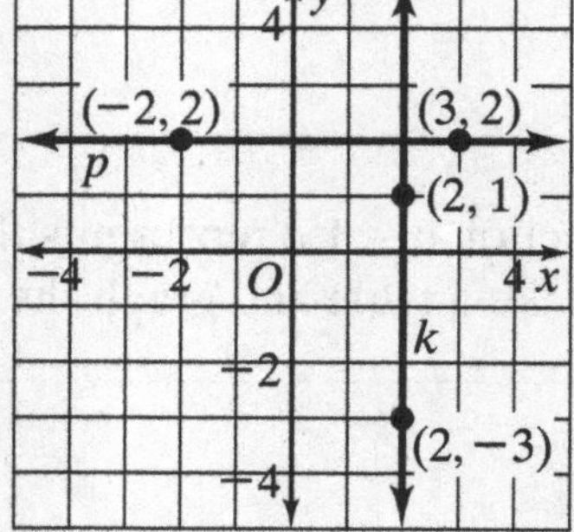

Division by zero is ☐.

The slope of a vertical line is ☐.

b. line p

slope = $\dfrac{2 - \square}{\square - 3} = \dfrac{\square}{\square} = \square$

The slope of a horizontal line is ☐.

Name ______________________ Class ______________ Date ______________

❸ Finding Slope From a Table Graph the data in the table. Connect the points with a line. Then find the rate of change.

Distance (mi)	Cost ($)
100	25
200	50
300	75
400	100

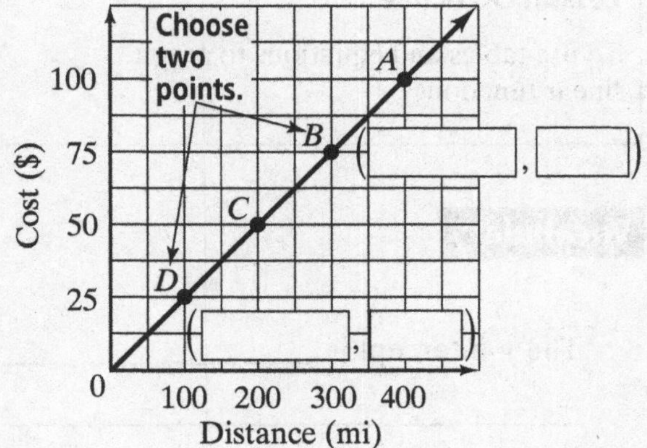

rate of change = slope = $\dfrac{\text{change in } \square}{\text{change in } \square}$

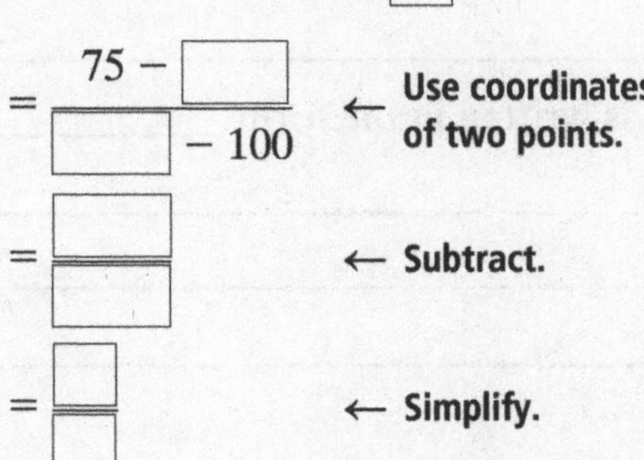

$= \dfrac{75 - \square}{\square - 100}$ ← **Use coordinates of two points.**

$= \dfrac{\square}{\square}$ ← **Subtract.**

$= \dfrac{\square}{\square}$ ← **Simplify.**

The cost increases by $ ☐ for every ☐ miles traveled.

Quick Check

1. Find the slope of each line.

a.

(2, 4)
(−3, 2)

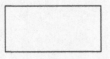

b.

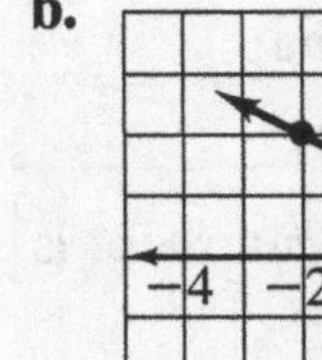

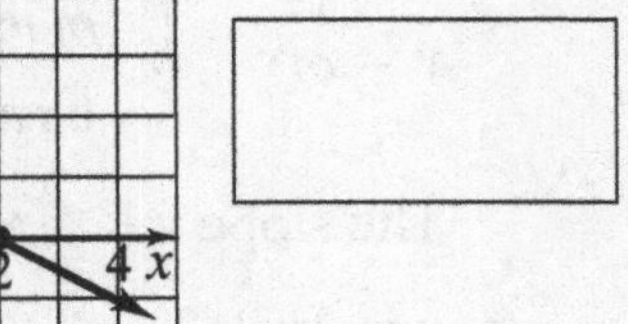

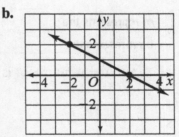

2. Find the slope of a line through the points (3, 1) and (3, −2). State whether the slope is zero or undefined.

3. Graph the data in the table and connect the points with a line. Then find the slope.

x	−1	0	1	2
y	2	0	−2	−4

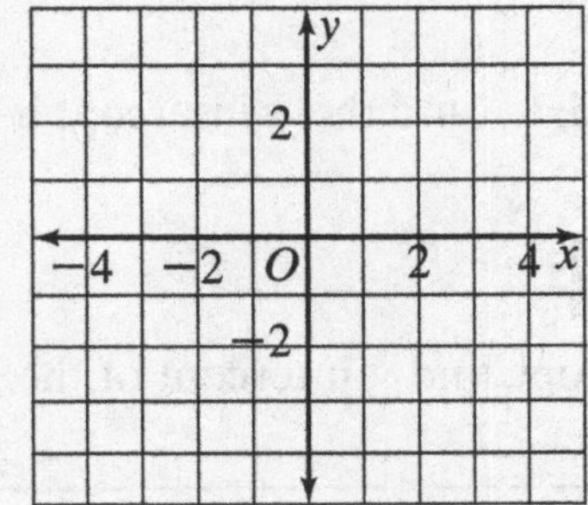

Slope = ☐

Name ______________________ Class ______________ Date ______________

Lesson 7-6

Graphing Linear Functions

Lesson Objective	**Common Core Standards**
To use tables and equations to graph linear functions	Expressions and Equations: 8.EE.6

Vocabulary

The *y*-intercept is ______________________________

____

An equation written in slope-intercept form is written in the form ______________

____

A linear function is ______________________________

____

Example

1 Finding Slope and *y*-intercept Find the slope and *y*-intercept of the graph of each function.

a. $y = 3x + 7$

$y = 3x + 7$

$\uparrow \quad \uparrow$

$y = mx + b$ ***m* represents the** ☐.

***b* represents the** ☐.

The slope is ☐ and the *y*-intercept is ☐.

b. $y = 3x + 7$

$y = \frac{3}{4}x - 5$

$\uparrow \quad \uparrow$

$y = mx + b$

The slope is ☐ and the *y*-intercept is ☐.

Quick Check

1. Find the slope and *y*-intercept of the graph of $y = x - 3$.

____

Name ______________________ Class ______________ Date ______________

Example

❷ Graphing Functions of the Form $y = mx$ The amount that Amber earns from her job is given by the function $y = 7x$, where y represents her earnings and x represents the number of hours she works. Graph $y = 7x$.

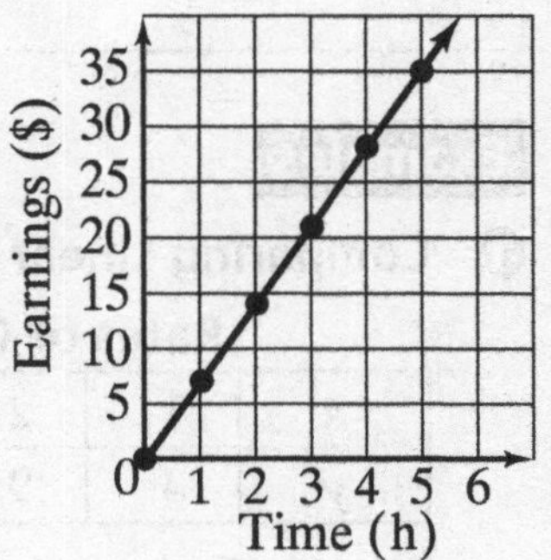

Use slope-intercept form.

The y-intercept is ☐ and the slope is ☐.

Move ☐ units ☐ from (0, 0) since the slope is positive and ☐ unit ☐. Repeat to find more points on the line.

Draw a line through the three points.

Quick Check

2. Graph the function $y = \frac{1}{5}x$.

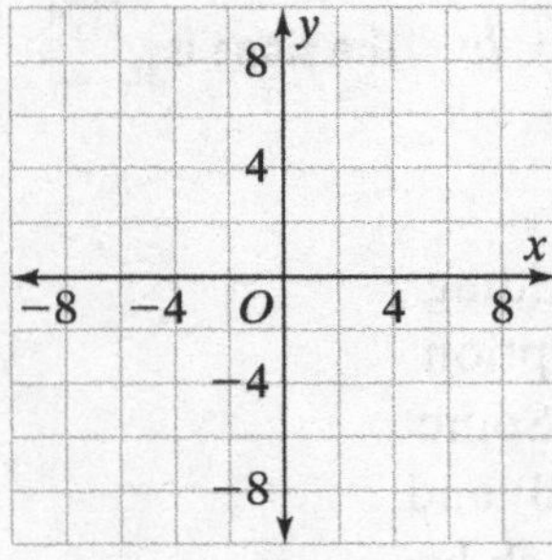

Name ____________________ Class ____________ Date ____________

Lesson 7-7

Comparing Functions

Lesson Objective	Common Core Standards
To compare properties of two functions represented in different ways	Expressions and Equations: 8.EE.5

Examples

1 Comparing Linear Functions Which function has a greater rate of change?

Rates of Change

x	1	2	3	4
y	4	9	14	19

$y = 6x + 1$

Step 1 Find the slope from the table. Use the points (1, 4) and (4, 19).

$$\text{slope} = \frac{\square - \square}{\square - \square} = \frac{\square}{\square} \text{ or } \square$$

Step 2 Find the slope from the equation using $y = mx + b$.

$y = 6x + 1$

↑

$y = mx + b$ **The slope is** $\square$.

Since $\square > \square$, the function $y = 6x + 1$ has a greater ______.

2 Comparing Initial Values of Linear Functions A company is deciding on its location for its annual employee appreciation dinner. A reception hall charges a \$300 rental fee and \$18 per person for meal service. Some rental rates for a hotel banquet room are the ordered pairs (20, 690) and (35, 1020) in the form (number of people, total cost in dollars). Which has the greater initial cost?

Reception Hall: The initial cost for the reception hall is represented by the ______ fee, which is ______.

Hotel Banquet Room: To find the initial cost of the hotel banquet room, use the ordered pairs to write an equation in slope-intercept form.

The ______ represents the initial cost.

Find the slope.

$$\text{slope} = \frac{\square - \square}{\square - \square}$$

$$= \frac{\square}{\square} \text{ or } 22$$

Find the y-intercept using $y = mx + b$.

$y = mx + b$

$690 = \square(20) + b$

$690 = \square + b$

$\square = b$

The initial cost for the hotel is ______.

Since ______ > ______, the ______ has a greater initial cost.

Name ________________________ Class ______________ Date ______________

❸ Comparing Nonlinear Functions Maria and Cory are both participating in a 6-mile bike-a-thon to raise money for charity. Sponsors can give a flat donation or pledge a certain amount of money for each mile they complete. Maria has $45 in flat donations and pledges totaling $12.50 per mile. Cory's donations are represented in the graph. Compare the functions.

Maria's Donations	Cory's Donations
increases	
not continuous	
Minimum	Minimum $30
Maximum $120	Maximum

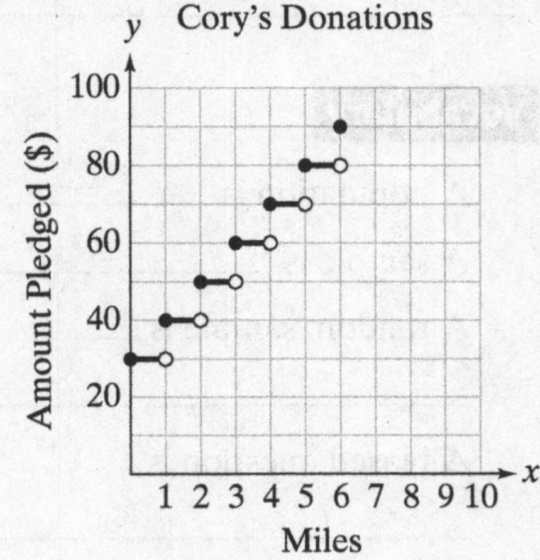

Quick Check

1. Which function has the greater rate of change?

x	1	3	4	6
y	5	13	17	25

$y = 2x + 1$

2. Vikram opened a savings account with $150. He deposits $150 every two weeks. Compare Vikram's account to Jack's account.

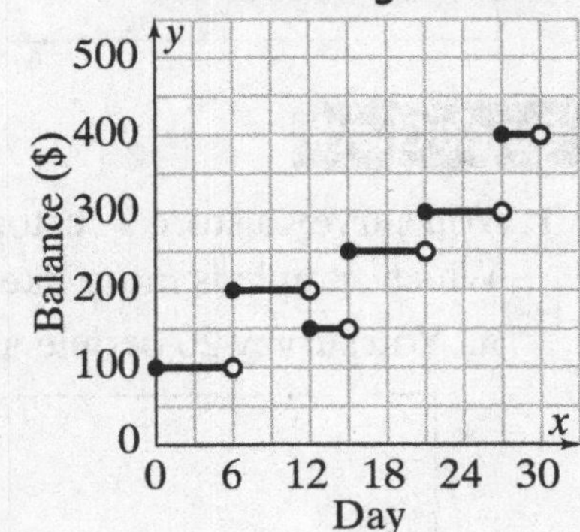

3. Steve's Scooter Rentals charges $17 per hour plus a $29 rental fee. Scooter World charges $48 for 1 hour and $108 for 4 hours. Both relationships are linear. Which company has the greatest initial cost?

Name ____________ Class ____________ Date ____________

Lesson 8-1

Random Samples and Surveys

Lesson Objective	**Common Core Standard**
To identify a random sample and to write a survey question	Statistics and Probability: 7.SP.1

Vocabulary

A population is ____________

A sample is ____________

A random sample is ____________

A biased question is ____________

Example

1 Identifying a Random Sample You survey students in your school about their snacking habits. Would you get a random sample if you questioned different English classes? Explain.

Quick Check

1. You survey a store's customers. You ask why they chose the store. Which sample is more likely to be random? Explain.

   a. You survey 20 people at the entrance from 5:00 P.M. to 8:00 P.M.

   b. You survey 20 people outside the entrance throughout the day.

Name ____________________ Class ____________ Date ____________

Example

❷ Identifying Biased Questions Is each question *biased* or *fair*? Explain.

a. "Which is a brighter color, pink, or green?"

This question is [ ]. The choices are presented equally.

b. "Is an electric pink shirt brighter than a green shirt?"

This question is [ ]. It implies that pink is brighter, thus influencing the responses.

Quick Check

2. Is each question *biased* or *fair*? Explain.

a. Do you prefer greasy meat or healthy vegetables on your pizza?

[ ]

b. Which pizza topping do you like best?

[ ]

Name ______________________ Class ______________ Date ______________

Lesson 8-2

Estimating Population Size

Lesson Objective	**Common Core Standard**
To estimate population size using proportions	Statistics and Probability: 7.SP.2

Vocabulary

The capture/recapture method is used to ______________________________________

____

Example

1 Using the Capture/Recapture Method Researchers know that there are 63 marked gazelles in an area. On a flight over the area, they count 19 marked gazelles and a total of 412 gazelles. Write a proportion to estimate the gazelle population.

$$\frac{\text{number of marked gazelles counted}}{\text{total number of gazelles counted}} = \frac{\text{total number of marked gazelles}}{\text{estimate of gazelle population}}$$

$$\frac{\square}{\square} = \frac{63}{x}$$ ← **Write a proportion.**

$$19x = 63 \cdot 412$$ ← **Write cross products.**

$$19x = \square$$ ← **Multiply.**

$$\frac{19x}{\square} = \frac{25{,}956}{\square}$$ ← **Divide each side by $\square$.**

$$x \approx \square$$ ← **Round to the nearest integer.**

There are about $\square$ gazelles in the area.

Check: You can use an estimate to check your answer.

$$\frac{19}{412} \approx \frac{\square}{\square}, \text{ or } \frac{1}{20}$$

$$\frac{1}{20} = \frac{63}{x}$$

$$x = 63 \times 20 = 1{,}260$$

Since this is close to 1,366, the answer is reasonable.

Name ______________________ Class ______________ Date ______________

Quick Check

1. Researchers know that there are 105 marked deer in an area. On a flight over the area, they count 35 marked deer and a total of 638 deer. Estimate the total deer population in the area.

Name ______________________ Class ______________ Date ____________

Lesson 8-3

Inferences

Lesson Objective	Common Core Standard
To use data from random samples to make inferences about populations	Statistics and Probability: 7.SP.2

Vocabulary

An inference is ____

____

Example

1 Drawing Inferences about a Population A clothing store selected a random sample of 20 customers and recorded the amount they spent on clothes. Based on the sample, what is the average, or mean, amount that customers spent on clothing?

Step 1 Find the average, or ☐, of the sample data.

$$\square = \frac{\text{sum of the data}}{\text{number of data items}}$$

$$= \frac{\square}{\square}$$

$$= \square$$

Random Sample of Amount Spent per Customer ($)				
25	72	10	125	29
96	46	21	17	31
84	63	19	35	9
146	28	57	82	65

Step 2 Use the average of the sample data to make an inference.

The average amount spent by customers in the sample is ☐, so the average amount spent by all customers is likely close to ☐.

Quick Check

1. A restaurant manager selected a random sample of 20 customers and recorded the amount they spent on their meal. Draw an inference about the percent of customers at the restaurant who spend more than $20.

____

____

____

____

Random Sample of Amount Spent per Customer ($)				
21	9	23	12	15
16	10	17	17	15
14	16	13	17	17
14	25	14	23	12

Name ______________________ Class ______________ Date ______________

Example

2 Comparing Random Samples There are 240 workers in a local factory. The factory owner surveys 3 random samples of 25 people each about which new work schedule they would like to adopt. The results are shown in the table.

Schedule	Sample 1	Sample 2	Sample 3
Schedule A	4	7	2
Schedule B	12	10	14
Schedule C	9	8	9

a. For each sample, predict how many votes Schedule B will get.

Use a proportion: $\frac{\text{votes for Schedule B in sample}}{\text{people in sample}} = \frac{\text{predicted votes for Schedule B}}{\text{people in factory}}$

Sample 1: $\frac{12}{25} = \frac{x}{240}$

$\square \cdot 240 = 25x$

$\square = 25x$

$\square \approx x$

Sample 2: $\frac{10}{25} = \frac{x}{240}$

$10 \cdot \square = 25x$

$\square = 25x$

$\square = x$

Sample 3: $\frac{14}{25} = \frac{x}{240}$

$14 \cdot \square = 25x$

$\square = 25x$

$\square \approx x$

Based on Sample 1, Schedule B will get about ☐ votes. Based on Sample 2, Schedule B will get about ☐ votes, and based on Sample 3, it will get about ☐ votes.

b. Describe the variation in the predictions.

The greatest prediction is ☐ votes, and the least prediction is ☐ votes. So the predictions vary by ☐ − ☐ = ☐ votes.

c. Make an inference about the number of votes Schedule B will get.

Find the mean of the predictions: $\frac{\square}{3} = \frac{\square}{3} = \square$.

Schedule B will get about ☐ votes.

Quick Check

2. The table shows the results of 3 random samples of 30 students each at a middle school with 420 students. The students were asked how many hours they spend online each week.

Hours Spent Online Per Week

Time (h)	Sample 1	Sample 2	Sample 3
< 5	16	13	11
≥ 5	14	17	19

a. For each sample, predict how many students in the school spend at least 5 hours online per week. ______________________

b. Describe the variation in the predictions. ______________________

c. Draw an inference about the number of students in at the school who spend at least 5 hours online per week.

____

____

Name ____________________ Class ____________ Date ____________

Lesson 8-4

Data Variability

Lesson Objective	**Common Core Standards**
To compare data about two populations by using measures of center and measures of variability	Statistics and Probability: 7.SP.3, 7.SP.4

Vocabulary

The interquartile range of a set of data is ______________________________

____

The mean absolute deviation of a data set measures ______________________

____

Example

1 Comparing Two Populations A gardener collects information about the heights of the flowers she grows. Compare the IQRs of the data sets, and use the comparison to make an inference about the plants.

IQR for Salvia:

☐ – ☐ = ☐

IQR for Marigolds:

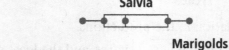

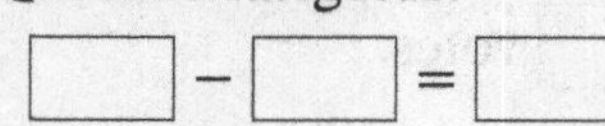

Salvia

Marigolds

8 9 10 11 12 13 14 15 16 17 18 19 20 21 22 23

Height of Plants (in.)

The IQRs of the data sets are ☐ ☐. So, you can infer that the heights of ☐ vary about as much as the heights of ☐.

Quick Check

1. A veterinarian collects data about the weights of the dogs she treats. Compare the medians of the data sets 1, and use the comparison to make an inference about the dogs.

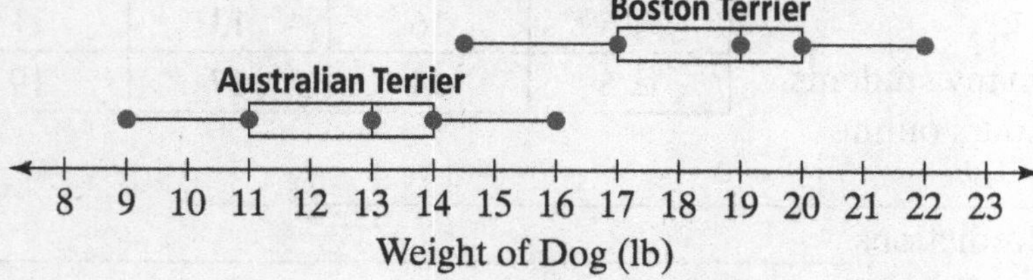

____

____

____

Name ______________________ Class ______________ Date ______________

Example

2 Determining Overlap of Data Sets The line plot at the right shows the ages of teens who participated in a junior archery competition.

a. Calculate the mean of each data set.

Girls: Mean $= \frac{\square}{\square} = \square$ **Boys:** Mean $= \frac{\square}{\square} = \square$

Participant Ages		
Girls		**Boys**
✗✗	13	✗
✗✗	14	
✗✗✗	15	
✗	16	✗✗
✗	17	✗✗✗
✗	18	✗✗
	19	✗✗

b. Determine the MAD for ages of girls in the competition.

Ages	13	13	14	14	15	15	15	16	17	18
Mean										
Distance	2	2	1	1	0	0	0	1	2	3

$\text{MAD} = \frac{\text{total distance}}{\text{number of data items}} = \frac{\square}{10} = \frac{\square}{5} = \square$

c. What number n multiplied by the MAD equals the difference between the means? What does this number tell you about the overlap of the data sets?

$\text{MAD} \cdot n =$ difference of means ← **Write an equation.**

$1.2n = 17 - \square$ ← **Substitute.**

$\square n = \square$ ← **Simplify.**

$\frac{1.2n}{\square} = \frac{2}{\square}$ ← **Divide each side by** $\square$.

$n = \square$ ← **Simplify.**

The difference between the means is $\square$ times the MAD. The multiple $\square$ is greater than 1, which indicates a $\square$ amount of overlap in the data sets.

Quick Check

2. The data table at the right shows the number of commercials during a random sample of hour-long shows on two television stations.

Commercials During Hour-Long Shows		
Station A		**Station B**
	32	✗
✗	33	
	34	✗✗✗
✗✗✗	35	✗✗
✗✗✗	36	✗✗
✗	37	✗✗
✗	38	
✗	39	

a. Calculate the mean of each data set.
Station A: $\square$ Station B: $\square$

b. Determine the MAD for Station A commercials. $\square$

c. What number n multiplied by the MAD equals the difference between the means? $n \approx \square$.

What does this number tell you about the overlap of the data sets?

____

____

Name ______________________ Class ______________ Date ____________

Lesson 9-1

Probability

Lesson Objective	**Common Core Standards**
To find the probability and the complement of an event	Statistics and Probability: 7.SP.5, 7.SP.7.a

Vocabulary and Key Concepts

Theoretical Probability

$$\text{theoretical probability} = P(\text{event}) = \frac{\text{number of } \boxed{} \text{ outcomes}}{\text{total number of } \boxed{} \text{ outcomes}}$$

An outcome is ______________________________

An event is ______________________________

The complement of an event is ______________________________

____

Examples

1 Finding Probability You select a letter at random from the letters F, G, H, and I. Find the probability of selecting a vowel. Express the probability as a fraction, a decimal, and a percent.

The event *vowel* has ☐ outcome, ☐, out of ☐ possible outcomes.

$P(\text{vowel}) = \frac{\boxed{}}{\boxed{}}$ ← **number of favorable outcomes** / ← **total number of possible outcomes**

$= \boxed{} = \boxed{}\%$ ← **Write as a decimal and percent.**

Name ______________________ Class ____________ Date ____________

❷ Finding Probabilities from 0 to 1 A jar contains 1 blue marble, 3 green marbles, 3 yellow marbles, and 4 red marbles. You randomly select a marble from the jar. Find each probability.

a. *P*(red)

There are ☐ possible outcomes. Since there are ☐ red marbles, there are ☐ favorable outcomes.

P(red) $\frac{\square}{\square}$ ← **number of favorable outcomes** ← **total number of possible outcomes**

b. *P*(orange)

The event *orange* has ☐ favorable outcomes.

P(orange) $\frac{\square}{\square}$, or ☐ ← **number of favorable outcomes** ← **total number of possible outcomes**

c. *P*(not orange)

P(not orange) + *P*(orange) = ☐ ← **The sum of the probabilities of an even and its complement is 1.**

P(not orange) + ☐ = ☐ ← **Substitute** ☐ **for *P*(orange).**

P(not orange) = ☐ ← **Simplify.**

Quick Check

1. Find *P*(consonant) as a fraction for the letters A, B, C, D, and E.

2. You roll a number cube once. Find each probability.

a. *P*(multiple of 3)

b. *P*(not multiple of 2)

c. *P*(9)

Name ____________ Class ____________ Date ____________

Lesson 9-2

Experimental Probability

Lesson Objective	Common Core Standards
To find experimental probability and to use simulations	Statistics and Probability: 7.SP.6, 7.SP.7, 7.SP.7.b

Vocabulary and Key Concepts

Experimental Probability

$$P(\text{event}) = \frac{\text{number of times an event occurs}}{\text{total number of trials}}$$

Experimental probability is ________________________________

____

Examples

1 Finding Experimental Probability A manufacturer of computer parts checks 100 parts each day. On Monday, two of the checked parts are defective.

a. What is the experimental probability that a part is defective?

$P(\text{defective part}) = \frac{\square}{\square}$ ← **number of defective parts** / ← **total number of parts checked**

$= \frac{\square}{\square}$ ← **Simplify.**

The experimental probability is $\frac{\square}{\square}$.

b. Which is the best prediction of the number of defective parts in Monday's total production of 1,250 parts?

A. 13 **B.** 25 **C.** 125 **D.** 250

Let x represent the predicted number of defective parts.

defective → $\frac{1}{\square} = \frac{x}{\square}$ **← defective** / **total →** ... **← total** ← **Write a proposition.**

$\square = x$ ← **Solve the proportion.**

You can predict ☐ parts out of 1,250 parts to be defective. The correct answer is choice ☐.

Name ______________________ Class ______________ Date ______________

❷ **Simulating an Event** A dog breeder knows that it is equally likely that a puppy will be male or female. Use a simulation to find the experimental probability that, in a litter of four puppies, all four will be male.

Simulate the problem by tossing four coins at the same time. Assume that male and female puppies are equally likely. Let "heads" represent a female and "tails" represent a male. A sample of 16 tosses is shown below.

Trial	Male	Female
1	✓✓	✓✓
2	✓	✓✓✓
3	✓✓✓✓	
4	✓✓	✓✓
5	✓✓✓	✓
6	✓✓	✓✓
7	✓	✓✓✓
8	✓✓	✓✓

Trial	Male	Female
9	✓✓	✓✓
10	✓✓✓	✓
11	✓✓	✓✓
12	✓	✓✓✓
13	✓✓	✓✓
14		✓✓✓✓
15	✓✓	✓✓
16	✓✓✓	✓

$P(\text{exactly four males}) = \frac{\square}{\square}$ ← **number of times four tails occurs** / ← **total number of trials**

The experimental probability that, in a litter of four puppies, all four will be male is ☐.

Quick Check

1. In 60 coin tosses, 25 are tails. Find the experimental probability.

2. The simulation uses coins to predict the genders of a family of three children, with "H" representing a girl and "T" representing a boy. What is the experimental probability that 3 children are all boys?

T T H	T T T	(H T H)	H T T	(H T H)
T T H	(H H T)	H T T	T H T	H H H
(H H T)	T T H	(T H H)	(H T H)	T H T
T H T	T H T	T H T	H H H	H H H

Name ______________________ Class ______________ Date ____________

Lesson 9-3

Sample Spaces

Lesson Objective	**Common Core Standards**
To make and use sample spaces and to use the counting principle	Statistics and Probability: 7.SP.8, 7.SP.8.b

Vocabulary and Key Concepts

The Counting Principle

Suppose there are *m* ways of making one choice and *n* ways of making a second choice. There are ☐ × ☐ ways to make the first choice followed by the second choice.

Example If you can choose a shirt in 5 sizes and 7 colors, then you can choose ☐ × ☐, or ☐, shirts.

A sample space is ____

____

Example

1 Finding a Sample Space

a. A spinner is divided into five equal sections labeled A–E. Make a table to show the sample space for spinning the spinner twice. Write the outcomes as ordered pairs.

☐

b. Find the probability of spinning at least one D.

There are ☐ outcomes with at least one D. There are ☐ possible outcomes. So, the probability of spinning at least one D is $\frac{☐}{☐}$.

Quick Check

1. Give the sample space for tossing two coins. Find the probability of getting two heads. ☐

Name ______________________ Class ______________ Date ______________

Examples

2 Using a Tree Diagram Suppose you can go west or northwest by train, bus, or car.

a. Draw a tree diagram to show the sample space for your journey.

Train — West: Train, ______
Train — Northwest: ______, Northwest

Bus — West: Bus, ______
Bus — Northwest: ______, Northwest

Car — West: Car, ______
Car — Northwest: ______, Northwest

← There are ____ possible outcomes.

b. What is the probability of a random selection that results in a bus trip west?

There is ______ favorable outcome (bus, ______) out of ______ possible outcomes. The probability is ____.

3 Using the Counting Principle How many kinds of coin purses are available if the purses come in small or large sizes and colors red, blue, yellow, and black?

Size	Colors
small	red
large	blue
	yellow
	black

Size		Color		
number of choices	×	number of choices		
____	×	____	=	____

There are ____ different kinds of coin purses available.

Quick Check

2. a. Suppose an airplane is added as another choice in Example 2. Draw a tree diagram to show the sample space.

b. Find the probability of selecting an airplane at random for your journey.

3. A manager at the Deli Counter decides to add chicken to the list of meat choices. How many different sandwiches are now available?

THE DELI COUNTER SANDWICHES

FRESH BREADS	DELI MEATS
Rye	Roast Beef
Wheat	Turkey
White	Ham
Pita	Pastrami
Wrap	Salami
	Liverwurst

Name ________________ Class ____________ Date ____________

Lesson 9-4

Compound Events

Lesson Objective	**Common Core Standards**
To find the probability of independent and dependent events	Statistics and Probability: 7.SP.8, 7.SP.8.a, 7.SP.8.b

Vocabulary and Key Concepts

Probability of Independent Events

If A and B are independent events, then $P(A, \text{then } B) =$ ☐ × ☐.

Probability of Dependent Events

If event B depends on event A, then $P(A, \text{then } B) =$ ☐ × ☐.

A compound event ____________________

Two events are independent if ____________________

____

Two events are dependent if ____________________

____

Examples

1 Probability of Independent Events A spinner has equal sections labeled 1 to 10. Suppose you spin twice. Find $P(2, \text{then } 5)$.

A. $\frac{1}{10}$ **B.** $\frac{1}{5}$ **C.** $\frac{1}{40}$ **D.** $\frac{1}{100}$

The two events are independent. There are ☐ possibilities on each spin.

$P(2, \text{then } 5) = P(2) \times$ ☐ ← **Spinning 2 is the first event. Spinning 5 is the second event.**

$= \frac{1}{10} \times \frac{☐}{☐} = \frac{☐}{☐}$ ← **Substitute. Then multiply.**

The probability that you will spin a 2 and then a 5 is ☐. The correct answer is choice ☐.

Name ______________________ Class ______________ Date ______________

❷ **Probability of Dependent Events** You select two cards at random from those with the letters on them as shown below. The two cards do not show vowels. Without replacing the two cards, you select a third card. Find the probability that you select a card with a vowel after you select the two cards without vowels.

P R O B A B I L I T Y

There are ______ remaining after you select the first two cards.

$P(\text{vowel}) = \frac{\square}{\square}$ ← **number of remaining cards with vowels** / ← **total number of remaining cards**

The probability of selecting a vowel for the third card is ______.

❸ **Probability of Dependent Events** A bag contains 3 red marbles, 4 white marbles, and 1 blue marble. You draw one marble. Without replacing it, you draw a second marble. What is the probability that the two marbles you draw are red followed by white?

The two events are dependent. After the first selection, there are ______ marbles to choose from.

$P(\text{red, then white}) = P(\text{red}) \times$ ______ ← **Use the formula for dependent events.**

$= \frac{3}{8} \times \frac{\square}{\square}$ ← **Substitute.**

$= \frac{\square}{\square} = \frac{\square}{\square}$ ← **Multiply. Then simplify.**

The probability that the two marbles are red and then white is ______.

Quick Check

1. You and a friend play a game twice. Assume the probability of winning is $\frac{1}{2}$. Find $P(\text{win, then lose})$.

2. Use the cards in Example 2. You select a B card at random. Without replacing the B card, you select a second card. Find $P(\text{Y})$.

3. Suppose 52 cards, two each lettered A–Z, are put in a bucket. You select a card. Without replacing the first card, you select a second one. Find $P(\text{J, then J})$.

Name ______________________ Class ______________ Date ____________

Lesson 9-5 Simulating Compound Events

Lesson Objective	Common Core Standard
To design and use simulations to estimate the probability of compound events	Statistics and Probability: 7.SP.8.c

Vocabulary

A simulation is ______________________________

Each trial of a simulation ______________________________

Examples

1 Designing a Simulation A laundry company inserts a coupon for one free box of detergent inside $\frac{1}{5}$ of its detergent boxes. Design a simulation that can be used to estimate the probability that a customer will need to buy at least 3 boxes to get a coupon.

Step 1 Choose a simulation tool.

$\frac{\square}{5}$ of the boxes include coupons, so use a tool that has $\square$ equally likely outcomes. A five-section spinner would be appropriate.

Step 2 Decide which outcomes are favorable.

$\frac{\square}{5}$ of the outcomes should represent a box with a coupon. Let spinning a 1 represent a box with a coupon.

Step 3 Describe a trial.

For each trial, spin until you get a $\square$ Keep track of the number of times you spin the spinner. This number represents the number of boxes the customer must buy to get a coupon for a free box.

2 Using a Simulation to Estimate Probability Perform 20 trials of the simulation you designed in Example 1. Then estimate the probability that a customer will need to buy at least 3 boxes of detergent to get a coupon.

The table shows the results of 20 trials of the simulation. Of the 20 trials, $\square$ resulted in 3 or more boxes. So, the experimental probability that a customer will need to buy at least 3 boxes to get a coupon is approximately $\frac{\square}{\square}$, or $\frac{\square}{\square}$.

Boxes Needed to Get a Coupon	Frequency
1	IIII
2	I
3 or more	~~IIII~~ ~~IIII~~ ~~IIII~~

Name ______________________ Class ______________ Date ____________

❸ **Using Random Digits as a Simulation Tool** In an election, 43% of voters chose Governor Smith. Use random digits as a simulation tool to estimate the probability that a journalist will have to interview more than 2 voters before finding one who voted for Smith.

43% of voters, or $\frac{\square}{100}$, chose Smith.

Use a simulation tool with ☐ equally likely outcomes.
You can use 2-digit random numbers from 0 to 99.
☐ of the possible outcomes should represent votes for Smith. Use the numbers 00 to 42.
Each row of random numbers represents one trial.
If either or both numbers are between ☐ and ☐, the journalist will need to interview 1 or 2 voters.
If neither number is between 00 and ☐, the journalist will need to interview more than 2 voters.
Out of 10 trials, ☐ resulted in more than 2 voters being interviewed. So, the probability that a journalist will have to interview more than 2 voters before finding one who voted for Smith is approximately $\frac{\square}{10}$, or $\frac{\square}{\square}$.

Random Numbers		Outcome
02	85	← ☐ voters
70	13	← ☐ voters
97	56	← ☐ voters
32	24	← ☐ voters
60	58	← ☐ voters
41	30	← ☐ voters
29	12	← ☐ voters
62	83	← ☐ voters
54	78	← ☐ voters
20	18	← ☐ voters

Quick Check

1. One-fourth of the deer in a population has a certain disease. Design a simulation for estimating the probability that a scientist will need to test no more than 3 deer before finding one with the disease.

____

____

____

____

____

2. Perform 20 trials of the simulation in Quick Check 1. Estimate the probability that a scientist will need to test no more than 3 deer before finding one that has the disease.

____

3. **Medicine** In the U.S., 42% of blood donors have type A blood. Use the random numbers at the right as a tool to estimate the probability that it will take at least 4 donors to find one with type A blood.

____

Medicine			
91	04	81	49
72	45	45	96
54	93	14	81
70	28	66	00
67	37	29	45
33	77	57	22
58	84	14	80
49	45	20	59
78	05	88	88
21	83	16	98

Name ______________________ Class ______________ Date ______________

Lesson 10-1

Angle Measures

Lesson Objective	**Common Core Standard**
To write and solve equations to find unknown angle measures	Geometry: 7.G.5

Vocabulary

An angle is ____

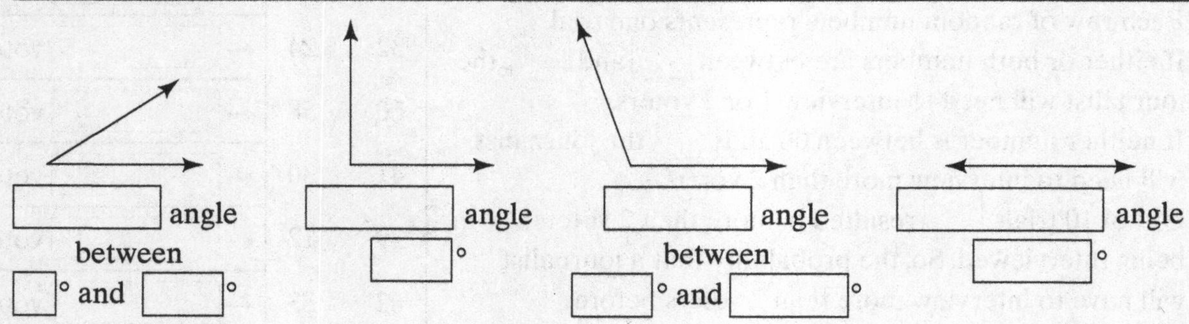

Adjacent angles are ____

Circle an angle adjacent to ∠1.

Vertical angles are ____

Circle a vertical angle to ∠1.

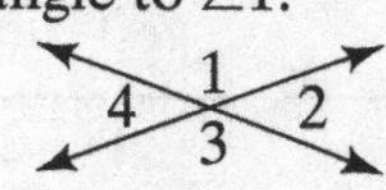

If the sum of the measure of two angles is 90°, the angles are ____________. If the sum is 180°, the angles are ____________.

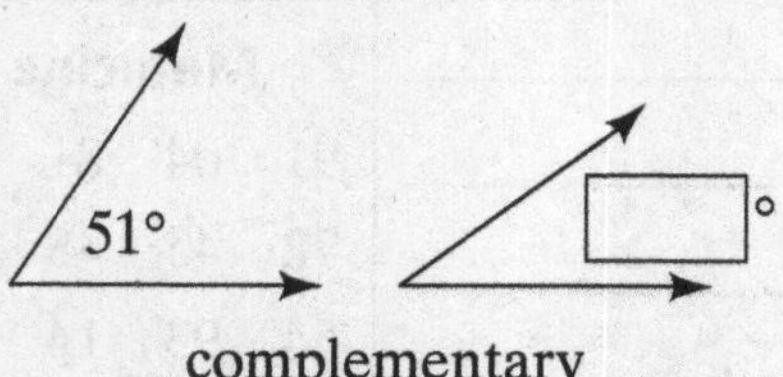

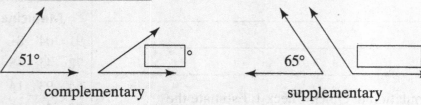

65° ____°

supplementary

Congruent angles are ____

Name ______________________ Class ______________ Date ______________

Examples

1 Finding Supplements and Complements Write and solve an equation to find the measures of the two angles described at the right.

$6x + (19x + 5) = 180$ ← **The angles are supplementary.**

$(6x + \square) + 5 = 180$ ← **Use the $\square$ Property.**

$\square + 5 = 180$ ← **Combine like terms.**

$\square + 5 - \square = 180 - \square$ ← **Subtract $\square$ from each side.**

$\square = \square$ ← **Simplify.**

$\frac{\square}{\square} = \frac{175}{\square}$ ← **Divide.**

$x = 7$ ← **Simplify.**

19x + 5°

6x

Calculate the angle measures.

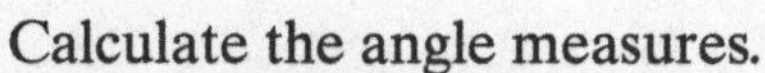

$6(\square) = \square$ and $19(\square) + 5 = \square$

The angle measures are $\square$° and $\square$°.

2 Finding Angle Measures In the diagram, $m\angle 3 = 32°$. Find the measures of $\angle 1$, $\angle 2$, and $\angle 4$.

1 2 3 4

$m\angle 2 + 32° = \square$ ← **$\angle 2$ and $\angle 3$ are $\square$.**

$m\angle 2 + 32° - 32° = \square - 32°$ ← **Subtract 32° from each side.**

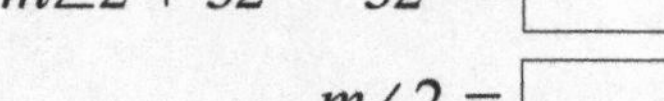

$m\angle 2 = \square$ ← **Simplify.**

$m\angle 1 = \square$ ← **$\angle 1$ and $\angle 3$ are $\square$ angles.**

$m\angle 4 = \square$ ← **$\angle 2$ and $\angle 4$ are $\square$ angles.**

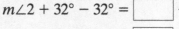

Quick Check

1. Write and solve an equation to find the measures of the two angles described at the right. $\square$

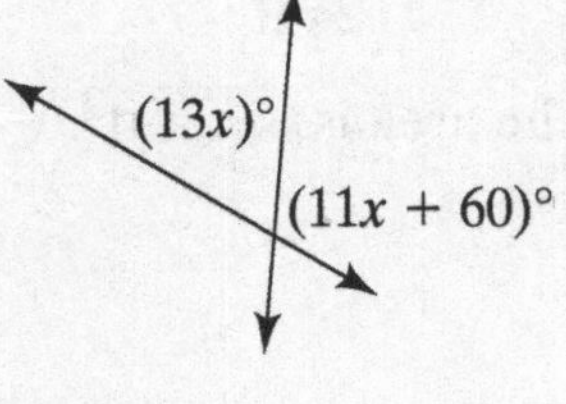

2. In the diagram at the right, $m\angle 8 = 72°$. Find the measures of $\angle 5$, $\angle 6$, and $\angle 7$.

Name ______________________ Class ______________ Date ____________

Lesson 10-2

Area of a Parallelogram

Lesson Objective	Common Core Standard
To find the area of a parallelogram and to relate perimeter and area	Expressions and Equations: 7.G.6

Vocabulary and Key Concepts

Area of a Parallelogram

The area of a parallelogram is equal to the product of any [ ] b and the corresponding [ ] h.

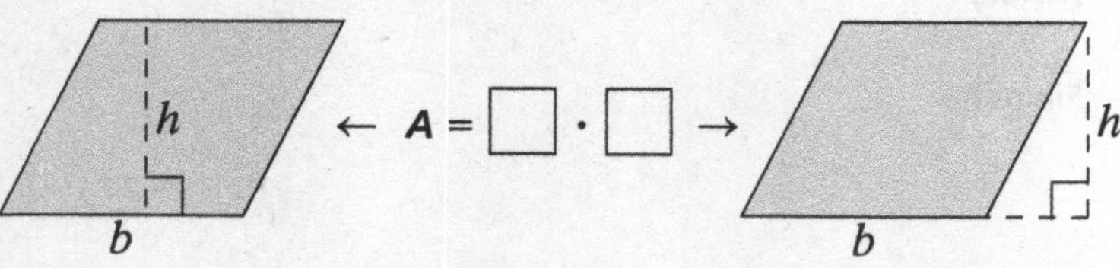

The height of a parallelogram is ______________________________

____

____

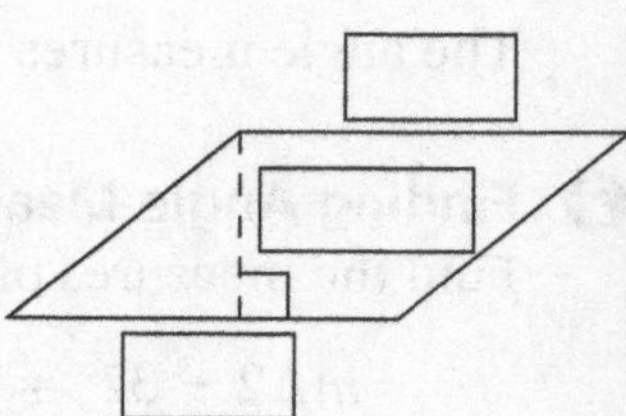

Examples

1 Finding the Area of a Parallelogram Find the area of the parallelogram.

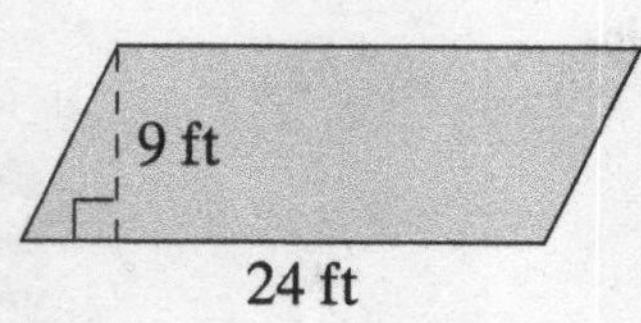

$A =$ [ ][ ] ← **Use the area formula.**

$=$ ([ ])([ ]) ← **Substitute.**

$=$ [ ] ← **Simplify.**

The area is [ ] ft^2.

Name ______________________ Class ______________ Date ______________

❷ **Relating Perimeter and Area** Jacob wants to fence in a rectangular dog run in his back yard. He has 46 feet of fencing and wants the dog run to be as large as possible. Which dimensions should he use?

A. length of 9 ft and width of 14 ft **B.** length of 10 ft and width of 14 ft
C. length of 11 ft and width of 12 ft **D.** length of 12 ft and width of 12 ft

Since all answer choices give the length l and the width w, you can calculate both the perimeter $2l + 2w$, and the area ☐.

Perimeter	**Area**	
☐ (9) + ☐ (14) = ☐	☐ ☐ ☐ = ☐	← **Perimeter is correct; find the area.**
☐ (10) + ☐ (14) = ☐		← **Perimeter is greater than 46 ft.**
☐ (11) + ☐ (12) = ☐	☐ ☐ ☐ = ☐	← **Perimeter is correct; the area in choice A is** ☐.
☐ (12) + ☐ (12) = ☐		← **Perimeter is greater than 46 ft.**

The rectangle with a length of ☐ ft and a width of ☐ ft will have the correct perimeter and the greatest area. The correct answer is choice ☐.

Quick Check

1. Find the area of the parallelogram.

☐

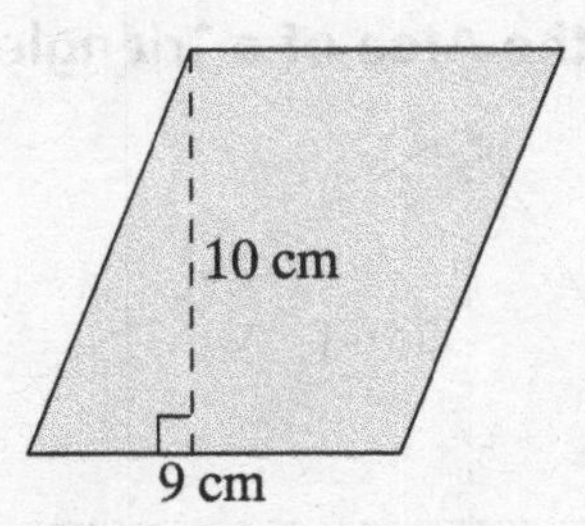

2. What is the perimeter of the rectangle?

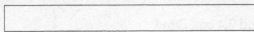

☐

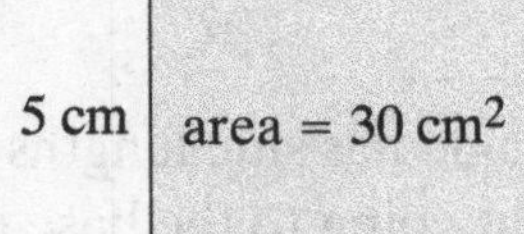

Name ____________________ Class ____________ Date ____________

Lesson 10-3

Area of a Triangle

Lesson Objective	Common Core Standard
To find the area of a triangle and to relate side lengths and area	Geometry: 7.G.6

Vocabulary and Key Concepts

Area of a Triangle

The area of a triangle is equal to half the product of any ______ and the corresponding ______.

$A = \frac{1}{2}\square\square$

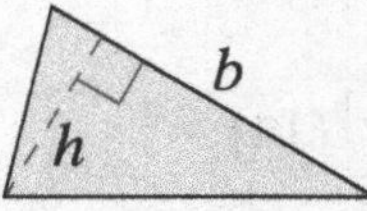

The height of a triangle ____

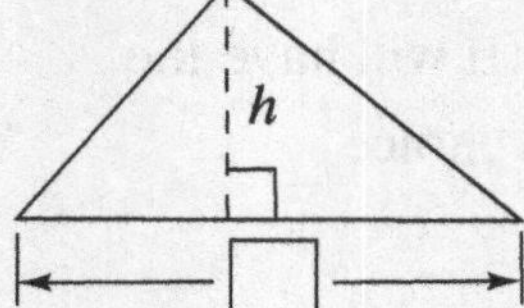

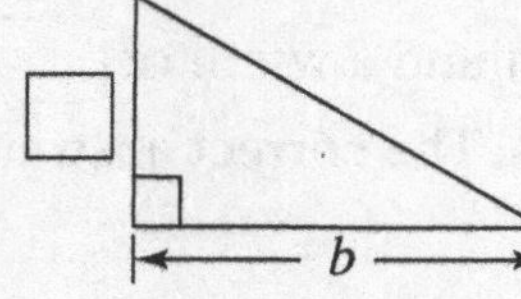

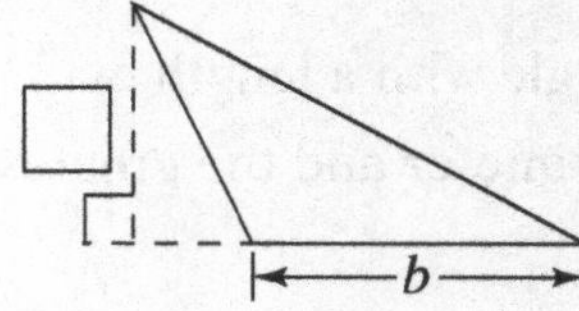

Examples

1 Finding the Area of a Triangle Find the area of each triangle.

a.

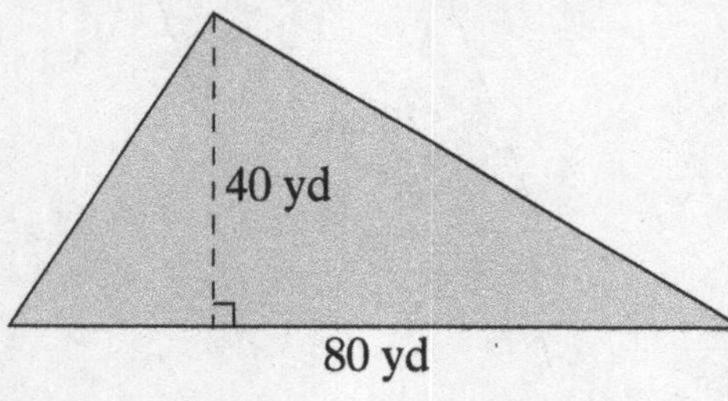

$A = \frac{1}{2}\square\square$ ← **Use the area formula.**

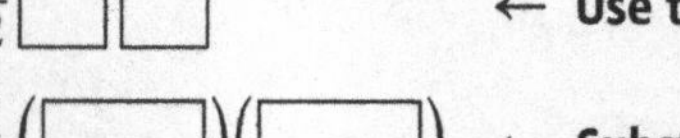

$= \frac{1}{2}(\square)(\square)$ ← **Substitute.**

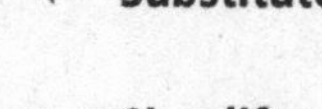

$= \square$ ← **Simplify.**

The area is ______ yd^2.

b. The triangle has side lengths of 16.2 cm, 15.4 cm, and 2.4 cm. Draw the height going to the base of length 2.4 cm. The height is 15 cm.

$A = \square bh$ ← **Use the area formula.**

$= \square\square\square$ ← **Substitute.**

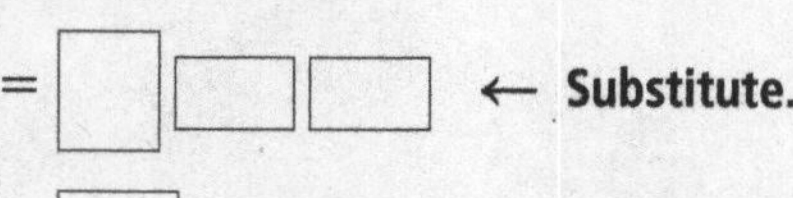

$= \square$ ← **Simplify.**

The area is ______ cm^2.

Name ______________________ Class ______________ Date ______________

❷ **Relating Side Lengths and Area** Triangle A below has sides three times as long as the sides of Triangle B. How does the area of Triangle A compare to the area of Triangle B?

Triangle A

$b =$ ☐ in., $h =$ ☐ in.

$A = \frac{1}{2}(\square)(\square)$

$= \square$

Triangle B

$b =$ ☐ in.; $h =$ ☐ in.

$A = \frac{1}{2}(\square)(\square)$

$= \square$

The area of Triangle A is ☐ in^2. The area of Triangle B is ☐ in^2. So, the area of Triangle A is ☐ times greater than the area of Triangle B.

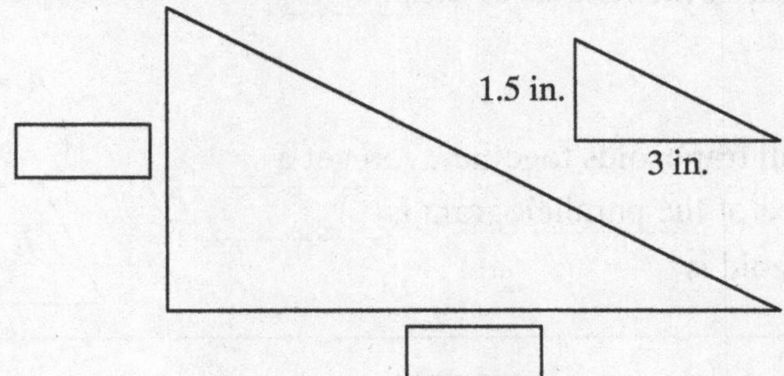

Quick Check

1. Find the area of each triangle.

a.

26.8 m
12 m
19 m
36 m

☐

b.

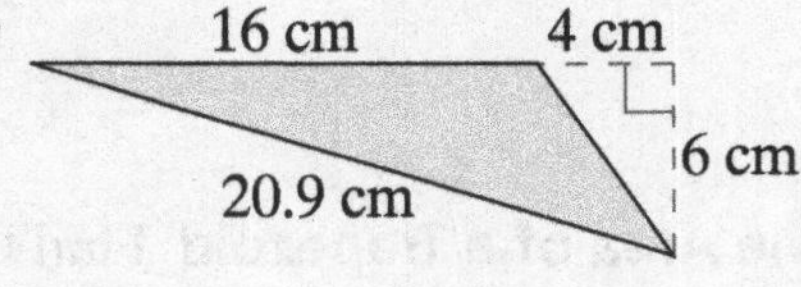

☐

2. What is the unknown side length of the triangle? ☐

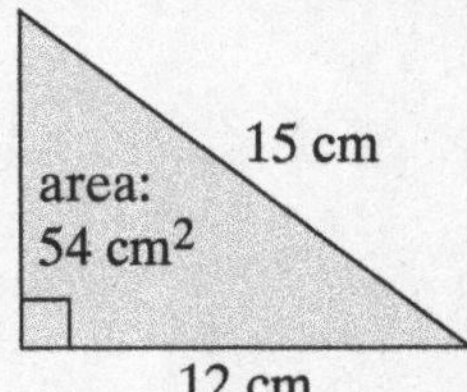

Name ____________ Class ____________ Date ____________

Lesson 10-4

Areas of Other Figures

Lesson Objective	**Common Core Standard**
To find the area of a trapezoid and the areas of irregular figures	Expressions and Equations: 7.G.6

Vocabulary and Key Concepts

Area of a Trapezoid

The area of a trapezoid is ☐ the product of the ☐ and the sum of the lengths of the ☐.

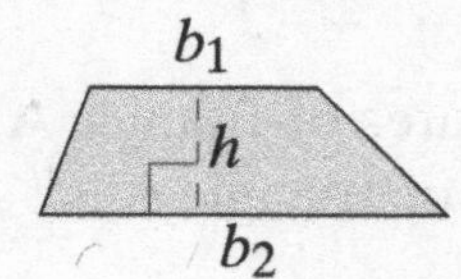

$A = \frac{1}{2}☐(☐ + ☐)$

If you put two identical trapezoids together, you get a parallelogram.The area of the parallelogram is ☐.
The area of one trapezoid is ☐.

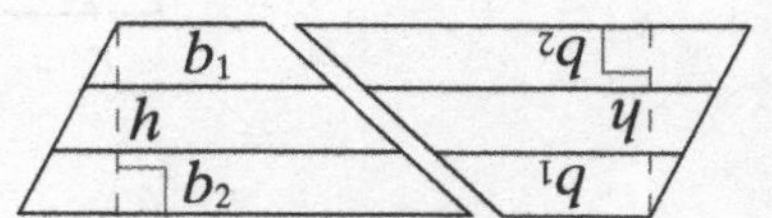

The bases of a trapezoid are ____________

The height of a trapezoid is ____________

____

Examples

1 Finding the Area of a Trapezoid Find the area of the trapezoid.

$A = \frac{1}{2}☐(☐ + ☐)$ ← **Use the area formula for a trapezoid.**

$= \frac{1}{2}(☐)(☐ + ☐)$ ← **Substitute for h, b_1, and b_2.**

$= \frac{1}{2}(☐)(16)$ ← **Add.**

$= ☐$ ← **Multiply.**

The area is ☐ cm^2.

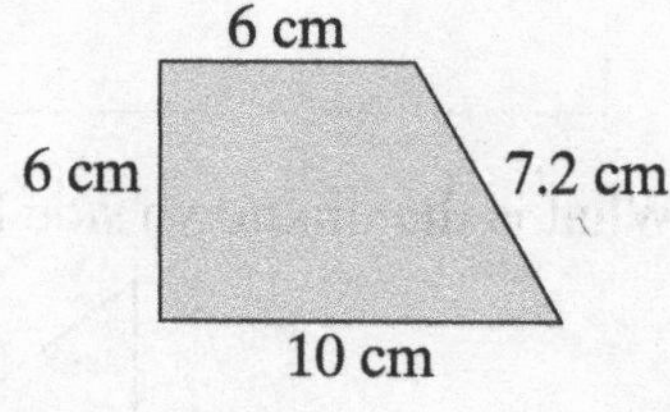

Name ____________________ Class ____________ Date ____________

❷ **Geography** Estimate the area of the figure by finding the area of the trapezoid.

$A = \frac{1}{2}\square(\square + b_2)$ ← **Use the area formula for a trapezoid.**

$= \frac{1}{2}(\square)(\square + \square)$ ← **Substitute for *h*, b_1, and b_2.**

$= \frac{1}{2}(\square)(\square)$ ← **Add.**

$= \square$ ← **Multiply.**

The area of the figure is about $\square$ ft².

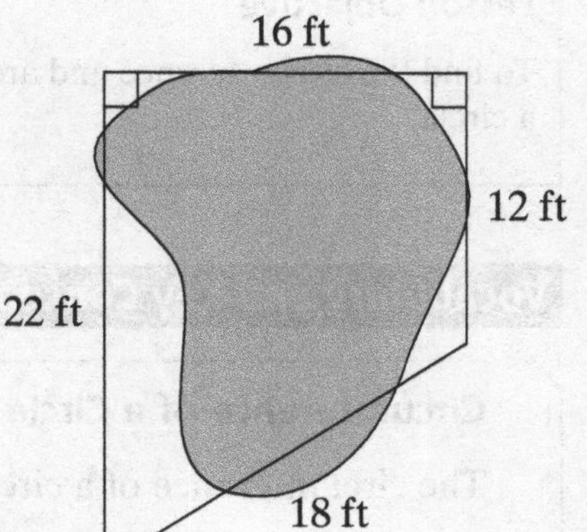

Quick Check

1. Find the area of each trapezoid.

a.

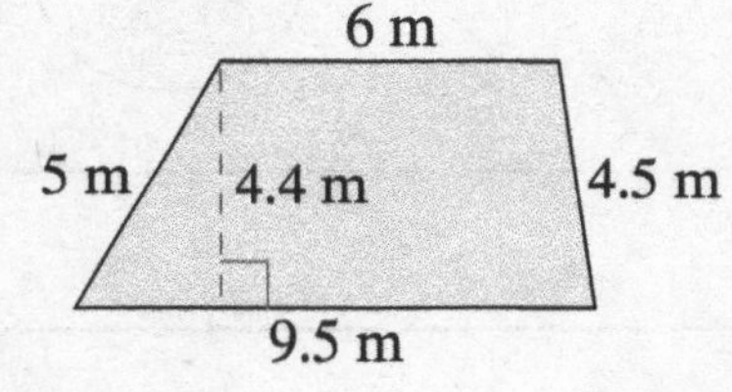

$\square$ m²

b.

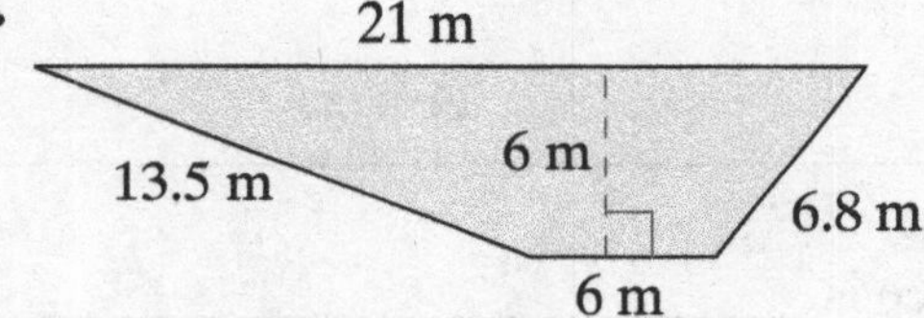

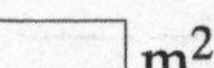

$\square$ m²

2. Estimate the area of the figure by finding the area of the trapezoid.

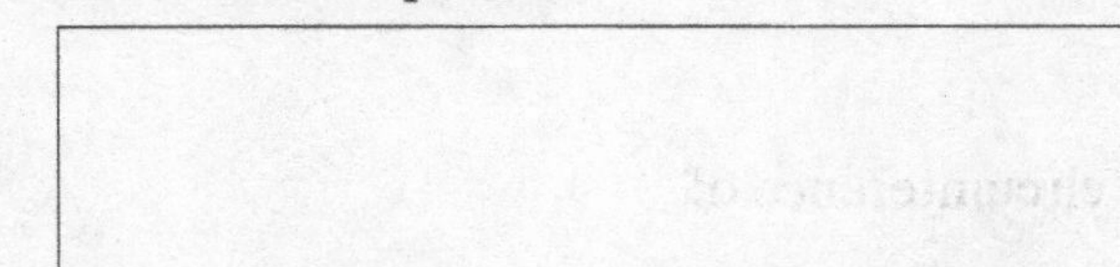

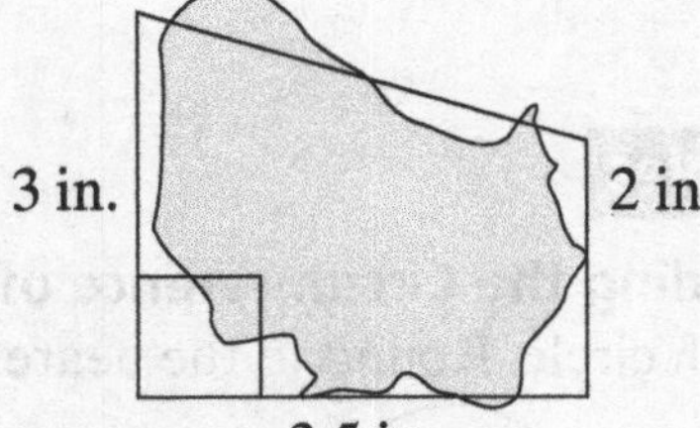

Name ____________________ Class ____________ Date ____________

Lesson 10-5

Circumference and Area of a Circle

Lesson Objective	**Common Core Standard**
To find the circumference and area of a circle	Expressions and Equations: 7.G.4

Vocabulary and Key Concepts

Circumference of a Circle

The circumference of a circle is ☐ times the ☐.

$$C = \pi d = 2\pi r$$

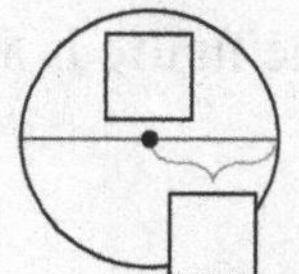

Area of a Circle

The area of a circle is the product of ☐ and the square of the ☐.

$$A = \pi r^2$$

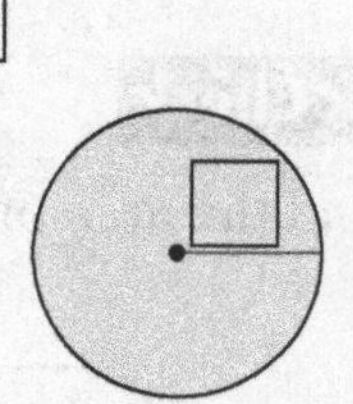

Circumference is ____

____

Pi (π) is ____

____

Examples

1 Finding the Circumference of a Circle Find the circumference of each circle. Round to the nearest tenth.

a.

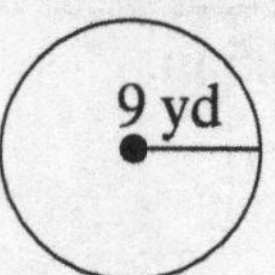

b.

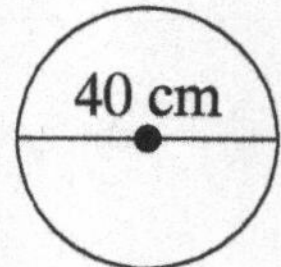

a.		b.
$C =$ ☐	← **Use the formula for circumference.** →	$C =$ ☐
$= 2\pi$ (☐)	← **Substitute.** →	$= \pi$ (☐)
$=$ ☐	← **Use a calculator.** →	$=$ ☐

The circumference is approximately ☐ yd.

The circumference is approximately ☐ cm.

Name ______________________ Class ______________ Date ______________

❷ Finding the Area of a Circle A pizza has a diameter of 28 cm. What is the area of the pizza? Round to the nearest tenth.

$r = \frac{\square}{2} = \square$ ← **The radius is half the diameter.**

$A = \square$ ← **Use the formula for the area of a circle.**

$= \pi \left(\square\right)^2$ ← **Substitute $\square$ for the radius.**

$\approx \square$ ← **Use a calculator.**

$\approx \square$ ← **Round the solution to the nearest tenth.**

The area of the pizza is approximately $\square$ cm^2.

Quick Check

1. Find the circumference of the circle. Round to the nearest tenth.

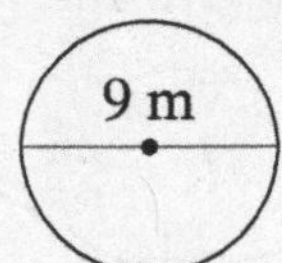

$\square$ m

2. Find the area of the circle. Round to the nearest square unit.

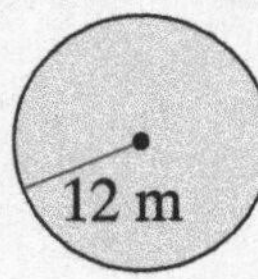

$\square$ m^2

Name ______________________ Class ______________ Date ______________

Lesson 11-1

Angles and Parallel Lines

Lesson Objective	**Common Core State Standard**
To identify parallel lines and the angles formed by parallel lines and transversals	Geometry: 8.G.5

Vocabulary and Key Concepts

Transversals and Parallel Lines

When a transversal intersects two parallel lines,

- [ ] angles are congruent, and
- [ ] angles are congruent.

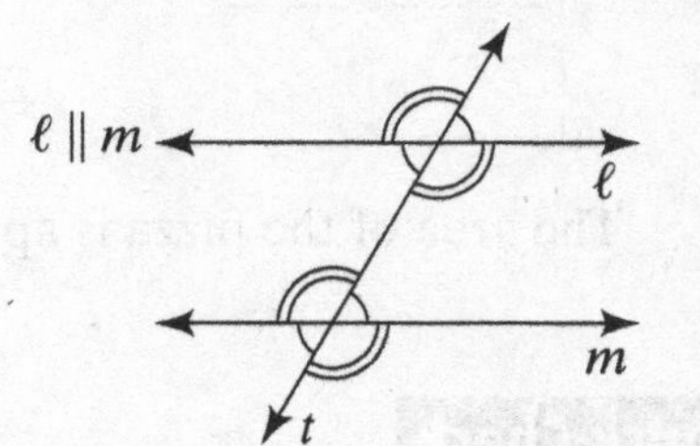

A transversal is ______________________

____

Corresponding angles lie ______________________

____

Examples: ∠1 and [ ] ∠2 and [ ]
∠3 and [ ] ∠4 and [ ]

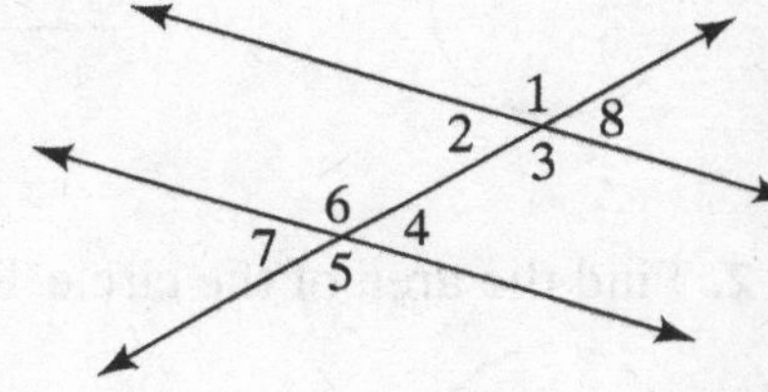

Alternate interior angles lie ______________________

____

Examples: ∠3 and [ ] ∠4 and [ ]

Examples

Use this diagram for Examples 1 and 2.

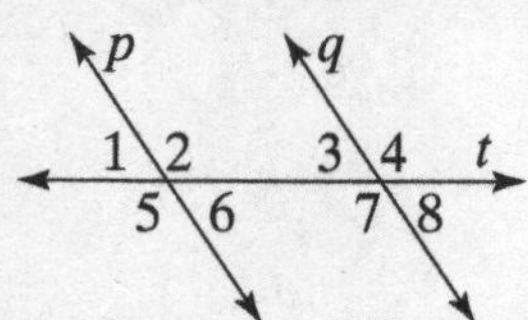

1 Identifying Angles Identify each pair of corresponding angles and each pair of alternate interior angles.

∠1 and [ ], ∠2 and [ ], ∠5 and [ ], ∠6 and [ ] are pairs of [ ] angles.

∠2 and [ ], ∠3 and [ ] are pairs of [ ] angles.

❷ Finding Angle Measures If p is parallel to q, and $m\angle 3 = 56°$, find $m\angle 6$ and $m\angle 1$.

$m\angle 6 = m\angle 3 =$ ☐ ← ☐ **angles are congruent.**

$m\angle 1 = m\angle 3 =$ ☐ ← ☐ **angles are congruent.**

❸ Identifying Parallel Lines In the diagram below, $m\angle 5 = 80°$, $m\angle 6 = 80°$, and $m\angle 7 = 80°$. Explain why p and q are parallel and why s and t are parallel.

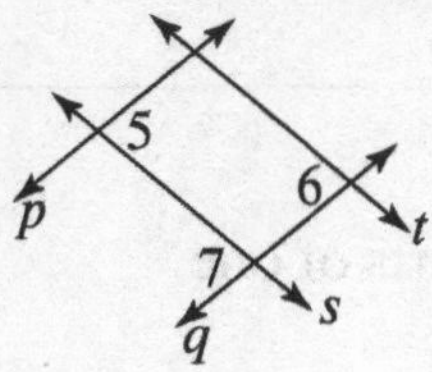

$p \parallel q$ because $\angle 5$ and $\angle 7$ are congruent ☐ angles.

$s \parallel t$ because $\angle 6$ and $\angle 7$ are congruent ☐ angles.

Quick Check

1. Use the diagram for Examples 1 and 2. Identify each pair of angles as *corresponding, alternate interior,* or *neither*.

a. $\angle 3, \angle 6$

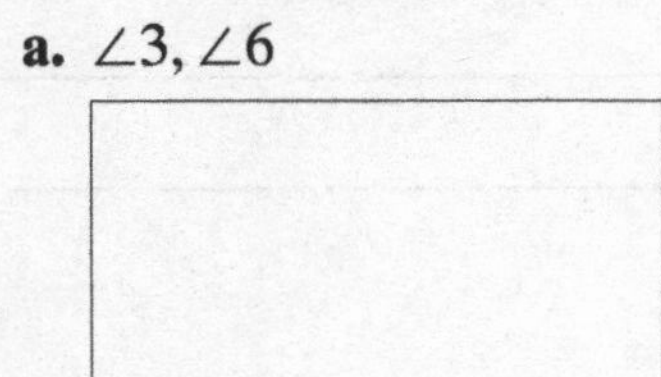

b. $\angle 2, \angle 7$

c. $\angle 1, \angle 8$

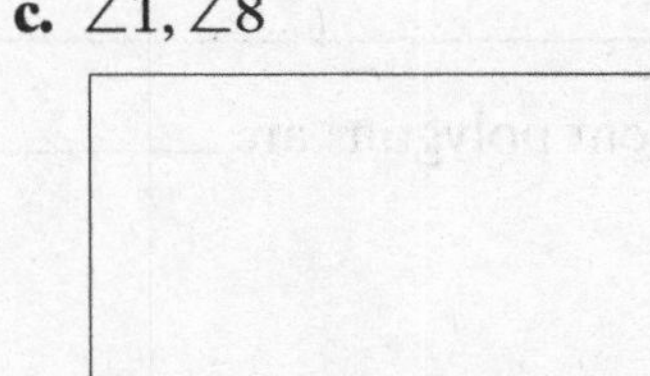

2. In the diagram for Examples 1 and 2, $m\angle 3 = 117°$. Find $m\angle 6$ and $m\angle 5$.

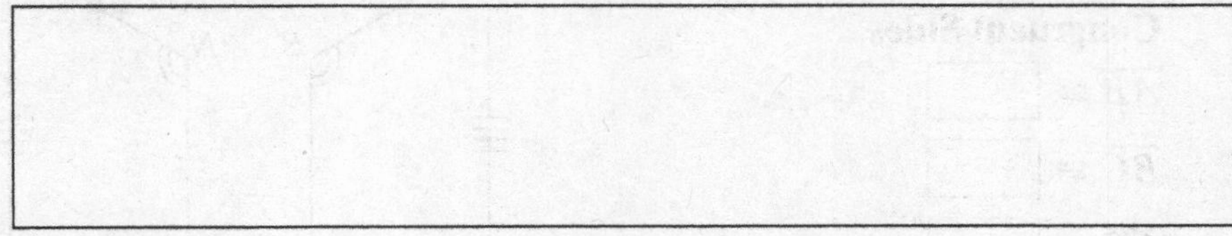

3. Transversal t is perpendicular to lines ℓ and m. Explain how you know $\ell \parallel m$.

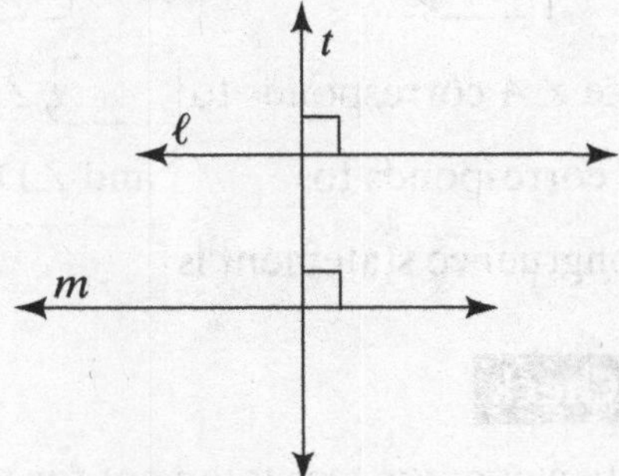

Name ______________________ Class ______________ Date ____________

Lesson 11-2

Congruent Figures

Lesson Objective	**Common Core State Standard**
To identify congruent figures and use them to solve problems	Geometry: 8.G.2

Vocabulary and Key Concepts

Showing Triangles Are Congruent

To demonstrate that two triangles are congruent, show that the following parts of one triangle are congruent to the corresponding parts of the other triangle.

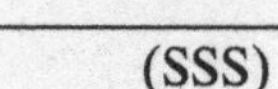

(SSS) (SAS) (ASA)

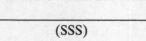

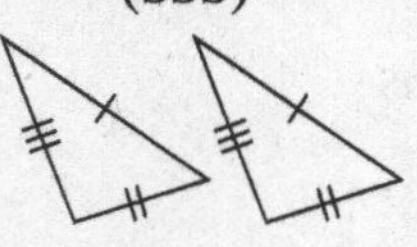

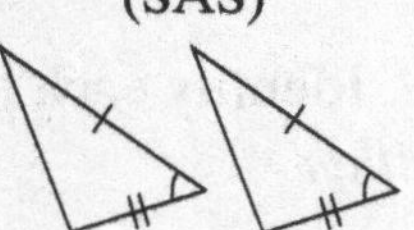

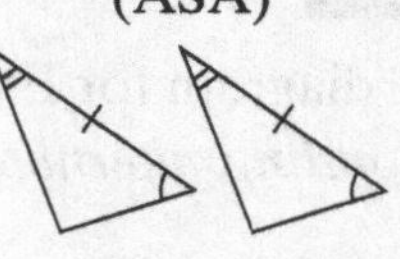

Congruent polygons are ____

Example

1 Writing Congruence Statements Write a congruence statement for the congruent figures at the right.

Congruent Angles	**Congruent Sides**
$\angle A \cong$ ☐	$\overline{AB} \cong$ ☐
$\angle B \cong$ ☐	$\overline{BC} \cong$ ☐
$\angle C \cong$ ☐	$\overline{CD} \cong$ ☐
$\angle D \cong$ ☐	$\overline{DA} \cong$ ☐

A B C D M N O P

Since $\angle A$ corresponds to ☐, $\angle B$ corresponds to ☐, $\angle C$ corresponds to ☐, and $\angle D$ corresponds to ☐, a congruence statement is ☐ $\cong$ ☐.

Quick Check

1. Write a congruence statement for the congruent figures at the right.

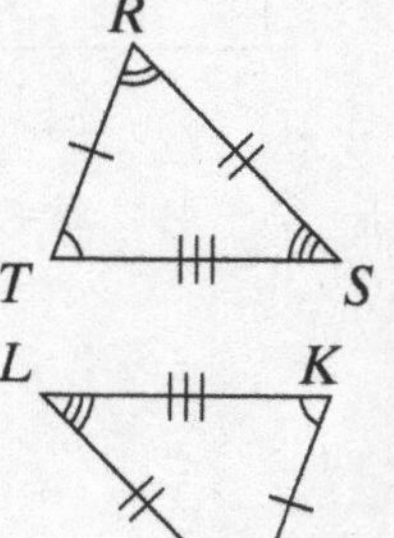

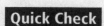

Name ______________________ Class ______________ Date ______________

Examples

❷ Congruent Triangles Show that the triangles are congruent.

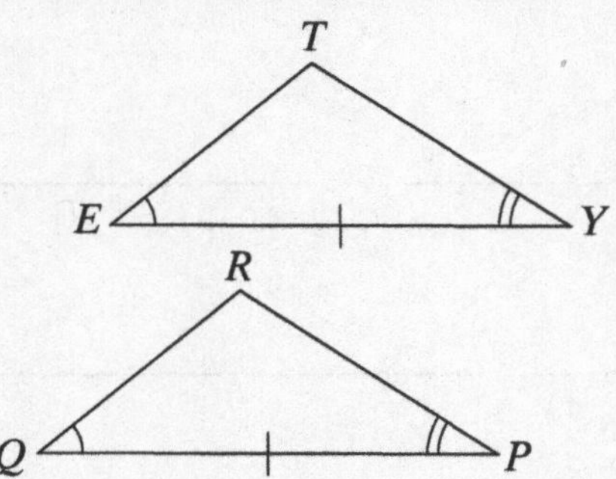

$\angle Q \cong \angle E$ [ ]

$\overline{QP} \cong \overline{EY}$ [ ]

$\angle P \cong \angle Y$ [ ]

$\triangle QPR \cong \triangle EYT$ [ ]

❸ Surveying A surveyor drew the diagram at the right to find the distance from J to I across the canyon. $\triangle GHI \cong \triangle KJI$. What is the distance $\overline{JI}$?

50°, G, 36 ft, 40°, 48 ft, J, I, H, 58 ft, K

Corresponding parts of congruent triangles are [ ]. Since $\overline{JI}$ corresponds to $\overline{HI}$,

$\overline{JI}$ = [ ] ft.

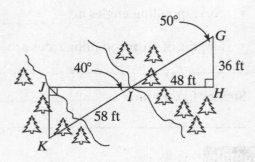

Quick Check

2. Show that each pair of triangles is congruent.

a.

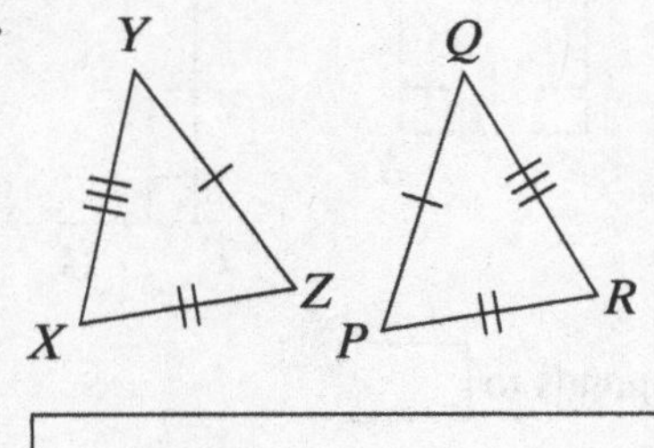

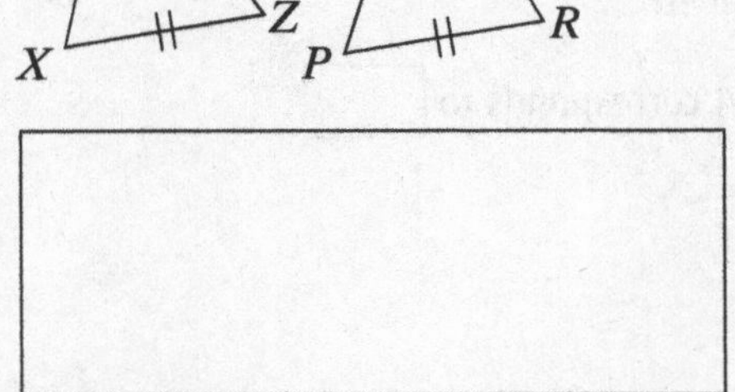

b.

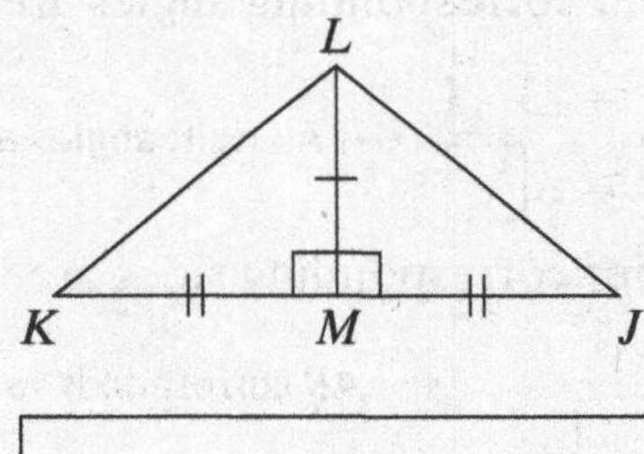

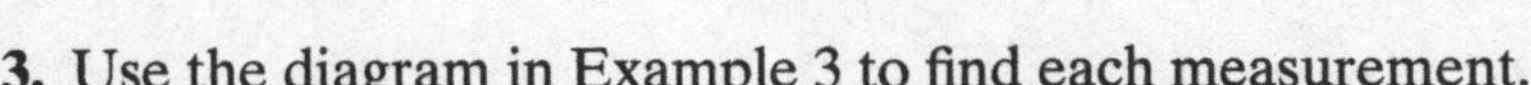

3. Use the diagram in Example 3 to find each measurement.

a. $\overline{JK}$

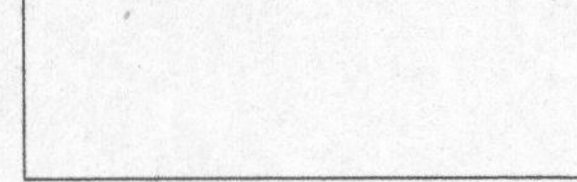

b. $m\angle K$

c. $m\angle GIH$

[ ]

Name ________________ Class ________________ Date ________________

Lesson 11-3

Similar Figures

Lesson Objective	**Common Core State Standard**
To identify similar figures and to use proportions to find missing measurements in similar figures	Geometry: 8.G.4

Vocabulary and Key Concepts

Similar Polygons If two polygons are similar polygons, then

- corresponding angles are ______ and
- lengths of corresponding sides are ______.

Similar figures have ____

____

Example

1 Identifying Similar Polygons Is rectangle *ABCD* similar to rectangle *RSTU*? Explain.

First, check whether corresponding angles are congruent.

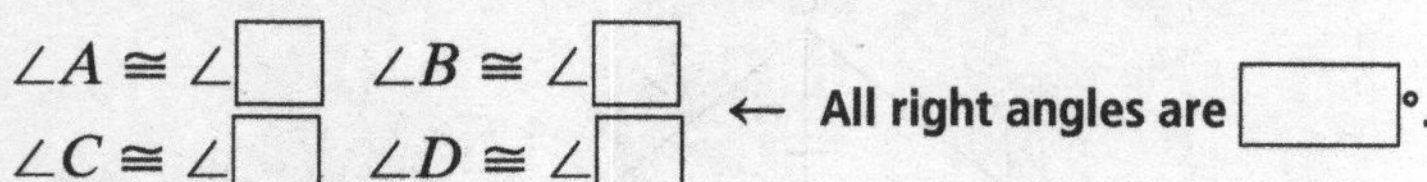

$\angle A \cong \angle$ ☐ $\angle B \cong \angle$ ☐ ← **All right angles are** ☐°.

$\angle C \cong \angle$ ☐ $\angle D \cong \angle$ ☐

Next, check whether corresponding sides are in proportion.

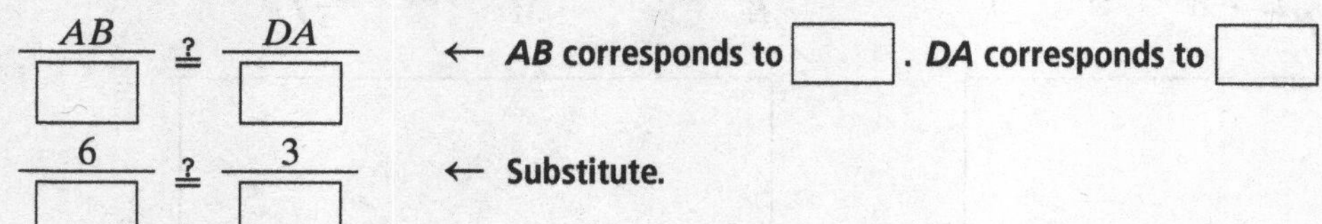

$\frac{AB}{☐} \stackrel{?}{=} \frac{DA}{☐}$ ← ***AB* corresponds to** ☐. ***DA* corresponds to** ☐.

$\frac{6}{☐} \stackrel{?}{=} \frac{3}{☐}$ ← **Substitute.**

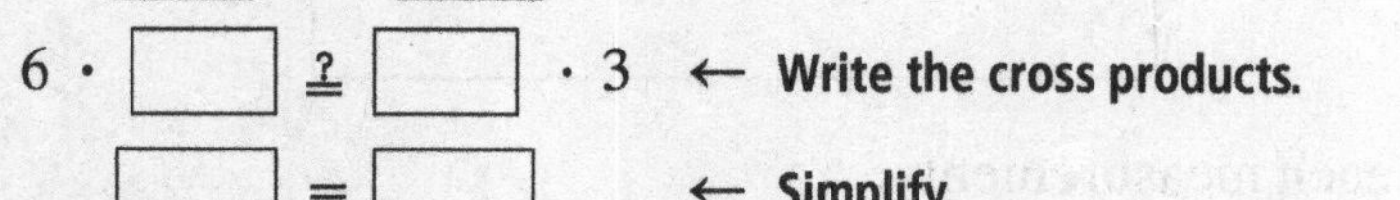

$6 \cdot$ ☐ $\stackrel{?}{=}$ ☐ $\cdot 3$ ← **Write the cross products.**

☐ = ☐ ← **Simplify.**

The corresponding sides ☐ in proportion, so rectangle *ABCD* is ☐ to rectangle *RSTU*.

Quick Check

1. Is rectangle *EFGH* similar to rectangle *PQRS*? Explain.

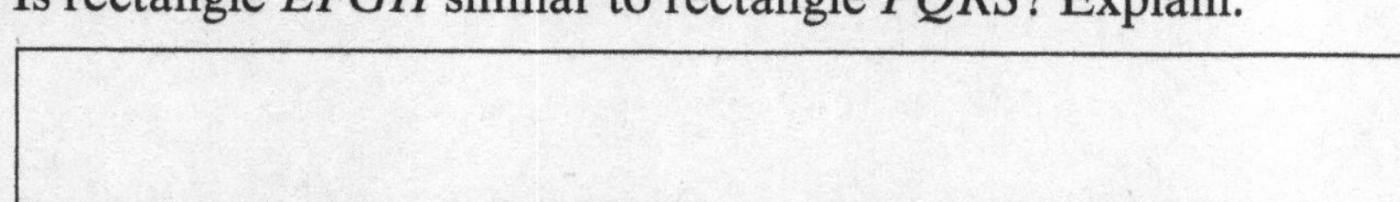

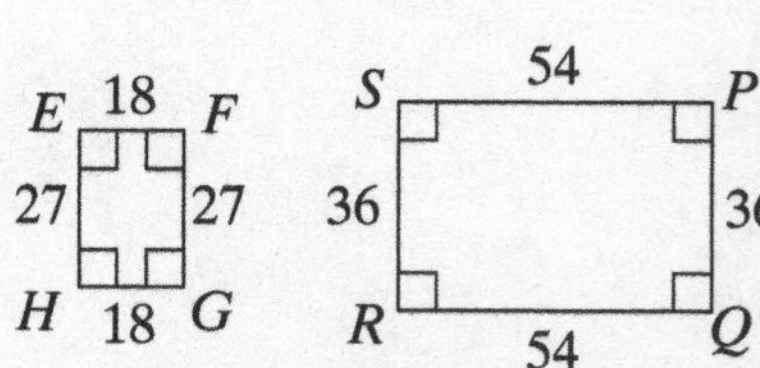

Name ____________________ Class ____________________ Date ____________________

Examples

❷ Application: Design Given that rectangle *EFGH* is similar to rectangle *WXYZ*, find *t*.

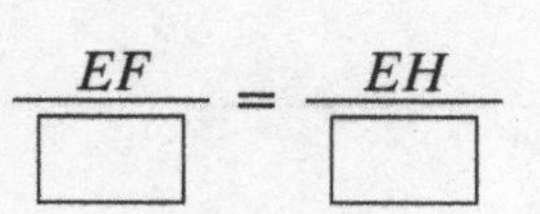

$\frac{EF}{\square} = \frac{EH}{\square}$ ← ***EF* corresponds to ☐.** ***EH* corresponds to ☐.**

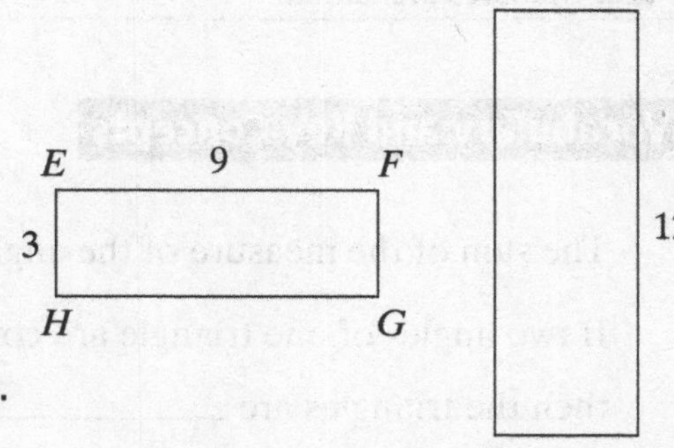

$\frac{9}{\square} = \frac{3}{\square}$ ← **Substitute.**

$9 \cdot \square = \square \cdot 3$ ← **Write the cross products.**

$\frac{\square}{9} = \frac{\square}{9}$ ← **Simplify. Then divide each side by 9.**

$t = \square$ ← **Simplify.**

❸ Overlapping Similar Triangles $\triangle RST \sim \triangle PSU$. Find the value of *d*.

Step 1 Separate the triangles.

Step 2 Write a proportion using corresponding sides of the triangles.

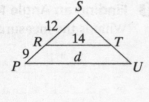

$\frac{SR}{\square} = \frac{RT}{\square}$ ← **Write a proportion.**

$\frac{12}{\square} = \frac{14}{\square}$ ← **Substitute.**

$12 \cdot \square = \square \cdot 14$ ← **Write the cross products.**

$\square = \square$ ← **Simplify.**

$\frac{\square}{12} = \frac{\square}{12}$ ← **Divide each side by 12.**

$d = \square$ ← **Simplify.**

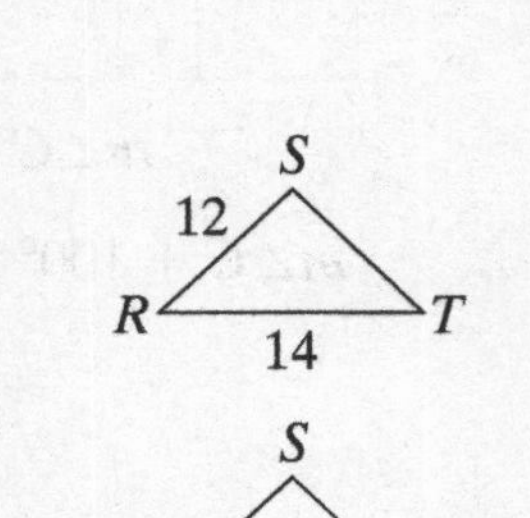

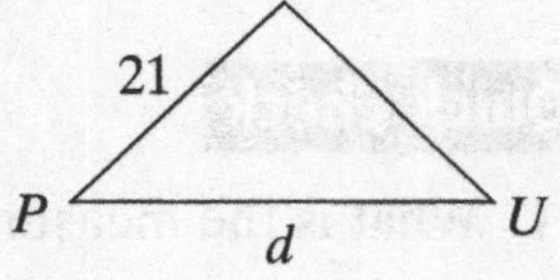

Quick Check

2. In Example 2, if the side lengths of *EFGH* are doubled, will the resulting polygon be similar to *EFGH*? Explain.

3. If *ST* is 13 ft in Example 3, what is the length of $\overline{SU}$?

Name ______________________ Class ______________ Date ______________

Lesson 11-4

Proving Triangles Similar

Lesson Objective	Common Core State Standard
To determine measures of the angles of triangles and use them to help prove that triangles are similar	Geometry: 8.G.5

Vocabulary and Key Concepts

The sum of the measure of the angles of any triangle is ______________________.

If two angles of one triangle are congruent to the corresponding angles of another triangle, then the triangles are ______________________.

Example

1 Finding an Angle Measure $\triangle BAC$ forms part of a bridge truss. What is the measure of $\angle C$?

$\square + \square + m\angle C = 180°$ ← **Angle sum of a triangle.**

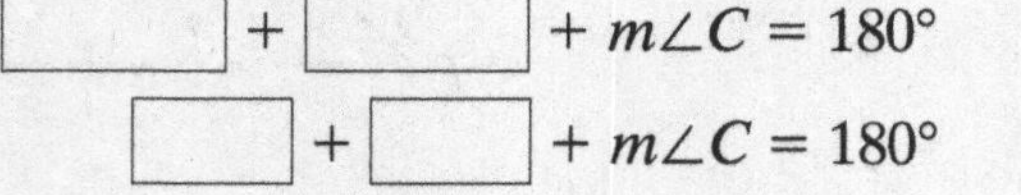

$\square + \square + m\angle C = 180°$ ← **Substitute.**

$m\angle C + \square = 180°$ ← **Simplify.**

$m\angle C + 100° - \square = 180° - \square$ ← **Subtract** $\square$ **from each side.**

$m\angle C = \square$ ← **Simplify.**

C, B 60°, 40° A

Quick Check

1. What is the measure of $\angle E$ in $\triangle DEF$?

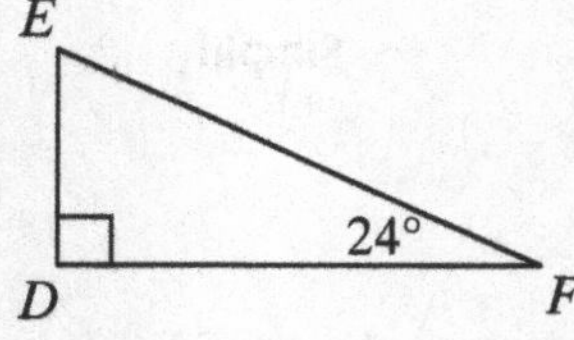

Name ____________________ Class ____________________ Date ____________________

Example

❷ Similar Triangles Show that the pair of triangles is similar.

Step 1 Use the angle sum of a ______ to find $m\angle R$.

$89° + 43° + m\angle R =$ ______

$132° + m\angle R =$ ______

$132 -$ ______ $+ m\angle R =$ ______ $-$ ______

$m\angle R =$ ______

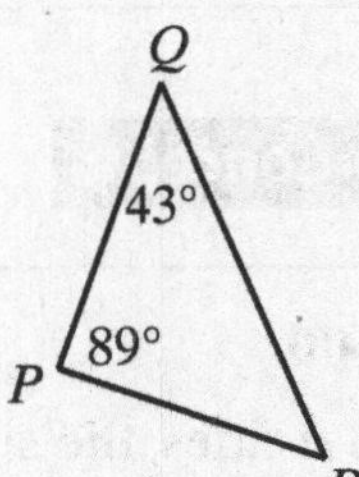

Step 2 Use AA similarity.

$\angle P \cong$ ______ ← **Each measures** ______.

$\angle R \cong$ ______ ← **Each measures** ______.

$\triangle PQR \sim \triangle LMK$ by Angle-Angle similarity.

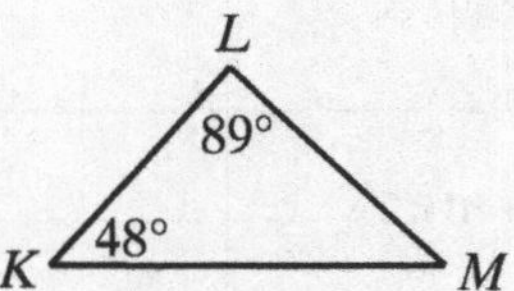

Quick Check

2. Show that each pair of triangles is similar.

a.

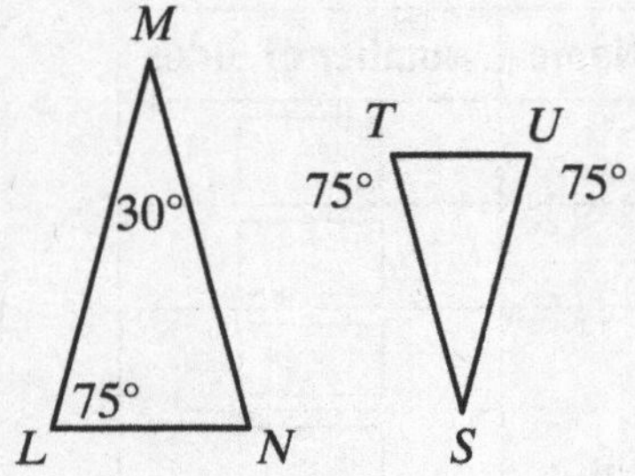

b.

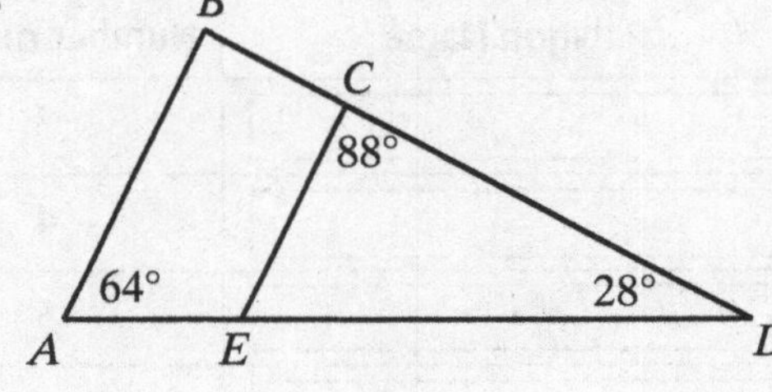

Name ______________________ Class ______________ Date ______________

Lesson 11-5

Angles and Polygons

Lesson Objective	**Common Core State Standard**
To find the angle measures of a polygon	Geometry: 8.G.5

Vocabulary and Key Concepts

Polygon Angle Sum

For a polygon with n sides, the sum of the measures of the interior angles is ______.

Exterior angles are ______________________________

____

Interior angles are ______________________________

____

Common Polygons

Polygon Name	Number of Sides	Polygon Name	Number of Sides
______	3	Octagon	___
______	4	Nonagon	___
______	5	Decagon	___
______	6	Dodecagon	___
Heptagon	___		

Example

1 Sum of the Interior Angle Measures Find the sum of the measures of the interior angles of an octagon.

An octagon has ___ sides.

$(n - 2)180° = (\square - 2)180°$ ← **Substitute ___ for *n*.**

$= \square°$ ← **Simplify.**

Quick Check

1. What is the sum of the measures of the interior angles of a heptagon? ___

Name ____________________ Class ____________ Date ____________

Examples

2 Angle Measures of a Polygon Find the missing angle measure in the hexagon.

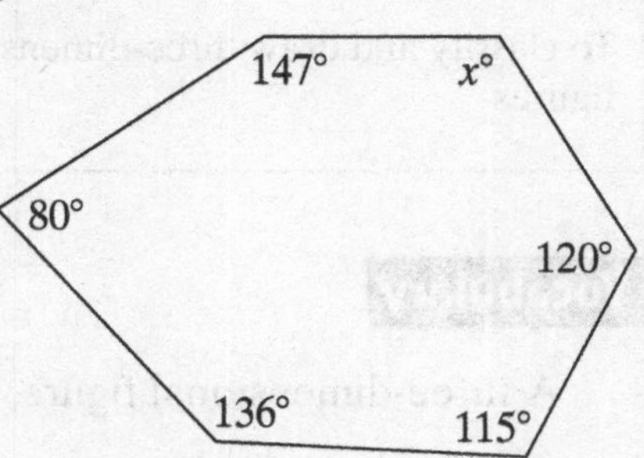

Step 1 Find the sum of the measures of the interior angles of a hexagon.

$(n-2)180° = (\square - 2)180°$ ← **Substitute** $\square$ **for** n.

$= \square$ ← **Simplify.**

Step 2 Write an equation.
Let x = the missing angle measure.

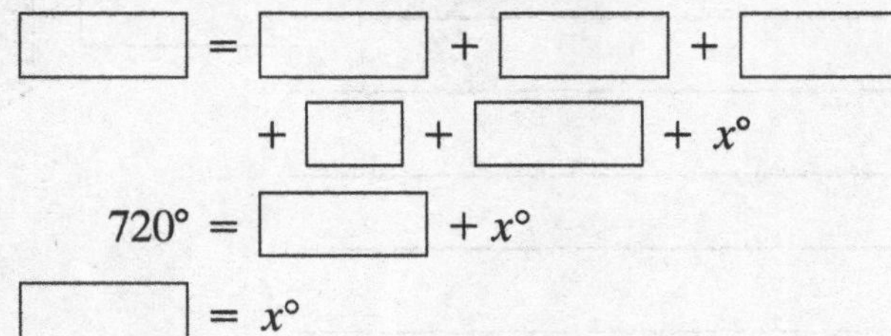

$\square = \square + \square + \square$
$+ \square + \square + x°$ ← **Write an equation.**

$720° = \square + x°$ ← **Add.**

$\square = x°$ ← **Subtract** $\square$ **from each side.**

The missing angle measure is $\square$.

3 Finding the Measure of an Exterior Angle $\angle 2$ is an exterior angle of $\triangle ABC$. What is $m\angle 2$?

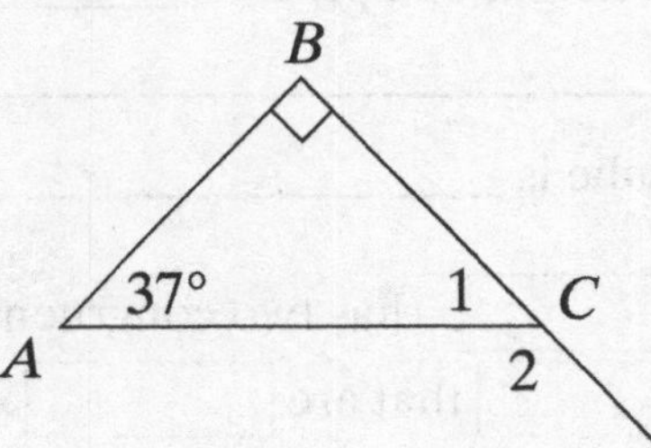

$m\angle 2 = m\angle A + m\angle B$ ← **Exterior angle of triangle**

$= \square$ ← **Substitute.**

$= \square$ ← **Simplify.**

$\angle 2$ measures 127°.

Check

By the angle sum of a triangle, $m\angle 1 = 180° - 90° - 37° = 53°$.

$\angle 1$ and $\angle 2$ are supplementary, so $m\angle 2 = 180° - 53° = 127°$. ✔

Quick Check

2. A hexagon has five angles with measures of 142°, 84°, 123°, 130°, and 90°. What is the measure of the sixth angle?

123°
130°
84°
142°
x°

3. In $\triangle RST$, $m\angle R = 63°$ and $m\angle S = 84°$. What is the measure of the exterior angle at vertex T?

Name ____________________ Class ____________ Date ____________

Lesson 12-1

Three-Dimensional Figures

Lesson Objective	Common Core Standard
To classify and draw three-dimensional figures	Geometry: Prepares for 7.G.3

Vocabulary

A three-dimensional figure, or solid, is ______________________________

____

A face is ______________________________

____

An edge is ______________________________

____

A prism is ______________________________

____

Prism

The bases of a prism are ______________________________

The height of a prism is ______________________________

____

A cube is ______________________________

A [ ] has two congruent parallel [ ] that are [ ].

The height of a cylinder is ______________________________

____

A [ ] has [ ] faces that meet at one point, a [ ], and a base that is a [ ].

A [ ] has one circular [ ] and one [ ].

A [ ] is the set of all points in space that are the same distance from a [ ] point.

Name ______________________ Class ______________ Date ______________

Examples

1 Naming Figures Name the geometric figure.

The figure is a [ ].

2 Drawing Three-Dimensional Figures Draw a pentagonal prism.

Step 1 Draw a [ ].

Step 2 Draw a second [ ] congruent to the first.

Step 3 Connect the vertices. Use [ ] for hidden edges.

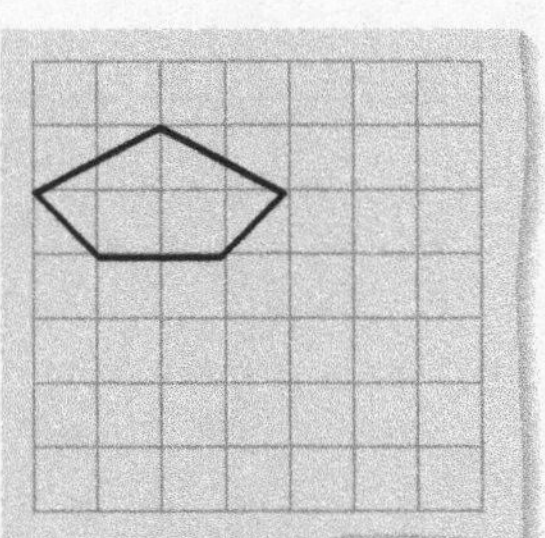

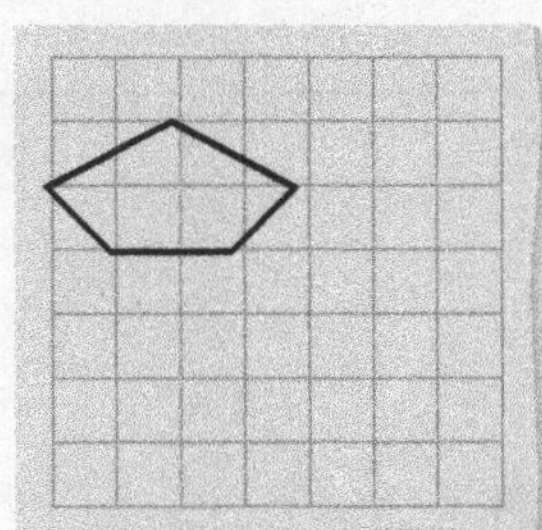

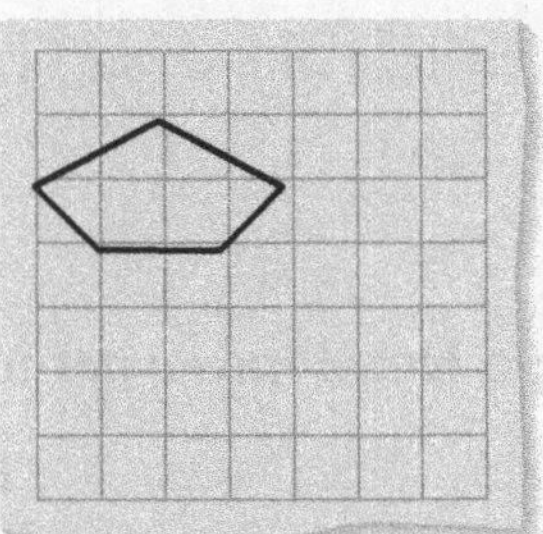

Quick Check

1. Name each figure.

a. 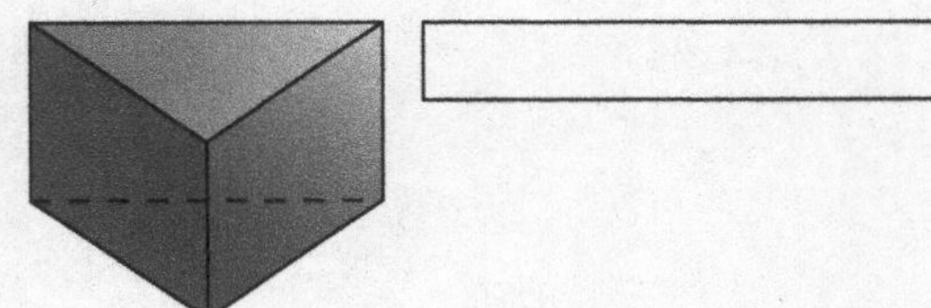

b. 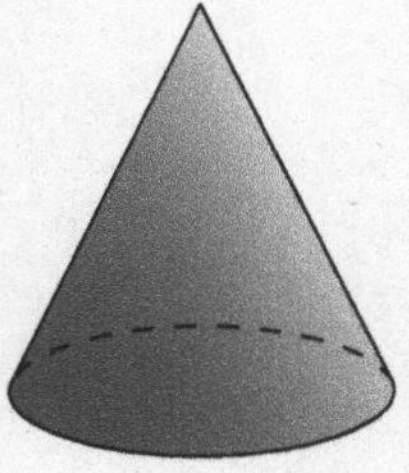

2. Use the grid to draw a triangular prism.

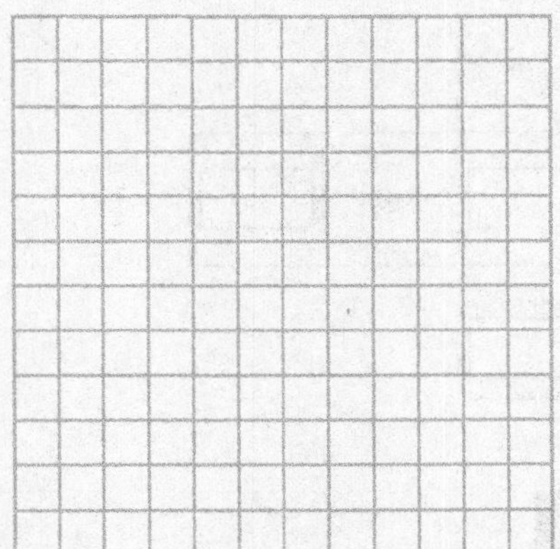

Name ______________________ Class ______________ Date ______________

Lesson 12-2

Surface Areas of Prisms and Cylinders

Lesson Objective	Common Core Standard
To find the surface areas of prisms and cylinders using nets	Geometry: 7.G.6

Vocabulary

A net is ____

The surface area of a prism is ______________________________

Example

1 Drawing a Net Draw a net for the cube.

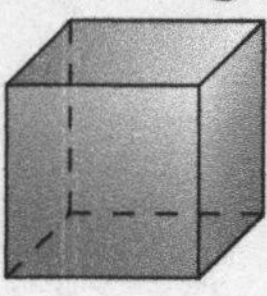

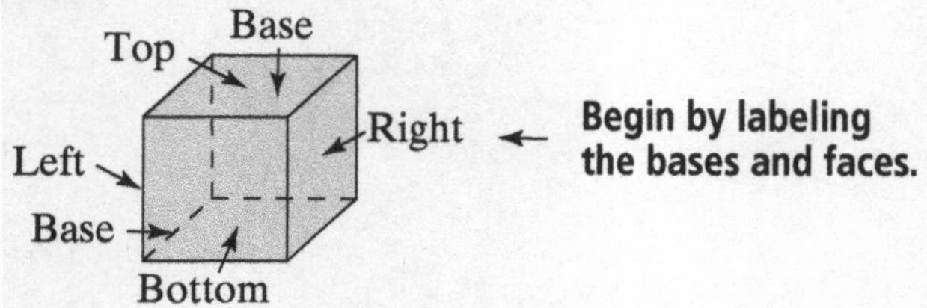

First, draw one base. Then, draw one face that connects both bases. Next, draw the other base. Draw and label the remaining faces.

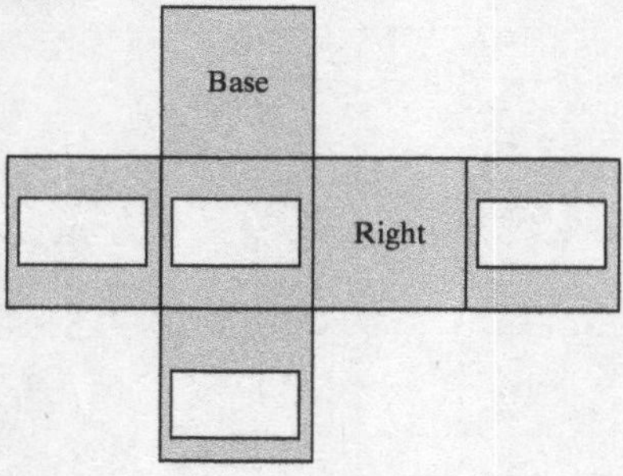

Quick Check

1. Draw a different net for the cube in Example 1.

Name ______________________ Class ______________ Date ______________

Examples

2 Finding the Surface Area of a Prism Find the surface area of the prism.

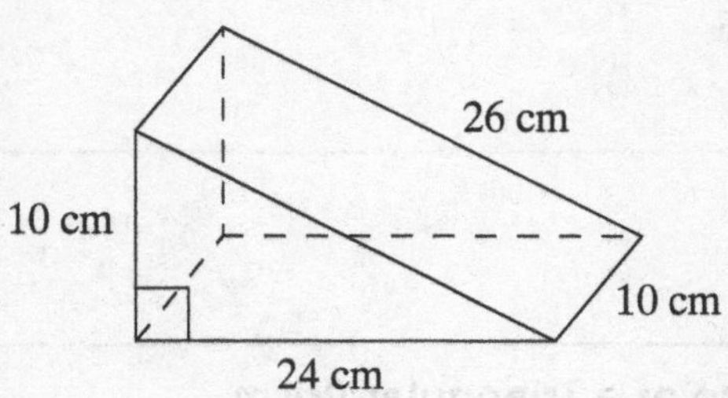

First, draw a net for the prism.

Back
26 cm
24 cm
Top
Bottom
Left side
Front

Then, find the total area of the five faces.

top	bottom	left side	front side	back side

$$10(\square) + 10(\square) + 10(\square) + \frac{1}{2}(\square)(\square) + \frac{1}{2}(\square)(\square) = \square$$

The surface area of the triangular prism is $\square$ cm^2.

3 Finding the Surface Area of a Cylinder Find the surface area of the cylinder. Round to the nearest tenth.

Step 1 Draw a net.

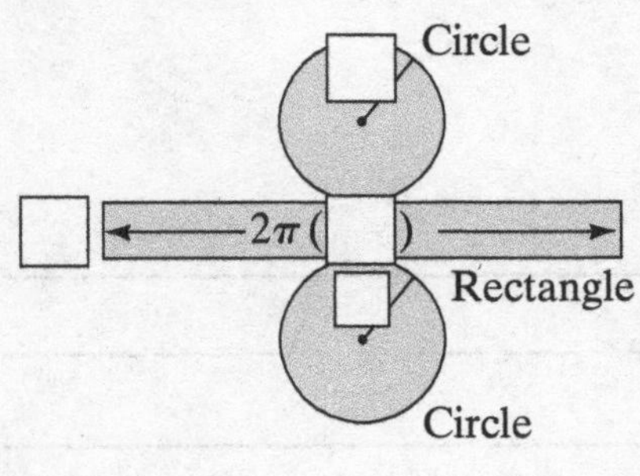

Step 2 Find the area of one circle.

$A = \pi r^2$

$= \pi(\square)^2$

$= \pi(\square)$

$\approx \square$

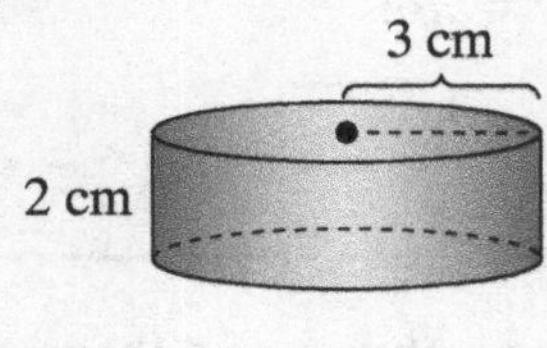

Step 3 Find the area of the rectangle.

$(2\pi r)\square = 2\pi(3)(\square) = \square\pi \approx \square$ cm^2

Step 4 Add the areas of the two circles and the rectangle.

Surface Area $= \square + \square + \square = \square$

The surface area of the cylinder is about $\square$ cm^2.

Quick Check

2. Find the surface area of the rectangular prism.

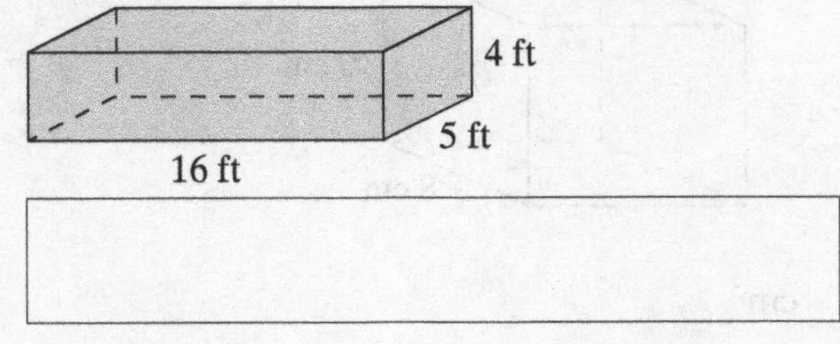

3. What is the surface area of the cylinder? Round to the nearest tenth.

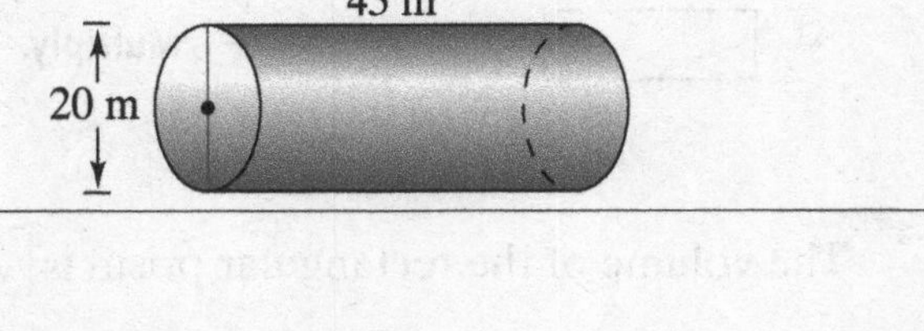

Name ______________________ Class ______________ Date ______________

Lesson 12-3

Volumes of Prisms and Cylinders

Lesson Objective	Common Core Standard
To find the volume of prisms and cylinders	Geometry: 7.G.6

Vocabulary and Key Concepts

Volume of a Rectangular Prism

V = area of base · [ ]

= Bh

= [ ]

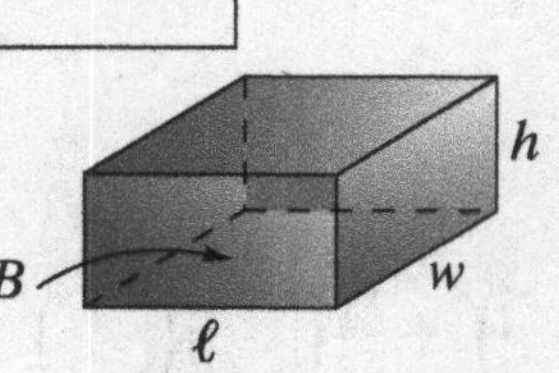

Volume of a Triangular Prism

V = area of base · height

= Bh

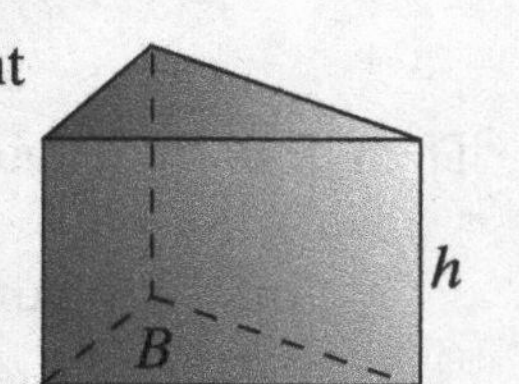

Volume of a Cylinder

V = area of base · [ ]

= Bh

= [ ]

The volume of a three-dimensional figure is ______________________________

____

A cubic unit is ______________________________

Examples

1 Finding the Volume of a Rectangular Prism Find the volume of the rectangular prism.

V = [ ] ← **Use the formula.**

= ([ ])([ ])([ ]) ← **Substitute.**

= [ ] ← **Multiply.**

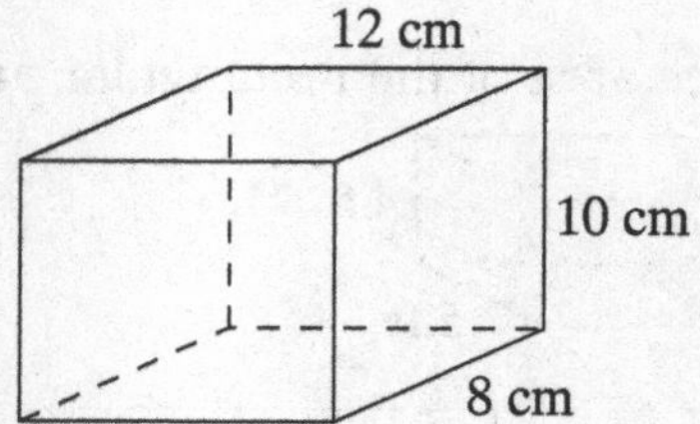

The volume of the rectangular prism is [ ] cm^3.

Name ______________________ Class ______________ Date ______________

❷ **Finding the Volume of a Triangular Prism** Find the volume of the triangular prism.

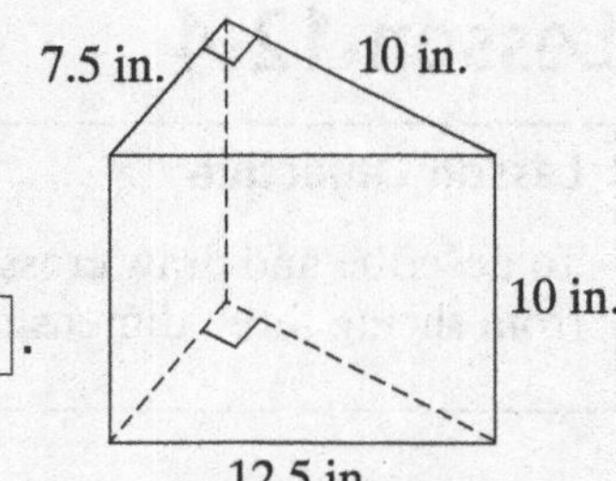

$V = Bh$ ← **Use the formula.**

$= \square (10)$ ← **Substitute *h* and $B = \frac{1}{2} \times 7.5 \times \square = \square$.**

$= \square$ ← **Multiply.**

The volume of the triangular prism is ______ cubic inches.

❸ **Finding the Volume of a Cylinder** A glass is 7.4 cm tall. The base of the glass has a diameter of 2.2 cm. Estimate the volume that the glass can hold if it is filled to the top. Then find the volume to the nearest cubic unit that the glass can hold if it is filled to the top.

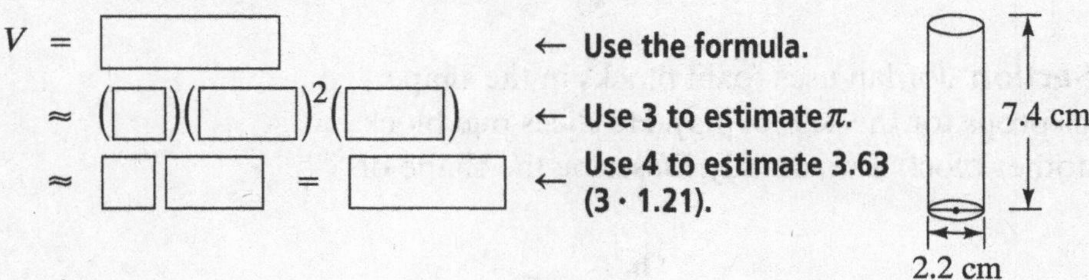

$V = \square$ ← **Use the formula.**

$\approx (\square)(\square)^2(\square)$ ← **Use 3 to estimate π.**

$\approx \square\ \square = \square$ ← **Use 4 to estimate 3.63 (3 · 1.21).**

The estimated volume is ______ cm^3.

Calculated volume: $V = \pi(\square)^2(\square) \approx \square$. ← **Use a calculator.**

The calculated volume is about ______ cm^3. ← **Round to the nearest whole number.**

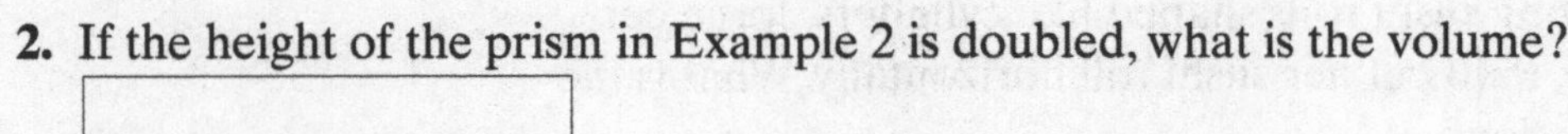

Quick Check

1. If the height of the prism in Example 1 is doubled, what is the volume?

2. If the height of the prism in Example 2 is doubled, what is the volume?

3. Estimate the volume of the cylinder. Then, find the volume to the nearest cubic centimeter.

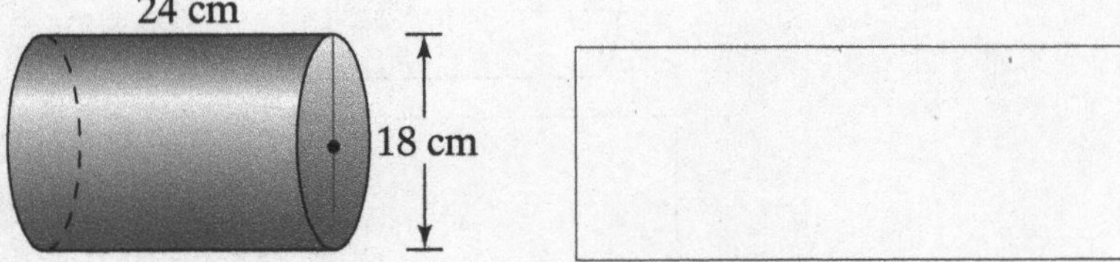

Name ______________________ Class ______________ Date ______________

Lesson 12-4

Cross Sections

Lesson Objective	Common Core Standard
To describe and draw cross sections that result from slicing three-dimensional figures	Geometry: 7.G.3

Vocabulary

If you slice through a three-dimensional object like this pyramid, you see a two-dimensional shape called a ______________ of the solid.

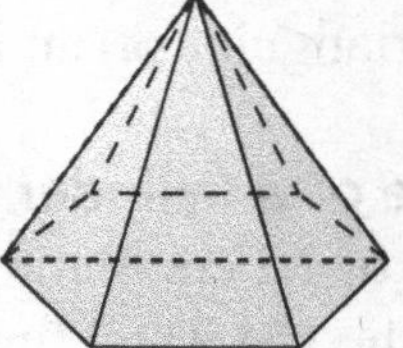

Example

1 Identifying a Cross Section Jordan uses foam blocks in the shape of a triangular prism as props for the school play. He slices one block vertically. He slices another block horizontally. Describe the shape of each cross section.

a.

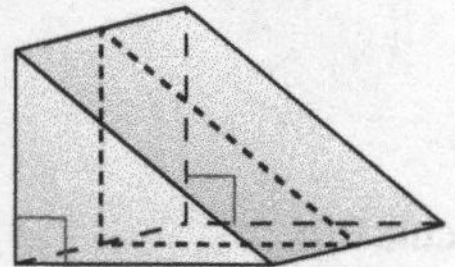

Vertical Slice

The vertical slice creates a triangular cross section.

b.

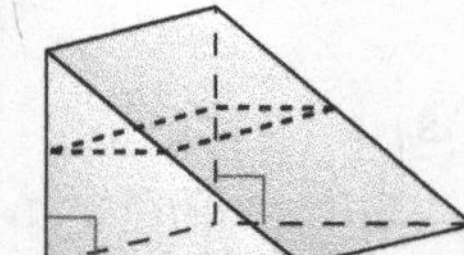

Horizontal Slice

The horizontal slice creates a rectangular cross section.

Quick Check

1. Jorge and Patti are eating sushi rolls shaped like cylinders. Jorge cut his sushi roll vertically. Patti cut her sushi roll horizontally. What is the shape of each cross section?

a.

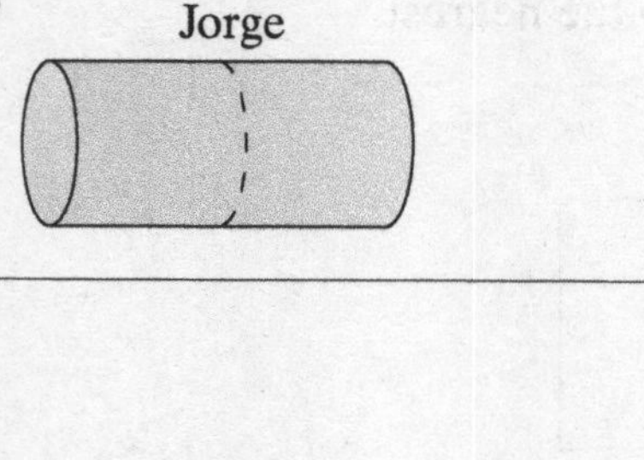

b.

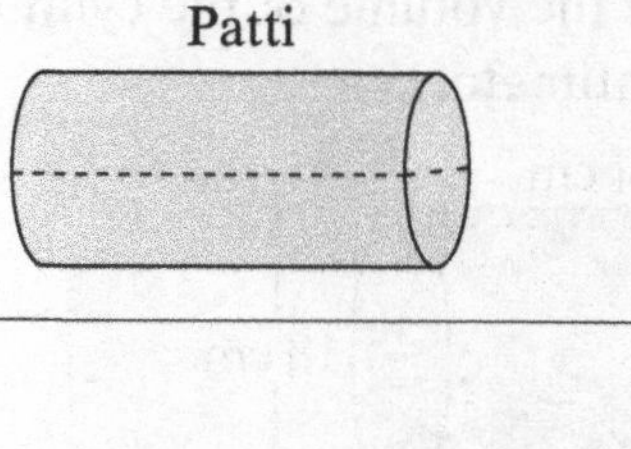

Name ____________________ Class ____________ Date ____________

Example

❷ Describing a Cross Section A carpenter is cutting wooden blocks in two ways. He slices some blocks with a vertical cut, from one corner diagonally to the opposite corner. He cuts other blocks horizontally. Draw and describe the cross section formed by the saw cutting the blocks of wood.

a. Vertical Cut

The saw will create a rectangular cross section with length equal to a line diagonally across the block width equal to the block's height.

b. Horizontal Cut

The saw will create a rectangular cross section with length equal to the length of the block and width equal to the block's width.

Quick Check

2. Describe the cross section formed by the slices through the hexagonal pyramid.

a.

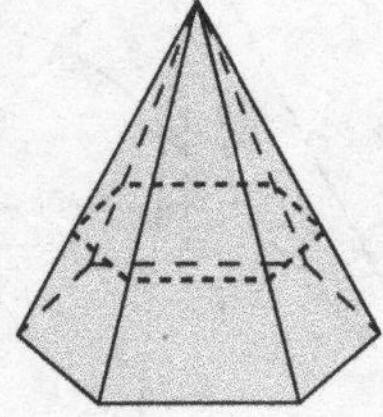

b.

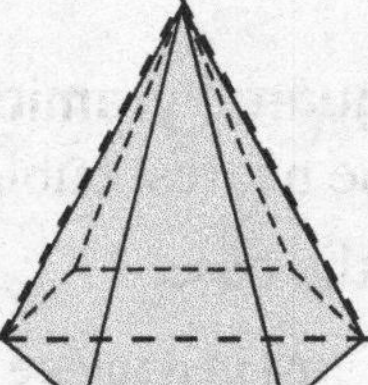

c. Reasoning Would any other slices through the pyramid produce a different type of cross section? If so, describe how the slice would have to be made.

____

____

Name ______________________ Class ______________ Date ______________

Lesson 12-5

Volumes of Pyramids and Cones

Lesson Objective	Common Core Standard
To find the volumes of pyramids and cones	Geometry: 8.G.9

Key Concepts

Volume of a Pyramid

The volume V of a pyramid is one third the product of the base area B and the height h.

$$V = \frac{1}{3}Bh$$

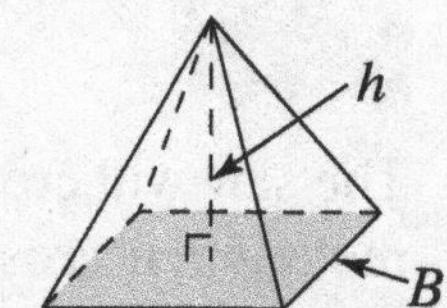

Volume of a Cone

The volume V of a cone is one third the product of the base area B and the height h.

$$V = \frac{1}{3}Bh$$

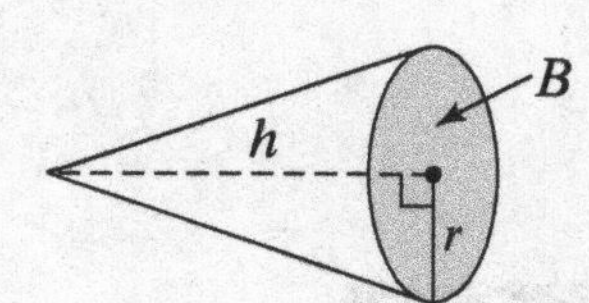

Examples

1 Finding Volume of a Square Pyramid Find the volume of this square pyramid to the nearest cubic foot.

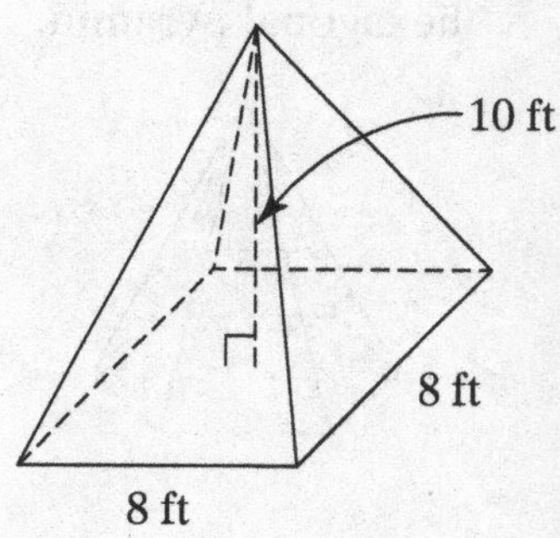

Step 1 Find the area of the base.

$B = \square$ ← **area of a square**

$= \square$ ← **Substitute $\square$ for s.**

$= \square$ ← **Simplify.**

Step 2 Use the base area to find the volume.

$V = \frac{1}{3}Bh$ ← **volume of a pyramid**

$= \frac{1}{3}(\square)(\square)$ ← **Substitute $\square$ for B and $\square$ for h.**

$\approx \square$ ← **Multiply.**

The volume of the pyramid is approximately $\square$ ft^3.

Name ____________________ Class ____________ Date ____________

❷ Using the Volume Formula Find the volume of this cone to the nearest cubic centimeter.

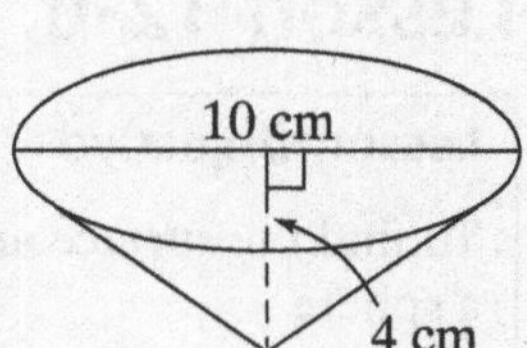

Step 1 Find the area of the base.

$B = \pi r^2$ ← **area of a circle formula**

$= \pi(\square)$ ← **Substitute** $\square$ **for *r*.**

$= \square$ ← **Simplify.**

Step 2 Use the base area to find the volume.

$V = \frac{1}{3}Bh$ ← **cone volume formula**

$= \frac{1}{3}(\square)\square$ ← **Substitute** $\square$ **for *B* and** $\square$ **for *h*.**

$= \square \frac{\square}{\square} \square$ ← **Multiply.**

≈ 105 ← **Simplify.**

To the nearest cubic centimeter, the volume of the cone is $\square$ cm^3.

Quick Check

1. Find the volume of the square pyramid at the right.

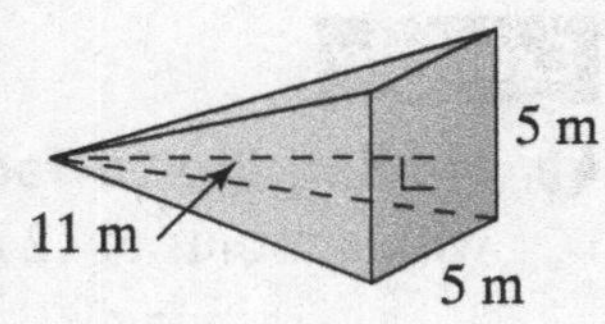

2. Find the volume of the cone at the right. Round to the nearest cubic meter.

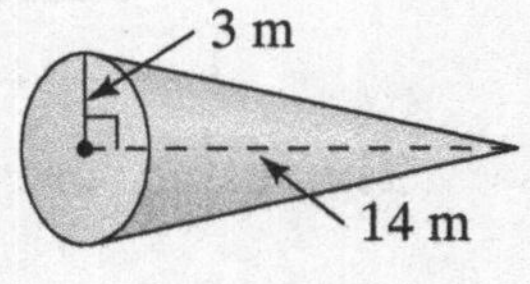

Name ______________________ Class ______________ Date ______________

Lesson 12-6

Spheres

Lesson Objective	Common Core Standard
To find the surface area and volume of a sphere	Geometry: 8.G.9

Vocabulary and Key Concepts

Surface Area and Volume of a Sphere

The surface area of a sphere is four times the product of π and the square of the radius r.

$$S.A. = 4\pi r^2$$

The volume of a sphere is four thirds of the product of π and the radius r cubed.

$$V = \frac{4}{3}\pi r^3$$

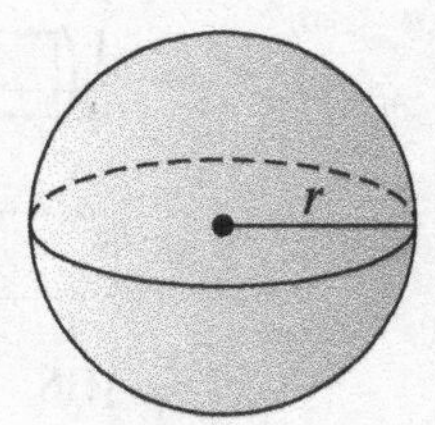

A sphere is ____

____

Example

1 Finding the Surface Area of a Sphere Find the surface area of a sphere with a radius of 12 m to the nearest whole unit.

S.A. = ☐ ← **surface area of a sphere**

$= 4\pi(\square)^2$ ← **Substitute** ☐ **for** ***r*****.**

$= \square\,\pi$ ← **Simplify.**

$\approx$ ☐ ← **Use a calculator.**

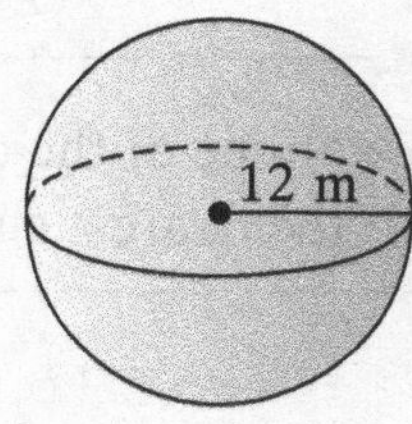

The surface area of the sphere is about ☐.

Quick Check

1. A sphere has a radius of 7 ft. Find its surface area to the nearest square foot.

☐

Name ______________ Class ______________ Date ______________

Example

❷ **Finding the Volume of a Sphere** A standard men's basketball has a diameter of 9.39 inches. What is the volume of a standard men's basketball to the nearest cubic inch?

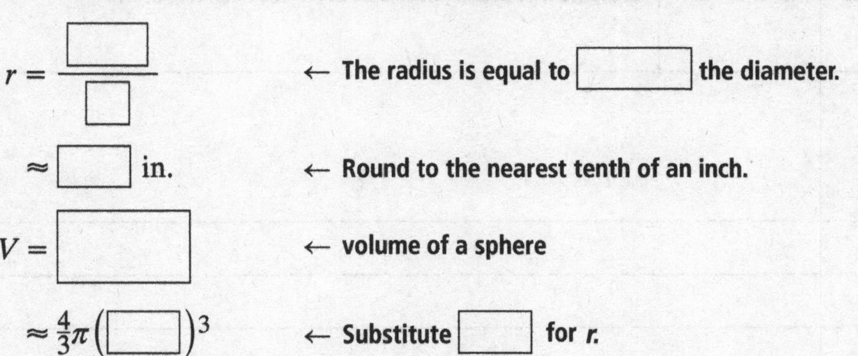

$r = \frac{\square}{\square}$ ← The radius is equal to ☐ the diameter.

$\approx \square$ in. ← Round to the nearest tenth of an inch.

$V = \square$ ← volume of a sphere

$\approx \frac{4}{3}\pi(\square)^3$ ← Substitute ☐ for r.

$\approx \square$ ← Use a calculator.

The volume of a standard men's basketball is about ☐.

Check for Reasonableness Use 3 for π and 5 for r. The volume is about $\frac{4}{3}(3)(5)^3$ in.^{3}, or ☐. The answer ☐ reasonable.

Quick Check

2. A globe in a brass stand has a diameter of 40 in. What is the volume of the globe to the nearest cubic inch?

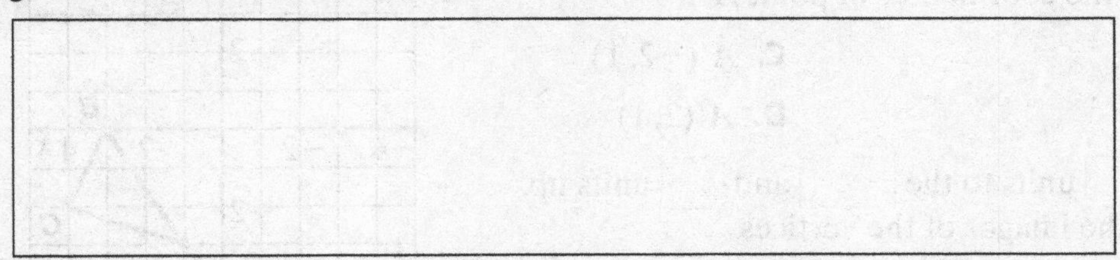

Name ______________________ Class ______________ Date ____________

Lesson 13-1

Translations

Lesson Objective	Common Core Standards
To graph and describe translations in the coordinate plane	Geometry: 8.G.1, 8.G.1.a, 8.G.1.b, 8.G.1.c, 8.G.3

Vocabulary

A transformation is ____

____

A translation is ____

____

An image is ____

____

Example

1 Graphing a Translation

Multiple Choice If $\triangle ABC$ is translated 3 units to the left and 2 units up, what are the coordinates of point A'?

A. $A'(-2, -1)$ **C.** $A'(-2, 1)$

B. $A'(2, -1)$ **D.** $A'(2, 1)$

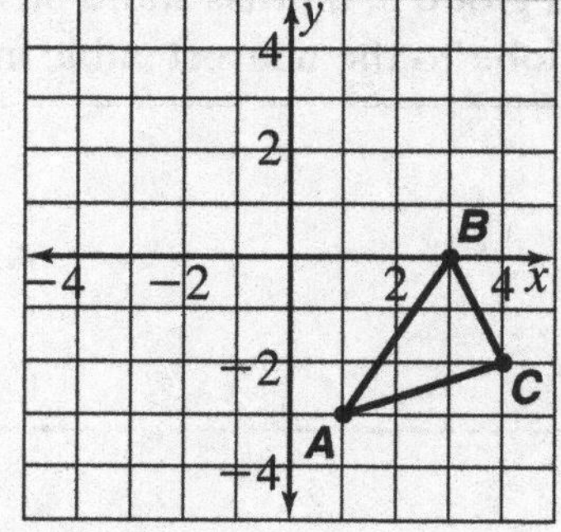

Slide each vertex ☐ units to the ☐ and ☐ units up. Label and connect the images of the vertices.

The correct answer is choice ☐.

Quick Check

1. $\triangle JKL$ has vertices $J(0, 2)$, $K(3, 4)$, $L(5, 1)$. Translate $\triangle JKL$ 4 units to the left and 5 units up. What are the coordinates of point J'?

☐

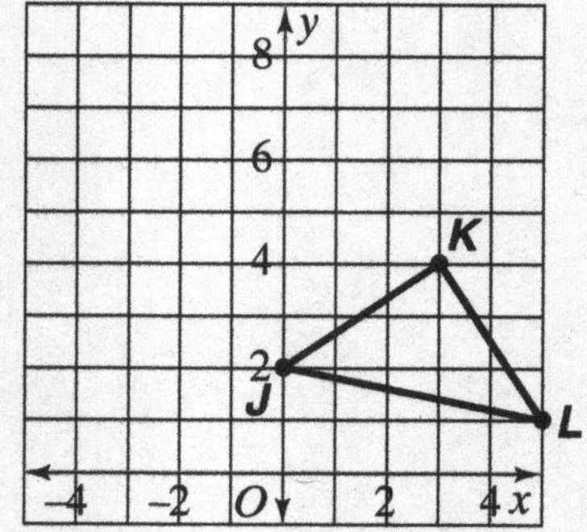

Name ______________________ Class ______________ Date ____________

Example

2 Describing a Translation Write a rule to describe the translation of $G(-5, 3)$ to $G'(-1, -2)$.

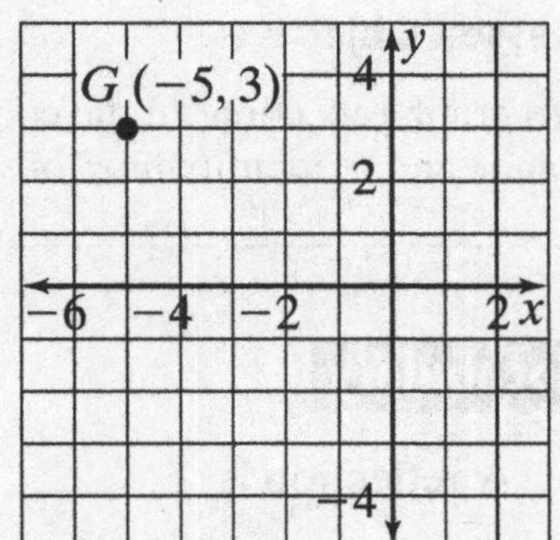

Point G moves ☐ units to the right and ☐ units down. So, the translation adds ☐ to the x-coordinate and subtracts ☐ from the y-coordinate.

The rule is ☐ → ☐.

Quick Check

2. Write a rule that describes the translation shown on the graph.

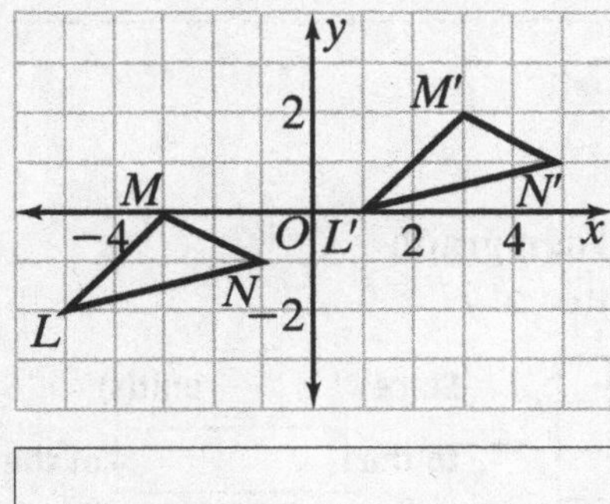

☐

Name ______________________ Class ______________ Date ______________

Lesson 13-2

Reflections and Symmetry

Lesson Objective	Common Core Standards
To graph reflections in the coordinate plane and to identify lines of symmetry	Geometry: 8.G.1, 8.G.1.a, 8.G.1.b, 8.G.1.c, 8.G.3

Vocabulary

A reflection is ______________________

A line of reflection is ______________________

A line of symmetry is ______________________

A figure can be reflected over a line so that its image matches the original figure if it has ______________________

Example

1 Graphing Reflections of a Point Graph the point $H(-4, 5)$. Then graph its image after it is reflected over the y-axis. Name the coordinates of H'.

The coordinates of H' are (☐, ☐).

H, 6, 4, 2, −4, −2, 2, 4, y, x

Since *H* is ☐ **unit(s) to the** ☐ **of the *y*-axis, *H'* is** ☐ **unit(s) to the** ☐ **of the *y*-axis.**

Quick Check

1. Graph the point $D(-2, 1)$. Then graph its image after it is reflected over the y-axis. Name the coordinates of D'.

☐

y, 2, −2, O, 2, x, −2

Name ______________________ Class ____________ Date ____________

Example

2 Graphing Reflections of a Shape $\triangle BCD$ has vertices $B(-3, 1)$, $C(-2, 5)$, and $D(-5, 4)$. Graph $\triangle BCD$ and its image after a reflection over the x-axis. Name the coordinates of the vertices of $\triangle B'C'D'$.

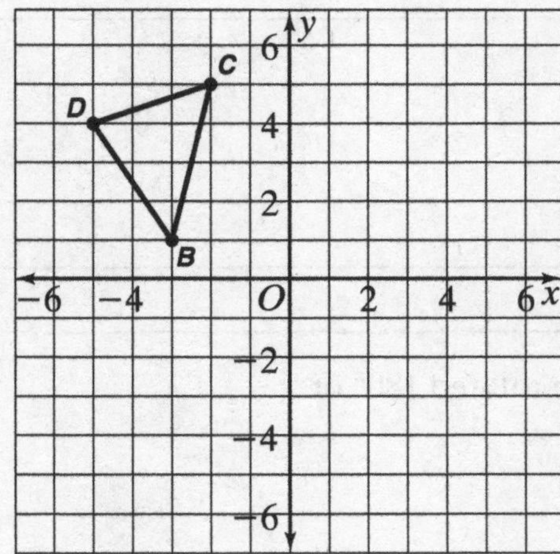

Since *B* is ☐ unit(s) ☐ the *x*-axis, *B′* is ☐ unit(s) ☐ the *x*-axis.

Reflect the other vertices.

Draw $\triangle B'C'D'$.

The coordinates of the vertices are B'(☐, ☐), C'(☐, ☐), and D'(☐, ☐).

Quick Check

2. $\triangle EFG$ has vertices $E(4, 3)$, $F(3, 1)$, and $G(1, 2)$. Graph $\triangle EFG$ and its image after a reflection over the x-axis. Name the coordinates of the vertices of $\triangle E'F'G'$.

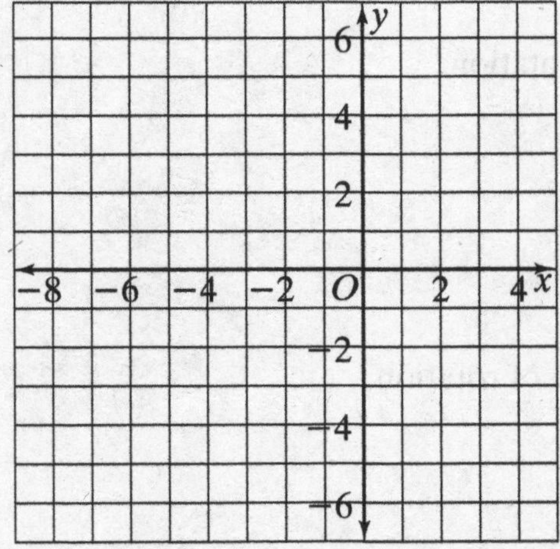

☐

Name ______________________ Class ______________ Date ____________

Lesson 13-3

Rotations

Lesson Objective	**Common Core Standards**
To graph rotations and identify rotational symmetry	Geometry: 8.G.1, 8.G.1.a, 8.G.1.b, 8.G.1.c, 8.G.3

Vocabulary

A rotation is ______________________________

The center of rotation is ______________________________

The angle of rotation is ______________________________

A figure has [ ] if it can be rotated 180° or less and exactly match its original figure.

Example

1 Rotational Symmetry Does this figure have rotational symmetry? If so, give the angle of rotation.

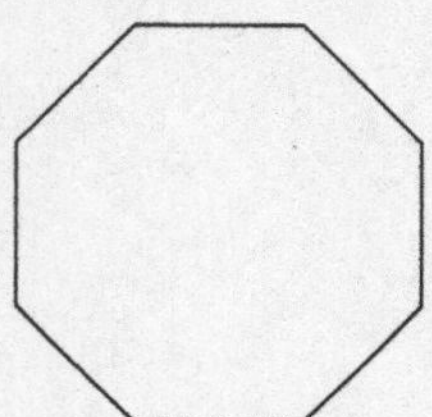

The image matches the original after [ ] of a complete rotation.

$\frac{1}{8} \cdot 360° = \square°$

The angle of rotation is $\square°$.

Quick Check

1. If the figure below has rotational symmetry, find the angle of rotation. If it does not, write *no rotational symmetry*.

Name ______________________ Class ______________ Date ______________

Example

❷ Graphing Rotations Draw the image of rectangle $ABCD$ after a rotation of 90° about the origin.

Step 1 Draw and trace.

- Draw rectangle $ABCD$ with vertices $(3, 2)$, $(-3, 2)$, $(-3, -2)$, and $(3, -2)$. Place a piece of tracing paper over your graph.
- Trace the vertices of the rectangle, the x-axis, and the y-axis.
- Place your pencil at the origin to rotate the paper.

Step 2 Rotate and mark each vertex.

- Rotate the tracing paper 90° counterclockwise. The axes should line up.
- Mark the position of each vertex by pressing your pencil through the paper.

Step 3 Complete the new figure.

- Remove the tracing paper.
- Draw the rectangle.
- Label the vertices to complete the figure.

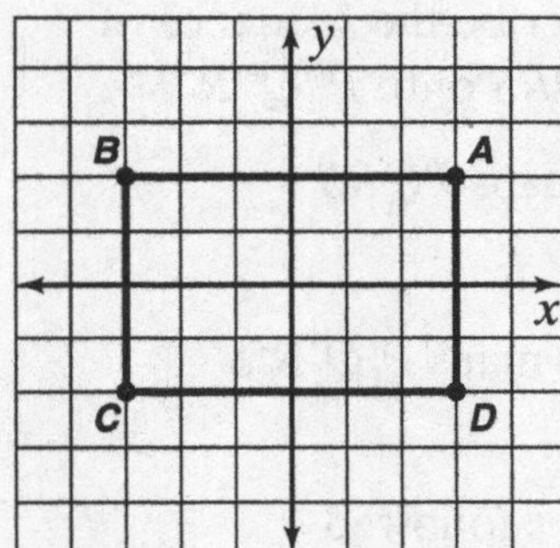

Quick Check

2. Draw the image of $\triangle ABD$ after a rotation of the given number of degrees about the origin. Name the coordinates of the vertices of the image.

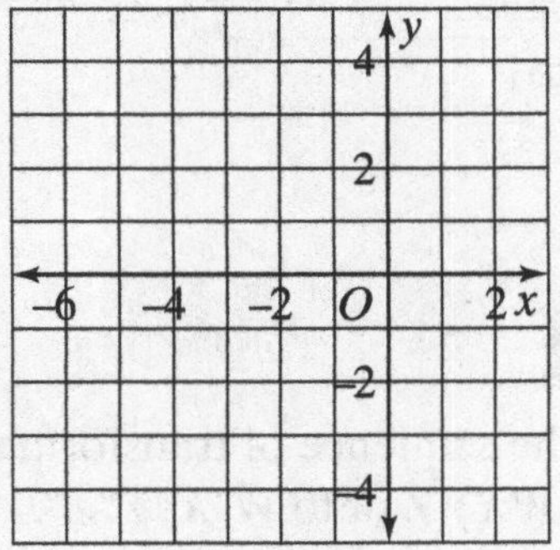

a. 180°

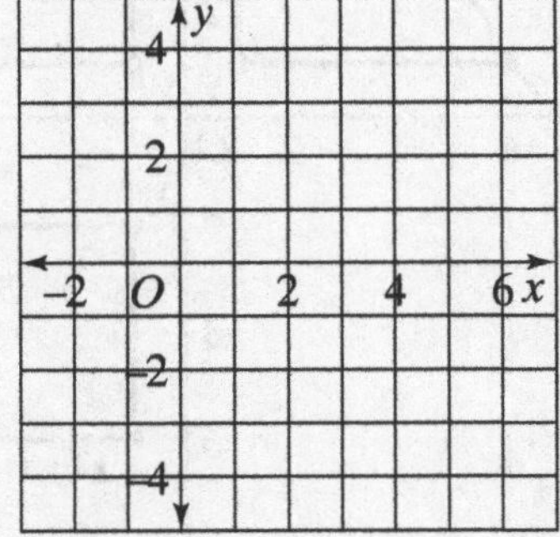

b. 270°

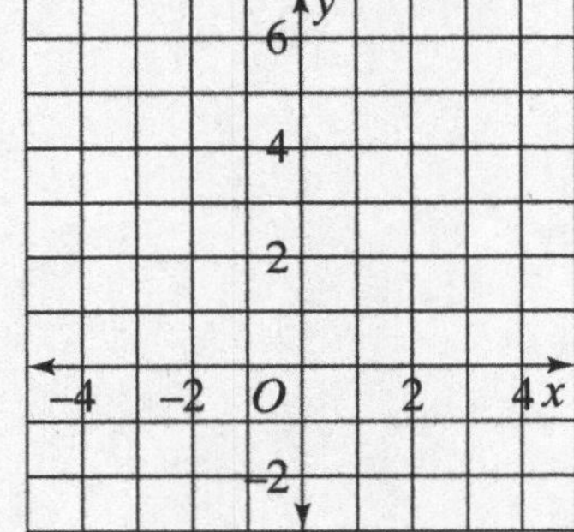

Name ____________________ Class ____________ Date ____________

Lesson 13-4

Transformations and Congruence

Lesson Objective	**Common Core Standard**
To describe a sequence of transformations that maps one figure onto another; to determine whether two figures are congruent by using a sequence of transformations	Geometry: 8.G.2

Vocabulary

You can use a sequence of transformations to [ ] one figure onto another.

Example

1 Recognizing a Series of Transformations The three trapezoids are congruent. Describe the sequence of transformations that maps $PQRS$ onto $P'''Q'''R'''S'''$.

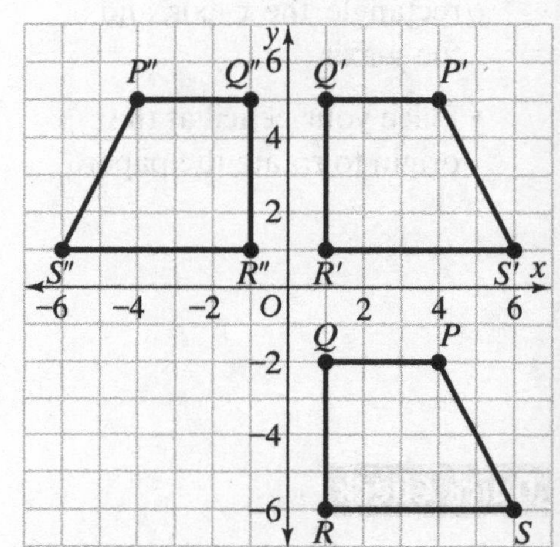

A translation [ ] units [ ] maps $PQRS$ onto [ ].

A reflection over the [ ]-axis maps $P'Q'R'S'$ onto [ ].

So, a translation [ ] units [ ], followed by a [ ] over the [ ]-axis, maps $PQRS$ onto [ ].

Quick Check

1. Describe the sequence of transformations that maps $WXYZ$ onto $W''X''Y''Z''$.

[ ]

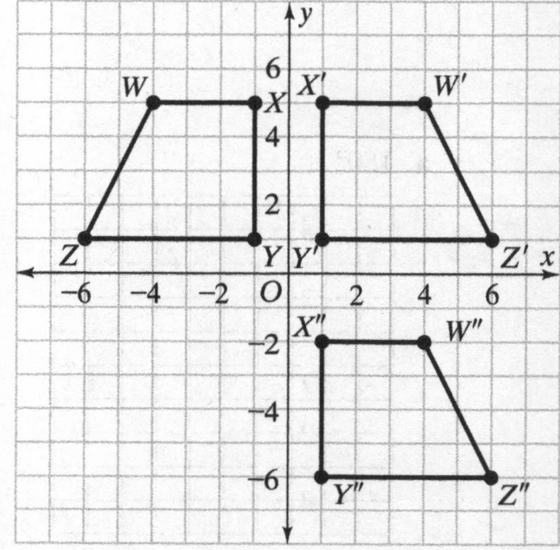

Name ____________________ Class ____________ Date ____________

Example

❷ Using Transformations to Determine Congruence

Determine whether the two triangles in the diagram are congruent. If they are congruent, write a congruence statement. If they are not congruent, explain why.

$\triangle ABC$ and $\triangle XYZ$ have ________ orientations and are on ________ sides of the y-axis.

So, first ________ $\triangle ABC$ over the ____-axis to get $\triangle$ ________.

Then, ________ the reflected image $\triangle$ ________ ________ units ________ to map it onto $\triangle$ ________.

Finally, write your congruence statement:

____

____

____

____

Quick Check

2. Determine whether $\triangle ABC$ is congruent to $\triangle QRS$. If the triangles are congruent, tell what sequence of transformations will map $\triangle ABC$ onto $\triangle QRS$. Then write a congruence statement. If they are not congruent, explain why.

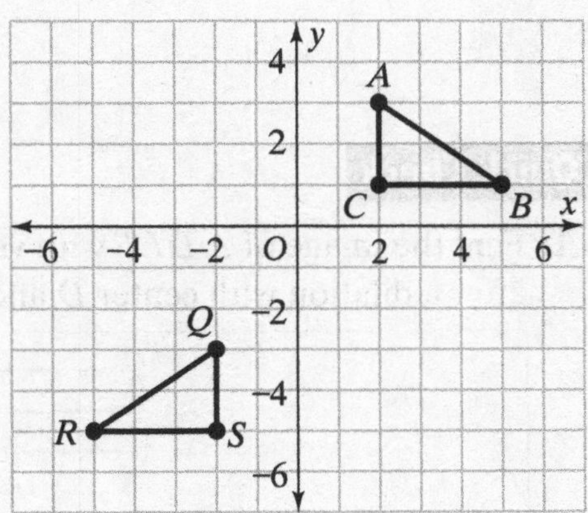

____

____

____

____

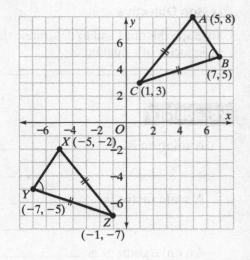

Name ____________________ Class ____________ Date ____________

Lesson 13-5

Dilations

Lesson Objective	Common Core Standards
To graph dilations and to determine the scale factor of a dilation	Geometry: 8.G.3, 8.G.4

Vocabulary

A dilation is ____

____

A scale factor is ____

____

An enlargement is ____

A reduction is ____

Example

1 Finding a Dilation Find the image of $\triangle ABC$ after a dilation with center A and a scale factor of 3.

$\triangle A'B'C'$ is the image of $\triangle ABC$ after a dilation with center A and a scale factor of 3. $\triangle ABC$ ☐ $\triangle A'B'C'$.

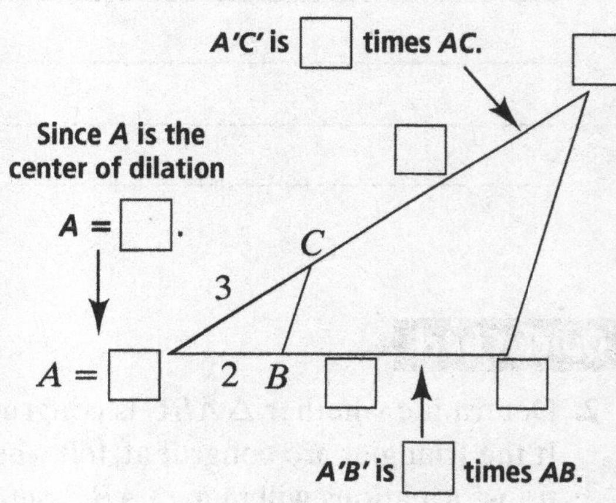

Quick Check

1. Find the image of $\triangle DEF$ with vertices $D(-2, 2)$, $E(1, -1)$, and $F(-2, -1)$ after a dilation with center D and a scale factor of 2.

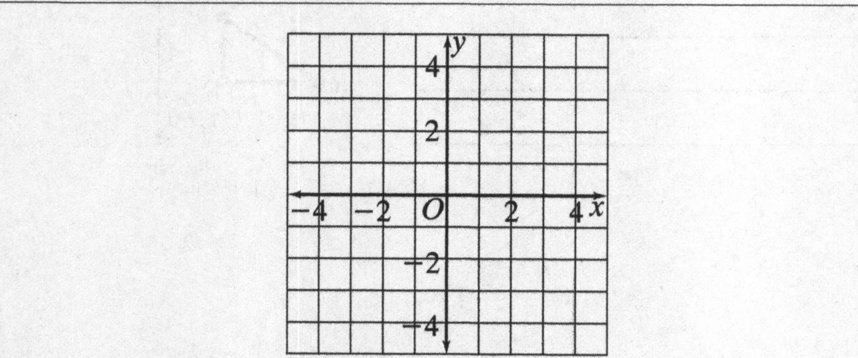

Name ______________________ Class ______________ Date ______________

❷ **Graphing Dilation Images** Find the coordinates of the vertices of the image of quadrilateral $WXYZ$ after a dilation with center (0, 0) and a scale factor of $\frac{1}{2}$. Then graph the image. Quadrilateral $WXYZ$ has vertices $W(-2, -1)$, $X(0, 2)$, $Y(4, 2)$, and $Z(4, -1)$.

Step 1 Multiply the x- and y-coordinates of each point by $\frac{1}{2}$.

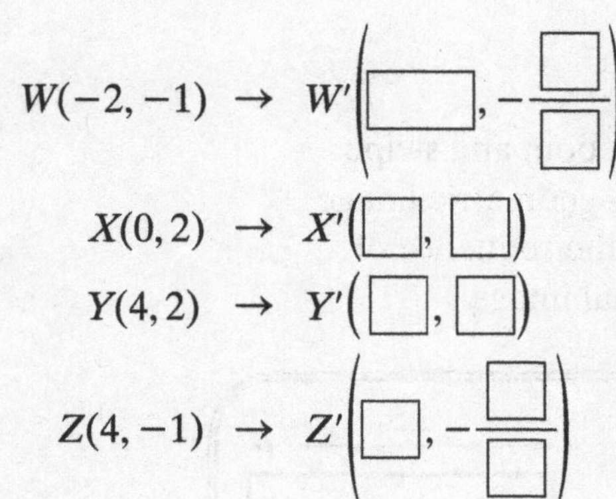

$W(-2, -1) \rightarrow W'(\square, -\frac{\square}{\square})$

$X(0, 2) \rightarrow X'(\square, \square)$

$Y(4, 2) \rightarrow Y'(\square, \square)$

$Z(4, -1) \rightarrow Z'(\square, -\frac{\square}{\square})$

Step 2 Graph the image.

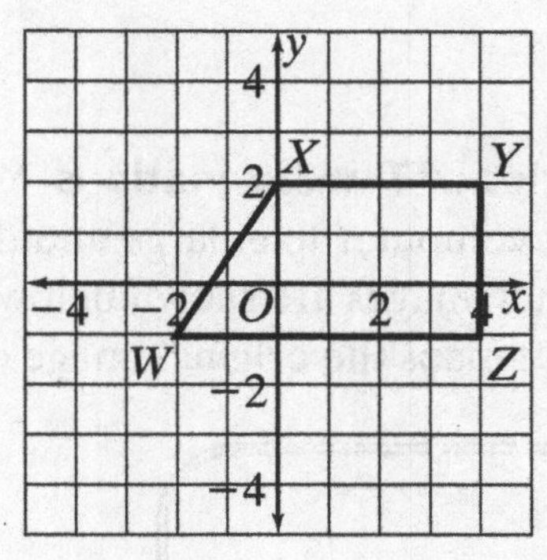

❸ **Finding a Scale Factor** $\triangle Q'P'R'$ is a dilation of $\triangle QPR$. What is the scale factor of the dilation?

image → $\frac{Q'P'}{QP} = \frac{\square + \square}{\square} = \square$
original →

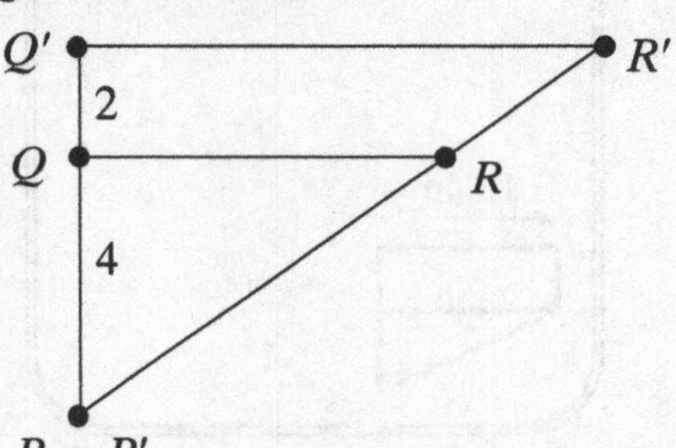

The scale factor is ______. It is ______ than 1, so the dilation is a(n) ______.

Quick Check

2. $ABCD$ has vertices $A(0, 0)$, $B(0, 3)$, $C(3, 3)$, and $D(3, 0)$. Find the coordinates of the vertices of the image of $ABCD$ after a dilation with a scale factor of $\frac{4}{3}$. Then graph the image.

3. Figure $EFGH$ shows the outline of a yard. Figure $E'F'G'H'$ is a doghouse. Figure $E'F'G'H'$ is a dilation image of figure $EFGH$. Find the scale factor. Is the dilation an enlargement or a reduction?

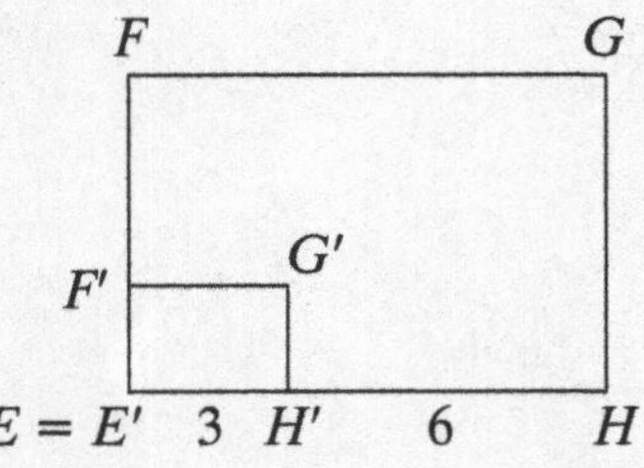

Name ______________________ Class ______________ Date ______________

Lesson 13-6

Transformations and Similarity

Lesson Objective	Common Core Standard
To describe a sequence of transformations that maps one figure onto another; to determine whether two figures are similar by using a sequence of transformations	Geometry: 8.G.4

Example

1 Recognizing a Series of Transformations You use the zoom and swipe features on a tablet computer to enlarge and then move a geometric image. The original and final images are shown below. Describe the sequence of transformations that maps the original image onto the final image

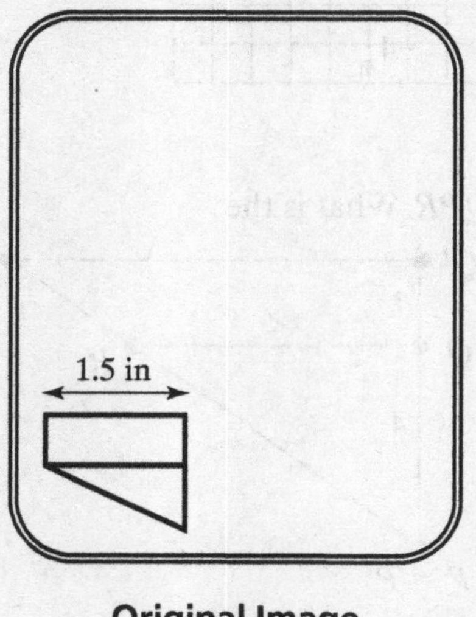

Original Image

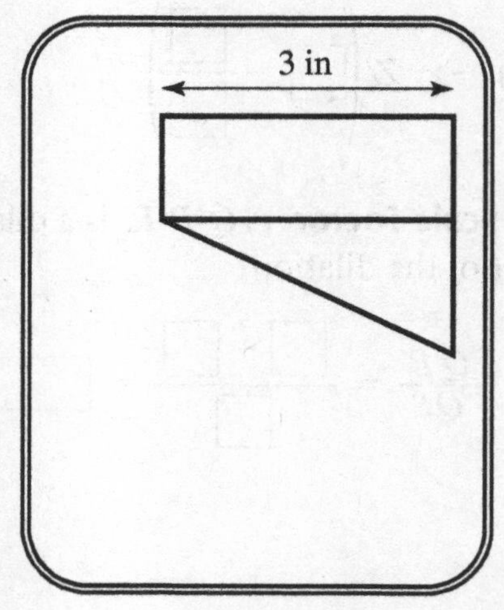

Final Image

The zoom was a ______ with a scale factor of ______.

Swiping the image mapped the original image in the direction ______ and then ______ onto the final zoomed-in image.

Name ______________________ Class ______________ Date ______________

Quick Check

1. Using a computer, a graphic designer moves a company logo from the top left of a page to the bottom center of the page and then enlarges the logo, as shown below. Describe the sequence of transformations that maps the original logo onto the final logo.

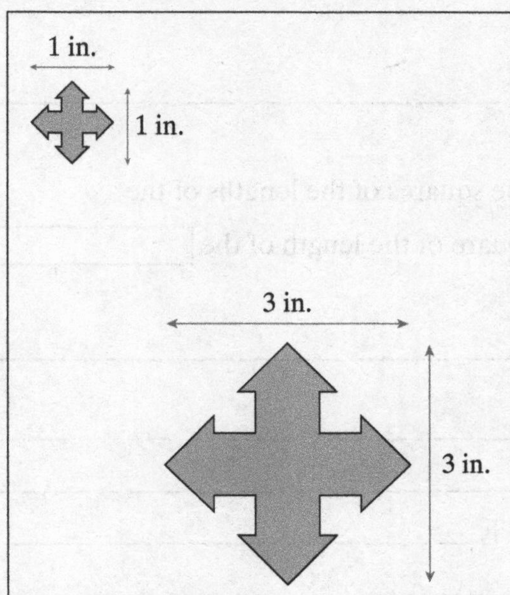

Name ______________________ Class ______________ Date ______________

Lesson A-1

The Pythagorean Theorem

Lesson Objective	
To use the Pythagorean Theorem to find the length of the hypotenuse of a right triangle	

Vocabulary and Key Concepts

The Pythagorean Theorem

In any right triangle, the sum of the squares of the lengths of the [ ] is equal to the square of the length of the [ ].

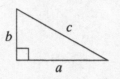

b, c, a

$a^2 + b^2 =$ [ ]

The legs of a right triangle are ______________________________

____

The hypotenuse of a right triangle is ______________________________

____

Examples

1 **Finding the Hypotenuse** Find the length of the hypotenuse of a right triangle with legs of 6 ft and 8 ft.

[ ]	← **Use the Pythagorean Theorem.**
$\square^2 + \square^2 = c^2$	← **Substitute [ ] for *a* and [ ] for *b***
$\square + \square = c^2$	← **Simplify.**
$\square = c^2$	← **Add.**
$\sqrt{\square} = \sqrt{\square}$	← **Find the positive square root of each side.**
$\square = c$	← **Simplify.**

The length of the hypotenuse is [ ] ft.

Name ______________________ Class ______________ Date ______________

❷ **Multiple Choice** The bottom of a ladder is 10 ft from the side of a building. The top of the ladder is 24 ft from the ground. How long is the ladder.

A. 22 ft **B.** 26 ft **C.** 30 ft **D.** 34 ft

$\square$ ← **Use the Pythagorean Theorem.**

$\square^2 + \square^2 = \square^2$ ← **Substitute**

$\square + \square = c^2$ ← **Simplify.**

$\square = c^2$ ← **Add.**

$\sqrt{\square} = \sqrt{\square}$ ← **Find the positive square root of each side.**

$\square = c$ ← **Simplify.**

The ladder is $\square$ ft long. The correct answer is choice $\square$.

Quick Check

1. Find the length of the hypotenuse of a right triangle with legs of 12 cm and 16 cm.

2. A bridge has 22-ft horizontal members and 25-ft vertical members. Find the length of each diagonal member to the nearest foot.

Name ______________ Class ______________ Date ______________

Lesson A-2

Using the Pythagorean Theorem

Lesson Objective	
To use the Pythagorean Theorem to find the missing measurements of triangles	

Example

1 Finding a Leg of a Right Triangle Find the missing leg length of the triangle below.

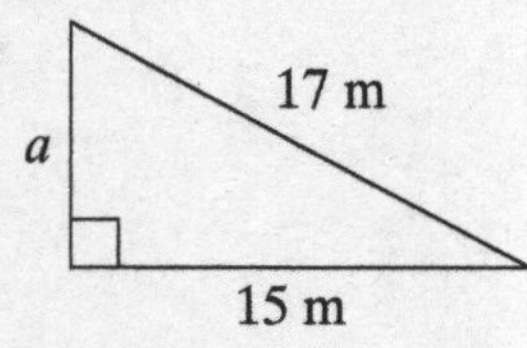

$\square$ ← **Use the Pythagorean Theorem.**

$\square^2 + \square^2 = \square^2$ ← **Substitute** $\square$ **for** ***b*** **and** $\square$ **for** ***c*****.**

$a^2 + \square = \square$ ← **Simplify.**

$a^2 = \square$ ← **Subtract.**

$\sqrt{\square} = \sqrt{\square}$ ← **Find the positive square root of each side.**

$a = \square$ ← **Simplify.**

The length of the other leg is $\square$ m.

Quick Check

1. The hypotenuse of a right triangle is 20.2 ft long. One leg is 12.6 ft long. Find the length of the other leg to the nearest tenth.

Name ______________________ Class ______________ Date ______________

Example

2 **Multiple Choice** You are riding on a carousel. You choose a horse near the outer edge of the carousel. Your friend is standing on the ground. Before the carousel starts moving, your friend is 9 m from you and 11 m from the center of the carousel. To the nearest tenth of a meter, how far are you from the center of the carousel?

A. 5.2 m **B.** 6.3 m **C.** 7.5 m **D.** 8.8 m

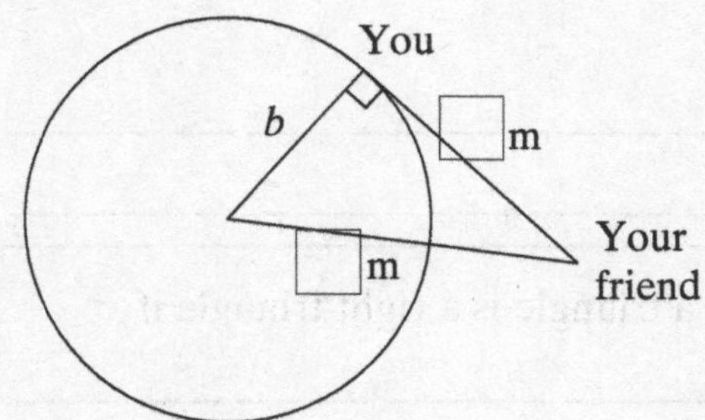

$\square$ ← **Use the Pythagorean Theorem.**

$\square^2 + \square^2 = \square^2$ ← **Substitute** $\square$ **for** ***a*** **and** $\square$ **for** ***c*****.**

$\square + b^2 = \square$ ← **Simplify.**

$b^2 = \square$ ← **Subtract.**

$\sqrt{\square} = \sqrt{\square}$ ← **Find the positive square root of each side.**

[√] $\square$ [=] $\square$ ← **Use a calculator.**

$b \approx \square$ ← **Simplify.**

You are about ______ m from the center of the carousel. The correct answer is choice ______.

Quick Check

2. Construction The bottom of an 18-ft ladder is 5 ft from the side of a house. Find the distance from the top of the ladder to the ground. Round to the nearest tenth of a foot.

Name ________________ Class ________________ Date ________________

Lesson A-3

Converse of the Pythagorean Theorem

Lesson Objective	
To solve problems using the Triangle Inequality Theorem and the Converse of the Pythagorean Theorem	

Vocabulary and Key Concepts

Triangle Inequality Theorem

The sum of ________________________________

is greater than ________________________________

According to the Converse of the Pythagorean Theorem, a triangle is a right triangle if

____

Example

1 Using the Triangle Inequality Theorem Is it possible to construct a triangle with the given side lengths? Explain.

a. 8 yd, 12 yd, 5 yd

☐ + ☐ ☐ 5

☐ + ☐ ☐ 8

☐ + ☐ ☐ 12

Yes. The sum of any two lengths is ☐ the third length.

b. 25 mm, 14 mm, 8 mm

☐ + ☐ ☐ 8

☐ + ☐ ☐ 14

☐ + ☐ ☐ 25

No. The sum of ☐ and ☐ is *not* greater than ☐.

Quick Check

1. Is it possible to construct a triangle with the given side lengths? Explain.

   a. 6 mi, 10 mi, 20 mi ☐

   b. 1.5 m, 2.5 m, 3.5 m ☐

Example

❷ Identifying a Right Triangle Determine whether the triangle is a right triangle. Explain.

$a^2 + b^2 \stackrel{?}{=} c^2$ ← **Use the Pythagorean Theorem.**

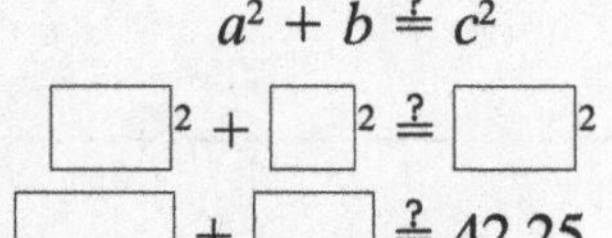

$\square^2 + \square^2 \stackrel{?}{=} \square^2$ ← **Substitute** ☐ **for *a*,** ☐ **for *b*, and** ☐ **for *c*.**

$\square + \square \stackrel{?}{=} 42.25$ ← **Simplify. Use a calculator.**

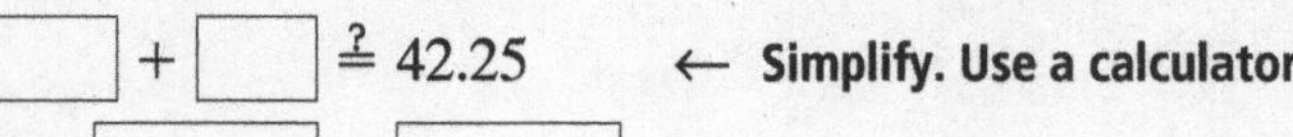

$\square = \square$

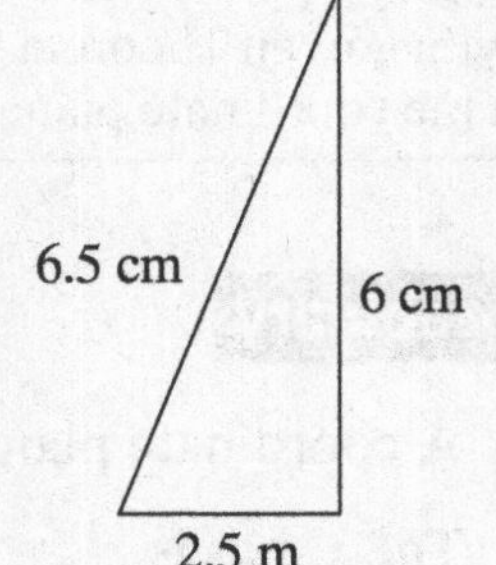

The equation is true, so the triangle is a ☐ triangle.

Quick Check

2. Determine whether the given lengths can be side lengths of a right triangle. Explain.

a. 10 in., 24 in., 26 in. ☐

b. 8 cm, 9 cm, 12 cm ☐

Example

❸ A carpenter has built two adjoining walls of a room and wants to make sure the walls meet at a 90° angle in the corner. One wall is 16 feet long and the other wall is 12 feet long. He measures the diagonal between the walls to be 20 feet. Do the walls meet at a right angle?

$a^2 + b^2 \stackrel{?}{=} c^2$ ← **Use the Pythagorean Theorem.**

$\square^2 + \square^2 \stackrel{?}{=} \square^2$ ← **Substitute** ☐ **for *a*,** ☐ **for *b*, and** ☐ **for *c*.**

$\square + \square \stackrel{?}{=} \square$ ← **Simplify.**

$\square = \square$

The equation is true, so the given lengths form a right triangle. The walls meet at a 90° angle in the corner.

Quick Check

3. A triangular field has boundary lines that are 40 yd, 75 yd, and 85 yd long. Determine whether the boundary lines form a right triangle. Explain.

☐

Name ______________________ Class ______________ Date ____________

Lesson A-4

Distance in the Coordinate Plane

Lesson Objective	
To graph points and to use the Pythagorean Theorem to find distances in the coordinate plane	

Vocabulary

A coordinate plane is ______________________

The *x*-axis is ______________________

The *y*-axis is ______________________

Quadrants are ______________________

The origin is ______________________

An [ ] gives the coordinates of the location of a point.

The [ ] tells the number of horizontal units a point is from the origin.

The [ ] tells the number of vertical units a point is from the origin.

Example

1 Finding Distance on a Coordinate Plane Find the distance between points $A(-2, 4)$ and $B(4, -4)$.

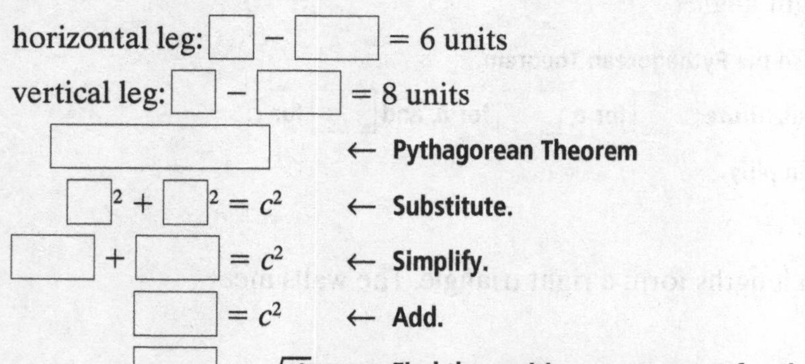

horizontal leg: [ ] − [ ] = 6 units
vertical leg: [ ] − [ ] = 8 units
[ ] ← Pythagorean Theorem
[ ]^2 + [ ]^2 = c^2 ← Substitute.
[ ] + [ ] = c^2 ← Simplify.
[ ] = c^2 ← Add.
[ ] = $\sqrt{c^2}$ ← Find the positive square root of each side.
[ ] = c

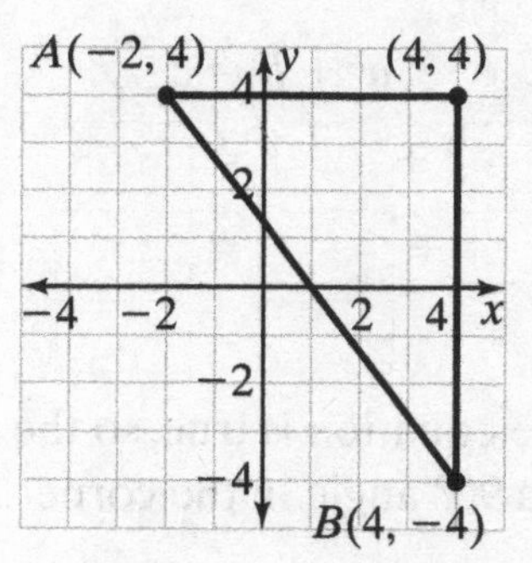

The distance between $A(-2, 4)$ and $B(4, -4)$ is [ ] units.

❷ **Multiple Choice** The park is 4 kilometers west of the bus station. The grocery store is 7 kilometers south of the bus station. To the nearest kilometer, how far is the grocery store from the park?

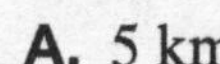

A. 5 km **C.** 7 km

B. 6 km **D.** 8 km

y Bus Station
Park
x
Grocery Store

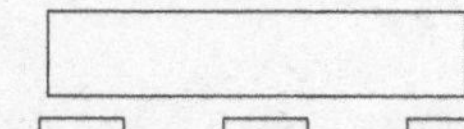 ← **Use the Pythagorean Theorem.**

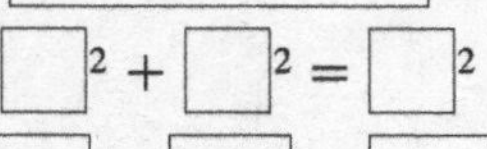 ← **Substitute**

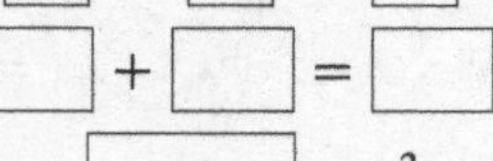 ← **Simplify.**

 ← **Add.**

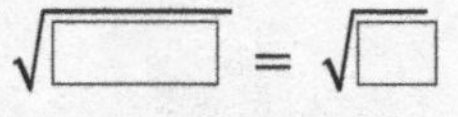 ← **Find the positive square root of each side.**

 ← **Use a calculator.**

 ← **Simplify.**

The correct answer is choice ☐.

Quick Check

1. Find the distance between points (2, 1) and (7, 9). If necessary, round to the nearest tenth.

2. Your school is 3 miles south of your house. The park is 5 miles east of your school. To the nearest mile, how far is your house from the park?

A Note to the Student:

This section of your workbook contains a series of pages that support your mathematics understandings for each chapter and lesson presented in your student edition.

- Practice pages provide additional practice for every lesson.
- Guided Problem Solving pages lead you through a step-by-step solution to an application problem in each lesson.
- Vocabulary pages contain a variety of activities to increase your reading and math understanding, ranging from graphic organizers to vocabulary review puzzles.

Name ______________________ Class ______________ Date ______________

Practice 1-1

Comparing and Ordering Integers

Name the integer represented by each point on the number line.

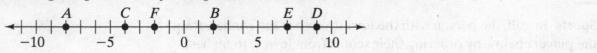

A C F B E D

−10 −5 0 5 10

1. *A* _____ **2.** *B* _____ **3.** *C* _____ **4.** *D* _____ **5.** *E* _____ **6.** *F* _____

Compare. Use <, >, or =.

7. −8 ☐ 8 **8.** 4 ☐ −4 **9.** −5 ☐ 1 **10.** −8 ☐ 0

11. −6 ☐ −2 **12.** −1 ☐ −3 **13.** −4 ☐ 0 **14.** −3 ☐ 2

Graph each integer and its opposite on the number line.

15. −9

−8 −6 −4 −2 0 2 4 6 8

16. 5

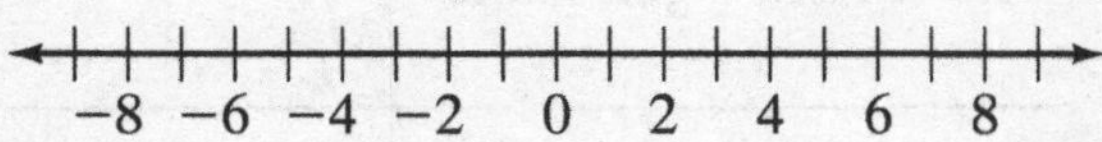

17. 8

−8 −6 −4 −2 0 2 4 6 8

18. −2

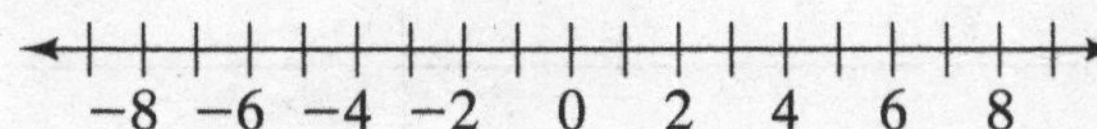

Find the opposite of each number. You may find a number line helpful.

19. 2 _____ **20.** −3 _____ **21.** −38 _____ **22.** (−2 + 2) _____

23. −44 _____ **24.** (5 + 2) _____ **25.** −16 _____ **26.** (7 − 3) _____

Write an integer to represent each situation.

27. a gain of 5 yards _____

28. a debt of $5 _____

29. a temperature of 100°F _____

30. 135 feet below sea level _____

Name ______________________ Class ______________ Date ______________

1-1 • Guided Problem Solving

GPS Student Page 7, Exercise 48:

Sports In golf, the person with the lowest score is the winner. Rank the players below by ordering their scores from lowest to highest.

Player	Score
T. Woods	−12
V. Singh	−4
E. Els	+10
P. Mickelson	−3
R. Goosen	−5

Understand

1. Who wins in a golf game?

____

2. How will you determine the lowest number?

____

Plan and Carry Out

3. Draw a number line. Plot each score. Which number is the farthest to the left of zero on the number line?

____

4. What is the order of all five numbers? ______________

5. Rank the players from lowest score to highest score.

____

____

Check

6. Is the person with the highest score last? Is the person with the lowest score first?

____

Solve Another Problem

7. Anne had the following golf scores this week: −6, +5, −4, +13, −2, +4, +6, −11. Which was her best score? Which was her worst score?

____

Name ______________________ Class ______________ Date ______________

Practice 1-2

Adding and Subtracting Integers

Use a number line to find each sum.

1. $8 + (-4)$ ______

2. $2 + (-3)$ ______

3. $7 - 6$ ______

4. $(-4) + (-8)$ ______

5. $3 + (-2)$ ______

6. $15 + (-8)$ ______

Find each sum.

7. $-2 + (-3)$ ______

8. $8 - 7 + 4$ ______

9. $8 + (-5)$ ______

10. $15 + (-3)$ ______

11. $-16 + 8$ ______

12. $7 + (-10)$ ______

13. $-9 + (-5)$ ______

14. $-12 + 14$ ______

Find each difference.

15. $9 - 26$ ______

16. $-4 - 15$ ______

17. $21 - (-7)$ ______

18. $27 - (-16)$ ______

19. $-16 - (-43)$ ______

20. $47 - 19$ ______

21. $-156 - 98$ ______

22. $-192 - 47$ ______

23. $0 - (-51)$ ______

24. $-63 - 89$ ______

25. $-12 - (-21)$ ______

26. $92 - (-16)$ ______

Use >, <, or = to complete each statement.

27. $-9 - (-11)$ ☐ 0

28. $-17 + 20$ ☐ 0

29. $11 - (-4)$ ☐ 0

30. $28 - 19$ ☐ 0

31. $52 + (-65)$ ☐ 0

32. $-28 - (-28)$ ☐ 0

Solve.

33. The highest and lowest temperatures ever recorded in Africa are 136°F and −11°F. The highest temperature was recorded in Libya, and the lowest temperature was recorded in Morocco. What is the difference in these temperature extremes?

____

34. The highest and lowest temperatures ever recorded in South America are 120°F and −27°F. Both the highest and lowest temperatures were recorded in Argentina. What is the difference in these temperature extremes?

____

Name ____________________ Class ____________ Date ____________

1-2 • Guided Problem Solving

GPS Student Page 13, Exercise 27:

Temperature The hottest temperature ever recorded in the United States was 134°F, measured at Death Valley, California. The coldest temperature, −80°F, was recorded at Prospect Creek, Alaska. What is the difference between these temperatures?

Understand

1. Circle the information you will need to solve the problem.
2. What are you being asked to do?

   ____
3. Which word tells you what operation to perform?

   ____

Plan and Carry Out

4. Write a subtraction expression for the problem.

   ____
5. Subtracting a negative number is the same as adding what type of number?

   ____
6. Write an addition expression that is the same as the expression you wrote in Step 4.

   ____
7. What is the difference between these temperatures?

   ____

Check

8. What is 134°F − 214°F?

   ____

Solve Another Problem

9. At 6:00 A.M. the temperature was 25°F. At 9:00 P.M. the temperature was −13°F. What was the difference in the temperature?

   ____

Name ______________________ Class ______________ Date ____________

Practice 1-3

Multiplying and Dividing Integers

Complete each statement. Then write two examples to illustrate each relationship.

1. positive ÷ positive = ?
2. negative · positive = ?
3. positive · positive = ?
4. negative ÷ negative = ?
5. negative ÷ positive = ?
6. positive · positive = ?
7. positive ÷ negative = ?
8. negative · negative = ?

Estimate each product or quotient.

9. $-72 \cdot 57$
10. $-92 \cdot (-41)$
11. $-476 \div 90$
12. $-83 \cdot 52$
13. $538 \div (-63)$
14. $-803 \cdot (-106)$
15. $49 \cdot 61$
16. $479 \div (-61)$

Find each product or quotient.

17. $-\frac{36}{9}$
18. $-\frac{52}{4}$
19. $(-5) \cdot (-20)$
20. $-\frac{63}{9}$
21. $(-15) \cdot (2)$
22. $-\frac{22}{2}$
23. $(13) \cdot (-6)$
24. $-\frac{100}{5}$
25. $(-60) \cdot (-3)$
26. $-\frac{240}{30}$
27. $(43) \cdot (-8)$
28. $-\frac{169}{13}$

Name ____________________ Class ____________ Date ____________

1-3 • Guided Problem Solving

GPS Student Page 19, Exercise 35:

Hobbies A scuba diver is 180 ft below sea level and rises to the surface at a rate of 30 ft/min. How long will the diver take to reach the surface?

Understand

1. Circle the information you will need to solve the problem.
2. What are you being asked to do?

____

____

Plan and Carry Out

3. Will you multiply or divide to solve this problem?

____

4. How far below sea level is the diver?

____

5. How fast is the diver rising?

____

6. How long will the diver take to reach the surface?

____

Check

7. What is 30 ft/min × 6 min? Does your answer equal the original distance below sea level?

____

Solve Another Problem

8. A rock climber climbs down into the Grand Canyon at a rate of 2 ft/min. How long will it take him to climb down 50 ft?

____

Name ____________________ Class ____________ Date ____________

Practice 1-4

Fractions and Decimals

Write each fraction as a decimal.

1. $\frac{3}{5}$ ________ 2. $\frac{7}{8}$ ________ 3. $\frac{7}{9}$ ________

4. $\frac{5}{16}$ ________ 5. $\frac{1}{6}$ ________ 6. $\frac{5}{8}$ ________

7. $\frac{1}{3}$ ________ 8. $\frac{2}{3}$ ________ 9. $\frac{9}{10}$ ________

10. $\frac{7}{11}$ ________ 11. $\frac{9}{20}$ ________ 12. $\frac{3}{4}$ ________

13. $\frac{4}{9}$ ________ 14. $\frac{9}{11}$ ________ 15. $\frac{11}{20}$ ________

Write each decimal as a mixed number or fraction in simplest form.

16. 0.6 ________ 17. 0.45 ________ 18. 0.62 ________

19. 0.8 ________ 20. 0.325 ________ 21. 0.725 ________

22. 4.75 ________ 23. 0.33 ________ 24. 0.925 ________

25. 3.8 ________ 26. 4.7 ________ 27. 0.05 ________

28. 0.65 ________ 29. 0.855 ________ 30. 0.104 ________

31. 0.47 ________ 32. 0.894 ________ 33. 0.276 ________

Order from least to greatest.

34. $0.\overline{2}, \frac{1}{5}, 0.02$

____

35. $1.\overline{1}, 1\frac{1}{10}, 1.101$

____

36. $\frac{6}{5}, 1\frac{5}{6}, 1.\overline{3}$

____

37. $4.\overline{3}, \frac{9}{2}, 4\frac{3}{7}$

____

38. A group of gymnasts were asked to name their favorite piece of equipment. 0.33 of the gymnasts chose the vault, $\frac{4}{9}$ chose the beam, and $\frac{1}{7}$ chose the uneven parallel bars. List their choices in order of preference from greatest to least.

____

Name ____________________ Class ____________ Date ____________

1-4 • Guided Problem Solving

GPS Student Page 24, Exercise 28:

Biology DNA content in a cell is measured in picograms (pg). A sea star cell has $\frac{17}{20}$ pg of DNA, a scallop cell has $\frac{19}{25}$ pg, a red water mite cell has 0.19 pg, and a mosquito cell has 0.024 pg. Order the DNA contents from greatest to least.

Understand

1. What are you being asked to do?

 ____

2. To order fractions and decimals, what must you do first?

 ____

 ____

Plan and Carry Out

3. Write the fraction $\frac{17}{20}$ as a decimal. __________
4. Write the fraction $\frac{19}{25}$ as a decimal. __________
5. Which organism has the smallest DNA content? __________
6. Which organism has the largest DNA content? __________
7. Order the DNA contents from greatest to least.

 ____

Check

8. Write 0.19 and 0.024 as fractions in simplest form. Order the DNA contents from greatest to least. Does your order check with that of Step 7?

 ____

 ____

Solve Another Problem

9. A solution calls for 0.25 oz of water, $\frac{2}{3}$ oz of vinegar, 0.6 oz of carbonate, and $\frac{9}{16}$ oz of lemon juice. Order the amounts from least to greatest.

 ____

Name ______________________ Class ______________ Date ______________

Practice 1-5

Rational Numbers

Compare. Use <, >, or =.

1. $-\frac{2}{9}$ ☐ $-\frac{4}{9}$
2. $-\frac{1}{6}$ ☐ $-\frac{2}{3}$
3. $-\frac{5}{12}$ ☐ $-\frac{3}{4}$
4. -1.2 ☐ -2.1
5. -0.6 ☐ -0.52
6. -1.23 ☐ -1.25
7. -5.3 ☐ $-5.\overline{3}$
8. $-3\frac{1}{4}$ ☐ -3.25
9. $-4\frac{2}{5}$ ☐ -4.12

Order from least to greatest.

10. $\frac{5}{4}, 1.5, -\frac{3}{2}, -0.5$

    ____

11. $\frac{1}{11}, -0.9, 0.069, \frac{1}{10}$

    ____

12. $0.1\overline{2}, -\frac{11}{12}, -\frac{1}{6}, -0.1$

    ____

13. $\frac{2}{3}, 0.6, -\frac{5}{6}, -6.6$

    ____

14. $1.312, 1\frac{3}{8}, -1\frac{3}{10}, -1.33$

    ____

15. $1, \frac{4}{5}, -\frac{8}{9}, -1$

    ____

Evaluate. Write in simplest form.

16. $\frac{y}{z}$, for $y = -6$ and $z = -20$ ______________
17. $\frac{2y}{-z}$, for $y = -5$ and $z = -12$ ______________
18. $\frac{y+z}{2z}$, for $y = -4$ and $z = 8$ ______________
19. $\frac{-2y+1}{-z}$, for $y = 3$ and $z = 10$ ______________

Compare.

20. The temperature at 3:00 A.M. was −17.3°F. By noon the temperature was −17.8°F. At what time was it the coldest?

    ____

21. Samuel is $\frac{5}{8}$ in. taller than Jackie. Shelly is 0.7 in. taller than Jackie. Who is the tallest?

    ____

Name ____________________ Class ____________ Date ____________

1-5 • Guided Problem Solving

GPS Student Page 29, Exercise 29:

Animals About $\frac{1}{25}$ of a toad's eggs survive to adulthood. About 0.25 of a frog's eggs and $\frac{1}{5}$ of a green turtle's eggs survive to adulthood. Which animal's eggs have the highest survival rate?

Understand

1. Circle the information you will need to solve the problem.
2. What are you being asked to do?

 ____

 ____

3. In order to find the greatest number, what must you do first?

 ____

Plan and Carry Out

4. Write $\frac{1}{25}$ as a decimal. ____________________
5. Write $\frac{1}{5}$ as a decimal. ____________________
6. Which is the largest decimal, 0.04, 0.2, or 0.25? ____________________
7. Which animal's eggs have the highest survival rate? ____________________

Check

8. What fraction is 0.25 equal to? Is it the greatest value?

 ____

Solve Another Problem

9. In order to organize the nails in a garage, Anne and Jeff measured the nails. Anne used fractions to measure her 3 groups of nails and found that they were $\frac{3}{5}$ in., $\frac{7}{12}$ in., and $\frac{4}{9}$ in. Jeff used decimals to measure his two groups and found that they were 0.62 in., and 0.31 in. Which nail is the longest?

 ____

Name ______________________ Class ______________ Date ______________

Practice 1-6

Adding and Subtracting Rational Numbers

Find each sum.

1. $2.5 + (-7.9)$
2. $-2.92 + (-1.25)$
3. $-12.1 + 4.8$
4. $-\frac{3}{8} + \frac{1}{2}$
5. $-1\frac{1}{5} + \left(-\frac{1}{2}\right)$
6. $-6\frac{1}{8} + 1\frac{1}{4}$
7. $20\frac{5}{16} + (-12\frac{1}{4})$
8. $-100.04 + (-4.01)$
9. $-8.33 + 7.17$

Find each difference.

10. $3.7 - (-12.4)$
11. $-5.55 - (-1.25)$
12. $-14.6 - 6.4$
13. $-\frac{5}{12} - \frac{1}{2}$
14. $2\frac{5}{8} - 2\frac{1}{4}$
15. $-4\frac{1}{4} - \left(-\frac{1}{2}\right)$
16. $90\frac{7}{16} - \left(-12\frac{1}{4}\right)$
17. $-5.04 - (-12.08)$
18. $-10.65 - 20.75$
19. What is the difference between -30.7 and -8.5?

____

20. The melting point of sodium is 208°F. The melting point of mercury is -37.7°F. What is the difference in melting points of these two elements?

____

Name ______________________ Class ______________ Date ____________

1-6 • Guided Problem Solving

GPS Student Page 36, Exercise 22:

A diver climbs a 12 ft tower and walks $6\frac{3}{4}$ ft to the end of the diving board. Then he jumps $5\frac{1}{2}$ft above the board and dives into the water. The water level is $1\frac{1}{4}$ft below the base of the tower. How far does the diver travel from the top of the dive to the water?

Understand

1. Circle the information you will need to solve the problem.
2. What are you being asked to do?

____

____

3. What number is not needed to solve the problem? Explain.

____

____

Plan and Carry Out

4. What will you do first? ______________________
5. Do you need to rename any fractions or mixed numbers?

____

6. What is the sum of $5\frac{1}{2}$ and $1\frac{1}{4}$ ______________________
7. Will your final answer be negative or positive? Explain.

____

____

8. How far does the diver travel from the top of the dive to the water? ______________________

Check

9. How can you check your answer? ______________________

____

Solve Another Problem

10. Kirk began a carpentry project with $4\frac{1}{2}$ lb of nails. He gave $2\frac{1}{3}$ lb to his brother. Later he found he needed 3 lb of nails to finish the project. Write his shortage of nails as a signed number.

____

Name ______________________ Class ______________ Date ______________

Practice 1-7

Multiplying Rational Numbers

Find each product. Write your answers in simplest form.

1. $2\frac{3}{4} \cdot 1\frac{1}{2}$

2. $-\frac{3}{5} \cdot \frac{7}{9}$

3. $\left(1\frac{7}{8}\right)\left(-\frac{3}{5}\right)$

4. $\left(-\frac{4}{5}\right)\left(-2\frac{3}{4}\right)$

5. $2\frac{1}{3} \cdot \left(-\frac{1}{5}\right)$

6. $\left(-4\frac{1}{3}\right)\left(\frac{5}{6}\right)$

7. $\left(\frac{3}{8}\right)\left(2\frac{1}{9}\right)$

8. $-1\frac{1}{5} \cdot \left(\frac{1}{2}\right)$

9. $\left(1\frac{1}{4}\right)\left(1\frac{3}{4}\right)$

Find each product.

10. $-1.3 \cdot (-4.8)$

11. $(12.5)\,(-0.2)$

12. $(4.9)(3.4)$

13. $-3.7(5.4)$

14. $-6.5 \cdot (3.5)$

15. $(8.7)(-2.1)$

16. $(-7.1)(-1.7)$

17. $9.3 \cdot (6.3)$

18. $(-10.06)(-6)$

19. Maggie went on a hot air balloon ride. At its highest altitude, the balloon was at 1,500 feet, but Maggie's ride was at $\frac{1}{3}$ of that altitude most of the time. What was the altitude for most of Maggie's ride?

20. An open parachute can descend $7\frac{3}{4}$ yards in one second. At that rate, what number represents the direction and distance it descends in 6 seconds?

Name ______________________ Class ______________ Date ____________

1-7 • Guided Problem Solving

GPS Student Page 42, Exercise 27:

Mental Math Richard's cell phone bill is $29.99 a month. Each month this amount is automatically taken from his checking account. In 6 months, what is the change to his checking account for his cell phone bills?

Understand

1. What information are you given? ______________________
2. What are you being asked to do? ______________________
____
3. What number represents the amount automatically taken from the checking account each month? ______________________

Plan and Carry Out

4. How can you estimate the answer? ______________________
____
5. What operation will you use to find the change to his checking account? ______________________
6. Will the answer be positive or negative number? Explain.
____
7. What is the change to his checking account for his cell phone bills? ______________________

Check

8. Explain how you can use mental math to check your answer.
____
____
9. Does your answer check?
____

Solve Another Problem

10. You have $10\frac{1}{2}$ pounds of flour in a bin. If you use $\frac{1}{2}$ pound of flour in each of 6 recipes, what will be the amount of flour remaining in the bin?
____

Name ______________________ Class ____________ Date ____________

Practice 1-8

Dividing Rational Numbers

Find each quotient. Write your answers in simplest form.

1. $-4\frac{1}{2} \div \frac{1}{4}$ ____________

2. $1\frac{9}{10} \div \left(-\frac{5}{8}\right)$ ____________

3. $1\frac{1}{8} \div 2\frac{1}{2}$ ____________

4. $6\frac{1}{3} \div \frac{2}{3}$ ____________

5. $\left(-\frac{3}{5}\right) \div \left(-1\frac{1}{3}\right)$ ____________

6. $\frac{9}{10} \div \left(-\frac{3}{4}\right)$ ____________

7. $\left(-\frac{5}{8}\right) \div \left(-\frac{3}{4}\right)$ ____________

8. $-3\frac{1}{4} \div 1\frac{1}{2}$ ____________

9. $\left(-2\frac{1}{5}\right) \div 10$ ____________

Find each quotient.

10. $-73.1 \div 4.3$ ____________

11. $2.73 \div (-0.7)$ ____________

12. $(-8.75) \div (-2.5)$ ____________

13. $4.44 \div (-3.7)$ ____________

14. $0.072 \div 0.08$ ____________

15. $-76.44 \div 9.1$ ____________

16. $(-0.115) \div (-0.23)$ ____________

17. $5.94 \div -11$ ____________

18. $(-0.802) \div (-4.01)$ ____________

19. Zain owes $1,312.50 for a new computer. An equal amount will be taken from his bank account each month for $10\frac{1}{2}$ months. How much will be taken out each month?

____

20. A marine biologist is measuring the temperature of a lake at 6 equally spaced depths. She makes her measurements at a point where the lake is 33.6 feet deep. What signed number represents the distance and direction of the first measurement from the lake's surface?

____

Name ____________ Class ____________ Date ____________

1-8 • Guided Problem Solving

GPS Student Page 47, Exercise 25:

Lucille had 48 oz of dried blueberries. Each batch of muffins uses 3.6 oz of dried blueberries. After making several batches, 30 oz of the dried blueberries are left. How many batches of muffins did she make?

Understand

1. What information are you given? ____________

2. What are you being asked to do? ____________

3. How many steps must you do to solve the problem? ____________

Plan and Carry Out

4. What operation(s) will you use to solve the problem? ____________

5. How many ounces of blueberries did Lucille use for the batches she made? ____________

6. How will you find the number of batches Lucille made? ____________

7. How many batches of muffins did she make? ____________

Check

8. How can you check your answer? ____________

9. Does your answer check? ____________

Solve Another Problem

10. Charlie made apple-walnut cakes. He had 40 oz of walnuts and used $6\frac{1}{2}$ ounces for each cake. If he has 14 oz walnuts left, how many cakes did he bake?

____

Name ____________________ Class ____________ Date ____________

Practice 1-9

Irrational Numbers and Square Roots

Find the two square roots of each number.

1. 81
2. $\frac{9}{49}$
3. $\frac{1}{121}$
4. 289

Estimate the value of each expression to the nearest integer and to the nearest tenth.

5. $\sqrt{5}$
6. $-\sqrt{10}$
7. $\sqrt{3}$
8. $-\sqrt{245}$
9. $-\sqrt{21}$
10. $-\sqrt{52}$

Which number is greater?

11. $\sqrt{60}$, 7.5
12. $\sqrt{35}$, 6.1
13. $\sqrt{44}$, 4.5
14. $\sqrt{84}$, 9.3

Find each square root. Round to the nearest tenth if necessary.

15. $\sqrt{130}$
16. $\sqrt{8}$
17. $\sqrt{144}$
18. $\sqrt{160}$
19. $\sqrt{182}$
20. $\sqrt{256}$
21. $\sqrt{301}$
22. $\sqrt{350}$

Identify each number as *rational* or *irrational*.

23. $\sqrt{16}$
24. $\sqrt{11}$
25. $\sqrt{196}$
26. $\frac{4}{5}$
27. $0.\overline{712}$
28. -8
29. $\sqrt{3}$
30. 5.2
31. 0.1010010001 ...
32. $-\sqrt{25}$
33. $\sqrt{306}$
34. 2.7064

Use $s = 20\sqrt{273 + T}$ to estimate the speed of sound s in meters per second for each Celsius temperature *T*. Round to the nearest integer.

35. 37°C
36. −1°C
37. 15°C
38. −18°C

Name ______________________ Class ______________ Date ______________

1-9 • Guided Problem Solving

GPS Student Page 54, Exercise 39:

Ferris Wheels The formula $d = 1.23\sqrt{h}$ represents the distance in miles d you can see from h feet above ground. On the London Eye Ferris Wheel, you are 450 ft above ground. To the nearest tenth of a mile, how far can you see?

Understand

1. What are you being asked to find?

____

____

____

Plan and Carry Out

2. What is the formula?

____

3. What is the height?

____

4. Substitute known values into the formula.

____

5. Simplify using a calculator. Round to the nearest tenth.

____

Check

6. Use estimation to check your answer.

____

____

____

____

Solve Another Problem

7. The formula $d = 1.23\sqrt{h}$ represents the distance in miles d you can see from h feet above ground. At the top of the Ferris wheel at Cedar Point, you are 140 ft above ground. To the nearest tenth of a mile, how far can you see?

____

Name ____________________ Class ____________ Date ____________

Practice 1-10

Cube Roots

Find the cube root of each number.

1. 64 ________ **2.** 729 ________ **3.** −343 ________

4. $\frac{1}{8}$ ________ **5.** −1,000 ________ **6.** $\frac{27}{64}$ ________

Solve each equation by finding the value of *x*.

7. $x^3 = -1$ ________ **8.** $x^3 = 216$ ________ **9.** $x^3 = 1{,}728$ ________

10. $x^3 = \frac{8}{27}$ ________ **11.** $x^3 = \frac{64}{125}$ ________ **12.** $x^3 = \frac{125}{512}$ ________

Find the side length of each cube.

13.

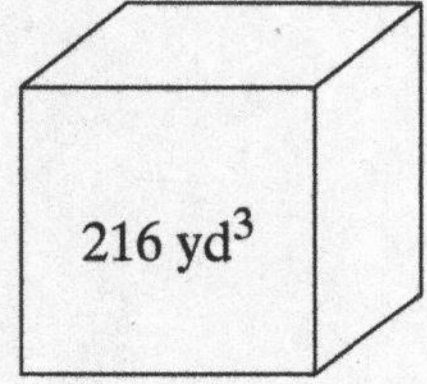

____

14.

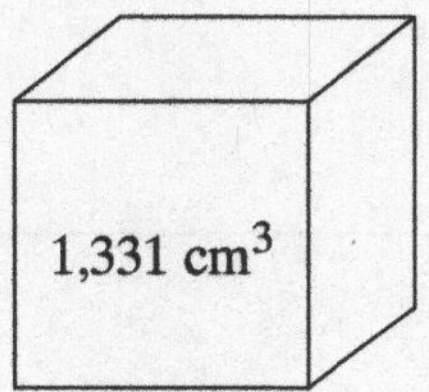

____

15. A bottle of cologne comes in a cube-shaped box that has a volume of 64 cubic inches. What is the length of one side of the box?

____

16. A cube-shaped shipping crate has a volume of 27 cubic feet. What are the dimensions of the crate?

____

17. What is a reasonable estimate for the volume of a number cube: 8 cm³, 27 in³, or 1 ft³?

____

18. A cube-shaped terrarium has a volume of $\frac{27}{64}$ cubic feet. What is the length of its sides?

____

Name ______________________ Class ______________ Date ______________

1-10 • Guided Problem Solving

GPS Student Page 57, Exercise 21:

Find the cube root of 0.216.

Understand

1. When you cube a number, how many times is the number used as a factor?

____

2. What is a cube root?

____

____

Plan and Carry Out

3. Write 0.216 as a fraction.

____

4. What is the cube root of the numerator?

____

5. What is the cube root of the denominator?

____

6. What is the cube root of the fraction?

____

7. Write the fraction as a decimal.

____

Check

8. Find the cube of your answer. Is it equal to 0.216?

____

Solve Another Problem

9. Find the cube root of 0.125.

____

Name ______________________ Class ______________ Date ______________

1A: Graphic Organizer

For use before Lesson 1-1

Study Skill As you begin a new textbook, look through the table of contents to see what kind of information you will be learning during the year. Notice that some of the topics were introduced last year. Get a head start by reviewing your old notes and problems.

Write your answers.

1. What is the chapter title? ______________________
2. How many lessons are there in this chapter? ______________
3. What is the topic of the Test-Taking Strategies page? ______________
4. Complete the graphic organizer below as you work through the chapter.
   - In the center, write the title of the chapter.
   - When you begin a lesson, write the lesson name in a rectangle.
   - When you complete a lesson, write a skill or key concept in a circle linked to that lesson block.
   - When you complete the chapter, use this graphic organizer to help you review.

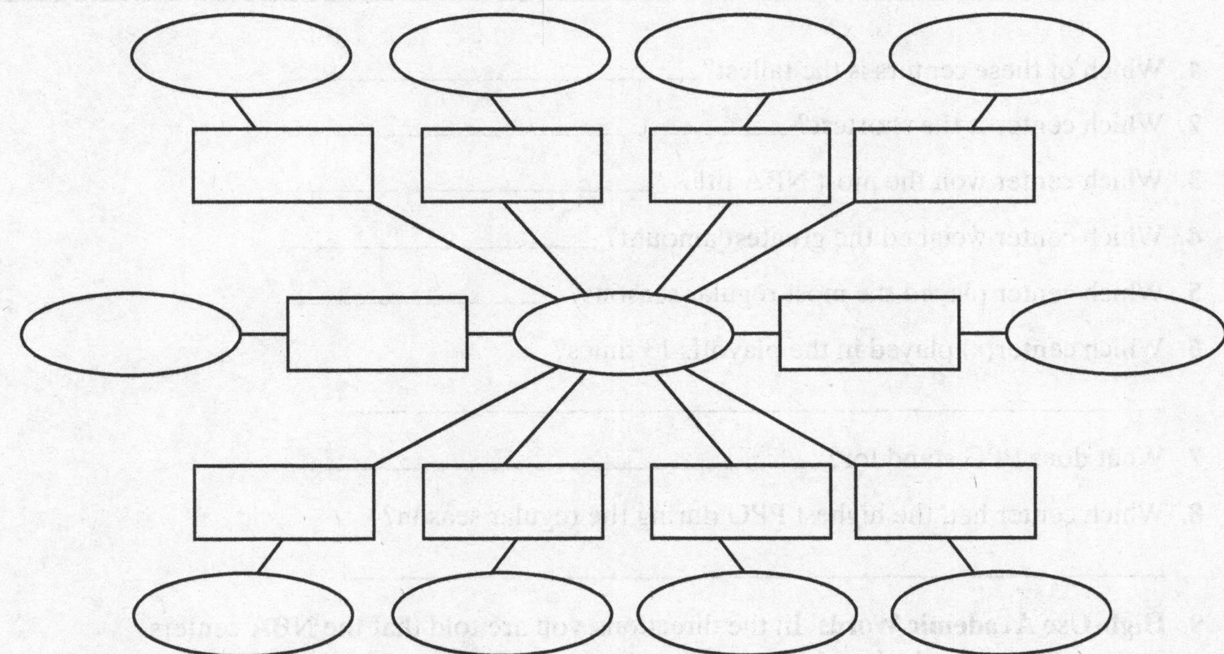

Name ______________________ Class ______________ Date ______________

1B: Reading Comprehension

For use after Lesson 1-5

Study Skill Practice reading charts and tables in books, magazines, or newspapers since information is often organized this way.

The table below contains information about four of the highest-ranked centers in the history of the National Basketball Association (NBA).

Use the table below to answer the questions.

Player	Height, Weight	Number of Seasons to Playoffs	Points Per Game (PPG) During Regular Season	PPG During Playoffs	NBA Titles	Age at Retirement
Kareem Abdul-Jabbar	7 ft 2 in. 267 lb	20 to 18	24.6	24.3	6	42
Wilt Chamberlain	7 ft 1 in. 275 lb	14 to 13	30.1	22.5	2	37
Shaquille O'Neal	7 ft 1 in. 325 lb	19 to 17	23.7	24.3	4	39
Bill Russell	6 ft 10 in. 220 lb	13 to 13	15.1	16.2	11	35

1. Which of these centers is the tallest? ______________
2. Which center is the shortest? ______________
3. Which center won the most NBA titles? ______________
4. Which center weighed the greatest amount? ______________
5. Which center played the most regular seasons? ______________
6. Which center(s) played in the playoffs 13 times?

   ____

7. What does PPG stand for? ______________
8. Which center had the highest PPG during the regular season?

   ____

9. **High-Use Academic Words** In the directions, you are told that the NBA centers in the table are *ranked* the highest. What does it mean to *rank*?

   a. to show clearly

   b. to determine the relative position of

Name ______________________ Class ______________ Date ______________

1C: Reading/Writing Math Symbols

For use after Lesson 1-6

Study Skill Finish one homework assignment before beginning another. Sometimes it helps to start with the most difficult assignment first.

Match the symbol in Column A with its meaning in Column B.

Column A	Column B
1. $\cdot$	A. division
2. $>$	B. degrees
3. $\div$	C. is greater than
4. $\lvert\,\rvert$	D. multiplication
5. $^\circ$	E. is less than
6. $<$	F. absolute value

Each of the following expressions uses a bar symbol in a different way. Explain the meaning of the bar in each expression.

7. $\frac{8}{11}$ ______________________

8. -6.5 ______________________

9. $0.\overline{35}$ ______________________

10. $14 - 9$ ______________________

Name ______________________ Class ______________ Date ______________

1D: Visual Vocabulary Practice

For use after Lesson 1-7

Study Skill If a word is not in the glossary, use a dictionary to find its meaning.

Concept List

absolute value	opposites
additive inverses	rational numbers
Commutative Property of Addition	repeating decimals
Distributive Property	terminating decimals
integers	

Write the concept that best describes each exercise. Choose from the concept list above.

1. $\frac{4}{7}, 3.4, -2, 6\frac{1}{3}$ ______________	**2.** $-17, 0, 8$ ______________	**3.** $\lvert -6 \rvert = 6$ $\lvert 6 \rvert = 6$ ______________
4. $\lvert -6 \rvert + -6 = 0$ $7.5 + (-7.5) = 0$ ______________	**5.** 26.387 41.0 306.904 ______________	**6.** $8(2^3 + 16) = 8(2^3) + 8(16)$ ______________
7. $b + c = c + b$ ______________	**8.** -12 and 12 -9.6 and 9.6 -40 and 40 ______________	**9.** $43.\overline{7} = 43.77\ldots$ $2.\overline{18} = 2.181818\ldots$ $1.\overline{302} = 601.302302302\ldots$ ______________

Name ____________________ Class ____________ Date ____________

1E: Vocabulary Check

For use after Lesson 1-5

Study Skill Strengthen your vocabulary. Use these pages and add cues and summaries by applying the Cornell Notetaking style.

Write the definition for each word or term at the right. To check your work, fold the paper back along the dotted line to see the correct answers.

____________________	absolute value
____________________	integers
____________________	repeating decimal
____________________	rational number
____________________	additive inverses

Vocabulary and Study Skills

Name ________________ Class ________________ Date ________________

1E: Vocabulary Check (continued)

For use after Lesson 1-5

Write the vocabulary word or term for each definition. To check your work, fold the paper forward along the dotted line to see the correct answers.

the distance of a number from 0 on the number line ________________

the set of positive whole numbers, their opposites, and 0 ________________

a decimal with one or more digits that repeat without end ________________

a number that can be written as a quotient of two integers, where the divisor is not 0 ________________

any two numbers whose sum is 0 ________________

Name ______________________ Class ______________ Date ______________

1F: Vocabulary Review Puzzle

For use with the Chapter Review

Study Skill Vocabulary is an important part of every subject you learn. Review new words and their definitions using flashcards.

Find each of the following words in the word search. Circle the word and then cross it off the word list. Words can be displayed forwards, backwards, up, down, or diagonally.

absolute value	integers	ordering	additive inverse
decimal	inverses	repeating	
opposites	rational	commutative	
terminating	distributive	multiplication	

O	E	E	U	L	A	V	E	T	U	L	O	S	B	A	A
D	Y	D	C	G	A	A	Q	V	E	N	S	R	O	N	D
R	W	I	U	L	T	I	P	L	I	V	E	P	I	O	D
E	X	S	K	R	L	A	N	R	V	P	F	T	L	I	I
R	A	T	I	O	N	A	L	M	E	Q	L	E	R	T	T
T	N	R	S	U	R	U	E	A	D	V	I	R	J	A	I
I	J	I	Q	E	V	I	T	A	T	U	M	M	O	C	V
O	N	B	Z	S	T	I	F	K	R	S	R	I	R	I	E
N	L	U	E	K	N	I	P	M	R	H	Z	N	D	L	I
L	M	T	U	G	D	V	S	E	N	N	V	A	E	P	N
B	N	I	X	U	G	M	G	O	H	X	R	T	R	I	V
I	N	V	E	R	S	E	S	S	P	H	F	I	I	T	E
C	V	E	S	M	T	S	N	H	K	P	P	N	N	L	R
M	B	R	C	N	N	F	R	C	S	P	O	G	G	U	S
D	E	C	I	M	A	L	X	R	Z	O	A	P	D	M	E

Name ______________________ Class ______________ Date ____________

Practice 2-1

Scientific Notation

Write each number in scientific notation.

1. 45 ________ **2.** 250 ________ **3.** 90 ________ **4.** 670 ________

5. 4,100 ________ **6.** 500 ________ **7.** 43,200 ________ **8.** 97,100 ________

9. 38,050 ________ **10.** 480,000 ________ **11.** 900,000 ________ **12.** 8,750,000 ________

Write each number in standard form.

13. 3.1×10^1 ________ **14.** 8×10^2 ________ **15.** 4.501×10^4 ________ **16.** 9.7×10^6 ________

17. 2.86×10^5 ________ **18.** 3.58×10^6 ________ **19.** 8.1×10^1 ________ **20.** 9.071×10^2 ________

21. 4.83×10^9 ________ **22.** 2.73×10^8 ________ **23.** 2×10^5 ________ **24.** 8.09×10^4 ________

Order each set of numbers from least to greatest.

25. $8.9 \times 10^2, 6.3 \times 10^3, 2.1 \times 10^4, 7.8 \times 10^5$

____

26. $2.1 \times 10^4, 2.12 \times 10^3, 3.46 \times 10^5, 2.112 \times 10^2$

____

27. A mulberry silkworm can spin a single thread that measures up to 3,900 ft in length. Write the number in scientific notation.

____

Write each number in scientific notation.

28. 0.025 ________ **29.** 0.00003 ________ **30.** 0.00197 ________ **31.** 0.000407 ________

Write each number in standard form.

32. 8.1×10^{-3} ________ **33.** 3.42×10^{-5} ________ **34.** 9.071×10^{-6} ________ **35.** 2×10^{-4} ________

Name ______________________ Class ______________ Date ______________

2-1 • Guided Problem Solving

GPS Student Page 69, Exercise 33:

Astronomy When the sun emits a solar flare, the blast wave can travel through space at 3×10^6 km/h. Use the formula $d = rt$ to find how far the wave will travel in 30 min.

Understand

1. What does each of the variables stand for in the formula?

   ____

2. What are you being asked to find?

   ____

Plan and Carry Out

3. Which variable are you solving for in the formula? __________

4. To write the rate in standard form, which way and how many places will you move the decimal point? What is the rate in standard form?

   ____

5. Convert 30 minutes to hours. __________

6. Substitute what you know into the formula and solve.

   ____

7. Write the distance back into scientific notation. Which way will you move the decimal point and how many places?

   ____

Check

8. How can you check to see if your answer is reasonable?

   ____

   ____

Solve Another Problem

9. A state animal shelter had 4.2×10^4 unwanted animals dropped off last year. If the goal of the shelter is to decrease the number by one-sixth this year, how many fewer animals will enter the shelter? Write your answer in scientific notation.

   ____

Name ______________________ Class ______________ Date ______________

Practice 2-2

Exponents and Multiplication

Write each expression using a single exponent.

1. $3^2 \cdot 3^5$
2. $1^3 \cdot 1^4$
3. $(-3)^{12} \cdot (-3)^5$
4. $0.8^3 \cdot 0.8$
5. $(-1.3)^2 \cdot (-1.3)^4$
6. $4.5^8 \cdot 4.5^2$
7. $3^3 \cdot 3 \cdot 3^4$
8. $2^2 \cdot 2^2 \cdot 2^2$
9. $5 \cdot 5^4 \cdot 5^3$

Simplify each expression.

10. $a^1 \cdot a^2$
11. $m^5 \cdot m$
12. $(-y)^3 \cdot (-y)^2$
13. $(3x) \cdot (3x)$
14. $4d \cdot 9d^8$
15. $x^2y \cdot xy^2$
16. $10jk^5 \cdot 3j^3k^2$
17. $2p^3q^2 \cdot 3p^2q^3$
18. $5x^2 \cdot x^6 \cdot x^3$

Replace each ? with =, <, or >.

19. 3^8 ? $3 \cdot 3^7$
20. 49 ? $7^2 \cdot 7^2$
21. $5^3 \cdot 5^4$? 25^2

22. A square has a side length of $7x^4$ in. Find the area of the square.

23. The formula for the volume of a rectangular prism is $V = \ell \cdot w \cdot h$. What is the volume of a prism with length $2x^2$ mm, width $4x$ mm, and height x^3 mm?

24. One meter is equal to 10^2 centimeters. One kilometer is equal to 10^3 meters. How many centimeters are in one kilometer?

Name ______________________ Class ____________ Date ____________

2-2 • Guided Problem Solving

GPS Student Page 75, Exercise 34:

Geometry The formula for the area of a square is $A = s^2$. What is the area of a square with sides that are $3x^2$ cm?

Understand

1. What are you being asked to do? ______________________

2. What do you know? ______________________

____

Plan and Carry Out

3. Write the formula for the area of the square as a multiplication sentence.

____

4. Substitute the side length of the square for s in the formula you wrote in Problem 3.

____

5. Rewrite the formula by using the Commutative Property of Multiplication to group numbers and to group variables that have the same base.

____

6. How do you multiply numbers or variables that have the same base?

____

7. What is the area of the square in simplest form?

____

Check

8. How can you check your answer? ______________________

____

____

____

Solve Another Problem

9. What is the area of a rectangle whose length is $5x$ ft and whose width is $8x^2$ ft?

____

Name ______________________ Class ______________ Date ______________

Practice 2-3

Multiplying with Scientific Notation

Find each product. Write the answers in scientific notation.

1. $(3 \times 10^4)(5 \times 10^6)$ ____________
2. $(7 \times 10^2)(6 \times 10^4)$ ____________
3. $(4 \times 10^5)(7 \times 10^8)$ ____________
4. $(9.1 \times 10^6)(3 \times 10^9)$ ____________
5. $(8.4 \times 10^9)(5 \times 10^7)$ ____________
6. $(5 \times 10^3)(4 \times 10^6)$ ____________
7. $(7.2 \times 10^8)(2 \times 10^3)$ ____________
8. $(1.4 \times 10^5)(4 \times 10^{11})$ ____________

Choose the most reasonable unit to describe the quantity.
Then use scientific notation to describe the quantity using the other unit.

9. The mass of a bicycle is about 6 _____. (g, kg) ____________
10. The length of a school bus is 12 _____. (m, km) ____________
11. Double the number 4.6×10^{15}. Write the answer in scientific notation.

____

12. Triple the number 2.3×10^3. Write the answer in scientific notation.

____

13. A company manufactures 3.2×10^4 cell phones per month. How many cell phones does it manufacture per year?

____

14. Yosemite National Park covers about 7.6×10^5 acres. There are about 4.36×10^4 square feet in one acre. How many square feet does the national park cover?

____

Name ______________________ Class ____________ Date ____________

2-3 • Guided Problem Solving

GPS Student Page 79, Exercise 20:

Geography The Sahara is a desert of about 3.5 million square miles. There are about 2.79×10^7 square feet in a square mile. About how many square feet does the Sahara cover? Write your answer in scientific notation.

Understand

1. What are you being asked to do?

____

____

2. What form will your answer be in? ____________________

Plan and Carry Out

3. Write 3.5 million in standard form. ____________________
4. Write 3.5 million in scientific notation. ____________________
5. To convert from square miles to square feet, what operation will you use?

____

6. Write the conversion for square feet to square miles.

____

7. Convert the square miles of the Sahara to square feet.

____

Check

8. Use another method to solve the problem. Does your answer check?

____

____

____

Solve Another Problem

9. The human body contains about 3.2×10^4 microliters of blood per pound of body weight. How many microliters of blood would a 185-pound man have circulating in his body? Write your answer in scientific notation.

____

Name ______________________ Class ______________ Date ______________

Practice 2-4

Exponents and Division

Simplify each expression.

1. 8^{-2}
2. $(-3)^0$
3. 5^{-1}
4. 18^0
5. 2^{-5}
6. 3^{-3}
7. 2^{-3}
8. 5^{-2}
9. $\frac{4^4}{4}$
10. $8^6 \div 8^8$
11. $-\frac{(3)^6}{(3)^8}$
12. $\frac{8^4}{8^0}$
13. $1^{15} \div 1^{18}$
14. $7 \div 7^4$
15. $-\frac{(4)^8}{(4)^4}$
16. $\frac{10^9}{10^{12}}$
17. $\frac{b^{12}}{b^4}$
18. $\frac{g^9}{g^{15}}$
19. $x^{16} \div x^7$
20. $v^{20} \div v^{25}$

Complete each equation.

21. $\frac{1}{3^5} = 3^{?}$
22. $-\frac{1}{(2)^7} = -2^{?}$
23. $\frac{1}{x^2} = x^{?}$
24. $-\frac{1}{125} = (-5)^{?}$
25. $\frac{1}{1{,}000} = 10^{?}$
26. $\frac{5^{10}}{?} = 5^5$
27. $\frac{z^{?}}{z^8} = z^{-3}$
28. $\frac{q^5}{?} = q^7$

Is each statement true or false? Explain your reasoning.

29. $(-1)^3 = 1^{-3}$
30. $3^{-1} \cdot 3^{-1} = 3^1$
31. $2^2 \cdot 2^{-2} = 1$
32. $7^2 \cdot (-7)^3 = (-7)^{-6}$

Name ______________________ Class ______________ Date ____________

2-4 • Guided Problem Solving

GPS Student Page 85, Exercise 24:

Earth Science Earth's crust is divided into large pieces called tectonic plates. The Pacific tectonic plate is moving northwest at a rate of about 4^{-2} m each year. At this rate, how long will it take the plate to move 4^6 m (about 2.5 miles)?

Understand

1. The equation $d = rt$ represents the relationship between distance d, rate r, and time t. What measurements are given in the problem?

   ____

2. What measurement are you asked to find?

   ____

Plan and Carry Out

3. Solve the equation $d = rt$ for t.

   ____

4. Substitute the values that are known into the equation for t.

   ____

5. What is the common base?

   ____

6. When dividing powers with the same base, what do you do to the exponents?

   ____

7. Solve the equation for t.

   ____

Check

8. Solve the problem by writing the numbers in standard form. Does your answer check?

   ____

Solve Another Problem

9. A rectangular plot of land covers an area of 2^{13} square feet. You measure the length of the plot to be 2^7 feet. What is the width?

   ____

Name ______________________ Class ______________ Date ______________

Practice 2-5

Dividing with Scientific Notation

Divide. Write each quotient in scientific notation.

1. $\frac{6.8 \times 10^7}{3.4 \times 10^5}$ ________

2. $\frac{7.3 \times 10^3}{4.5 \times 10^6}$ ________

3. $\frac{2.6 \times 10^5}{5.1 \times 10^3}$ ________

4. $\frac{1.9 \times 10^{-4}}{3.3 \times 10^1}$ ________

5. $\frac{7.9 \times 10^5}{2.3 \times 10^3}$ ________

6. $\frac{6.2 \times 10^7}{5.6 \times 10^{-8}}$ ________

7. $\frac{8.2 \times 10^5}{6}$ ________

8. $\frac{12}{4.3 \times 10^2}$ ________

9. $\frac{3.4 \times 10^7}{9}$ ________

Which of the following numbers is greater?

10. 5.2×10^4 or 5.8×10^3 ________

11. 6×10^3 or 8×10^{-3} ________

12. 3.42×10^6 or 3.24×10^6 ________

13. 8.1×10^{-7} or 8.1×10^{-8} ________

Estimate how many times larger the first number is than the second number.

14. 6×10^{12} and 2×10^{10} ________

15. 4×10^9 and 8×10^5 ________

16. The height of the thermosphere is about 2.95×10^5 feet above Earth. There are 5,280 feet in 1 mile. About how many miles above earth is the thermosphere?

____

17. The speed of light is about 3.0×10^8 m/s. The speed of sound is about 3.4×10^2 m/s. How much faster does light travel than sound?

____

18. The distance between Los Angeles, California, and Washington, D.C., is 4.3×10^6 m. The distance between New York City, New York, and Washington, D.C., is 3.6×10^5 m. How much farther is Los Angeles from Washington, D.C., than New York City?

____

Name ______________________ Class ______________ Date ______________

2-5 • Guided Problem Solving

GPS Student Page 93, Exercise 19:

The sun's diameter is 1.39×10^6 kilometers. Earth's diameter is 1.28×10^4 kilometers. How many times greater is the sun's diameter than Earth's diameter?

Understand

1. Which diameter is larger? ______________________

2. What are you being asked to find?

____

____

Plan and Carry Out

3. The diameters are in scientific notation, and the numbers 1.28 and 1.39 are close in value, so what do you need to compare?

____

4. When dividing powers with the same base, what do you do to the exponents?

____

5. Subtract the exponents and write the power in standard form.

____

6. How many times greater is the sun's diameter than Earth's?

____

Check

7. What strategy could you use to check your answer?

____

____

Solve Another Problem

8. When you donate a pint of blood, you lose about 2.3×10^{12} red blood cells. If your body can produce about 2×10^6 red blood cells per second, about how many seconds would it take for your body to replenish the red blood cells lost through donation? Write your answer in standard form.

____

Name ______________________ Class ______________ Date ______________

2A: Graphic Organizer

For use before Lesson 2-1

Study Skill Your textbook includes a Skills Handbook with extra problems and questions. Working these exercises is a good way to review material and prepare for the next chapter.

Write your answers.

1. What is the chapter title? ______________________
2. How many lessons are there in this chapter? ______________
3. What is the topic of the Test-Taking Strategies page?

____

4. Complete the graphic organizer below as you work through the chapter.
   - In the center, write the title of the chapter.
   - When you begin a lesson, write the lesson name in a rectangle.
   - When you complete a lesson, write a skill or key concept in a circle linked to that lesson block.
   - When you complete the chapter, use this graphic organizer to help you review.

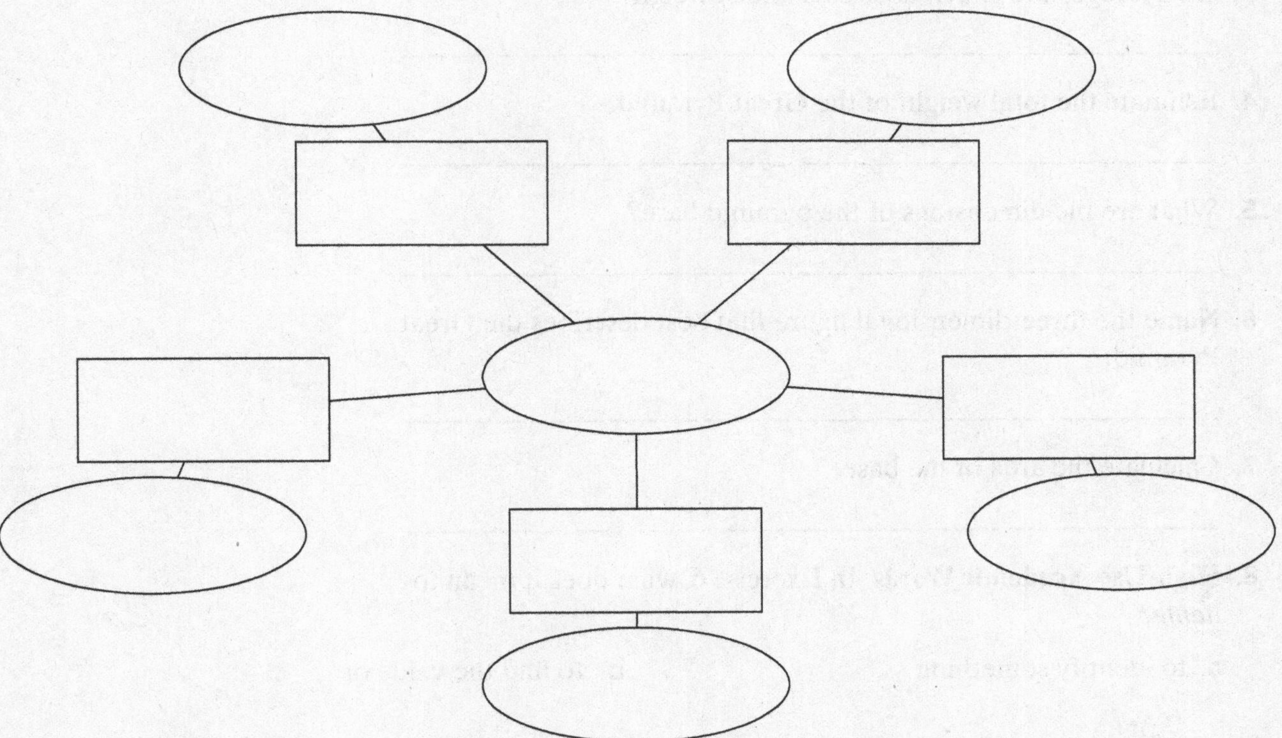

Vocabulary and Study Skills

Name ____________________ Class ____________ Date ____________

2B: Reading Comprehension

For use after Lesson 2-3

Study Skill Attitude is everything.

Read the paragraph below and answer the questions that follow.

The Great Pyramid of Giza, one of the Seven Wonders of the World, is located just outside the city of Cairo, Egypt. It was built between 2589 and 2566 B.C. by the pharaoh Khufu. The walls are set at an incline of approximately 52 degrees. The square base is 745 feet on each side and the height is 449 feet. The pyramid is oriented to face the four cardinal directions: north, south, east, and west. It is composed of more than 2.3 million stone blocks that weigh about 2.5 tons each on average. The heaviest stones weigh almost 9 tons.

1. How long did it take to build the Great Pyramid?

____

2. About how many stone blocks were used? Give your answer in scientific notation.

____

3. On average, how much does each block weigh?

____

4. Estimate the total weight of the Great Pyramid.

____

5. What are the dimensions of the pyramid base?

____

6. Name the three-dimensional figure that best describes the Great Pyramid.

____

7. Calculate the area of the base.

____

8. **High-Use Academic Words** In Exercise 6, what does it mean to *name*?

a. to identify something

b. to find the value of

Name ______________________ Class ______________ Date ______________

2C: Reading/Writing Math Symbols

For use after Lesson 2-5

Study Skill Appreciate your efforts even when you have yet to see them pay off.

Match each expression in Column A to its meaning in Column B.

Column A	Column B
1. $6^{(4-2)}$	A. $11 \cdot 11 \cdot 11$
2. $(3^2)^4$	B. 1
3. 6^{-2}	C. a^4
4. 0.06×10^4	D. 600
5. 11^3	E. $\frac{1}{6^2}$
6. $(-6a)^0$	F. 3^8
7. $\frac{a^6}{a^2}$	G. 6^2

Write each statement using appropriate mathematical symbols.

8. five raised to the *n* plus three power

____

9. The square root of 168 is approximately thirteen.

____

10. *y* is equal to three times *x* plus eleven.

____

11. eight and sixty-five hundredths, multiplied by ten raised to the ninth power

____

12. the quantity seven plus *z*, squared

____

13. the quantity eight minus 3 raised to the negative third power.

____

14. the quantity five to the eighth power, raised to the third power

____

Name ______________________ Class ______________ Date ______________

2D: Visual Vocabulary Practice

For use after Lesson 2-5

Study Skill Making sense of mathematical symbols is like reading a foreign language that uses different letters.

Concept List

9,000,000	constant	c^4
coefficient	6^3	a^{-n}
400	like terms	4.34×10^{-2}

Write the concept that best describes each exercise. Choose from the concept list above.

1. $\frac{6^9}{6^6}$ ______	**2.** The factor in scientific notation that multiplies a power of 10. ______	**3.** 0.0434 ______
4. $\frac{1}{a^n}$ ______	**5.** $2y$ and $-8y$ in the expression $2y + 3y^2 - 8y - 5$ ______	**6.** -4 in the expression $-\frac{4}{5}x^5 - 6x^4 + 4x - 4$ ______
7. 9×10^6 in standard form. ______	**8.** $c \times c \times c \times c$ ______	**9.** $\frac{8 \times 10^5}{2 \times 10^3}$ ______

Name ____________ Class ____________ Date ____________

2E: Vocabulary Check

For use after Lesson 2-5

Study Skill Strengthen your vocabulary. Use these pages and add cues and summaries by applying the Cornell Notetaking style.

Write the definition for each word or term at the right. To check your work, fold the paper back along the dotted line to see the correct answers.

______________________________ scientific notation

______________________________ standard form

______________________________ base

______________________________ squared

______________________________ power

Name ______________________ Class ______________ Date ____________

2E: Vocabulary Check (continued)

For use after Lesson 2-5

Write the vocabulary word or term for each definition. To check your work, fold the paper forward along the dotted line to see the correct answers.

a number where the first factor is greater than or equal to one and the second factor is a power of 10 ______________________

a number not written as a product of factors ______________________

in the expression, 5^2, what 5 represents ______________________

a number taken to the second power ______________________

in the expression of a^n, what n represents ______________________

Name ________________________ Class ______________ Date ______________

2F: Vocabulary Review Puzzle

For use with the Chapter Review

Study Skill Read problems carefully. Pay special attention to exponents when working with polynomials.

Complete the crossword puzzle below. For help, use the Glossary in your textbook.

Here are the words you will use to complete this crossword puzzle:

distributive	constant
binomial	polynomial
variable	exponent
coefficient	scientific notation
like terms	monomial

ACROSS

2. may be one term or the sum or difference of two or more terms
5. the numerical factor in any term of a polynomial
8. a polynomial with two terms
9. terms with exactly the same variable factors
10. tells how many times a number, or base, is used as a factor

DOWN

1. a way to write a number as two factors, the second of which is always a power of ten
3. $a(b + c) = ab + ac$ is an example of the ______ Property.
4. $4m$, for example
6. a term in a polynomial that does not contain a variable
7. a letter that stands for a number

Name ______________________ Class ______________ Date ______________

Practice 3-1

Evaluating and Writing Algebraic Expressions

Evaluate each expression using the values $m = 7$, $r = 8$, and $t = 2$.

1. $5m - 6$ ______________
2. $4m + t$ ______________
3. $r \div t$ ______________
4. $m \times t$ ______________
5. $5t + 2m$ ______________
6. $r \times m$ ______________
7. $3m - 5t$ ______________
8. $(m \times r) \div t$ ______________
9. mrt ______________
10. Write an algebraic expression for the nth term of the table below.

A	0	1	2	3	4	5	n
B	3	5	7	9	11	13	?

____

Write a word phrase for each algebraic expression.

11. $n + 16$ ______________
12. $3.2n$ ______________
13. $25.6 - n$ ______________
14. $n \div 24$ ______________
15. $\frac{45}{n}$ ______________
16. $15.4 - n$ ______________

Write an algebraic expression for each word phrase.

17. 12 more than m machines ______________
18. six times the daily amount of fiber f in your diet ______________
19. your aunt's age a minus 25 ______________
20. the total number of seashells s divided by 10 ______________
21. You and four friends plan a surprise party. Each of you contributes the same amount of money m for food.
    a. Write an algebraic expression for the total amount of money contributed for food. ______________
    b. Evaluate your expression for $m = \$5.25$. ______________

Name ______________________ Class ______________ Date ____________

3-1 • Guided Problem Solving

GPS Student Page 106, Exercise 38:

Estimation This section of a page from a telephone directory shows a column with 11 names in 1 inch. Each page has four 10-inch columns. Write an algebraic expression for the approximate number of names in p pages of the directory.

6-4462 **Daalling V** 8 Everett All..........
2-3302 [illegible] R..........
4-1775 **Dabady V** 94 Burns de All........
2-0014 **Dabagh L** 13 Lanca ter R.......
6-3356 **Dabagh W** Dr 521 eston All..
4-7322 **Dabar G** 98 River A..............
6-1530 **Dabarera F** 34 Ros land All....
2-2279 **Dabas M** 17 Riversi e R..........
4-9978 **D'Abate D** 86 Moss Hill Rd All..
2-6745 **D'Abate G** 111 Sou Central R
4-5456 **Dabbous H** 670 Wa ren Dr All..
6-3064 **Dabbraccio F** 151 entury All..
6-2257 **Dabby D** 542 Waln All..........
2-9987 [illegible] Green R..
6-5643 **Dabcovich M** 72 Main All..........

Understand

1. What are you being asked to do?

____

____

2. What is an algebraic expression?

____

____

3. What does p represent?

____

____

Plan and Carry Out

4. How many names are in 1 in. of one column? ____________
5. How many names are in one 10-in. column? ____________
6. How many names are in four 10-in. columns? ____________
7. How many names are listed on one page? ____________
8. How many names are listed on p pages? ____________
9. Write an algebraic expression for the approximate number of names in p pages of the directory. ____________

Check

10. Substitute $p = 1, 2,$ and 3 in the expression and solve. Does your expression provide reasonable values?

____

Solve Another Problem

11. The yearbook committee can fit 1 student picture in one inch of a row. If there are eight 6-inch rows on each page, write an expression for the approximate number of pictures that can fit on p pages.

____

Name ________________ Class ________________ Date ________________

Practice 3-2

Simplifying Expressions

Simplify each expression.

1. $12 - \frac{2}{3}m + 4 - \frac{3}{4}m$ **2.** $a - 2 + 13 + 8a$ **3.** $10q - 2q + 3 - 9$

4. $8 - g - 2 + 5g$ **5.** $2.2k + 5 + 7.9k + 8$ **6.** $-4r - 2r - 6 - 4$

7. $0.2(15 - 3t) - 1.8$ **8.** $7x - 5(3x + 12)$ **9.** $\frac{1}{3}(9z - 27) + 12$

Factor each expression completely.

10. $42r - 18$ **11.** $100 - 50d$ **12.** $24x + 64$ **13.** $-9y - 39$

14. $60 - 24x$ **15.** $9w - 81$ **16.** $132 + 77t$ **17.** $16y - 56$

Use >, <, or = to make each statement true.

18. $-4 + p + 2$ ● $4p + 2 \cdot 4 - 3p$ ________________

19. $2m + 2n - 5$ ● $6 + 2(m + n) - 11$ ________________

20. $3x + 4 - 4x + 2$ ● $3(5 - x) + 2x$ ________________

21. Find the perimeter of a rectangle with length $3c - 5$ and width $2c$. Simplify your answer.

____

Name ____________________ Class ____________ Date ____________

3-2 • Guided Problem Solving

GPS Student Page 111, Exercise 39:

Earning Money You work 40 hours a week and earn d dollars an hour. You get a raise of $3 an hour plus a $13 bonus in the first week. Write and simplify the expression that shows the amount you will earn in the week.

Understand

1. What are you being asked to do?

____

____

2. What does it mean to simplify an expression?

____

____

3. What does d stand for?

____

____

Plan and Carry Out

4. At first, how much do you earn an hour? ____________
5. How much do you earn an hour after your raise? ____________
6. How many hours do you work in a week? ____________
7. Write an expression to show how much you earn a week. ____________
8. How much was your bonus? ____________
9. How much did you earn the first week? Write and simplify the expression.

____

Check

10. Substitute $d = 5$ in the expression. Does your expression seem reasonable?

____

Solve Another Problem

11. You make 40 shirts a week and earn p dollars per shirt. You get a raise of $1.50 a shirt plus a $22 bonus in the first week. Write and simplify the expression that shows the amount you will earn in the week.

____

Name ____________________ Class ____________ Date ____________

Practice 3-3

Solving One-Step Equations

Solve each equation. Check your answer.

1. $n + 2 = 5$ ________
2. $x - 1 = -3$ ________
3. $7 = a + 2$ ________
4. $p + 2 = -6$ ________
5. $-18 = -\frac{y}{2}$ ________
6. $\frac{y}{16} = 3$ ________
7. $-56 = 8r$ ________
8. $9w = -63$ ________

Use a calculator, paper and pencil, or mental math. Solve each equation.

9. $-3v = -48$ ________
10. $13 = -\frac{x}{4}$ ________
11. $28 = -4a$ ________
12. $-\frac{t}{42} = 3$ ________
13. $t + 43 = 28$ ________
14. $-19 = r + 6$ ________
15. $25 = r + 7$ ________
16. $13 = 24 + c$ ________

Write and solve an equation to represent each situation.

17. The odometer on your family car reads 20,186.7 after going 62.3 miles. How many miles were on the odometer before going 62.3 miles?

____

18. Michael bought a $25.00 gift for a friend. After he bought the gift, Michael had $176.89. Write and solve an equation to calculate how much money Michael had before he bought the gift.

____

19. This spring it rained a total of 11.5 inches. This was 3 inches less than last spring. Write and solve an equation to find the amount of rain last season.

____

20. One of the largest flowers, the Rafflesia, weighs about 15 lb. How many Rafflesia flowers can be placed in a container that can hold a maximum of 240 lb?

____

21. "Heavy water" is a name given to a compound used in some nuclear reactors. Heavy water costs about $1,500 per gallon. If a nuclear plant spent $10,500 on heavy water, how many gallons of heavy water were bought?

____

Name ______________________ Class ______________ Date ______________

3-3 • Guided Problem Solving

GPS Student Page 117, Exercise 22:

Biology A student collects 12 ladybugs for a science project. This is 9 fewer than the number of ladybugs the student collected yesterday. Write and solve an equation to find the number of ladybugs the student collected yesterday.

Understand

1. Circle the information you will need to solve the problem.
2. What are you being asked to do?

   ____

   ____

3. What will your variable represent?

   ____

   ____

Plan and Carry Out

4. How many ladybugs did the student collect today? ____________
5. Determine a variable for the number of ladybugs the student collected yesterday. ____________
6. Write an expression for the phrase; *9 fewer than the number of ladybugs the student collected yesterday.* ____________
7. Write an equation that compares the answer to step 4 with the answer to Step 6. ____________
8. Solve the equation written in Step 7. ____________
9. How many ladybugs did the student collect yesterday? ____________

Check

10. Substitute the answer to Step 9 into the equation for the variable and solve.

    ____

Solve Another Problem

11. Jason is 72 in. tall. If Kenny is 15 in. shorter than Jason, write and solve an equation for the height of Kenny.

    ____

Name ______________________ Class ____________ Date ____________

Practice 3-4

Exploring Two-Step Equations

Define a variable and write an algebraic expression for each phrase.

1. six times the price of gas minus 20

____

2. one-half the distance from Boston to New York minus 25

____

3. two fewer than five times the number of eggs needed in the recipe

____

4. 10 megabytes less than the number of megabytes in a computer, divided by 6

____

Solve each equation using number sense.

5. $10 + 5h = 25$

6. $8s - 8 = 64$

7. $3y + 78 = 81$

8. $2g + 4 = 12$

9. $5j + 5 = 15$

10. $3w + 8 = 20$

11. $\frac{h}{2} + 1 = 4$

12. $\frac{g}{g} + 12 = 16$

13. $2 + \frac{b}{7} = 3$

14. For a walk-a-thon a sponsor committed to give you a flat fee of $5 plus $2 for every mile you walk. Write an expression for the total amount you will collect from your sponsor at the end of the walk-a-thon. Then evaluate your expression for 20 miles walked.

____

Name ____________________ Class ____________ Date ____________

3-4 • Guided Problem Solving

GPS Student Page 124, Exercise 39:

Food You are helping to prepare food for a large family gathering. You can slice 2 zucchinis per minute. You need 30 sliced zucchinis. How long will it take you to finish, if you have already sliced 12 zucchinis?

Understand

1. Circle the information you will need to solve the problem.
2. What are you being asked to do?

   ____

   ____

3. What will your variable represent?

   ____

Plan and Carry Out

4. How many sliced zucchinis do you need? ____________
5. How many sliced zucchinis do you already have? ____________
6. Write and simplify an expression for the number of zucchinis you still need to slice. ____________
7. To calculate the number of minutes it will take to slice the remaining zucchinis, what number will you divide your answer to Step 7 by? ____________
8. Write an equation to solve the problem. ____________
9. How long will it take you to finish slicing the remaining zucchinis? ____________

Check

10. Multiply your answer to Step 9 by your answer to Step 7. Does your answer match your result from Step 6?

    ____

Solve Another Problem

11. Jordan skates 6 mi/h. Today she has already skated 8 miles. Her goal is to skate a total of 20 miles. How much longer does she have to skate to reach her goal?

    ____

Name ______________________ Class ______________ Date ______________

Practice 3-5

Solving Two-Step Equations

Solve each equation. Then check your answer.

1. $7m + 8 = 71$ ______
2. $\frac{y}{7} + 6 = 11$ ______
3. $12y + 2 = 146$ ______
4. $\frac{m}{9} - 17 = 21$ ______
5. $\frac{y}{-12} + 1 = 6$ ______
6. $2a - 1 = 19$ ______
7. $\frac{c}{9} - 8 = 17$ ______
8. $-4t + 16 = 24$ ______
9. $\frac{b}{-2} - 8 = -6$ ______
10. $3d + 14 = 11$ ______
11. $\frac{z}{17} - 1 = 8$ ______
12. $\frac{e}{5} - 14 = 21$ ______
13. $\frac{f}{-9} + 4 = 2$ ______
14. $-2y + 16 = 10$ ______
15. $4w - 26 = 82$ ______
16. $\frac{j}{19} - 2 = -5$ ______

Solve each equation.

17. $3n - 8 = 4$ ______
18. $\frac{n}{5} - 4 = 11$ ______
19. $2n - 3 = 9$ ______
20. $1 + \frac{n}{4} = 9$ ______

Match each sentence with a two-step equation.

21. Half of the height of a tree minus five equals fifteen. ______
22. Two less than three times the number of feet of fencing required equals twelve feet. ______
23. Eight less than the quotient of Dave's golf score and four equals negative five. ______
24. Three times Gail's age increased by two years equals twelve years. ______

A. $3n - 2 = 12$

B. $3n + 2 = 12$

C. $\frac{n}{2} - 5 = 15$

D. $\frac{n}{4} - 8 = -5$

Name ____________________ Class ____________ Date ____________

3-5 • Guided Problem Solving

GPS Student Page 129, Exercise 32:

Jobs You earn $20 per hour landscaping a yard. You pay $1.50 in bus fare each way. How many hours must you work to earn $117?

Understand

1. Circle the information you will need to solve the problem.
2. What are you being asked to do?

   ____

   ____

3. How much do you spend in bus fare to go to and from work? ____________

Plan and Carry Out

4. Write an expression for the amount of money you make after *h* hours.

   ____

5. Write an expression for the amount of money you have after you pay for bus fare.

   ____

6. How much money do you need to earn? ____________
7. Write an equation that can be solved for *h*. ____________
8. Solve the equation. ____________
9. How many hours must you work to earn $117? ____________

Check

10. Substitute the answer in Step 9 into the equation for the variable and solve.

    ____

Solve Another Problem

11. You charge $6 per hour to babysit one child. You charge an additional $2 per hour for each additional child. The Taylors have 4 children. How many hours would you have to babysit the Taylors' children to earn $84?

    ____

Name ______________ Class ______________ Date ______________

Practice 3-6

Solving Multi-Step Equations

Solve each equation. Check the solution.

1. $2x - 3 + 4x = 39$

2. $0.7w + 16 + 4w = 27.28$

3. $-6(m + 1) = 24$

4. $\frac{2}{3}(k - 8) = 52$

5. $4(1.5c + 6) - 2c = -9$

6. $0.5n + 17 + n = 20$

7. $2(2.5b - 9) + 6b = -7$

8. $3(\frac{3}{4}a + 3) + 6 = 87$

9. $20 = -4(f + 6) + 14$

10. $9a - 4 + 3(a - 11) = 23$

11. **You want to join the tennis team. You go to the sporting goods store with $100. If the tennis racket you want costs $80 and the tennis balls cost $4 per can, how many cans of tennis balls can you buy?**

12. **Johnny wants to ship a package to his friend. A shipping company charges $2.49 for the first pound and $1.24 for each additional pound. If it cost Johnny $11.17 to ship the package, how much did his package weigh?**

Name ______________________ Class ______________ Date ____________

3-6 • Guided Problem Solving

GPS Student Page 137, Exercise 22:

Jobs An employee earns $7.00 an hour for the first 35 hours worked in a week and $10.50 for any hours over 35. One week's paycheck (before deductions) was for $308.00. How many hours did the employee work?

Understand

1. How much per hour does the employee make for the first 35 hours? ____________
2. How much per hour does the employee make after 35 hours of work? ____________
3. How much was the week's paycheck? ____________
4. What is it you are asked to find?

____

Plan and Carry Out

5. Write an equation for this situation. Multiply the hourly rate by 35 hours. Add the overtime rate multiplied by an unknown, x. Set this sum equal to the total amount of the check.

____

6. Solve for x, the number of overtime hours the employee worked.

____

7. What do you have to do to find the total hours worked?

____

8. How many total hours did the employee work? ____________

Check

9. Does the answer check? Is 35 times $7 plus the overtime hours times $10.50 equal to the total check?

____

Solve Another Problem

10. A college student has a long-distance phone card. The phone-card rate for the first 100 minutes is 12 cents per minute and then goes to 15 cents per minute after that. If the student had a long distance charge of $21, how many total minutes did the student talk?

____

Name ______________________ Class ______________ Date ______________

Practice 3-7

Solving Equations With Variables on Both Sides

Solve each equation. Check the solution.

1. $10 + 12y = 2y + 40$

2. $6(c + 4) = 4c - 18$

3. $0.5m + 6.4 = 4.9 - 0.1m$

4. $14b = 16(b + 12)$

5. $7 + \frac{2}{5}y = \frac{3}{5}y - 4$

6. $9(d - 4) - 8 = 5d$

7. $12j = 16(j - 8)$

8. $0.7p + 4.6 = 7.3 - 0.2p$

9. $6(f + 5) + 8 = 2f$

10. $4 = -2(4.5p + 25)$

11. Jace owns twice as many DVDs as Louis. Bo has sixty fewer DVDs than five times Louis's collection. If Jace and Bo have the same amount of DVDs, how many DVDs are in Louis's collection?

12. Deborah has two paintings in her portfolio and paints three more each week. Kai has twelve paintings in her portfolio and paints two more each week. After how many weeks will Deborah and Kai have the same number of paintings?

Name ______________________ Class ______________ Date ____________

3-7 • Guided Problem Solving

GPS Student Page 141, Exercise 17:

Efren leaves home at 9 A.M. and walks 4 miles per hour. His brother, Gregory, leaves half an hour later and runs 8.5 miles per hour in the same direction as Efren. Predict the time at which Gregory will catch up to Efren.

Understand

1. What is the distance formula? ______________________
2. What can you say about the distance each boy will have traveled when Gregory catches up to Efren? ______________________

____

Plan and Carry Out

3. Write an expression for the distance Gregory travels per hour. Let h stand for time in hours. ______________________
4. Write an expression for the distance Efren travels per hour plus the distance he will have traveled when Gregory leaves the house.

____

5. Write an equation setting the distance expressions in Steps 3 and 4 equal. ______________________
6. Solve for h. Use your answer to estimate the time at which Gregory will catch up to Efren. ______________________

____

____

Check

7. Solve the expressions in Steps 3 and 4 for your value of h. Are the distances equal? ______________________

____

Solve Another Problem

8. Roshonda begins riding her bike home from school at 3:00 P.M., traveling 12 miles per hour. James leaves school in a bus a quarter of an hour later and travels 35 miles per hour in the same direction. At about what time will James catch up to Roshonda?

____

____

Name ______________________ Class ____________ Date ____________

Practice 3-8

Types of Solutions of Linear Equations

Show whether each equation has one solution, infinitely many solutions, or no solution. Justify your answer.

1. $8c = 6 + 5c$

2. $2x + 7 = -8x - 9 + 10x$

3. $-2(b - 4) = -2b + 8$

4. $0.6(2h - 4) = 2.4 + 1.2h$

5. $-6a - 15 = -3(a - 7)$

6. $\frac{1}{2}(4z + \frac{1}{4}) = 2(z + \frac{1}{16})$

7. $3 - 7t = -5t + 3 - 2t$

8. $-3x + 6 = -3(x + 3)$

9. $4(0.8g + 1.5) = 2(3 + 1.6g)$

10. $1 + \frac{2}{3}w + \frac{1}{2} = 2w$

11. One restaurant offers two large pizzas for the same price as two medium pizzas and a $6 pitcher of drinks. The medium pizza costs $3 less than the large pizza. How much could a large pizza cost? Justify your answer.

12. Four less than a number equals four times the sum of a number and 2. Is this statement true for only one number, for all numbers, or for no numbers? Explain your reasoning.

Name ______________________ Class ______________ Date ______________

3-8 • Guided Problem Solving

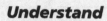

GPS Student Page 148, Exercise 20a:

Geometry Greg is buying fabric from a store. He has the choice of buying fabric that is 2 feet wide or 3 feet wide. The diagrams show how much fabric of each type he can buy for *d* dollars. For what value(s) of *d* is the perimeter of both choices the same?

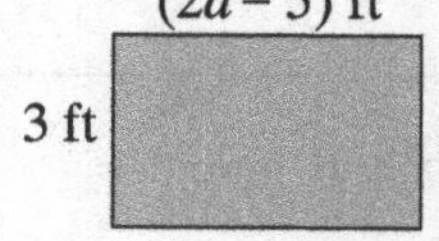

Understand

1. What is the formula for the perimeter of a rectangle?

____

2. What is it you are asked to find?

____

____

Plan and Carry Out

3. Write an expression for the perimeter of the 3-ft wide fabric.

____

4. Write an expression for the perimeter of the 2-ft wide fabric.

____

5. Write an equation setting the perimeter expressions in Steps 3 and 4 equal. ______________

6. Transform the equation into its simplest form. ______________

7. The lengths of the fabrics must be positive numbers of units. How does this affect the possible values of *d*? ______________

____

Check

8. Evaluate the expressions in Steps 3 and 4 for several different values of *d*. Are the perimeters equal? ______________

Solve Another Problem

9. For what value(s) of *s* is the perimeter of both isosceles triangles the same? ______________

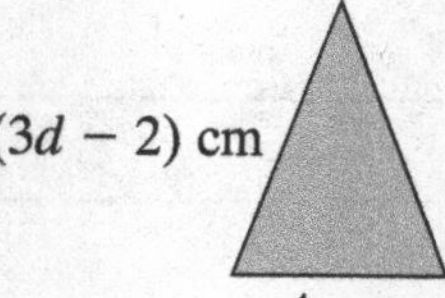

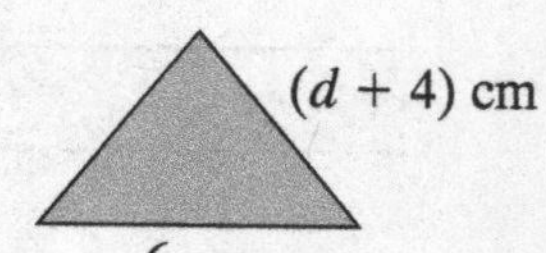

Name ______________________ Class ______________ Date ____________

3A: Graphic Organizer

For use before Lesson 3-1

Study Skill Develop consistent study habits. Block off the same amount of time each evening for schoolwork. Plan ahead by setting aside extra time when you have a big project or test coming up.

Write your answers.

1. What is the chapter title? ______________________
2. How many lessons are there in this chapter? ______________
3. What is the topic of the Test-Taking Strategies page? __________
4. Complete the graphic organizer below as you work through the chapter.
   - In the center, write the title of the chapter.
   - When you begin a lesson, write the lesson name in a rectangle.
   - When you complete a lesson, write a skill or key concept in a circle linked to that lesson block.
   - When you complete the chapter, use this graphic organizer to help you review.

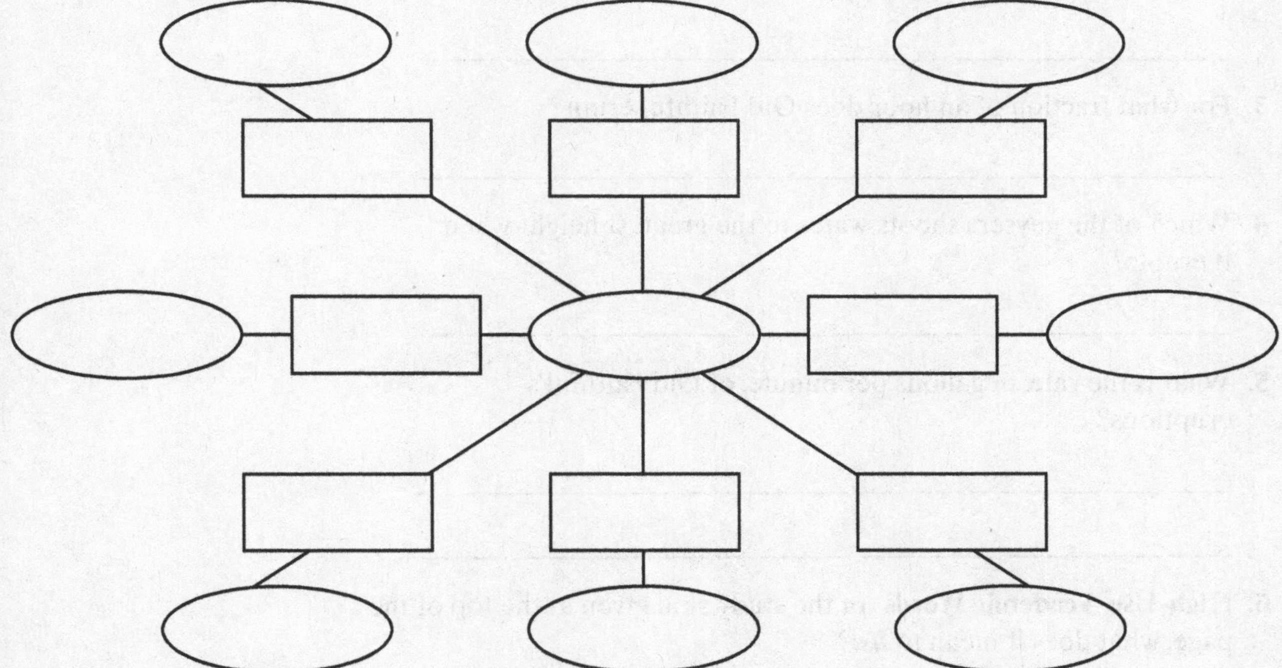

Vocabulary and Study Skills

Name ______________________ Class ______________ Date ______________

3B: Reading Comprehension

For use after Lesson 3-5

Study Skill Never go to class unprepared. List your assignments, books needed, and supplies to help you prepare.

Read the paragraph and answer the questions.

Old Faithful is the most famous geyser at Yellowstone National Park. It erupts approximately every $1\frac{1}{4}$ hours for up to 5 minutes. When it erupts, a mixture of water and steam shoots into the air as high as 170 feet. The amount of water expelled during each eruption ranges from 10,000 to 12,000 gallons. Giant Geyser and Steamboat Geyser, two other geysers at Yellowstone, shoot water to heights of 200 feet and 380 feet, respectively.

1. What is the paragraph about?

____

2. Which number in the paragraph is written as a mixed number?

____

3. For what fraction of an hour does Old Faithful erupt?

____

4. Which of the geysers shoots water to the greatest height when it erupts?

____

5. What is the rate, in gallons per minute, of Old Faithful's eruptions?

____

____

6. High-Use Academic Words In the study skill given at the top of the page, what does it mean to *list*?

a. to enumerate

b. to locate on a map

Name ______________________ Class ______________ Date ______________

3C: Reading/Writing Math Symbols For use after Lesson 3-1

Study Skill Mathematics builds on itself, so build a strong foundation.

Match each expression with its word form.

1. $x - 3$

2. $4m$

3. $\frac{7}{x}$

4. $m + 6$

5. $m \div 5$

A. six more than a number

B. the quotient of a number and five

C. a number decreased by three

D. seven divided by a number

E. four multiplied by a number

Write a mathematical expression for each word description.

6. nine less than the product of eleven and x

____

7. a number plus four minus thirteen

____

8. the quotient of x and 4

____

9. the absolute value of a number

____

Write two different word phrases for each of the following expressions.

10. $x - 10$

____

____

11. $5m$

____

____

12. $-8 + p$

____

____

Name _______________ Class _______________ Date _______________

3D: Visual Vocabulary Practice

For use after Lesson 3-3

Study Skill Making sense of mathematical symbols is like reading a foreign language that uses different letters.

Concept List

Addition Property of Equality	Subtraction Property of Equality
Division Property of Equality	Multiplication Property of Equality
variable	inverse operations
algebraic expression	like terms
coefficient	

Write the concept that best describes each exercise. Choose from the concept list above.

1. If $5 - y = 2 - 3y$, then $5 - y + 3y = 2 - 3y + 3y$. _______________	**2.** $t + 8$ $7r$ $3 - y$ _______________	**3.** $16n$ and $3n$ are; $18p$ and $27r$ are not _______________
4. z in the equation $\frac{2z}{5} = 12$ _______________	**5.** If $6 + w = 9w$, then $6 + w - w = 9w - w$. _______________	**6.** 4 in the equation $4x = 12$ _______________
7. If $5b = 3$, then $\frac{5b}{5} = \frac{3}{5}$. _______________	**8.** addition and subtraction represent this in $7x + 12 = 183$ $7x + 12 - 12 = 183$ _______________	**9.** If $3t \div 9 = 32$, then $3t \div 9 \cdot 9 = 32 \cdot 9$. _______________

Name ______________________ Class ______________ Date ____________

3E: Vocabulary Check

For use after Lesson 3-3

Study Skill Strengthen your vocabulary. Use these pages and add cues and summaries by applying the Cornell Notetaking style.

Write the definition for each word or term at the right. To check your work, fold the paper back along the dotted line to see the correct answers.

Definition	Term
______________________	variable
______________________	algebraic expression
______________________	like terms
______________________	coefficient
______________________	inverse operations

Vocabulary and Study Skills

Name ______________________ Class ______________ Date ______________

3E: Vocabulary Check (continued)

For use after Lesson 3-3

Write the vocabulary word or term for each definition. To check your work, fold the paper forward along the dotted line to see the correct answers.

a symbol that represents one or more numbers ______________________

a mathematical expression with at least one variable ______________________

terms that have the same variable factors ______________________

a numerical factor of a term with a variable ______________________

operations that undo each other ______________________

Name ______________________ Class ______________ Date ______________

3F: Vocabulary Review Puzzle

For use with the Chapter Review

Study Skill Use a notebook or a section of a loose-leaf binder for math assignments. Review problems that gave you trouble.

Unscramble each of the key words from the chapter to help you fill in the famous quote by Walt Disney. Match the letters in the numbered cells with the numbered cells at the bottom.

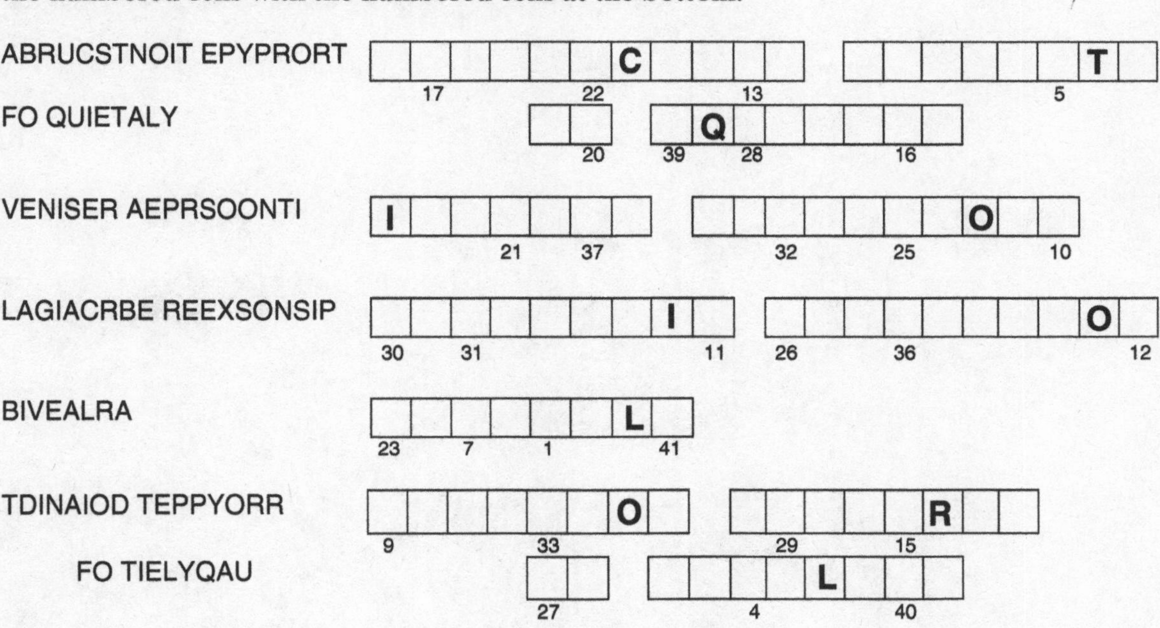

IICEOEFTNCF

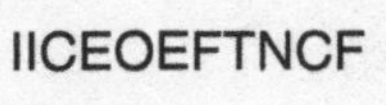

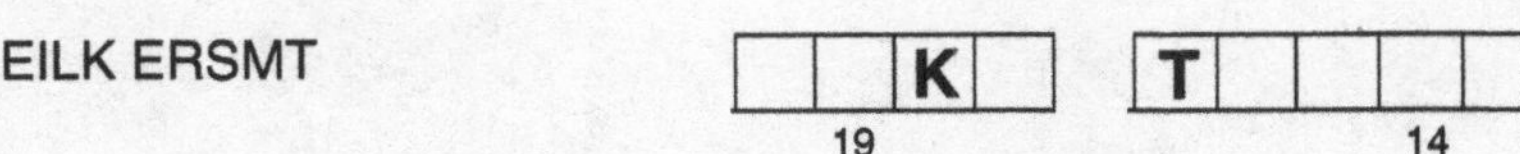

EILK ERSMT

IDNOSIIV ERPYROPT FO EUIYQTAL

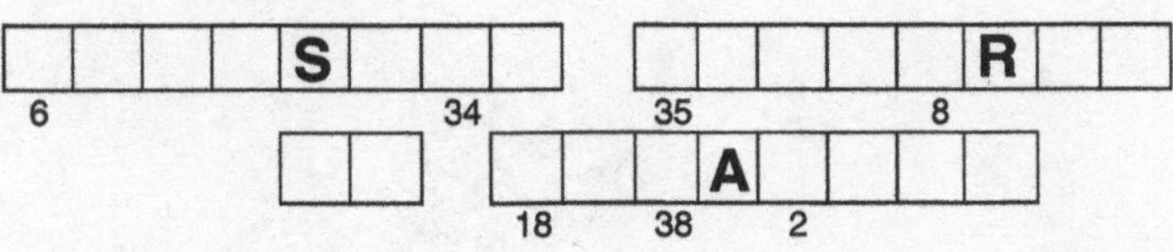

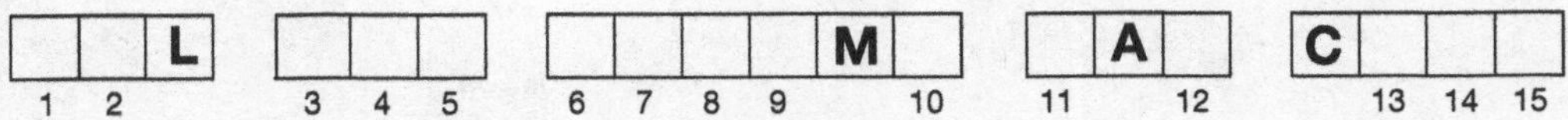

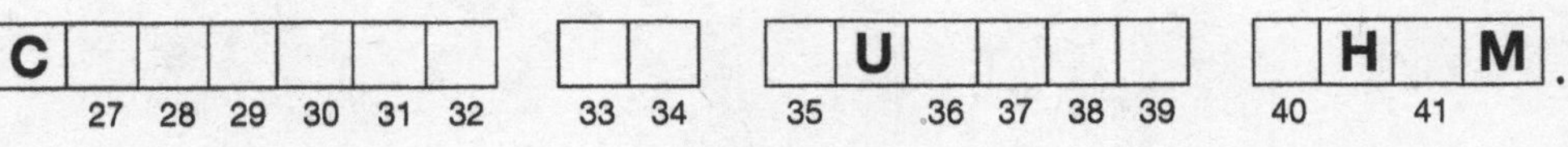

Vocabulary and Study Skills

Name ____________________ Class ____________ Date ____________

Practice 4-1

Graphing and Writing Inequalities

Graph the solution of each inequality on a number line.

1. $x \leq 3$

x: −4 −3 −2 −1 0 1 2 3 4

2. $t > 1$

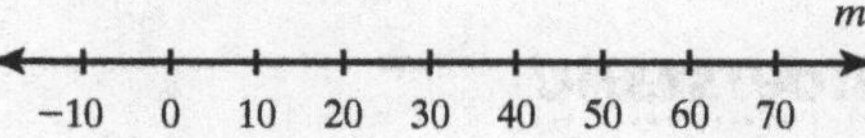

3. $q \geq -10$

q: −20 −10 0 10 20

4. $m < 50$

m: −10 0 10 20 30 40 50 60 70

For each inequality, tell whether the number in bold is a solution.

5. $x < 7$; **7** ____________

6. $p > -3$; **3** ____________

7. $k \geq 5$; **0** ____________

8. $3z \leq 12$; **4** ____________

9. $n - 5 > 3$; **6** ____________

10. $2g + 8 \geq 3$; **−1** ____________

Write an inequality for each graph.

11. ____________________

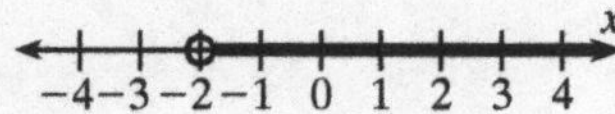

12. ____________________

z: −10 0 10 20 30 40 50 60 70

Write an inequality for each statement. Graph each solution on the number line shown.

13. You can walk there in 20 minutes or less.

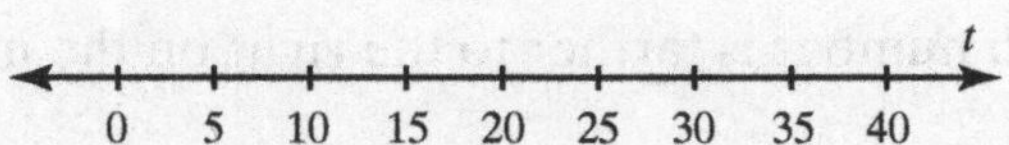

____

14. Each prize is worth over $150.

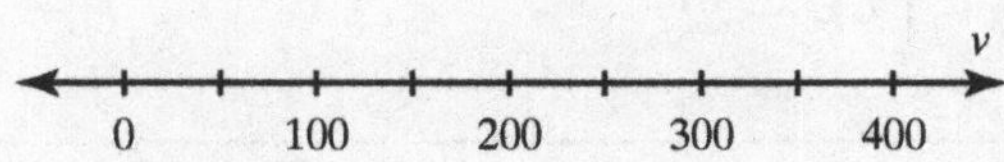

____

15. A species of catfish, *malapterurus electricus*, can generate up to 350 volts of electricity.

a. Write an inequality to represent the amount of electricity generated by the catfish.

____

b. Draw a graph of the inequality you wrote in **a.**

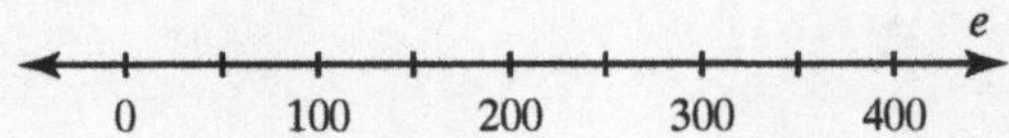

Name ____________________ Class ____________________ Date ____________________

4-1 • Guided Problem Solving

Student Page 159, Exercise 30:

Reasoning Explain why $-17 > -22$.

Understand

1. What are you being asked to do?

____

____

2. What visual representation can you use to help your explanation?

____

Plan and Carry Out

3. Graph -17 on a number line.

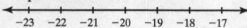

−23 −22 −21 −20 −19 −18 −17

4. Graph -22 on the same number line.

5. Which number is farther to the right on the number line?

____

6. Why is $-17 > -22$?

____

____

Check

7. Which mathematical definition did you use to explain that $-17 > -22$?

____

____

Solve Another Problem

8. Explain why $-8 < -5$.

____

____

Name ______________________ Class ______________ Date ____________

Practice 4-2

Solving Inequalities by Adding or Subtracting

Solve each inequality. Graph each solution.

1. $w + 4 < -2$

____

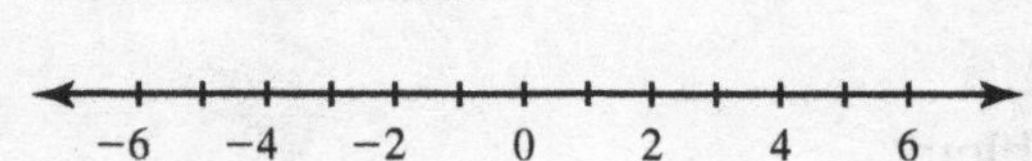

2. $a - 4 \geq 0$

____

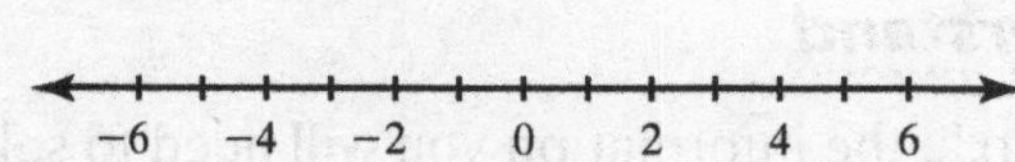

3. $a + 19 > 13$

____

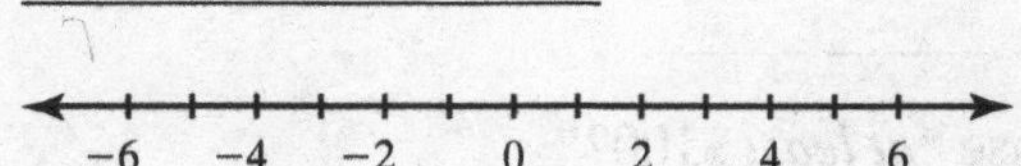

4. $x + 7 \leq 12$

____

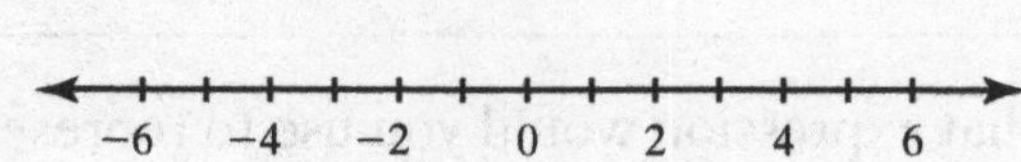

5. $a + 2 > -3$

____

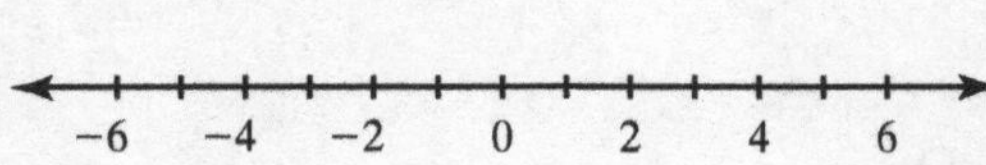

6. $t - 6 < 3$

____

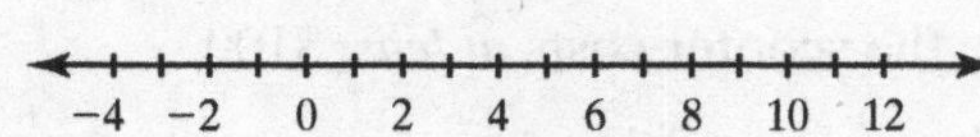

7. $r - 3.4 \leq 2.6$

____

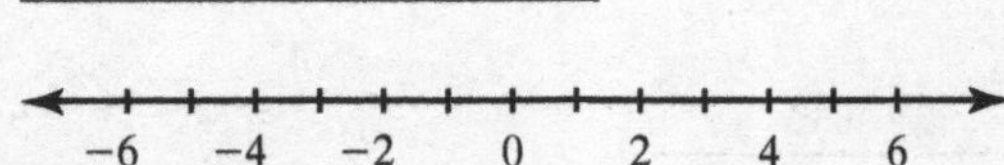

8. $a + 5.7 \geq -2.3$

____

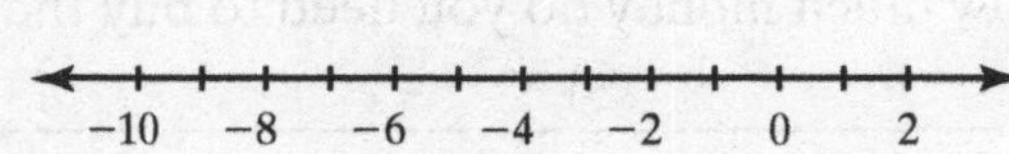

9. $h - 4.9 > -0.9$

____

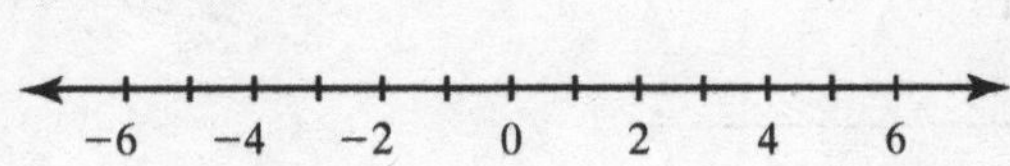

10. $y + 3.4 < -4.6$

____

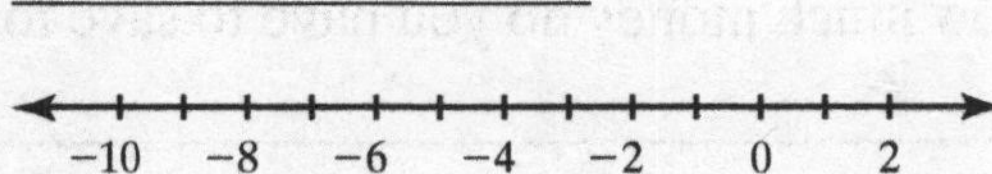

Write an inequality for each problem. Solve the inequality.

11. The school record for the most points scored in a football season is 85. Lawrence has 44 points so far this season. How many more points does he need to break the record?

____

____

____

12. The maximum weight limit for a fully loaded truck is 16,000 pounds. The truck you are loading currently weighs 12,500 pounds. How much more weight can be added and not exceed the weight limit?

____

____

Name ______________________ Class ______________ Date ____________

4-2 • Guided Problem Solving

GPS Student Page 162, Exercise 27:

Consumer Issues Your parents give you $35 for a scooter that costs at least $100. How much money do you have to save to buy the scooter?

Understand

1. Circle the information you will need to solve this problem.
2. What are you being asked to do?

   ____

   ____

3. What expression would you use to represent the phrase "*at least* $100?"

   ____

Plan and Carry Out

Suppose the scooter costs *at least* $100.

4. Write an expression for the amount of money you need to save, *s*, plus the amount of money your parents will give you.

   ____

5. How much money do you need to buy the scooter?

   ____

6. Write an inequality to solve for *s*. ______________________
7. Solve the inequality. ______________________
8. How much money do you have to save for the scooter?

   ____

Check

9. If you save $65, how much money will you have?

   ____

Solve Another Problem

10. You have to be at least 42 in. tall to ride the big roller coasters at the amusement park. You are 36 in. tall right now. How much more do you have to grow? Write and solve an inequality.

    ____

Name ________________ Class ________________ Date ________________

Practice 4-3

Solving Inequalities by Multiplying or Dividing

Solve each inequality. Graph each solution.

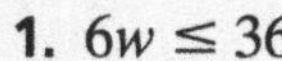

1. $6w \leq 36$

____

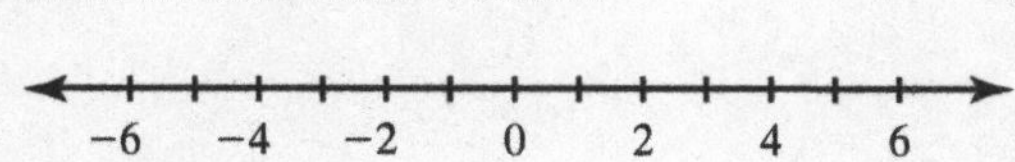

2. $10a \geq 40$

____

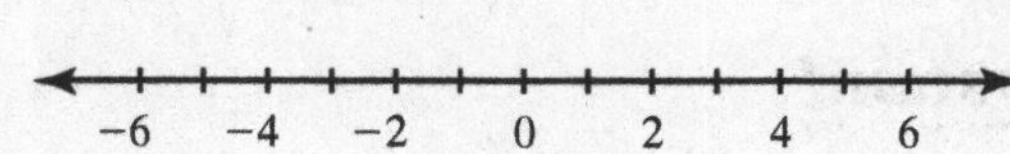

3. $\frac{f}{3} \leq -2$

____

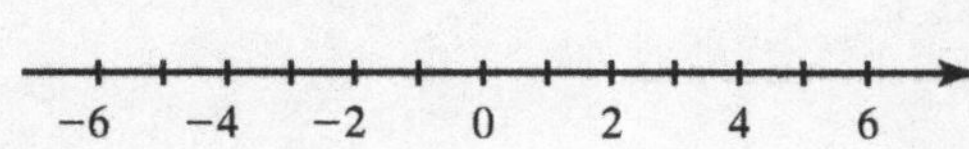

4. $\frac{v}{4} > 2$

____

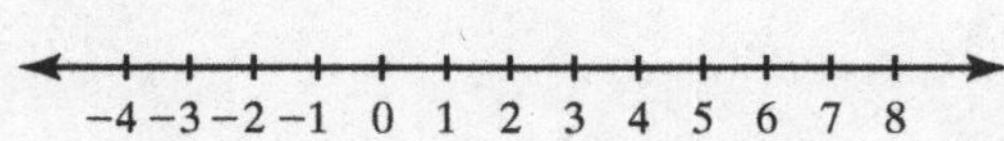

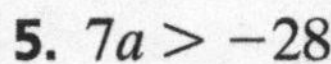

5. $7a > -28$

____

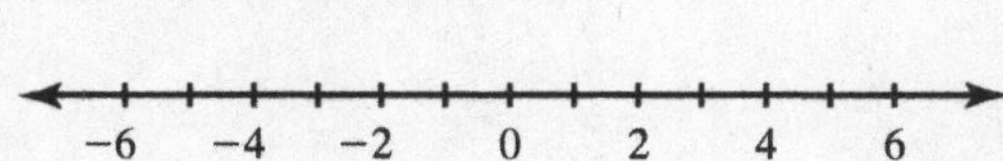

6. $-\frac{c}{3} \geq 3$

____

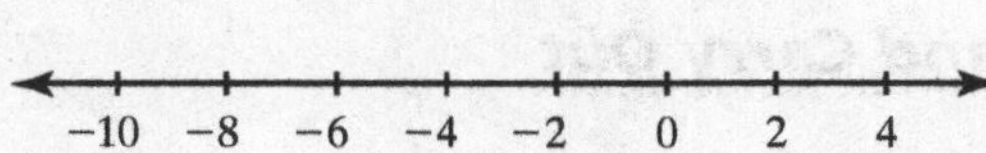

7. $\frac{f}{2} > -1$

____

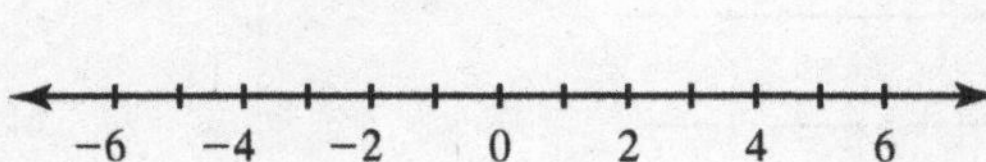

8. $9a \leq 63$

____

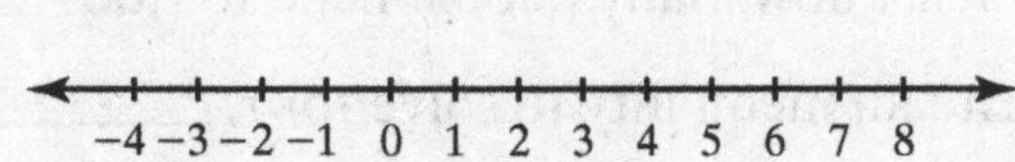

9. $4w \geq -12$

____

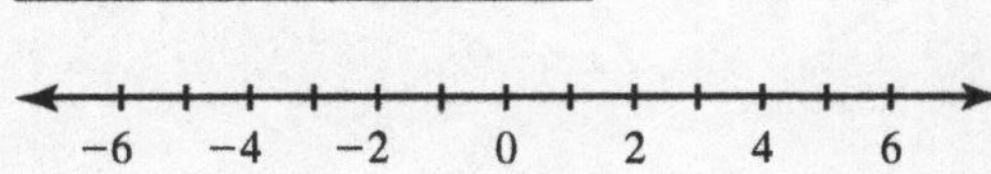

10. $-\frac{h}{2} \geq -5$

____

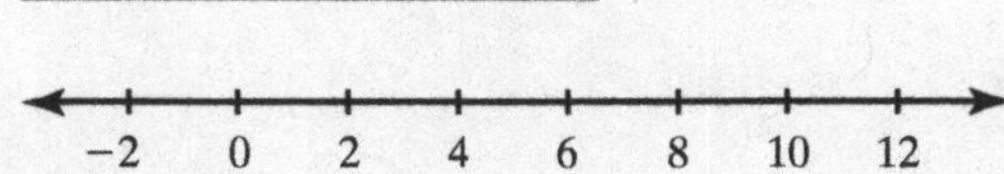

Write an inequality to solve each problem. Then solve the inequality.

11. Marcus wants to buy 5 baseballs. He has \$35. What is the most each baseball can cost?

____

____

____

12. Melinda charges \$4 per hour for babysitting. Mrs. Garden does not want to spend more than \$25 for babysitting. What is the maximum number of hours that she can have Melinda babysit?

____

____

____

Name ______________________ Class ______________ Date ______________

3-3 • Guided Problem Solving

GPS Student Page 168, Exercise 23:

Rides A roller coaster can carry 36 people per run. How many times does the roller coaster have to run to allow at least 10,000 people to ride?

Understand

1. Circle the information you will need to solve this problem.
2. What are you being asked to do?

   ____

   ____

3. What symbol would you use to represent the phrase *at least 10,000 people*?

   ____

Plan and Carry Out

4. Write an expression for the maximum number of people who could ride the roller coaster in *r* runs.

   ____

5. At least how many people need to ride? ______________
6. Write an inequality to solve for *r*. ______________
7. Solve the inequality. ______________
8. How many times does the roller coaster need to run?

   ____

Check

9. If the roller coaster runs 278 times, how many people will it have carried? Use a calculator to check your answer.

   ____

Solve Another Problem

10. Chicken is on sale for $1.99 per pound. The most you can spend is $20, and you must buy a whole number of pounds. How many pounds of chicken can you buy?

    ____

Name ______________________ Class ______________ Date ______________

Practice 4-4

Solving Two-Step Inequalities

Solve each inequality. Graph the solution. Write your answer in simplest form.

1. $-3 + 5n > -13$

2. $4 \geq \frac{z}{3} - 1$

3. $6 - 4b \leq 14$

4. $5t + 2 < 7$

5. $\frac{s}{4} + 3 \geq 9$

6. $-7b + 2 < 16$

Solve each inequality. Circle the letter of the inequality that is represented by each graph.

7. 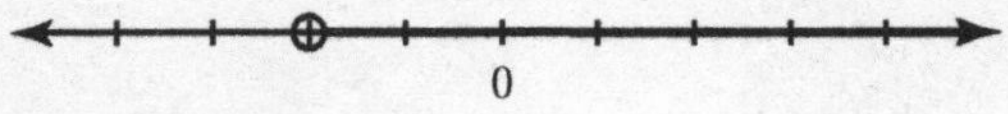

A. $4d - 3 < 9$

B. $-2d + 4 < 8$

8. 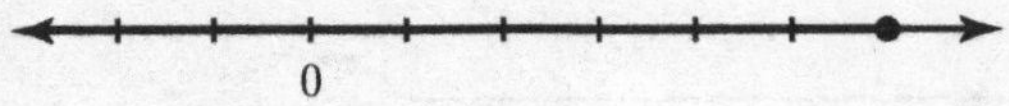

A. $6 - 1.5x \geq -3$

B. $-2.4x + 3.2 \geq -4$

9. Tasha gets $7.50 every week for walking the neighbor's dog daily. She also makes and sells bracelets for $2.50 each. She wants to earn at least $25 this week as vacation money. Write an inequality to find the number of bracelets she needs to make. Graph and describe the solutions.

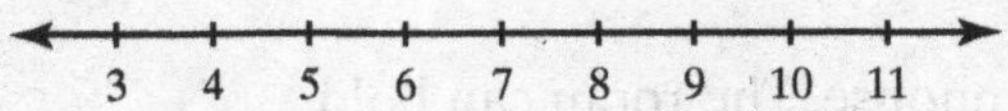

Name ____________________ Class ____________ Date ____________

4-4 • Guided Problem Solving

GPS Student Page 175, Exercise 27:

Event Planning A play is being presented in a school gymnasium that can hold a maximum of 600 people. One hundred twenty people can sit on the bleachers. Chairs will be set up in 15 equal rows. Describe the number of chairs that can be in each row.

Understand

1. Circle the information you will need to solve the problem.
2. What are you being asked to do? ____________________

Plan and Carry Out

3. What is the maximum number of people you must plan for? ____________________
4. Write an expression to show the number of chairs in each row, *c*. ____________________
5. How many people can sit on the bleachers? ____________________
6. What inequality can you use to solve for *c*? ____________________
7. How many chairs will be placed in each row? ____________________

Check

8. Explain why your answer is correct. ____________________

Solve Another Problem

9. Scott plans to fill an empty room in his greenhouse. The room can hold a maximum of 80 plants. Twenty plants can be hung from the ceiling racks. The rest of the plants can be placed in 4 equal rows on the table. Describe the number of plants that can be in each row.

____

Name ______________________ Class ______________ Date ______________

4A: Graphic Organizer

For use before Lesson 4-1

Study Skill You should fully understand the basic concepts in each chapter before moving on to more complex material. Be sure to ask questions when you are not comfortable with what you have learned.

Write your answers.

1. What is the chapter title? ______________________
2. How many lessons are there in this chapter? ______________________
3. What is the topic of the Test-Taking Strategies page? ______________________
4. Complete the graphic organizer below as you work through the chapter.
   - In the center, write the title of the chapter.
   - When you begin a lesson, write the lesson name in a rectangle.
   - When you complete a lesson, write a skill or key concept in a circle linked to that lesson block.
   - When you complete the chapter, use this graphic organizer to help you review.

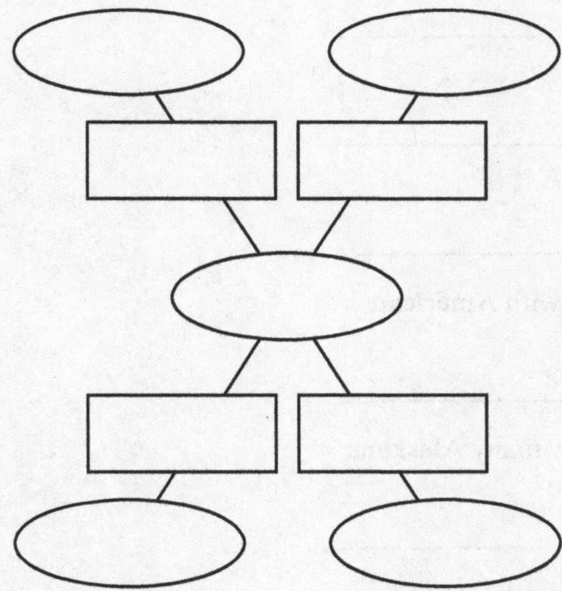

Vocabulary and Study Skills

Name ______________________ Class ______________ Date ______________

4B: Reading Comprehension

For use after Lesson 4-2

Study Skill As you learn more vocabulary, more concepts are within your reach.

Read the paragraph below and answer the questions that follow.

November is American Indian and Alaska Native Heritage Month. According to the U.S. Census Bureau, more than 4 million people in the United States identified themselves as American Indian or Alaska native in 2004. That is 1.5% of the total U.S. population. About 687,000 people with this heritage live in California, giving it the largest American Indian and Alaska native population of any state. However, $\frac{1}{5}$ of the Alaska population is American Indian or Alaska native. This is a much greater fraction than in California.

1. What is the subject of this paragraph?

____

____

2. What is the largest number in the paragraph?

____

3. What is the smallest number?

____

4. Which state has the greatest number of people with American Indian and Alaska native ancestry?

____

5. The population of Alaska is about 665,000. How many Alaskans have American Indian or Alaska native heritage?

____

6. Explain how California can have the greatest population but not the largest fraction of people with this ancestry.

____

7. **High-Use Academic Words** In Exercise 6, what does the word *explain* mean?

   a. to put or use in place of something else

   b. to give facts and details that make an idea easier to understand

Name ______________________ Class ______________ Date ____________

4C: Reading/Writing Math Symbols

For use after Lesson 4-3

Study Skill Read problems carefully. Pay special attention to units when working with measurements.

Match the abbreviation in Column A with the name of the unit in Column B.

Column A	Column B
1. 1b	**A.** mile
2. in.	**B.** pound
3. mi	**C.** calorie
4. s	**D.** gram
5. min	**E.** meter
6. cal	**F.** inch
7. g	**G.** minute
8. m	**H.** second

Describe what the symbol on each number line means.

9. 

10. 10

______________________ ______________________

11. 

12. 10

______________________ ______________________

Name ______________________ Class ______________ Date ______________

4D: Visual Vocabulary Practice

For use after Lesson 4-3

Study Skill Making sense of mathematical symbols is like reading a foreign language that uses different letters.

Concept List

Addition Property of Inequality	Subtraction Property of Inequality
Division Property of Inequality	Multiplication Property of Inequality
reciprocal	quotient
product	solution of an inequality
inequality	

Write the concept that best describes each exercise. Choose from the concept list above.

1. If $6x > 84$, then $\frac{6x}{6} > \frac{84}{6}$. ______________	**2.** $8 + x \geq 2x$ ______________	**3.** 15 in the equation $x \div 7 = 15$. 27 in the equation $\frac{m}{8} = 27$. ______________
4. For $\frac{1}{7}$, it is 7. For $\frac{8}{3}$, it is $\frac{3}{8}$. For 9, it is $\frac{1}{9}$. ______________	**5.** If $7m < 1 + 2m$, then $7m - 2m < 1 + 2m - 2m$. ______________	**6.** For 7 and 12, it is 84. For 14 and x, it is $14x$. ______________
7. In $x - 27 > 41$, then $x - 27 + 27 > 41 + 27$. ______________	**8.** $-2x + 1 < 4$ $-2x < 3$ $x > -\frac{3}{2}$ 0 represents this for $-2x + 1 < 4$. ______________	**9.** If $\frac{1}{9}z < 8$, then $9 \times (\frac{1}{9}z) < 9 \times 8$. ______________

Name ____________________ Class ______________ Date ____________

4E: Vocabulary Check

For use after Lesson 4-4

Study Skill Strengthen your vocabulary. Use these pages and add cues and summaries by applying the Cornell Notetaking style.

Write the definition for each word or term at the right. To check your work, fold the paper back along the dotted line to see the correct answers.

____________________ quotient

____________________ inequality

____________________ reciprocals

____________________ product

____________________ compound inequality

Name ______________________ Class ______________ Date ______________

4E: Vocabulary Check (continued)

For use after Lesson 4-4

Write the definition for each word or term at the right. To check your work, fold the paper forward along the dotted line to see the correct answers.

the solution to a division sentence ______________________

a mathematical sentence that contains $<, >, \leq, \geq$, or $\neq$ ______________________

two numbers whose product is 1 ______________________

the solution to a multiplication sentence ______________________

a number sentence with more than one inequality symbol ______________________

Name ______________________ Class ______________ Date ______________

4F: Vocabulary Review

For use with the Chapter Review

Study Skill Review notes that you have taken in class as soon as possible to clarify any points you missed and to refresh your memory.

Vocabulary and Study Skills

Circle the word that best completes the sentence.

1. A mathematical statement that contains $<$ or $>$ is called an (*equation, inequality*).
2. You use the (*Addition, Multiplication*) Property of Inequality if you add the same value to each side of an inequality.
3. Two numbers are (*inverses, reciprocals*) if their product is 1.
4. The solution to a division sentence is a (*quotient, divisor*).
5. If you use the (*Division, Subtraction*) Property of Inequality with a negative number, the direction of the inequality symbol is reversed.
6. You can use the (*Multiplication, Addition*) Property of Inequality to solve the inequality $m \div 6 < 29$.
7. You use the (*Subtraction, Division*) Property of Inequality if you take away the same value from each side of an inequality.
8. To solve an inequality involving addition, you use (*subtraction, reciprocals*).
9. When solving a two-step inequality, you need to get the (*variable, reciprocal*) along on one side of the inequality.
10. A (*variable, solution*) of an inequality is any value that makes the inequality true.
11. A number sentence is a (*compound, rational*) inequality if it has more than one inequality symbol.
12. The solution to a multiplication sentence is a (*product, difference*).

Name ______________________ Class ______________ Date ______________

Practice 5-1

Ratios

Write a ratio for each situation in three ways.

1. Ten years ago in Louisiana, schools averaged 182 pupils for every 10 teachers.

____

2. Between 1899 and 1900, 284 out of 1,000 people in the United States were 5–17 years old.

____

Use the chart below for Exercises 3–4.

Three seventh-grade classes were asked whether they wanted chicken or pasta served at their awards banquet.

Room Number	Chicken	Pasta
201	10	12
202	8	17
203	16	10

3. In room 201, what is the ratio of students who prefer chicken to students who prefer pasta?

____

4. Combine the totals for all three rooms. What is the ratio of the number of students who prefer pasta to the number of students who prefer chicken?

____

Write each ratio as a fraction in simplest form.

5. 12 to 18 ________ 6. 81 : 27 ________ 7. $\frac{6}{28}$ ________

Tell whether the ratios are *equivalent* or *not equivalent*.

8. 12 : 24, 50 : 100 ______________________

9. $\frac{22}{1}, \frac{1}{22}$ ______________________

10. 2 to 3, 24 to 36 ______________________

11. A bag contains green, yellow, and orange marbles. The ratio of green marbles to yellow marbles is 2 : 5. The ratio of yellow marbles to orange marbles is 3 : 4. What is the ratio of green marbles to orange marbles?

____

Name ____________________ Class ____________ Date ____________

5-1 • Guided Problem Solving

GPS Student Page 186, Exercise 27:

Cooking To make pancakes, you need 2 cups of water for every 3 cups of flour. Write an equivalent ratio to find how much water you will need with 9 cups of flour.

Understand

1. Circle the information you will need to solve.
2. What are you being asked to do?

 ____

 ____

3. Why will a ratio help you to solve the problem?

 ____

 ____

 ____

Plan and Carry Out

4. What is the ratio of the cups of water to the cups of flour? ____________
5. How many cups of flour are you using? ____________
6. Write an equivalent ratio to use 9 cups of flour. ____________
7. How many cups of water are needed for 9 cups of flour? ____________

Check

8. Why is the number of cups of water triple the number of cups needed for 3 cups of flour?

 ____

 ____

Solve Another Problem

9. Rebecca is laying tile in her bathroom. She needs 4 black tiles for every 16 white tiles. How many black tiles are needed if she uses 128 white tiles?

 ____

Name ______________________ Class ______________ Date ______________

Practice 5-2

Unit Rates and Proportional Reasoning

Write the unit rate for each situation.

1. travel 250 mi in 5 h

2. earn $75.20 in 8 h

3. read 80 pages in 2 h

4. type 8,580 words in 2 h 45 min

5. complete $\frac{3}{4}$ of a puzzle in $\frac{7}{8}$ h

6. drink $\frac{4}{5}$ L in $\frac{1}{4}$ h

Find each unit price. Then determine the better buy.

7. paper: 100 sheets for $.99
   500 sheets for $4.29

8. peanuts: 1 lb for $1.29
   12 oz for $.95

9. crackers: 15 oz for $1.79
   12 oz for $1.49

10. apples: 3 lb for $1.89
    5 lb for $2.49

11. mechanical pencils: 4 for $1.25
    25 for $5.69

12. bagels: 4 for $.89
    6 for $1.39

13. a. Yolanda and Yoko ran in a 100-yd dash. When Yolanda crossed the finish line, Yoko was 10 yd behind her. The girls then repeated the race, with Yolanda starting 10 yd behind the starting line. If each girl ran at the same rate as before, who won the race? By how many yards?

    b. Assuming the girls run at the same rate as before, how far behind the starting line should Yolanda be in order for the two to finish in a tie?

Name ______________________ Class ______________________ Date ______________

5-2 • Guided Problem Solving

GPS Student Page 191, Exercise 27a:

Geography Population density is the number of people per unit of area. Alaska has the lowest population density of any state in the United States. It has 626,932 people in 570,374 mi^2. What is its population density? Round to the nearest person per square mile.

Understand

1. What is *population density*?

   ____

   ____

2. What are you being asked to do?

   ____

3. What does the phrase *people per unit of area* imply?

   ____

   ____

   ____

Plan and Carry Out

4. What is the population of Alaska? ______________
5. What is the area of Alaska? ______________
6. Write a division expression for the population density. ______________
7. What is its population density? ______________
8. Round to the nearest person per square mile. ______________

Check

9. Why is the population density only about 1 person/mi^2?

   ____

   ____

Solve Another Problem

10. Mr. Boyle is buying pizza for the percussion band. The bill is $56.82 for 5 pizzas. If there are 12 members of the band, how much does the pizza cost per member? Round to the nearest cent.

    ____

Name ______________________ Class ______________ Date ______________

Practice 5-3

Proportions

Determine if the ratios in each pair are proportional.

1. $\frac{12}{16}, \frac{30}{40}$ ________
2. $\frac{8}{12}, \frac{15}{21}$ ________
3. $\frac{27}{21}, \frac{81}{56}$ ________
4. $\frac{45}{24}, \frac{75}{40}$ ________
5. $\frac{5}{9}, \frac{80}{117}$ ________
6. $\frac{15}{25}, \frac{75}{125}$ ________
7. $\frac{2}{14}, \frac{20}{35}$ ________
8. $\frac{9}{6}, \frac{21}{14}$ ________
9. $\frac{24}{15}, \frac{16}{10}$ ________
10. $\frac{3}{4}, \frac{8}{10}$ ________
11. $\frac{20}{4}, \frac{17}{3}$ ________
12. $\frac{25}{6}, \frac{9}{8}$ ________

Decide if each pair of ratios is proportional.

13. $\frac{14}{10} \stackrel{?}{=} \frac{9}{7}$ ________
14. $\frac{18}{8} \stackrel{?}{=} \frac{36}{16}$ ________
15. $\frac{6}{10} \stackrel{?}{=} \frac{15}{25}$ ________
16. $\frac{7}{16} \stackrel{?}{=} \frac{4}{9}$ ________
17. $\frac{6}{4} \stackrel{?}{=} \frac{12}{8}$ ________
18. $\frac{19}{3} \stackrel{?}{=} \frac{114}{8}$ ________
19. $\frac{5}{14} \stackrel{?}{=} \frac{6}{15}$ ________
20. $\frac{6}{27} \stackrel{?}{=} \frac{8}{36}$ ________
21. $\frac{27}{15} \stackrel{?}{=} \frac{45}{25}$ ________
22. $\frac{3}{18} \stackrel{?}{=} \frac{4}{20}$ ________
23. $\frac{5}{2} \stackrel{?}{=} \frac{15}{6}$ ________
24. $\frac{20}{15} \stackrel{?}{=} \frac{4}{3}$ ________

Solve.

25. During the breaststroke competitions of the 1992 Olympics, Nelson Diebel swam 100 meters in 62 seconds, and Mike Bowerman swam 200 meters in 130 seconds. Are the rates proportional?

____

26. During a vacation, the Vasquez family traveled 174 miles in 3 hours on Monday, and 290 miles in 5 hours on Tuesday. Are the rates proportional?

____

Name ____________ Class ____________ Date ____________

5-3 • Guided Problem Solving

GPS Student Page 195, Exercise 29:

Decorating A certain shade of green paint requires 4 parts blue to 5 parts yellow. If you mix 16 quarts of blue paint with 25 quarts of yellow paint, will you get the desired shade of green? Explain.

Understand

1. Circle the information you will need to solve.
2. What are you being asked to do?

 ____

 ____

3. Will a ratio help you to solve the problem? Explain.

 ____

 ____

Plan and Carry Out

4. What is the ratio of blue parts to yellow parts? ____________
5. What is the ratio of blue quarts to yellow quarts? ____________
6. Check to see if the cross products of the two ratios are equal.

 ____

7. Are the ratios the same? ____________
8. Will you get the desired shade of green? Explain.

 ____

Check

9. How do you know that the ratios are not the same?

 ____

Solve Another Problem

10. There are 15 boys and 12 girls in your math class. There are 5 boys and 3 girls in your study group. Determine if the boy to girl ratio is the same in study group as it is in your math class. Explain.

 ____

 ____

Name ______________________ Class ______________ Date ______________

Practice 5-4

Solving Proportions

Use mental math to solve for each value of *n*.

1. $\frac{n}{14} = \frac{20}{35}$ ______________
2. $\frac{9}{6} = \frac{21}{n}$ ______________
3. $\frac{24}{n} = \frac{16}{10}$ ______________
4. $\frac{3}{4} = \frac{n}{10}$ ______________

Solve each proportion using cross products.

5. $\frac{k}{8} = \frac{14}{4}$ $k =$ ______________
6. $\frac{u}{3} = \frac{10}{5}$ $u =$ ______________
7. $\frac{14}{6} = \frac{d}{15}$ $d =$ ______________
8. $\frac{5}{1} = \frac{m}{4}$ $m =$ ______________
9. $\frac{36}{32} = \frac{n}{8}$ $n =$ ______________
10. $\frac{5}{30} = \frac{1}{x}$ $x =$ ______________
11. $\frac{t}{4} = \frac{5}{10}$ $t =$ ______________
12. $\frac{9}{2} = \frac{v}{4}$ $v =$ ______________

Solve.

13. A contractor estimates it will cost $2,400 to build a deck to a customer's specifications. How much would it cost to build five similar decks?

    ____

14. A recipe requires 3 c of flour to make 27 dinner rolls. How much flour is needed to make 9 rolls?

    ____

Solve using a calculator, paper and pencil, or mental math.

15. Mandy runs 4 km in 18 min. She plans to run in a 15 km race. How long will it take her to complete the race?

    ____

16. Ken's new car can go 26 miles per gallon of gasoline. The car's gasoline tank holds 14 gal. How far will he be able to go on a full tank?

    ____

17. Eleanor can complete two skirts in 15 days. How long will it take her to complete eight skirts?

    ____

18. Three eggs are required to make two dozen muffins. How many eggs are needed to make 12 dozen muffins?

    ____

Name ______________________ Class ______________ Date ________

5-4 • Guided Problem Solving

GPS Student Page 202, Exercise 28:

There are 450 students and 15 teachers in a school. The school hires 2 new teachers. To keep the student-to-teacher ratio the same, how many students in all should attend the school?

Understand

1. What are you being asked to do?

____

____

2. Will a proportion help you to solve the problem? Explain.

____

____

____

Plan and Carry Out

3. Write a ratio for the current student-to-teacher ratio. ________
4. Write a ratio for the new student-to-teacher ratio. ________
5. Write a proportion using the ratios in Steps 3 and 4. ________
6. How many total students should attend the school?

____

Check

7. Are the two ratios equivalent? Explain.

____

____

Solve Another Problem

8. There are 6 black marbles and 4 red marbles in a jar. If you add 4 red marbles to the jar, how many black marbles do you need to add to keep the ratio of black marbles to red marbles the same?

____

Name ______________________ Class ______________ Date ______________

Practice 5-5

Similar Figures

$\triangle MNO \sim \triangle JKL$. Complete each statement.

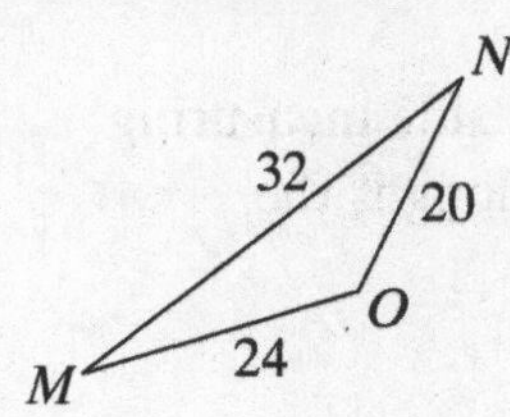

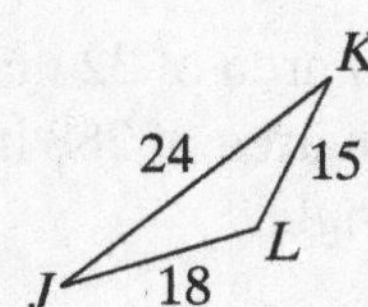

1. $\angle M$ corresponds to ______________.
2. $\angle L$ corresponds to ______________.
3. $\overline{JL}$ corresponds to ______________.
4. $\overline{MN}$ corresponds to ______________.
5. What is the ratio of the lengths of the corresponding sides? ______________

The pairs of figures below are similar. Find the value of each variable.

6. 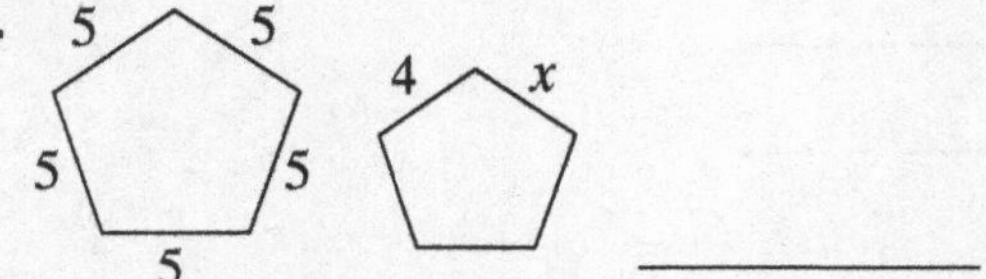

____

7. 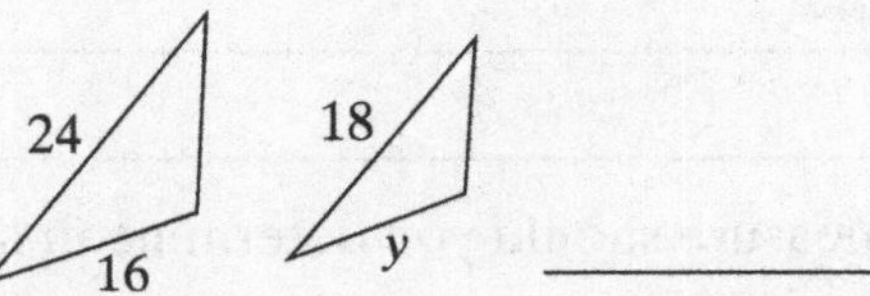

____

8. 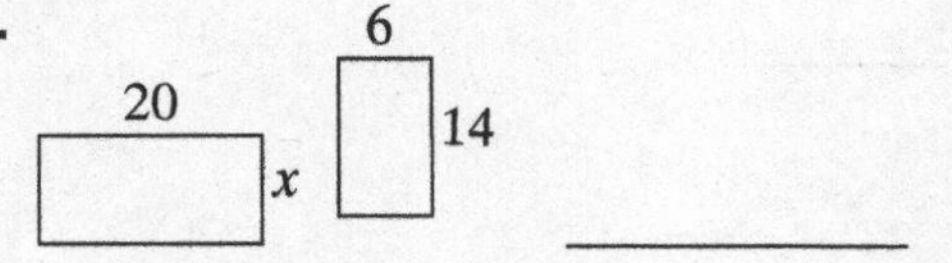

____

9. 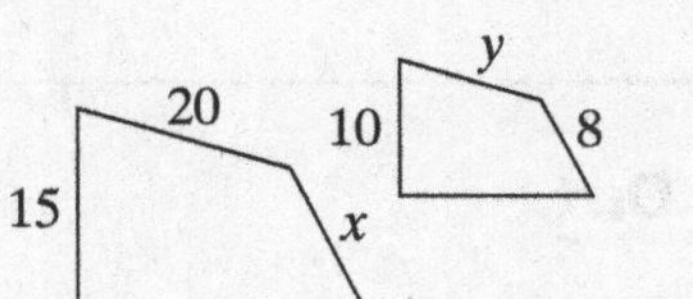

____

10. 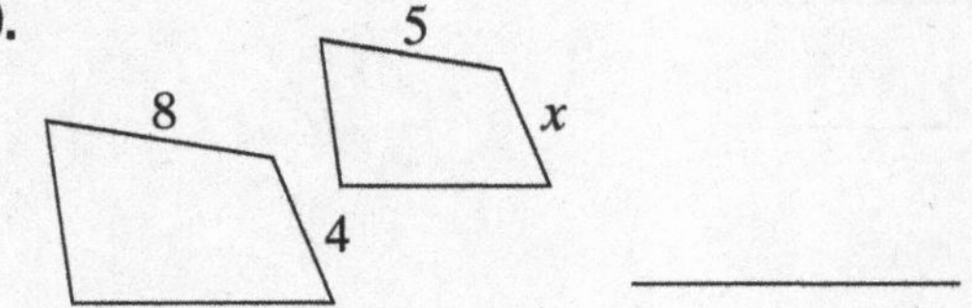

____

11. 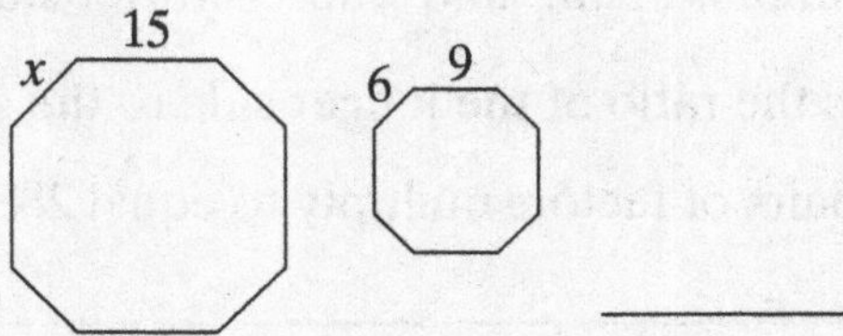

____

12. On a sunny day, if a 36-inch yardstick casts a 21-inch shadow, how tall is a building whose shadow is 168 ft?

____

13. Oregon is about 400 miles from west to east, and 300 miles from north to south. If a map of Oregon is 15 inches tall (from north to south), about how wide is the map?

____

Name ______________________ Class ______________ Date ______________

5-5 • Guided Problem Solving

GPS Student Page 209, Exercise 13:

Geometry A rectangle with an area of 32 in^2 has one side measuring 4 in. A similar rectangle has an area of 288 in^2. How long is the longer side in the larger rectangle?

Understand

1. What are you being asked to do?

 ____

2. Will a proportion that equates the ratio of the areas to the ratio of the shorter sides result in the desired answer? Explain.

 ____

 ____

 ____

3. What measure should you determine first?

 ____

 ____

Plan and Carry Out

4. What is the length of the longer side of the rectangle whose area is 32 $in.^2$ and whose shorter side is 4 in.? ________

5. What is the ratio of the longer side to the shorter side? ________

6. What pairs of factors multiply to equal 288?

 ____

7. Which pair of factors has a ratio of $\frac{2}{1}$? ________

8. What is the length of the longer side? ________

Check

9. Why must the ratio between the factors be $\frac{2}{1}$?

 ____

 ____

Solve Another Problem

10. A triangle with perimeter 26 in. has two sides that are 8 in. long. What is the length of the third side of a similar triangle which has two sides that are 12 in. long? ________

Name ____________________ Class ____________ Date ____________

Practice 5-6

Maps and Scale Drawings

The scale of a map is 2 cm : 21 km. Find the actual distances for the following map distances.

1. 9 cm ________
2. 12.5 cm ________
3. 14 mm ________
4. 3.6 m ________
5. 4.5 cm ________
6. 7.1 cm ________

A scale drawing has a scale of $\frac{1}{4}$ in. : 12 ft. Find the length on the drawing for each actual length.

7. 8 ft ________
8. 30 ft ________
9. 15 ft ________
10. 18 ft ________
11. 20 ft ________
12. 40 ft ________

Use a metric ruler to find the approximate distance between the towns.

13. Hickokburg to Kidville ________
14. Dodgetown to Earp City ________
15. Dodgetown to Kidville ________
16. Kidville to Earp City ________
17. Dodgetown to Hickokburg ________
18. Earp City to Hickokburg ________

Solve.

19. The scale drawing shows a two-bedroom apartment. The master bedroom is 9 ft × 12 ft. Use an inch ruler to measure the drawing.

   a. The scale is ________.

   b. Write the actual dimensions in place of the scale dimensions.

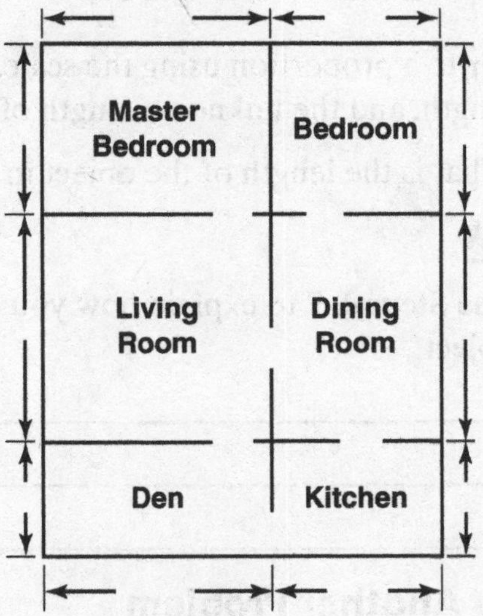

Name ____________________ Class ____________ Date ____________

5-6 • Guided Problem Solving

GPS Student Page 217, Exercise 23:

Writing in Math You are making a scale drawing with a scale of 2 in. = 17 ft. Explain how you find the length of the drawing of an object that has an actual length of 51 ft.

Understand

1. What are you being asked to do?

____

____

2. What points should you include in your explanation?

____

____

3. What is a scale?

____

____

Plan and Carry Out

4. What is the scale? ____________
5. What is the actual length of the object? ____________
6. Write a proportion using the scale, the actual length, and the unknown length of the drawing. ____________
7. What is the length of the object in a drawing? ____________

Check

8. Use Steps 4–7 to explain how you decided how long to draw the object.

____

____

____

Solve Another Problem

9. The length of the wing of a model airplane is 3 in. If the scale of the model to the actual plane is 1 in. = 25 ft, what is the length of the actual wing? ____________

Name ______________________ Class ______________ Date ______________

Practice 5-7

Proportional Relationships

Determine whether each table or graph represents a proportional relationship. Explain your reasoning.

1.

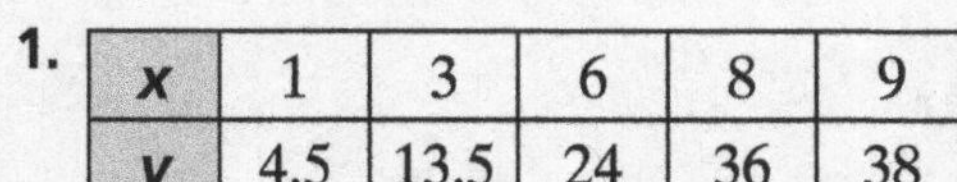

x	1	3	6	8	9
y	4.5	13.5	24	36	38

____

____

2.

x	1	5	8	11	12
y	$\frac{8}{5}$	$\frac{40}{5}$	$\frac{64}{5}$	$\frac{88}{5}$	$\frac{96}{5}$

____

____

3.

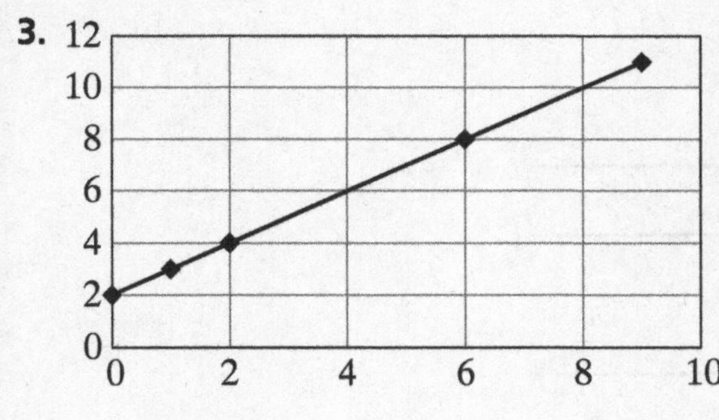

____

____

4.

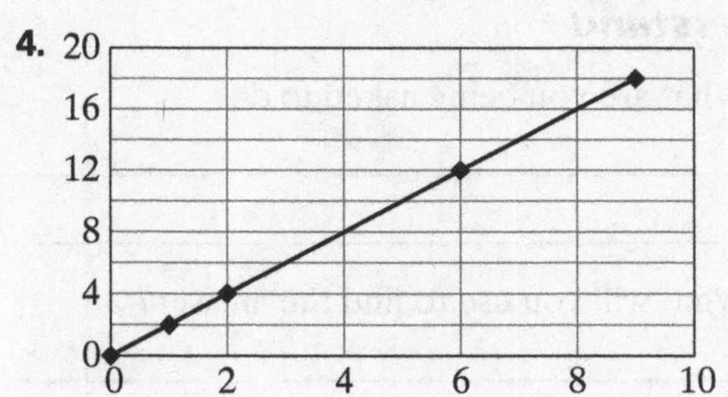

____

____

Find the constant of proportionality for each table of values.

5.

Roses	6	12	24
Price	\$22.50	\$45.00	\$90.00

$c =$ __________

6.

Tomatoes (lb)	3	7	9
Price	\$4.47	\$10.43	\$13.41

$c =$ __________

7.

Gallons	5	10	15
Miles	120	240	360

$c =$ __________

8.

Seconds	2	6	8
Feet	500	1,500	2,000

$c =$ __________

Write an equation using the constant of proportionality to describe the relationship.

9. A boat that has traveled 8 leagues from shore is 24 nautical miles out. Find the number of miles m in l leagues. __________

10. Four score years ago is 80 years past. Find the number of years y in s scores. __________

Name ______________________ Class ______________ Date ______________

5-7 • Guided Problem Solving

GPS Student Page 224, Exercise 15:

Error Analysis A salesperson showed the table below while explaining that oranges are the same price per pound, no matter what size bag they come in. Why is the salesperson wrong?

$	$8	$10	$20
lbs	4	6	10

Understand

1. What are you being asked to do?

____

____

2. What will you use to find the answer?

____

____

Plan and Carry Out

3. What is the unit price for 4 pounds of oranges? ______________
4. What is the unit price for 6 pounds of oranges? ______________
5. What is the unit price for 10 pounds of oranges? ______________
6. Why is the salesperson wrong?

____

____

Check

7. How can you check your answer?

____

____

Solve Another Problem

8. A customer thinks pizzas cost the same per slice at a local restaurant. Why is the customer wrong?

$	$8	$9	$12
Slices	10	12	16

____

____

Name ______________________ Class ______________ Date ______________

5A: Graphic Organizer

For use before Lesson 5-1

Study Skill As you read over the material in the chapter, keep a paper and pencil handy to write down notes and questions in your math notebook. Review notes taken in class as soon as possible.

Write your answers.

1. What is the chapter title? ______________________
2. How many lessons are there in this chapter? ______________________
3. What is the topic of the Test-Taking Strategies page? ______________________
4. Complete the graphic organizer below as you work through the chapter.
   - In the center, write the title of the chapter.
   - When you begin a lesson, write the lesson name in a rectangle.
   - When you complete a lesson, write a skill or key concept in a circle linked to that lesson block.
   - When you complete the chapter, use this graphic organizer to help you review.

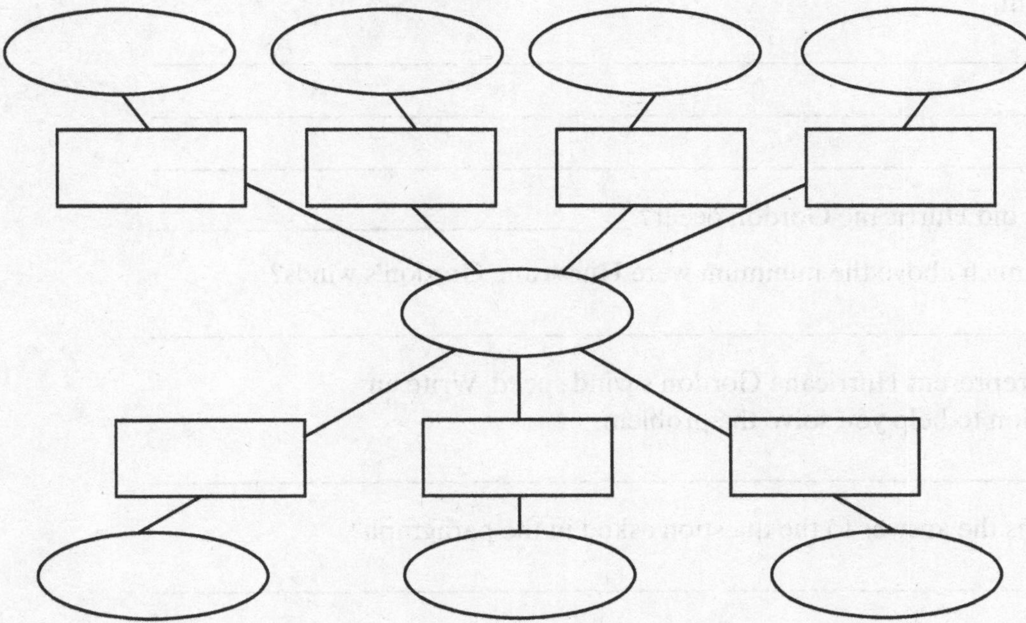

Name ______________________ Class ______________ Date ______________

5B: Reading Comprehension

For use after Lesson 5-3

Study Skill When you read mathematics, look for words like "more than," "less than," "above," "times as many," "divided by." These clues will help you decide what operation you need to solve a problem.

Read the paragraph and answer the questions that follow.

> A tropical storm is classified as a hurricane when it has wind speeds in excess of 74 mi/h. The winds of Hurricane Gordon (1994) reached 12.4 mi/h above the minimum. How fast were the winds of Hurricane Gordon?

1. What numbers are in the paragraph? ______________
2. What question are you asked to answer? ______________
____
3. What units will you use in your answer? ______________
4. Does a storm with winds of 74 mi/h qualify as a hurricane? Explain.
____
____
____
5. When did Hurricane Gordon occur? ______________
6. How much above the minimum were Hurricane Gordon's winds?
____
7. Let x represent Hurricane Gordon's wind speed. Write an equation to help you solve the problem.
____
8. What is the answer to the question asked in the paragraph?
____
9. **High-Use Academic Words** In Exercise 7, what does it mean to *solve*?
   a. to find an answer for
   b. to keep something going

Name ____________________ Class ____________ Date ____________

5C: Reading/Writing Math Symbols

For use after Lesson 5-4

Vocabulary and Study Skills

Study Skill When you take notes in any subject, use abbreviations and symbols whenever possible.

Write each statement or expression using the appropriate mathematical symbols.

1. the ratio of a to b ____________________
2. x to 4 is less than 5 to 2 ____________________
3. 4 more than 5 times n ____________________
4. $5:24$ is not equal to $1:5$ ____________________

Write each mathematical statement in words.

5. $x \leq 25$ ____________________
6. $|-20| > |15|$ ____________________
7. $1 \text{ oz} \approx 28 \text{ g}$ ____________________
8. $\frac{1}{3} = \frac{4}{12}$ ____________________

Match the symbolic statement or expression in Column A with its written form in Column B.

Column A	Column B
9. $k < 12$	A. 12 times x
10. $\lvert -5 \rvert$	B. negative 2 plus negative 4 is p
11. $n \geq 15$	C. the ratio of 4 to 8
12. $x = -4 + 5$	D. k is less than 12
13. $4:8$	E. the quotient of x and 9
14. $12x$	F. x equals negative 4 plus 5
15. $-2 + (-4) = p$	G. the absolute value of negative 5
16. $x \div 9$	H. n is greater than or equal to 15

Name ________________ Class ________________ Date ________________

5D: Visual Vocabulary Practice

For use after Lesson 5-6

Study Skill When you come across something you don't understand, view it as an opportunity to increase your brain power.

Concept List

cross products	equivalent ratios	indirect measurement
proportion	rate	scale
similar polygons	unit cost	unit rate

Write the concept that best describes each exercise. Choose from the concept list above.

1. $\frac{18}{16}$ and $4.5 : 4$ ________________	**2.** A 6-ft-tall person standing near a building has a shadow that is 60 ft long.This can be used to determine the height of the building. ________________	**3.** A bakery sells a dozen donuts for \$3.15. This can also be represented as $\frac{\$3.15}{12 \text{ donuts}}$. ________________
4. The expression "45 words per minute" represents this. ________________	**5.** $\frac{30}{75} = \frac{2}{5}$ ________________	**6.** For the equation $\frac{15}{16} = \frac{3z}{4}$, these are represented by 15×4 and $3z \times 16$. ________________
7. The equation $\frac{1}{2}$ in. = 50 mi represents this on a map. ________________	**8.** $\frac{\$4.25}{5 \text{ lb}} = \frac{\$0.85}{\text{lb}}$ ________________	**9.** [Rectangle 25.5 by 12; rectangle 8.5 by 4] 12 25.5 4 8.5 ________________

Name ____________________ Class ____________ Date ____________

5E: Vocabulary Check

For use after Lesson 5-7

Study Skill Strengthen your vocabulary. Use these pages and add cues and summaries by applying the Cornell Notetaking style.

Write the definition for each word or term at the right. To check your work, fold the paper back along the dotted line to see the correct answers.

Definition	Term
______________________________	polygon
______________________________	proportion
______________________________	unit rate
______________________________	ratio
______________________________	scale drawing

Name ______________________ Class ______________ Date ______________

5E: Vocabulary Check (continued)

For use after Lesson 5-7

Write the vocabulary word or term for each definition. To check your work, fold the paper forward along the dotted line to see the correct answers.

a closed figure formed by three or more line segments that do not cross ______________________

an equation stating that two ratios are equal ______________________

the rate for one unit of a given quantity ______________________

a comparison of two quantities by division ______________________

an enlarged or reduced drawing of an object that is similar to the actual object ______________________

Name ______________________ Class ______________ Date ______________

5F: Vocabulary Review Puzzle

For use with the Chapter Review

Study Skill Use a special notebook or section of a loose-leaf binder for math.

Complete the crossword puzzle. For help, use the Glossary in your textbook.

Here are the words you will use to complete this crossword puzzle:

equation	factor	figures	fraction
inequality	mixed number	prime	proportion
ratio	scale drawing		

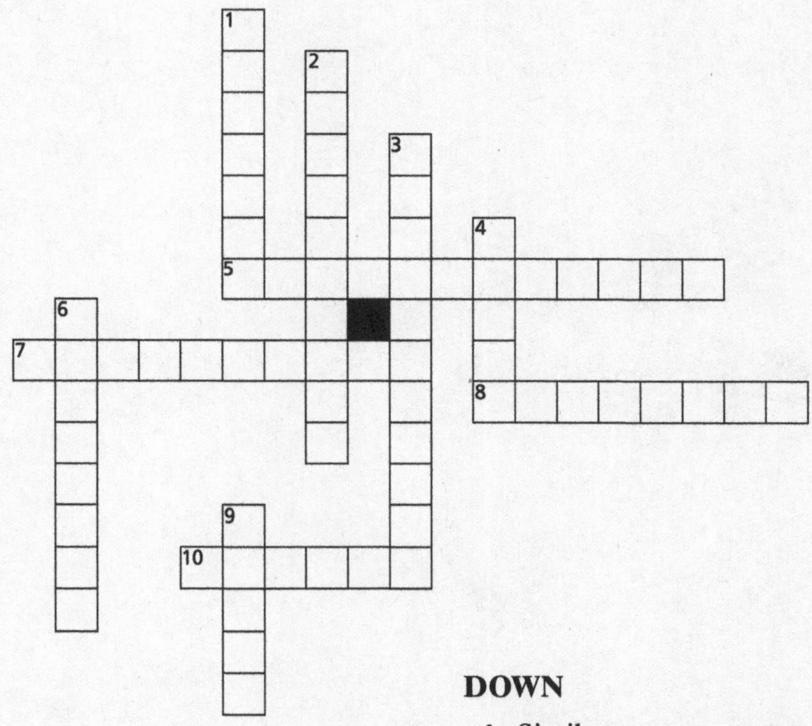

ACROSS

5. enlarged or reduced drawing of an object
7. equation stating two ratios are equal
8. a statement of two equal expressions
10. a whole number that divides another whole number evenly

DOWN

1. Similar ______________ have the same shape but not necessarily the same size.
2. a statement that two expressions are not equal
3. a number made up of a nonzero whole number and a fraction
4. a number with only two factors, one and itself
6. a number in the form $\frac{a}{b}$
9. a comparison of two numbers by division

Vocabulary and Study Skills

Name ______________________ Class ______________ Date ______________

Practice 6-1

Percents, Fractions, and Decimals

Write each percent as a fraction in simplest form and as a decimal.

1. 65% ________ **2.** 37.5% ________ **3.** 80% ________ **4.** 25% ________

5. 18% ________ **6.** 46% ________ **7.** 87% ________ **8.** 8% ________

9. 43% ________ **10.** 55% ________ **11.** 94% ________ **12.** 36% ________

Write each number as a percent. Round to the nearest tenth of a percent where necessary.

13. $\frac{8}{15}$ ________ **14.** $\frac{7}{50}$ ________ **15.** 0.56 ________

16. 0.0413 ________ **17.** $\frac{3}{8}$ ________ **18.** $\frac{7}{12}$ ________

19. 0.387 ________ **20.** 0.283 ________ **21.** $\frac{2}{9}$ ________

Write each number as a percent. Place the number into the puzzle without using the percent sign or decimal point.

22.

Across

1. 0.134
3. $\frac{53}{100}$
5. 0.565
7. $1\frac{7}{50}$
9. 0.456
10. 0.63
11. $\frac{11}{200}$
13. 0.58
14. $\frac{191}{200}$
16. 0.605

Down

2. 0.346
4. 0.324
5. $\frac{1}{2}$
6. 0.515
8. $\frac{33}{200}$
9. 0.4385
10. $\frac{659}{1,000}$
12. $\frac{1,087}{20,000}$
15. $\frac{14}{25}$

1.	2.			
			3.	4.
5.		6.		
		7.	8.	
	9.			
10.			11.	12.
13.				
14.		15.		
		16.		

Name ________________________ Class ________________ Date ______________

6-1 • Guided Problem Solving

GPS Student Page 236, Exercise 35:

Your teacher uses different methods of grading quizzes. Your quiz grades are 85%, $\frac{9}{10}$, $\frac{16}{20}$, 92%, $\frac{21}{25}$, and 79%.

a. Write your quiz grades in order from least to greatest.

b. Find the average percent grade of your quizzes.

Understand

1. What are you being asked to do in part (a)?

____

____

2. In order to compare the grades, what should you do first?

____

____

3. Besides knowing the grades of the quizzes, explain what else is needed to find the average.

____

Plan and Carry Out

4. What are all your grades in percent form?

____

5. Order the grades from smallest to largest.

____

6. What is the total of all your grades? ____________

7. Find the average percent grade of your six quizzes. ____________

Check

8. Does the average grade fall between the smallest and largest grade?

____

Solve Another Problem

9. Your classmate had quiz grades of 75%, $\frac{13}{20}$, $\frac{15}{25}$, 89%, $\frac{8}{10}$, and 81%. Order the grades from least to greatest and find the average.

____

Name ____________________ Class ____________ Date ____________

Practice 6-2

Solving Percent Problems Using Proportions

Use a proportion to solve.

1. 48 is 60% of what number? ____________

2. What is 175% of 85? ____________

3. What percent of 90 is 50? ____________

4. 76 is 80% of what number? ____________

5. What is 50% of 42.88? ____________

6. 96 is 160% of what number? ____________

7. What percent of 24 is 72? ____________

8. What is 85% of 120? ____________

9. What is 80% of 12? ____________

10. 56 is 75% of what number? ____________

Solve.

11. The sale price of a bicycle is $120. This is 75% of the original price. Find the original price.

____

12. The attendance at a family reunion was 160 people. This was 125% of last year's attendance. How many people attended the reunion last year?

____

13. A company has 875 employees. On "Half-Price Wednesday," 64% of the employees eat lunch at the company cafeteria. How many employees eat lunch at the cafeteria on Wednesdays?

____

14. There are 1,295 students attending a small university. There are 714 women enrolled. What percentage of students are women?

____

Name ______________________ Class ______________ Date ______________

6-2 • Guided Problem Solving

GPS Student Page 240, Exercise 34:

At the library, you find 9 books on a certain topic. The librarian tells you that 55% of the books on this topic have been signed out. How many books does the library have available on the topic?

Understand

1. Circle the information you will need to solve.
2. What are you being asked to do?

____

____

3. If 55% of the books on this topic have been signed out, what percent of the books on this topic have *not* been signed out?

____

Plan and Carry Out

4. Choose a variable to represent the total number of books the library has on the topic. ______________
5. How many books did you find on the topic? ______________
6. Write a proportion comparing the percent of books on this topic to the number of books in the library. ______________
7. Solve the proportion. ______________
8. How many books does the library have on the topic? ______________

Check

9. Is 55% of your answer plus 9 equal to your answer?

____

Solve Another Problem

10. There are 12,000 people attending a concert. You learn that 20% of the people who bought tickets to the concert did not attend. How many people bought tickets to the concert?

____

____

Name ____________________ Class ____________ Date ____________

Practice 6-3

Solving Percent Problems Using Equations

Write and solve an equation. Round answers to the nearest tenth.

1. What percent of 64 is 48?

2. 16% of 130 is what number?

3. 25% of what number is 24?

4. What percent of 18 is 12?

5. 48% of 83 is what number?

6. 40% of what number is 136?

7. What percent of 530 is 107?

8. 74% of 643 is what number?

9. 62% of what number is 84?

10. What percent of 84 is 50?

11. 37% of 245 is what number?

12. 12% of what number is 105?

Solve.

13. A cafe offers senior citizens a 15% discount off its regular price of $8.95 for the dinner buffet.
    a. What percent of the regular price is the price for senior citizens? ____________
    b. What is the price for senior citizens? ____________

14. According to a recent government study, the average 15-year-old male gets 11.4% of his daily caloric intake from sugar drinks. If that 15-year-old consumes 2,400 calories each day, how many calories come from sugar drinks? ____________

6-3 • Guided Problem Solving

GPS Student Page 244, Exercise 28:

Food You make 72 cookies for a bake sale. This is 20% of the cookies at the bake sale. How many cookies are at the bake sale?

Understand

1. Circle the information you will need to solve.
2. What are you being asked to do?

   ____

3. What word indicates an equal sign?

   ____

Plan and Carry Out

4. Choose a variable to represent the number of cookies at the bake sale. ____________
5. What number is 20% of the cookies at the bake sale? ________
6. Write an expression for the phrase, *20% of the cookies at the bake sale.* ____________
7. Write an equation using what you wrote in Steps 5 and 6 to find the number of cookies at the bake sale.

   ____

8. Solve the equation. ____________
9. How many cookies are at the bake sale? ____________

Check

10. Find 20% of your answer. Does it equal 72?

    ____

Solve Another Problem

11. You collect trading cards and so far you have 12 different cards. If this is 30% of the possible cards, how many cards are there to collect?

    ____

Name ______________________ Class ______________ Date ______________

Practice 6-4

Applications of Percent

Find the total cost.

1. $17.50 with a 7% sales tax ______________

2. $21.95 with a 4.25% sales tax ______________

3. The price of a pair of shoes is $85.99 before sales tax. The sales tax is 7.5%. Find the total cost of the shoes. ______________

Estimate a 15% tip for each amount.

4. $12.68 ______________

5. $18.25 ______________

6. $15.00 ______________

Find each commission.

7. 2% on $1,500 in sales ______________

8. 8% on $80,000 in sales ______________

9. 5% on $600 in sales ______________

Find the percent error.

A student in a science lab is measuring the density of various materials. Compare the student's finding to the actual density.

Substance	Density g/cm^3	Measured Density g/cm^3	Percent Error
concrete	2.4	2.46	**10.**
corn kernel	0.4	0.38	**11.**
copper	8.9	9.1	**12.**

Find the registration fee.

10. To cover office expenses, a gymnastics camp charges a registration fee that is 3.4% of the tuition. If tuition is $485, what is the fee? Round to the nearest cent. ______________

11. During peak summer season, a whitewater rafting company charges a 15% registration fee to reserve a 6-person raft that rents for $90. How much is the fee? ______________

Solve.

12. To recover a large chair in your home, you purchase $9\frac{1}{2}$ yards of upholstery fabric at $11.00 per yard. If there is a 7% sales tax, what is the total cost of the fabric?

____

Name ______________________ Class ______________ Date ____________

6-4 • Guided Problem Solving

GPS Student Page 252, Exercise 26:

Sales A store pays a 6% commission on the first $500 in sales and 8% on sales over $500. Find the commission on an $800 sale.

Understand

1. Circle the information you will need to solve.
2. Define commission.

____

____

3. Which operations do you need to use to solve this problem?

____

Plan and Carry Out

4. $800 = $500 + __?__ ______________
5. What is 6% of $500? ______________
6. What is 8% of $300? ______________
7. What is the commission on a $800 sale? ______________

Check

8. Find 10% of $500 and 10% of $300. Since 6% is a little more than half of 10%, what is half of 10% of 500? Add this with 10% of 30, since 8% is close to 10%. Does your answer make sense?

____

Solve Another Problem

9. Dan's uncle asks him to come work for him at his men's clothing store. He will pay him 5% on his first $1,000 in sales and 8% on sales above $1,000. How much will Dan earn if he sells $2,500 in merchandise?

____

____

Name ____________________ Class ____________ Date ____________

Practice 6-5

Simple Interest

Graph the total *simple* interest earned for each account over 5 years.

1. $1,300 at 6.9%

2. $11,500 at 12.50%

3. $450 at 3%

Find the simple interest earned in each account.

4. $2,000 at 4% for 6 months ____________________

5. $10,000 at 10% for 2 years ____________________

6. $500 at 3% for 3 months ____________________

7. $25,000 at 4.25% for 5 years ____________________

Compare the loans.

8. Compare two loans for $5,000. The 5-year loan has a 5% simple interest rate. The 6-year loan has a 4% simple interest rate. Which loan costs less? ____________________

9. You want to borrow $2,000. You can get 3-year loan with a 15% simple interest rate or a 5-year loan with a 10% simple interest rate. Which loan costs less? ____________________

10. You want to borrow $720. You can get a 2-year loan with an 8% simple interest rate or a 1-year loan with a 15% simple interest rate. Which loan costs less? ____________________

Solve.

11. You invest $5,000 in an account earning simple interest. The balance after 6 years is $6,200. What is the interest rate?

____

12. Suppose you have $300 to invest. One bank offers an annual simple interest rate of 4.5% for a 3-year investment. Another bank offers an annual simple interest rate of 6.8% for a 2-year investment. Which account will earn you more money?

____

Name ______________________ Class ______________ Date ____________

6-5 • Guided Problem Solving

GPS Student Page 256, Exercise 16:

You borrow \$500 at 18% simple annual interest. You make no payments for 6 months. How much do you owe after 6 months?

Understand

1. What is simple interest?

____

____

2. What are you being asked to do?

____

Plan and Carry Out

3. What is the formula for simple interest? ______________
4. What is the original principal? ______________
5. What is the interest rate? ______________
6. How much time in years has passed since the money was borrowed? ______________
7. Substitute the values into the formula. ______________
8. Including principal, how much do you owe after 6 months? ______________

Check

9. Find the total simple interest on the account after one year. How should this number compare to the interest you calculated above?

____

____

____

Solve Another Problem

10. You borrow \$1,050 at 16% annual interest. How much interest have you paid after 5 years?

____

Name ______________________ Class ______________ Date ______________

Practice 6-6

Finding Percent of Change

Find each percent of change. State whether the change is an increase or a decrease.

1. A $50 coat is put on sale for $35.

____

____

2. Mayelle earns $18,000 a year. After a raise, she earns $19,500.

____

____

3. Last year Anthony earned $24,000. After a brief lay-off this year, Anthony's income is $18,500.

____

____

4. In 1981, about $1.1 million was lost due to fires. In 1988, the loss was about $9.6 million.

____

____

5. In a recent year, certain colleges and universities received about $268 million in aid. Ten years later, they received about $94 million.

____

____

6. A coat regularly costing $125 is put on sale for $75.

____

____

7. Complete the table.

Enrollment in Center City Schools From 1995 to 2000

Year	Enrollment	Change from Last Year (number of students)	Change from Last Year (%)	Increase or Decrease
1995	18,500	—	—	—
1996	19,300			
1997	19,700			
1998	19,500			
1999	19,870			
2000	19,200			

Name ____________________ Class ____________ Date ____________

6-6 • Guided Problem Solving

GPS Student Page 261, Exercise 29:

Sports A football player gained 1,200 yd last season and 900 yd this season. Find the percent of change. State whether the change is an increase or a decrease.

Understand

1. What two numbers will you be comparing?

   ____

2. Did the football player gain more yards last season or this season?

   ____

3. What are you being asked to do?

   ____

Plan and Carry Out

4. What is the difference in the number of yards gained last season and this season? ____________
5. Write a proportion comparing the difference and the percent of change. ____________
6. What are the cross products? ____________
7. What number do you divide each side by? ____________
8. What is the percent of change? ____________
9. Is it a decrease or increase? ____________

Check

10. Explain your answer to step 9.

    ____

    ____

    ____

Solve Another Problem

11. In a previous game the school's star basketball player scored 25 points. In today's game he scored 40 points. What was the percent of change in the player's scoring? Is the change an increase or decrease?

    ____

Name ______________________ Class ______________ Date ______________

6A: Graphic Organizer

For use before Lesson 6-1

Study Skill As you read over the material in the chapter, keep a paper and pencil handy to write down notes and questions that you have.

Write your answers.

1. What is the chapter title? ______________________
2. How many lessons are there in this chapter? ______________________
3. What is the topic of the Test-Taking Strategies page? ______________________
4. Complete the graphic organizer below as you work through the chapter.
   - In the center, write the title of the chapter.
   - When you begin a lesson, write the lesson name in a rectangle.
   - When you complete a lesson, write a skill or key concept in a circle linked to that lesson block.
   - When you complete the chapter, use this graphic organizer to help you review.

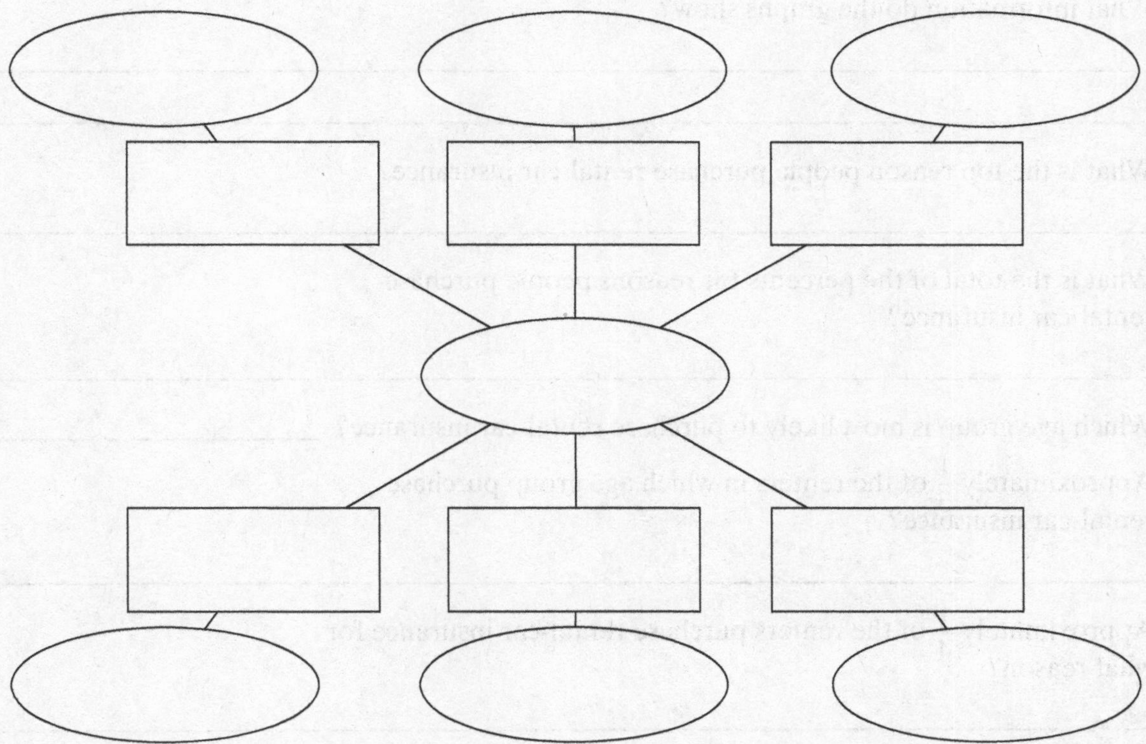

Vocabulary and Study Skills

Name ______________________ Class ______________ Date ______________

6B: Reading Comprehension

For use after Lesson 6-2

Study Skill Use a special notebook (or section of a loose-leaf binder) for your math handouts and homework. Keep your notebook neat and organized by reviewing its contents often.

Use the graphs shown below to answer the questions that follow.

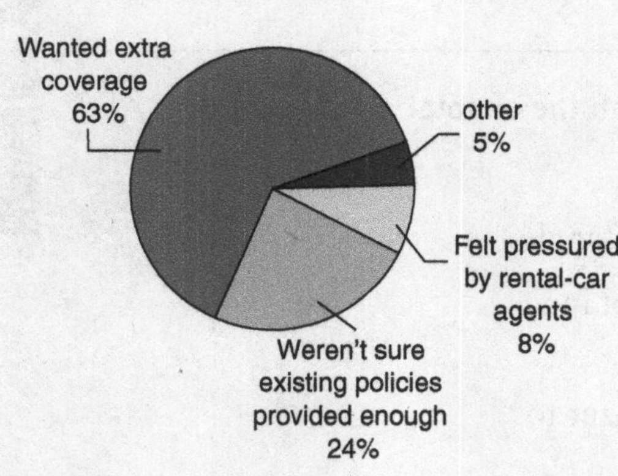

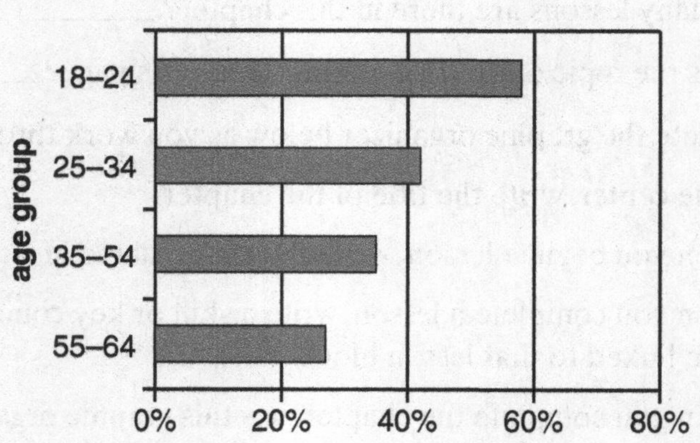

1. What information do the graphs show?

____

____

2. What is the top reason people purchase rental-car insurance?

____

3. What is the total of the percents for reasons people purchase rental-car insurance?

____

4. Which age group is most likely to purchase rental-car insurance? ______________

5. Approximately $\frac{1}{3}$ of the renters in which age group purchase rental-car insurance?

____

6. Approximately $\frac{1}{4}$ of the renters purchase rental-car insurance for what reason?

____

7. **High-Use Academic Words** In Exercise 1, what does the word *show* mean?

   a. to display　　　**b.** to put in a sequence

Name ______________________ Class ______________ Date ______________

6C: Reading/Writing Math Symbols

For use after Lesson 6-4

Study Skill When working on your math homework, use a pencil and have an eraser nearby.

Write each of the following using appropriate mathematical symbols and abbreviations.

1. 3 feet to 1 yard ______________
2. 47 and 6 tenths percent ______________
3. 37 percent is greater than $\frac{1}{3}$ ______________
4. 1 meter to 100 centimeters ______________
5. 106 percent ______________
6. $\frac{1}{4}$ is less than 26% ______________
7. 8 quarts to 2 gallons ______________
8. 93 and 32 hundredths percent ______________
9. the absolute value of negative 16 ______________
10. 78 out of 100 ______________

Write each of the following in words.

11. $|-7.3| = 7.3$

____

12. 30.08%

____

13. $50\% > \frac{2}{5}$

____

14. 2 h : 120 min

____

15. $\frac{55}{100}$

____

16. $\frac{1}{10} < 12\%$

____

Name ______________________ Class ______________ Date ______________

6D: Visual Vocabulary Practice

For use after Lesson 6-6

High-Use Academic Words

Study Skill When making a sketch, make it simple but make it complete.

Concept List

represent	graph	solve
model	explain	pattern
substitute	calculate	verify

Write the concept that best describes each exercise. Choose from the concept list above

1.

35% of 70 is
$0.35 \times 70 = 24.5$

____

2.

−3 −2 −1 0 1

____

3.

5 : 7
5 to 7
$\frac{5}{7}$

____

4.

$n + 76 \geq 64$
$n + 76 - 76 \geq 64 - 76$
$n \geq -12$

____

5.

Sales tax is a percent of a purchase price you must pay when buying certain items. The formula for sales tax is sales tax = tax rate × purchase price.

____

6.

If $\frac{t}{18} = \frac{7}{126}$, then $t = 1$.
Check: $1 \times 126 = 7 \times 18$

____

7.

A	B
3	15
6	30
9	45
12	60
15	75

____

8.

$7a = 161$; a is either 23 or 26

$7(21) \stackrel{?}{=} 147$ False
$7(23) \stackrel{?}{=} 161$ True

____

9.

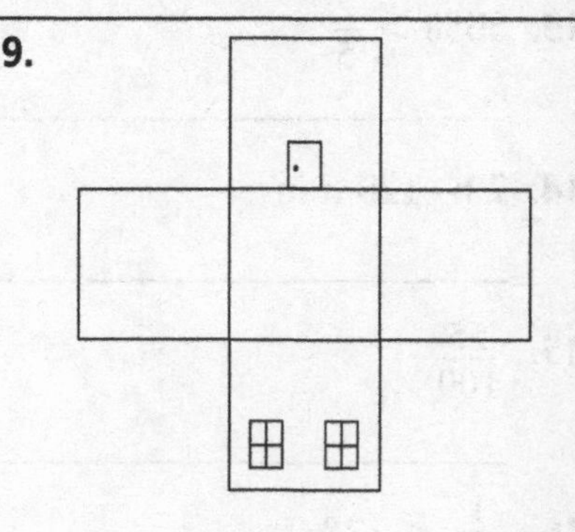

____

Name ____________________ Class ____________ Date ____________

6E: Vocabulary Check

For use after Lesson 6-6

Study Skill Strengthen your vocabulary. Use these pages and add cues and summaries by applying the Cornell Notetaking style.

Write the definition for each word or term at the right. To check your work, fold the paper back along the dotted line to see the correct answers.

____________________	commission
____________________	discount
____________________	markup
____________________	percent
____________________	percent of change

Vocabulary and Study Skills

Name ______________________ Class ______________ Date ______________

6E: Vocabulary Check (continued)

For use after Lesson 6-6

Write the vocabulary word or term for each definition. To check your work, fold the paper back along the dotted line to see the correct answers.

pay that is equal to a percent of sales ______________________

the difference between the original price and the sale price of an item ______________________

the difference between the selling price and the original cost ______________________

a ratio that compares a number to 100 ______________________

the percent a quantity increases or decreases from its original amount ______________________

Name ______________________ Class ______________ Date ______________

6F: Vocabulary Review

For use with the Chapter Review

Study Skill When you have to match words and descriptions from two columns, read the list of words and the definitions carefully and completely so you can quickly find the obvious matches. Then do the rest, one at a time. Cross out words and definitions as you use them.

Match the word in Column A with its definition in Column B.

Column A	Column B
1. percent	**A.** difference between the original price and the sale price
2. factor	**B.** equation stating two ratios are equal
3. discount	**C.** whole number that divides into another whole number evenly
4. ratio	**D.** difference between the selling price and the original cost of an item
5. proportion	**E.** comparison of two numbers by division
6. markup	**F.** ratio comparing a number to 100

Match the word in Column A with its definition in Column B.

Column A	Column B
7. mode	**G.** percent a quantity increases or decreases from its original amount
8. equation	**H.** enlarged or reduced drawing of an object
9. commission	**J.** statement that two expressions are equal
10. tip	**K.** number that occurs most often in a data set
11. scale drawing	**L.** percent of sales
12. percent of change	**M.** percent of a bill that you give to a person for providing a service

Name ____________________ Class ____________ Date ____________

Practice 7-1

Relating Graphs to Events

Each graph represents a situation. Match a graph with the appropriate situation.

a.
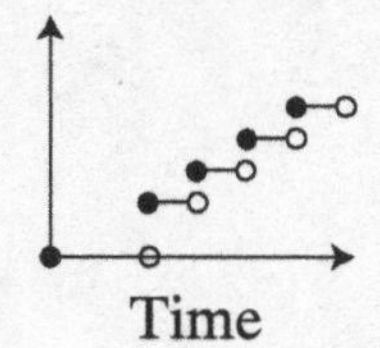

b.
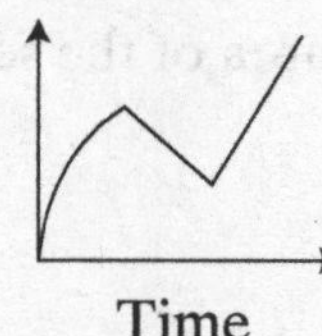

c.
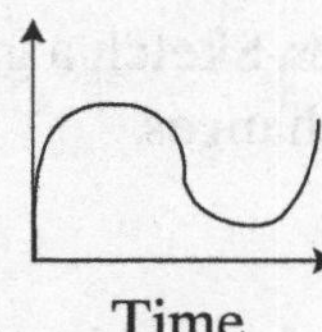

d.
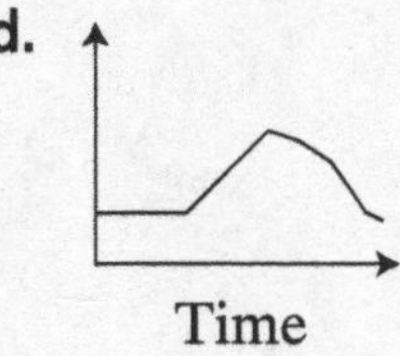

e.
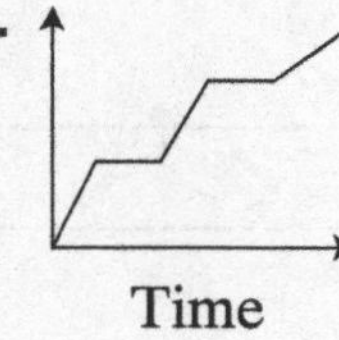

f.
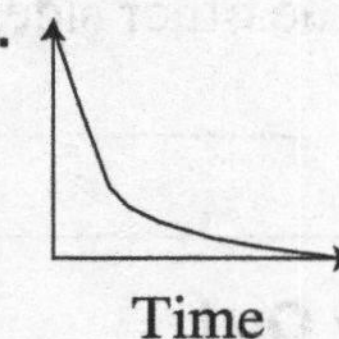

1. the amount of an unpaid library fine ____________
2. the height above ground of a skydiver during a dive ____________
3. one's adrenaline flow when receiving a fright ____________
4. the temperature of the air during a 24-h period beginning at 9:00 A.M. ____________
5. a jogger gradually increases speed, steadily decreases speed, then steadily increases speed ____________
6. elevator ride up with stops ____________
7. Look at graph b above. Suppose the total time shown is 6 min. Estimate the times when the graph is increasing, decreasing, linear, and nonlinear. ____________

Sketch and label a graph of each relationship.

8. the height of a football after it has been kicked

9. the distance traveled by a car that was traveling at 50 mph, but is now stopped by road construction

10. The function table at the right shows the distance in feet that an object falls over time.

Time (s)	Distance (ft)
1	16
2	64
3	144
4	256

Name ____________________ Class ____________________ Date ____________________

7-1 • Guided Problem Solving

GPS Student Page 273, Exercise 19:

Geometry As the length of the side of a square increases, the area of the square increases. Sketch a graph that shows the area of the square as the side length changes.

Understand

1. As the length of one side of a square increases, what happens to the lengths of the other sides?

____

____

Plan and Carry Out

2. What is the formula for the area of a square in terms of one side length? ____________________

3. Complete the chart.

Side Length	1	2	3	4	5
Area					

4. Draw a graph with the x-axis labeled "side length" and the y-axis labeled "area." Plot each of the values from Step 3, and draw a line connecting the points.

Check

5. Another way to find the area of a square is to multiply the length times the width. Are your calculations correct? ____________

Solve Another Problem

6. As the length of one side of a square increases, the perimeter of the square increases. Sketch a graph that shows the perimeter of a square as its side length increases in increments of one.

Name ____________ Class ____________ Date ____________

Practice 7-2

Functions

Use the function rule $y = 5x + 1$. Find each output.

1. $x = 3$ ________
2. $x = -6$ ________
3. $x = 8$ ________
4. $x = 1.5$ ________
5. $x = 0$ ________
6. $x = 30$ ________

7. **Measurement** The function rule $c = 2.54k$ gives the number of centimeters c that are equivalent to k inches. How many centimeters are equivalent to 4 inches? ________

8. **Cycling** The function rule $h = \frac{m}{5}$ gives the number of hours h that are needed to travel m miles at a speed of 5 miles per hour. How many hours are needed to travel 32 mi? ________

Complete the input-output table for each function.

9. $r = 2t - 1$

Input t	Output r
−2	
0	
2	
4	

10. $p = 2v + 12$

Input v	Output p
−0.4	
−0.2	
0	
0.1	

11. $k = 0.3n - 2$

Input n	Output k
−10	
−5	
0	
5	

12. **Unit Pricing** Complete the table of input-output pairs for the function $c = \frac{p}{8}$. The variable c represents the unit cost in dollars of a box of 8 granola bars. The variable p represents the price in dollars of a box of 8 granola bars.

Input p (dollars in price)	Output c (dollars in unit price)
4	
3.60	
3.48	

13. **Merchandising** The function $d = 3r + 5.25$ represents the cost in dollars d for a vase of r roses from a flower shop. Make a table of input-output pairs to show the cost for arrangements with 6, 9, and 12 rows.

Input r (number of roses)	Output d (cost of arrangement in dollars)
6	
9	
12	

Name ______________________ Class ______________ Date ______________

7-2 • Guided Problem Solving

GPS Student Page 278, Exercise 19:

Fruit smoothies cost $1.50 each plus $0.50 for each fruit mixed into the smoothie. The function $c = 1.5 + 0.5f$ gives the cost c of a smoothie with f fruits. Find the cost of a smoothie with 4 different fruits mixed in.

Understand

1. What do the variables represent?

____

____

2. Which variable is the input variable? ______________

3. Circle what you are asked to find.

Plan and Carry Out

4. How can you use a function to find the output when you are given an input?

____

____

5. Use the function to find the cost of a smoothie with 4 fruits mixed in.

____

Check

6. How could you find the answer another way?

____

____

Solve Another Problem

7. You spent $4.50 for admission to the fair. Each ride ticket costs $0.75. The function $c = 4.5 + 0.75t$ gives the cost of admission with t ride tickets. Find the cost of 6 ride tickets.

____

Name ________________ Class ________________ Date ________________

Practice 7-3

Proportional Relationships

Determine if the relationship is proportional.

1.

x	y
−6	−30
−3	−15
6	30
9	60

______

2.

a	b
20	10
40	20
60	30
80	40

______

3.

g	h
−8	−6
−4	−2
0	0
4	2

______

4.

r	s
8	12
16	20
24	28
32	36

______

5.

c	d
25	−10
35	−14
45	−18
55	−22

______

6.

v	w
120	24
150	0
180	36
210	40

______

7. **Bagels**
2 for $3
4 for $6
12 for $18

______

8. **Canoe Rentals**
1 hr for $6
2 hr for $10
3 hr for $12

______

9. **Berries**
3 lb for $9
5 lb for $15
10 lb for $30

______

10. **Bottles of Water**
6 for $4
12 for $8
24 for $16

______

11. **Ears of Corn**
4 for $3
6 for $4
12 for $7

______

12. **Bridge Tolls**
5 for $10
10 for $20
25 for $40

______

13. **Swimming** Evan pays $12 per month to belong to a gym so that he can swim in the gym's pool. Each time he swims he pays an additional $2. He uses the function $e = 2t + 12$ to track his monthly swimming expenses, where e represents total expenses and t represents number of times Evan swims. Make an input-output table, graph your results, and determine if the function has a proportional relationship. Explain.

______

______

Name ____________________ Class ______________ Date ____________

7-3 • Guided Problem Solving

GPS Student Page 283, Exercise 15:

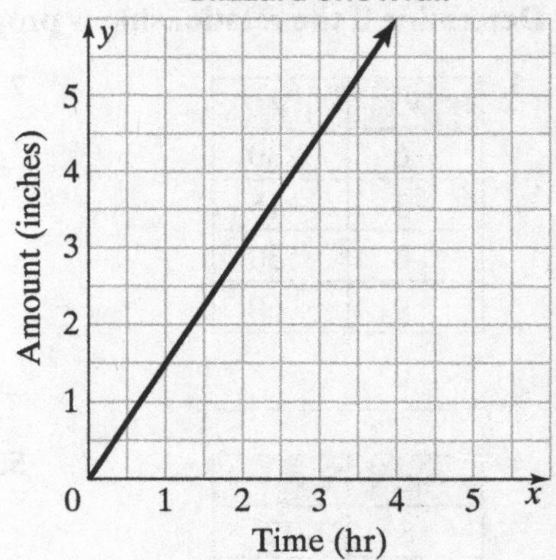

Data Analysis The graph shows the relationship between time and total snowfall for a December blizzard. Based on the graph, estimate how long it will take for the amount of snow to total 18 inches.

Understand

1. Is the relationship shown in the graph proportional or not proportional? ____________
2. What are the input and output values for this relationship?

 ____

 ____
3. What is the scale used on each axis of the graph?

 ____
4. Underline what you are being asked to do.

Plan and Carry Out

5. Find a point on the graph that corresponds to an amount of snowfall that is a factor of 18. Write the ordered pair for that point. ____________
6. What is the ratio in simplest form of input to output for the ordered pair you wrote in Step 5? ____________
7. What input value can you pair with 18 to make the same ratio? ____________
8. About how many hours did it take for 18 inches of snow to fall? ____________

Check

9. Divide 18 inches of snowfall by the number of hours. Compare the rate of inches per hour to the ordered pair for the input 1.

 ____

 ____

Solve Another Problem

10. The graph shows the relationship between time and total distance covered by a hiker. Based on the graph, estimate how long it will take for the hiker to cover 20 miles.

 ____

Cross Country Hike

Distance (mi)

0 1

Time (hr)

Name ____________________ Class ____________ Date ____________

Practice 7-4

Linear Functions

Determine if the function represented by the table is linear. Explain.

1.

x	3	5	7	11
y	6	9	12	18

____

2.

x	−4	−1	5	12
y	3	7	15	23

____

3.

x	6	0	−9	−12
y	−2	8	23	28

____

4.

x	−1	5	12	18
y	72	12	2	0

____

5.

x	84	5	−1	−4
y	1	−1	−5	−9

____

6.

x	25	15	0	−10
y	16	8	−4	−12

____

Determine whether the data for each function are *discrete* or *continuous*. Then make a table and graph for the function.

7. The function $I = 1.5h + 6$ represents the height (in inches) of water in a pool that contained 6 inches of water before the refilling began.

____

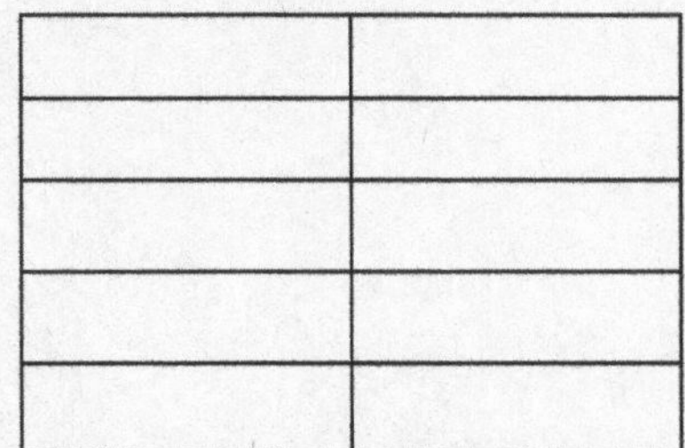

8. The function $c = 2.25b - 0.5$ represents the cost (in dollars) of b beverages at a snack bar after using a coupon.

____

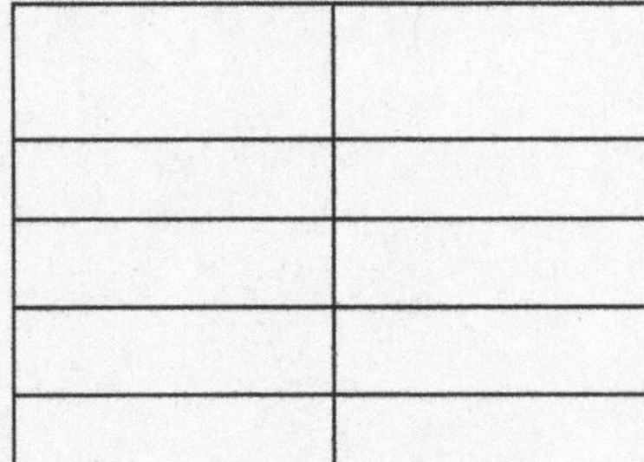

Name ________________________ Class ______________ Date ____________

7-4 • Guided Problem Solving

GPS Student Page 289, Exercise 11:

Science The height of a burning candle depends on how long the candle has been burning. For one type of candle, the function $h = 8 - \frac{1}{2}t$ gives the candle's height h (in centimeters) as a function of the time t the candle has burned (in hours). **a.** Graph the function. **b.** What was the original height of the candle? **c.** What is the greatest amount of time the candle can burn?

Understand

1. What are the input and output values for this relationship?

____

2. When the candle is at its original height, how many hours will it have burned? ____________

3. When the candle has burned the greatest amount of time, what will its height be? ____________

Plan and Carry Out

4. Make a table for input values of 0, 1, 2, and 3.

5. Use the table to graph the function. (Hint: Number the x-axis by 2s.)

6. Use the graph to answer these questions.

   a. What was the original height of the candle? ____________

   b. What is the greatest amount of time the candle can burn?

   ____

Check

7. Substitute your answers from Step 6 in the function equation. Solve for the corresponding values. Check that the pairs of values represent points on the graph you made in Step 5.

____

Solve Another Problem

8. While driving home from a water park, your distance from home depends upon how long you have been driving. The function $d = 9 - 0.6t$ gives the distance d (in miles) as a function of the time t (in minutes) that you have been driving.

   a. Graph the function.

   b. How far is the water park from your home? ____________

   c. How long will it take you to reach home? ____________

Name ______________________ Class ______________ Date ______________

Practice 7-5

Understanding Slope

Find the slope of each line.

1. 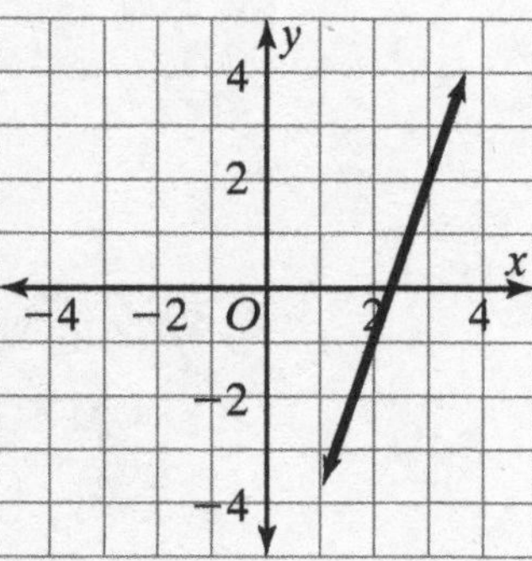

2. 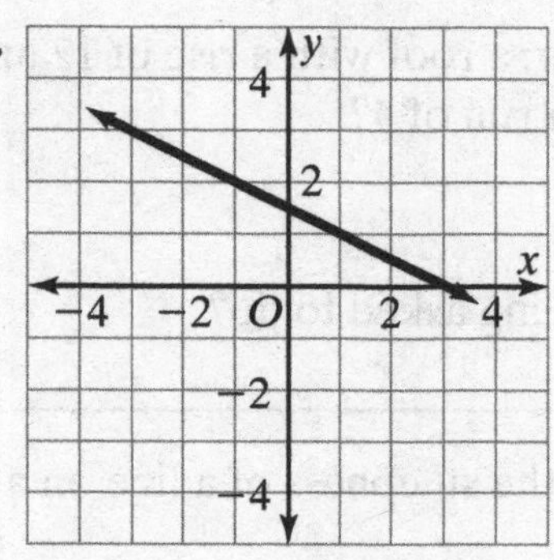

____

3. 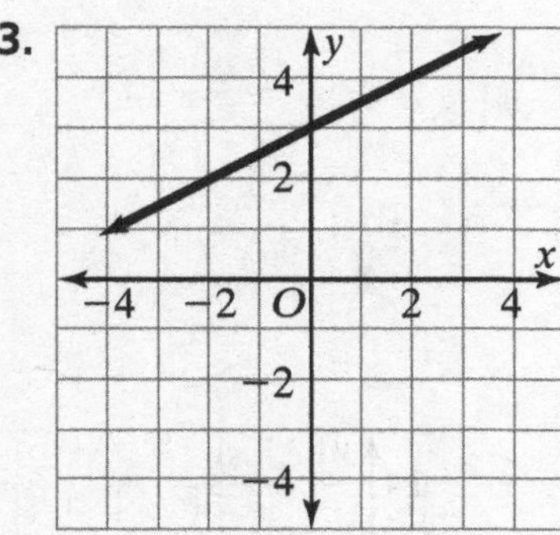

4. 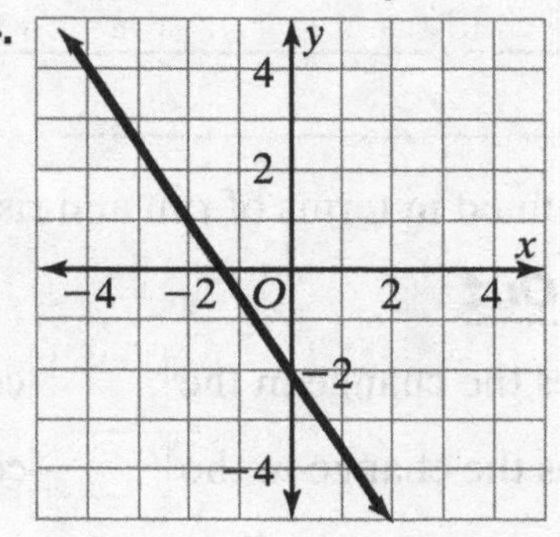

______________ ______________

The points from each table lie on a line. Use the table to find the slope of each line. Then graph the line.

5.

x	0	1	2	3	4
y	−3	−1	1	3	5

slope = ______________

6.

x	0	1	2	3	4
y	5	3	1	−1	−3

slope = ______________

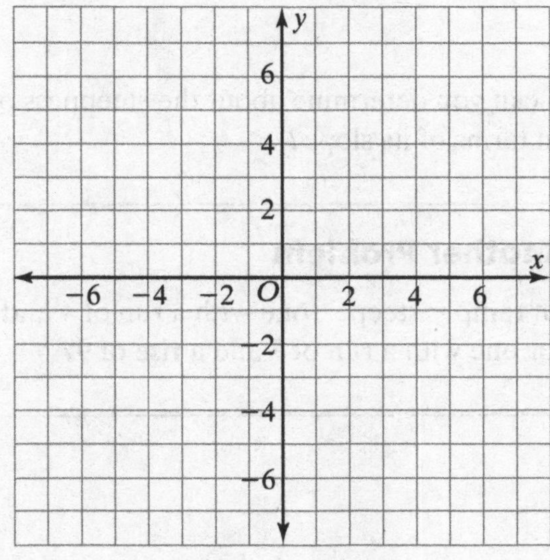

Name ______________________ Class ______________ Date ______________

7-5 • Guided Problem Solving

GPS Student Page 296, Exercise 12:

Which roof is steeper: a roof with a rise of 12 and a run of 7 or a roof with a rise of 8 and a run of 4?

Understand

1. What are you being asked to do?

____

2. What describes the steepness of a line on a coordinate plane?

____

3. What is a good way to visualize this problem?

____

____

4. How is slope defined in terms of run and rise? ______________

Plan and Carry Out

5. The rise involves the change in the ☐ -coordinates.
6. The run involves the change in the ☐ -coordinates.
7. Graph each slope on the coordinate plane.
8. Which roof is steeper?

____

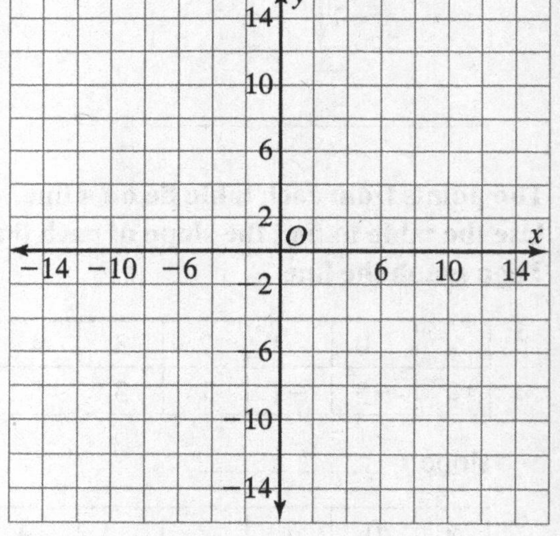

Check

9. What can you determine about the steepness of a line in terms of its slope?

____

Solve Another Problem

10. Which ramp is steeper: one with a run of 4 and a rise of 6, or one with a run of 7 and a rise of 9?

____

Name ______________________ Class ______________ Date ______________

Practice 7-6

Graphing Linear Functions

Find the slope and y-intercept of the graph of each function.

1. $y = x - 2$ ______
2. $y = -3x + 4$ ______
3. $y = \frac{4}{5}x + \frac{1}{5}$ ______
4. $y = -2x$ ______
5. $y = -\frac{2}{9}x - 8$ ______
6. $y = 6x + 1$ ______

Graph each linear function.

7. $f(x) = -x + 4$

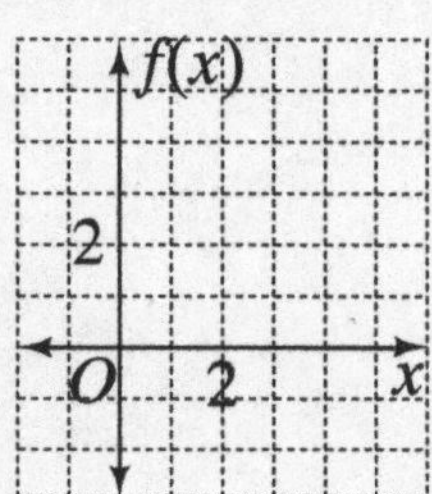

8. $f(x) = \frac{2}{3}x + 1$

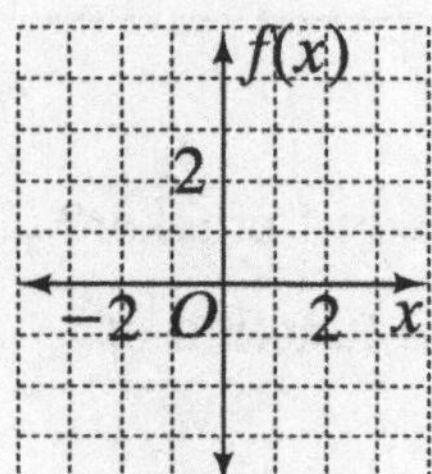

9. $f(x) = -2x + 1$

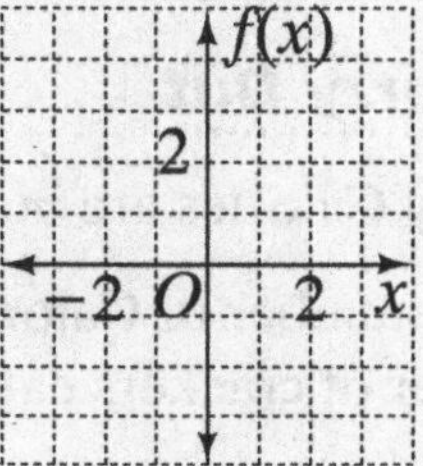

10. $y = \frac{1}{2}x + 3$

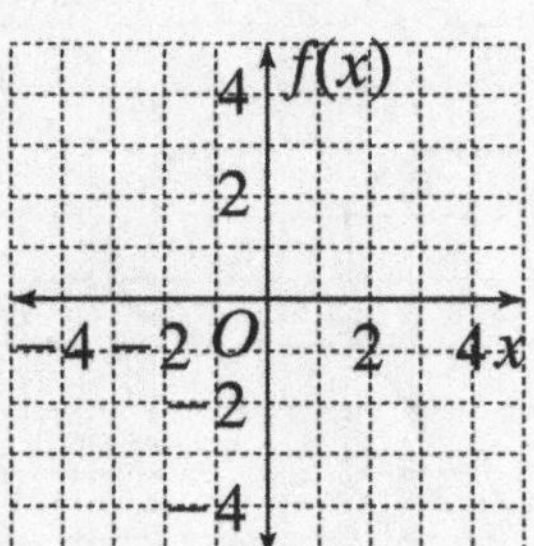

11. $y = -2 - 3x$

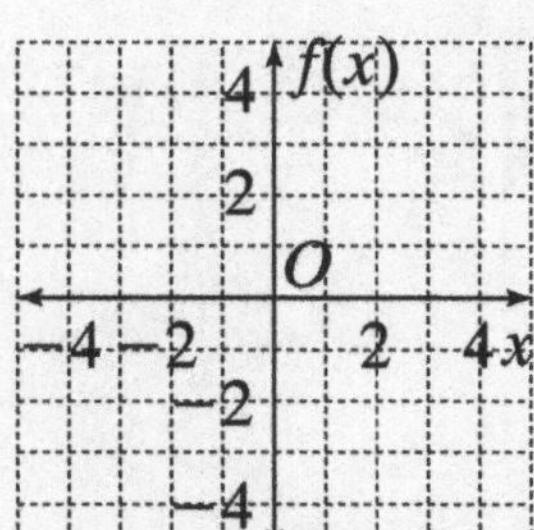

12. $y = 5 - 0.2x$

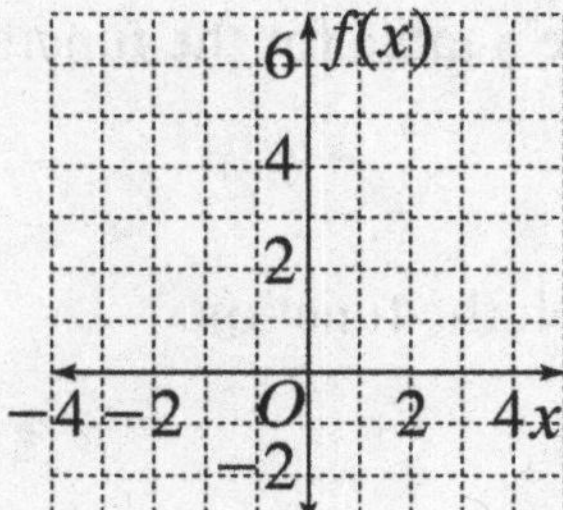

13. On a trip Alex averages 300 mi/day. The distance he covers (y) is a function of the number of days (x). Complete the table and graph the function.

Days	1	2	3	4
Miles				

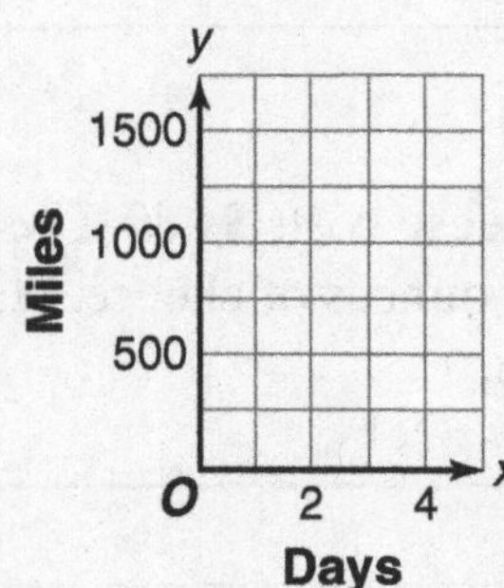

Name ______________________ Class ______________ Date ______________

7-6 • Guided Problem Solving

GPS Student Page 302, Exercise 23:

Nutrition Facts
Serving Size: 8 crackers (31g)
Serving Per Container: about 15

Amount Per Serving	
Calories 140	Calories from Fat 35
	% Daily Value
Total Fat 4g	**6%**
Saturated Fat 1g	**5%**
Monounsaturated Fat 1.5g	

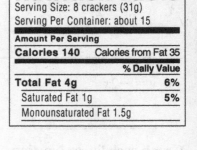

Nutrition The label at the right shows the nutrition facts for a package of crackers. Find how many Calories are in one cracker. The number of Calories consumed is a function of the number of crackers eaten. Make a table and a graph for the function.

Understand

1. What are you being asked to do? ______________________

____

____

Plan and Carry Out

2. How many Calories are in 8 crackers? _____ in 1 cracker? _____

3. Write the number of Calories consumed as a function of the number of crackers eaten.

____

____

4. Make a table for the function.

5. Graph the function.

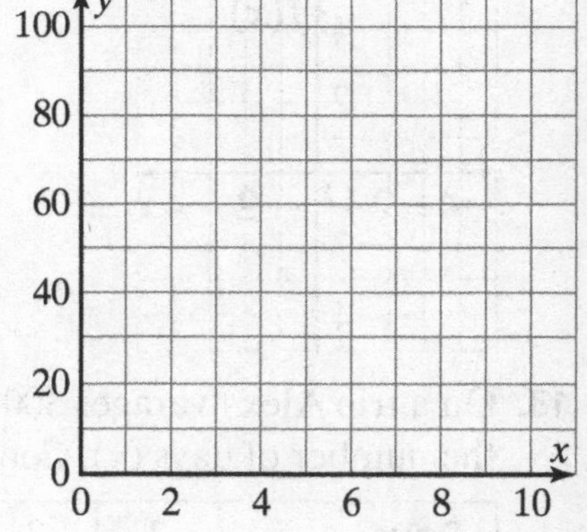

Check

6. How can you check your answer?

____

Solve Another Problem

7. A 16-ounce package of cheese costs $4.80. The cost is a function of the number of ounces of cheese. Make a table and graph for the function.

____

____

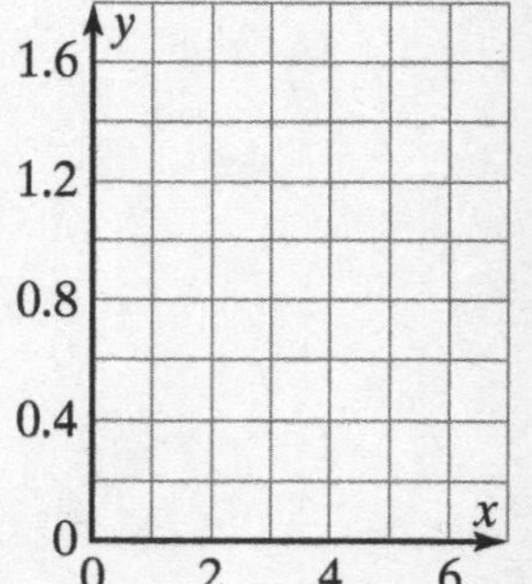

Name ______________________ Class ______________ Date ______________

Practice 7-7

Comparing Functions

1. Determine which function has the greater rate of change. ____________

Function 1

x	2	3	5	6
y	6	10	18	22

Function 2

$y = 3x + 8$

2. Determine which function has the greater initial value? ____________

Function 1

When the value of x is 0, the value of y is 3. Each time the value of x increases by 1, the value of y increases by 5.

Function 2

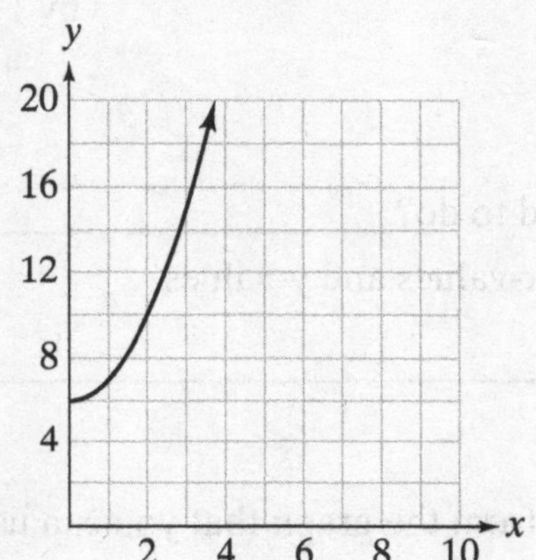

3. The repair costs for two mechanic shops are shown below. Which shop has the greater initial cost?

____

GT Auto Shop	Capital City Auto Service
• \$75 to run a diagnostic test • \$60 per hour for labor	The ordered pairs (2, 210) and (5, 435) are in the form (number of hours, total cost in dollars).

4. Which car gets better gas mileage (more miles per gallon)?

____

Mrs. Jackson's Car

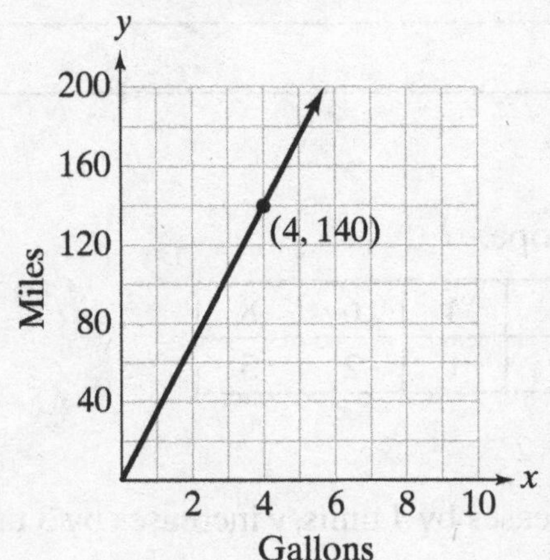

Mr. Padilla's Car

$m = 42g$ where m represents the number of miles and g represents the number of gallons

Name ____________________ Class ____________ Date ____________

7-7 • Guided Problem Solving

GPS Student Page 308, Exercise 13:

Order linear functions G, T, E, and W from least to greatest slope.

G:

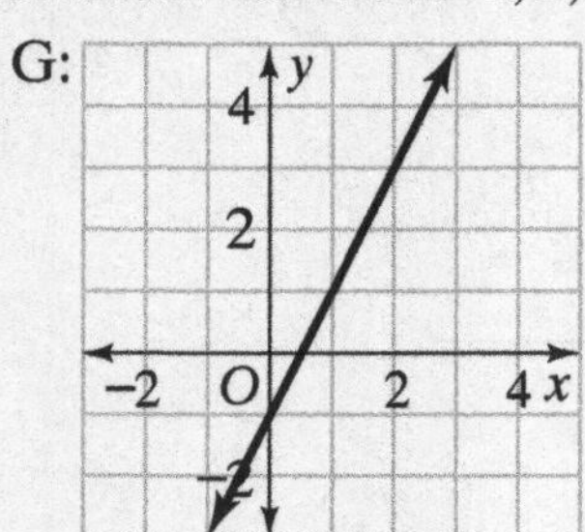

T:

x	−4	0	4	8
y	2	3	4	5

E: $y = \frac{5}{3}x + 2$

W: As x increases by 3 units, y increases by 1 unit.

Understand

1. What are you being asked to do? ____________________
2. Define slope in terms of x-values and y-values.

____

Plan and Carry Out

3. Name two ordered pairs from the graph that you can use to find the slope.

____

4. Name two ordered pairs from the table that you can use to find the slope.

____

5. Find the slope for functions G, T, E, and W. ____________
6. Order the functions from least to greatest slope. ____________

Check

7. How can you check your answer?

____

____

Solve Another Problem

8. Order the functions A, B, C, and D from least to greatest slope.

A:

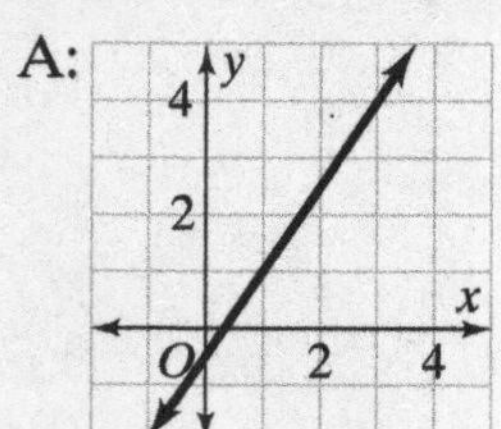

B:

x	2	4	6	8
y	0	1	2	3

C: $y = \frac{1}{4}x + 2$

D: As x increases by 4 units, y increases by 3 units.

Name ______________________ Class ______________ Date ______________

7A: Graphic Organizer

For use before Lesson 7-1

Study Skill Your textbook includes a Skills Handbook with extra problems and questions. Working these exercises is a good way to review material and prepare for the next chapter.

Write your answers.

1. What is the chapter title? ______________________
2. How many lessons are there in this chapter? ______________________
3. What is the topic of the Test-Taking Strategies page?

   ____
4. Complete the graphic organizer below as you work through the chapter.
   - In the center, write the title of the chapter.
   - When you begin a lesson, write the lesson name in a rectangle.
   - When you complete a lesson, write a skill or key concept in a circle linked to that lesson block.
   - When you complete the chapter, use this graphic organizer to help you review.

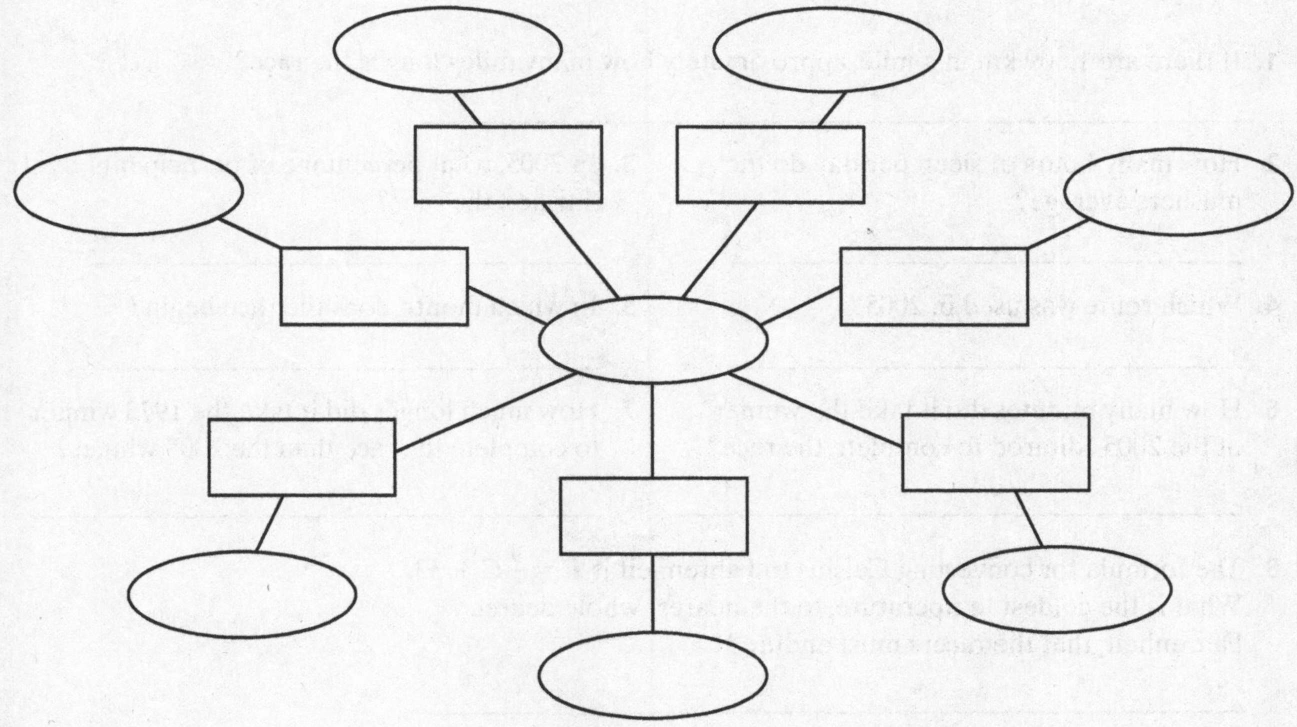

Vocabulary and Study Skills

Name ______________________ Class ______________ Date ______________

7B: Reading Comprehension

For use after Lesson 7-2

Study Skill Pay attention to detail when you read. Try to pick out the important points as you go along.

Read the paragraph below and answer the questions.

The Iditarod is an annual dog sledding competition that begins the first Saturday in March. This event, which covers about 1,850 km, begins in Anchorage and ends in Nome, Alaska. There are two possible routes: a northern route that is used in even-numbered years and a southern route that is used in odd-numbered ones. The weather is often unpredictable, with wind chill temperatures as low as −73°C. The drivers ("mushers") average approximately two hours of sleep each day. In 2005, there were 79 participants who started the race, but only 63 finished. Mushers are required to carry everything they need for the journey in their sleds. A fully loaded sled weighs approximately 150 lb. The first Iditarod was held in 1973 and it took the winner 20 days to complete. In 2005, the winner completed the course in 9 days, 18 hours, and 39 minutes.

1. If there are 1.609 km in a mile, approximately how many miles long is the race?

____

2. How many hours of sleep per day do the mushers average?

____

3. In 2005, what percentage of participants finished the race?

____

4. Which route was used in 2005?

____

5. In which month does the race begin?

____

6. How many minutes did it take the winner of the 2005 Iditarod to complete the race?

____

7. How much longer did it take the 1973 winner to complete the race than the 2005 winner?

____

8. The formula for converting Celsius to Fahrenheit is $F = \frac{9}{5}C + 32$. What is the coldest temperature, to the nearest whole degree Fahrenheit, that the racers must endure?

____

9. High-Use Academic Words What is a *detail*, as mentioned in the study skill?

a. small part or feature

b. a short statement of the main part

Name ______________________ Class ______________ Date ______________

7C: Reading/Writing Math Symbols

For use after Lesson 7-4

Study Skill Work in a well-lit, quiet spot with the proper materials.

Write the meaning of the following mathematical expressions or equations.

1. $f(3) = 2x$ ______________________

2. -12 ______________________

3. $\angle S \cong \angle R$ ______________________

4. $\frac{8}{\$5}$ ______________________

5. $(3, 9)$ ______________________

6. $y < 15$ ______________________

7. $(-16 + 4^2) = 0$ ______________________

8. $12 - x$ ______________________

9. $\sqrt{64} = 8$ ______________________

10. $|-41| = 41$ ______________________

11. $\frac{3}{4} = 75\%$ ______________________

12. $f(x) = x + 3$ ______________________

13. $\triangle ABC \cong \triangle DEF$ ______________________

14. $\pi \approx 3.14$ ______________________

15. $x^2 + 4$ ______________________

16. $\sqrt{48} \approx 7$ ______________________

17. $A = bh$ ______________________

Name ________________________ Class ________________ Date ________________

7D: Visual Vocabulary Practice

For use after Lesson 7-4

Study Skill Mathematics builds on itself, so build a strong foundation.

Concept List

functions	function rule	linear
linear function	nonlinear	nonlinear functions
vertices	proportional relationship	fourth quadrant

Write the concept that best describes each exercise. Choose from the concept list above.

1.

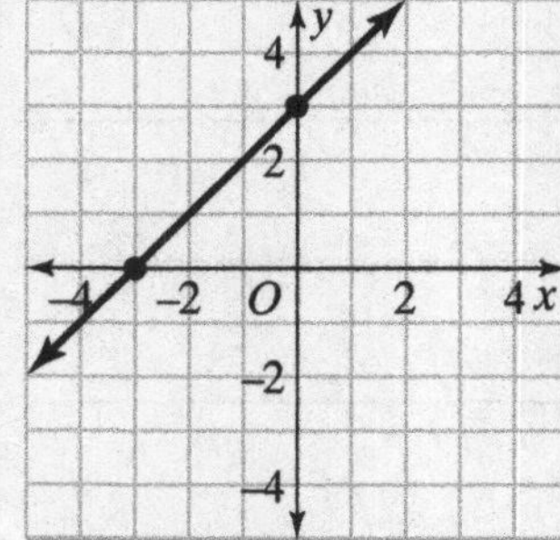

The type of change represented by the graph.

____

2.

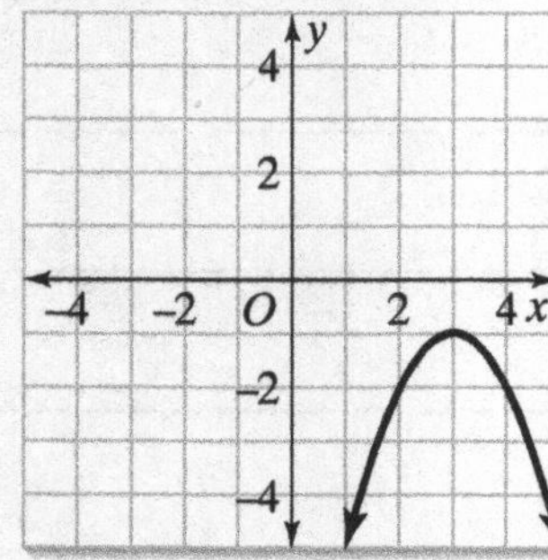

The type of change represented by the graph.

____

3.

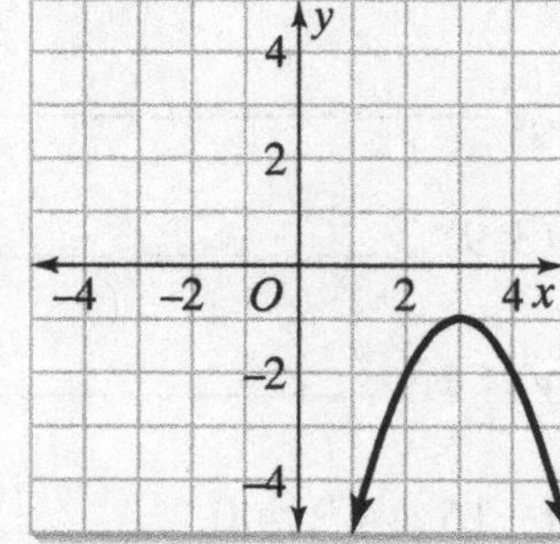

The location of the visible portion of the graph.

____

4. The points A, B, and C in triangle ABC

____

5.

$y = 3x^2 + 7$

$s = 8k^3 + 4$

____

6.

Cost	Pounds of Tomatoes
\$1.50	1
\$3.00	2
\$4.50	3
\$6.00	4

____

7. g is six added to the product of three and t

____

8. $g = 6 + 3t$

____

9.

$h = x^2 + 3$

$k = 4x + 2$

____

Name ________________________ Class ______________ Date ______________

7E: Vocabulary Check

For use after Lesson 7-5

Study Skill Strengthen your vocabulary. Use these pages and add cues and summaries by applying the Cornell Notetaking style.

Write the definition for each word or term at the right. To check your work, fold the paper back along the dotted line to see the correct answers.

______________________	linear
______________________	quadratic function
______________________	function rule
______________________	proportional relationship
______________________	function

Vocabulary and Study Skills

Name ______________________ Class ______________ Date ______________

7E: Vocabulary Check (continued)

For use after Lesson 7-5

Write the vocabulary word or term for each definition. To check your work, fold the paper back along the dotted line to see the correct answers.

change in data that forms a straight line when graphed ______________________

a nonlinear function in which the greatest exponent of a variable is 2 ______________________

an equation that describes a function ______________________

a relationship between inputs and outputs in which the ratio of inputs and outputs is always the same ______________________

a relationship that assigns exactly one output value for each input value ______________________

7F: Vocabulary Review

For use with the Chapter Review

Study Skill Take notes while you study. Use a highlighter to emphasize important material in your notes.

Circle the word that best completes the sentence.

1. A rule that assigns to each input value exactly one output value is a (*nonlinear function, function*).

2. A count of items, such as number of people or cars, is (*discrete, continuous*).

3. A function whose points lie on a straight line when the function is graphed is (*linear, nonlinear*).

4. A function whose points do not line on a straight line when the function is graphed is (*linear, nonlinear*).

5. Data where numbers between any two data values have meaning is (*discrete, continuous*).

6. Change in data is (*linear, nonlinear*) if it forms a straight line when graphed.

7. A (*coordinate, function rule*) is an equation that describes a function.

8. Slope intercept form is written as ($y = mx + b$, $y = Ax^2+Bx+C$).

9. Data that produces a curve when graphed is an example of (*linear, nonlinear*) change.

10. The (*x-intercept, y-intercept*) is the point where the graph crosses the y-axis.

11. A (*quadratic, proportional*) relationship is one in which the ratio of inputs and outputs is always the same.

Name ____________________ Class ____________ Date ____________

Practice 8-1

Random Samples and Surveys

You want to survey students in your school about their exercise habits. Tell whether the situations described in Exercises 1 and 2 are likely to give a random sample of the population. Explain.

1. You select every tenth student on an alphabetical list of the students in your school. You survey the selected students in their first-period classes.

2. At lunchtime you stand by a vending machine. You survey every student who buys something from the vending machine.

Is each question *biased* or *fair*? Rewrite biased questions as fair questions.

3. Do you think bike helmets should be mandatory for all bike riders?

4. Do you prefer the natural beauty of hardwood floors in your home?

5. Do you exercise regularly?

6. Do you eat at least the recommended number of servings of fruits and vegetables to ensure a healthy and long life?

7. Do you prefer the look and feel of thick lush carpeting in your living room?

8. Do you take a daily multiple vitamin to supplement your diet?

9. Do you read the newspaper to be informed about world events?

10. Do you feel that the TV news is a sensational portrayal of life's problems?

Name ____________________ Class ____________ Date ____________

8-1 • Guided Problem Solving

GPS Student Page 319, Exercise 19:

Parks Suppose you are gathering information about visitors to Yosemite National Park. You survey every tenth person entering the park.Would you get a random sample of visitors? Explain.

Understand

1. What is a random sample?

____

____

2. What are you being asked to do?

____

____

Plan and Carry Out

3. What is the population you are surveying?

____

4. Does every person in the population have an equal chance of being surveyed? ____________

5. Is this a random sample? Why or why not? ____________

____

Check

6. How else could you randomly survey the people at Yosemite National Park?

____

____

Solve Another Problem

7. You want to survey the people at the local pool about the food served in the snack shack. You decide to walk around the kiddy pool and survey parents. Is this a random sample? Why or why not?

____

____

____

Name ______________________ Class ____________ Date ____________

Practice 8-2

Estimating Population Size

Workers at a state park caught, tagged, and set free the species shown at the right. Later that same year, the workers caught the number of animals shown in the table below and counted the tagged animals. Use a proportion to estimate the park population of each species.

Tagged Animals	
Bears	12
Squirrels	50
Raccoons	23
Rabbits	42
Trout	46
Skunks	21

	Caught	Counted Tagged	Estimated Population
1. Bears	30	9	
2. Squirrels	1,102	28	
3. Raccoons	412	10	
4. Rabbits	210	2	
5. Trout	318	25	
6. Skunks	45	6	

A park ranger tags 100 animals. Use a proportion to estimate the total population for each sample.

7. 23 out of 100 animals are tagged

____

8. 12 out of 75 animals are tagged

____

9. 8 out of 116 animals are tagged

____

10. 5 out of 63 animals are tagged

____

11. 4 out of 83 animals are tagged

____

12. 3 out of 121 animals are tagged

____

13. 83 out of 125 animals are tagged

____

14. 7 out of 165 animals are tagged

____

Use a proportion to estimate each animal population.

15. Total ducks counted: 1,100
Marked ducks counted: 257
Total marked ducks: 960

____

16. Total alligators counted: 310
Marked alligators counted: 16
Total marked alligators: 90

____

Name ____________________ Class ____________ Date ____________

8-2 • Guided Problem Solving

GPS Student Page 322, Exercise 19:

Sharks A biologist is studying the shark population off the Florida coast. He captures, tags, and sets free 38 sharks. A week later, 8 out of 25 sharks captured have tags. He uses the proportion $\frac{25}{8} = \frac{38}{x}$ to estimate that the population is about 12.

a. **Error Analysis** Find the error in the biologist's proportion.

b. Estimate the shark population.

Understand

1. What are you being asked to do?

____

Plan and Carry Out

2. If x represents all the sharks off the coast of Florida, write the ratio of the sharks the biologist originally tagged to the number of all the sharks off the coast of Florida. ______

3. How many sharks did the biologist capture the second time? How many were tagged? ______

4. Write a ratio comparing the sharks the biologist found tagged and the number that were captured the second time. ______

5. Set the ratios from Steps 2 and 4 equal to form the correct proportion. ______

6. What is wrong with the biologist's proportion? ______

7. Solve this proportion to find the correct estimate. ______

Check

8. Explain why the biologist should have known the estimate was wrong.

____

____

Solve Another Problem

9. A ranger traps, tags, and releases 32 jackrabbits. Later she captures 12 jackrabbits, of which 4 are tagged. The ranger estimates that there are 96 jackrabbits in the area. Write a proportion and check the ranger's estimate. Is she correct?

____

Name ______________________ Class ______________ Date ______________

Practice 8-3

Inferences

The tables below show the number of hours a random sample of park visitors spent at the park during the months of January and June. Use the samples to make an inference about each measure. Support your answer.

Random Sample of Hours - January									
2	2	3	1	4	2	1	7	4	1
3	2	4	5	6	3	3	2	4	3

Random Sample of Hours - June									
2	3	4	2	5	4	9	1	5	3
1	8	2	6	4	3	7	6	8	5

1. the mean number of hours visitors spent in the park in January ______________

____

____

2. the mean number of hours visitors spent in the park in June ______________

____

____

3. Compare the mean number of hours visitors spent in the park in January to the mean number of hours visitors spent in the park in June.

____

____

____

____

About 450 people visit a local travel expo. A local travel agency owner surveys 3 random samples of 20 people each about their favorite vacation destinations. The table at the right shows the results.

	Sample 1	Sample 2	Sample 3
Beach	8	7	4
Mountains	9	6	10
City	3	7	6

4. For each sample, estimate how many people prefer to vacation in the mountains.

____

5. Describe the variation in the predictions. ____

6. Make an inference about the number of people who will prefer to vacation in the mountains.

____

____

Name ______________________ Class ______________ Date ______________

8-3 • Guided Problem Solving

GPS Student Page 329, Exercise 13:

Reasoning A government inspector takes 5 random samples of the same size from a shipment of eggs. She determines the mean weight of a dozen eggs in each sample. What can the inspector conclude if the mean weights of the samples are very close to each other?

Understand

1. What are you being asked to do? ______________________

2. How will you find the answer? ______________________

Plan and Carry Out

3. How do you find the mean weight of one sample of eggs? ______________________

4. What does the mean tell you about a sample?

5. What can you tell by comparing the means of all the samples? ______________________

6. What can you conclude if the mean weights of all the samples are very close to each other?

Check

7. How can you be sure your answer is correct? ______________________

Solve Another Problem

8. A poll taker interviews 10 random samples of 20 people each about the number of minutes they spend exercising each day. What can the poll taker conclude if the mean numbers of minutes spent exercising per day are very far apart? ______________________

Name ______________________ Class ______________ Date ______________

Practice 8-4

Data Variability

1. A biologist collects data about beard length on wild turkeys. Compare the IQRs of the data sets, and use the comparison to make an inference.

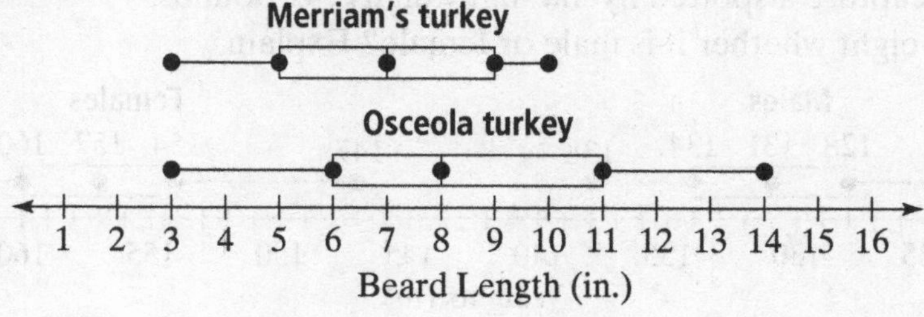

IQR for Merriam's wild turkey: ☐ IQR for Osceola wild turkey: ☐

What can you infer? Explain your reasoning.

____

____

____

The line plot at the right shows the number of homeruns hit by players in a homerun derby.

Homeruns		
Teens		Adults
✗✗	1	✗
✗✗	2	
✗	3	✗✗
✗	4	✗✗✗
✗✗	5	
	6	
✗	7	✗✗
	8	✗
	9	✗
✗	10	

2. Calculate the mean of each data set.

Teens: ☐

Adults: ☐

3. Determine the MAD for each data set.

Teens: ☐

Adults: ☐

4. What number n multiplied by the MAD equals the difference between the means?

MAD: ☐

5. What does this number tell you about the overlap of the data sets?

☐

Name ________________ Class ________________ Date ________________

8-4 • Guided Problem Solving

GPS Student Page 334, Exercise 12:

Reasoning Biologists capture a spotted hyena that weighs 142 pounds. Can you tell from its weight whether it is male or female? Explain.

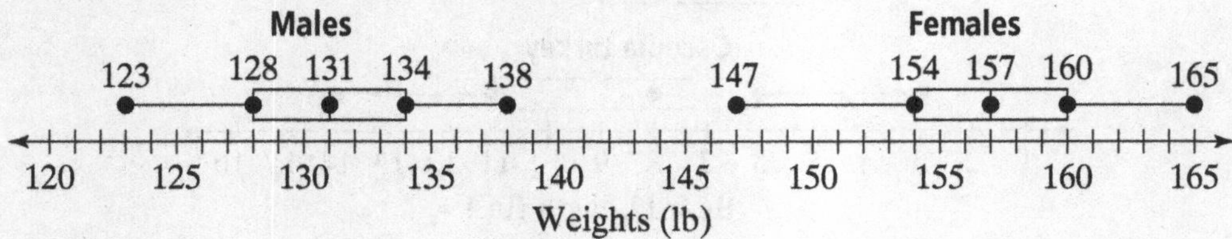

Understand

1. What are you being asked to do?

____

2. What will you use to find the answer? ________________

Plan and Carry Out

3. What is the maximum weight given for male spotted hyenas? ________

4. What is the minimum weight given for female spotted hyenas? ________

5. Does the weight of 142 pounds fit into either the male or female range? ________

6. Can you tell whether the spotted hyena is male or female based on its weight? Explain.

____

____

____

Check

7. Plot the weight 142 on the number line above.

Solve Another Problem

8. The box-plot below shows the scores of students. Based on the plot, can you tell if a student who scored 1,360 took the Study Skills course?

____

____

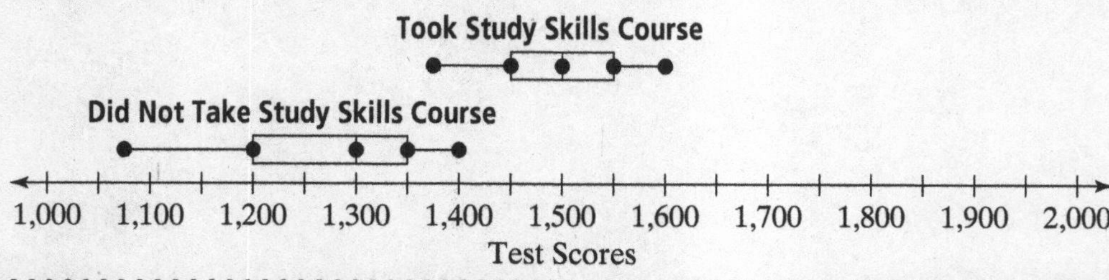

Name ________________ Class ____________ Date ____________

8A: Graphic Organizer

For use before Lesson 8-1

Study Skill As your teacher presents new material in the chapter, keep a paper and pencil handy to write down notes and questions. If you miss class, borrow a classmate's notes so you will not fall behind.

Write your answers.

1. What is the chapter title? ____________________
2. How many lessons are there in this chapter? ____________
3. What is the topic of the Test-Taking Strategies page? ____________
4. Complete the graphic organizer below as you work through the chapter.
   - In the center, write the title of the chapter.
   - When you begin a lesson, write the lesson name in a rectangle.
   - When you complete a lesson, write a skill or key concept in a circle linked to that lesson block.
   - When you complete the chapter, use this graphic organizer to help you review.

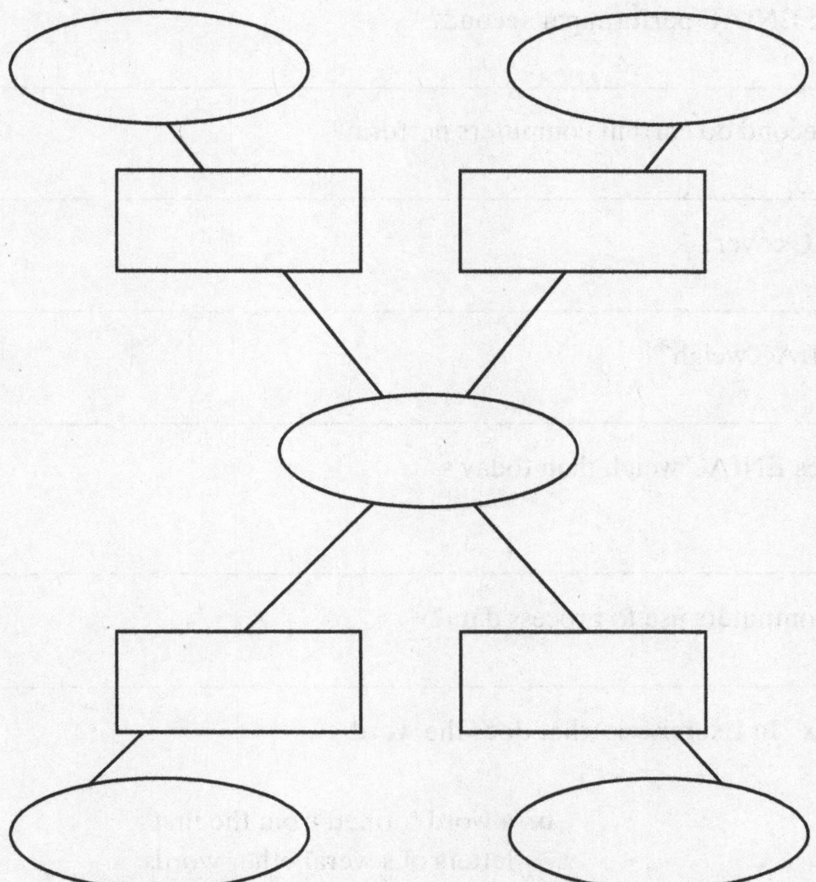

Name ______________________ Class ______________ Date ____________

8B: Reading Comprehension

For use after Lesson 8-3

Study Skill Take short breaks between assignments.

Read the paragraph and answer the questions.

In 1945, the first electronic computer was built. ENIAC, which stands for Electronic Numerical Integrator and Calculator, was able to do 5,000 additions per second. Current computers are capable of doing 100,000 times as many additions per second. ENIAC weighed approximately 30 tons and had a length of 40 feet and a width of 45 feet. Present-day computer notebooks weigh about 3 pounds. Unlike modern computers, which use microprocessors composed of thousands or millions of transistors, ENIAC used vacuum tubes to process data. It had about 18,000 tubes, each the size of a small light bulb.

1. What does the acronym ENIAC stand for?

____

2. How many years ago was ENIAC built?

____

3. How many additions could ENIAC perform per second?

____

4. How many additions per second do current computers perform?

____

5. How much area did ENIAC cover?

____

6. How many pounds did ENIAC weigh?

____

7. How many times more does ENIAC weigh than today's notebook computers?

____

8. What do today's modern computers use to process data?

____

9. **High-Use Academic Words** In Exercise 1, what does the word *acronym* mean?

   a. a certain way in which something appears

   b. a word formed from the first letters of several other words

Name ______________________ Class ______________ Date ______________

8C: Reading/Writing Math Symbols

For use after Lesson 8-4

Study Skill Make a realistic study schedule. Plan ahead when your teacher assigns a long-term project.

Some mathematical symbols have multiple meanings. Explain the meaning of the bar (−) in each of the following.

1. $2.\overline{3}$

____

2. $11 - 15$

____

3. $\overline{GH}$

____

4. $3 + (-7)$

____

5. $\frac{1}{5}$

____

____

The bar (−) takes on different meanings when used with other symbols. Explain the meaning of each symbol below.

6. $=$ ______________________

7. $\leq$ ______________________

8. $\cong$ ______________________

9. $\stackrel{?}{=}$ ______________________

10. $\neq$ ______________________

When they are vertical, the bars also take on different meanings. Explain the meaning of these symbols.

11. $|\ \ |$, as in $|-3| = 3$

____

12. $\|$, as in $m \parallel n$

____

Vocabulary and Study Skills

Name ______________________ Class ______________ Date ______________

8D: Visual Vocabulary Practice

For use after Lesson 8-4

Study Skill When interpreting an illustration, notice the information that is given and also notice what is not given. Do not make assumptions.

Concept List

biased question	proportion	variability
frequency table	line plot	population
sample	interquartile range (IQR)	inference

Write the concept that best describes each exercise. Choose from the concept list above.

1.

Measure of how much the data is spread out.

____

2.

Number of Sports Played by Students

Sports	Tally	Frequency
0	~~IIII~~	5
1	II	2
2	III	3
3	~~IIII~~ II	7

____

3.

Sandy conducted a survey at her college. She chose a random sample from all freshmen and asked how much time they study each week. The freshmen class represents this for the survey.

____

4.

A prediction or conclusion

____

5.

Books Read Last Month

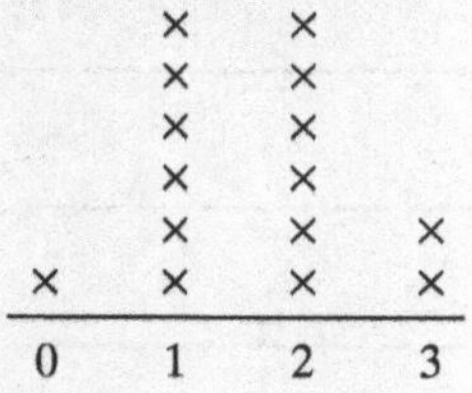

____

6.

Used to estimate population size.

____

7.

"Do you prefer lovable dogs or lazy cats?"

____

8.

Difference between upper and lower quartiles

____

9.

Derrick conducted a survey using the customers at a local ice cream shop. Derrick chose every 5th and 8th customer entering the shop to represent this.

____

Name ______________________ Class ______________ Date ______________

8E: Vocabulary Check

For use after Lesson 8-4

Study Skill Strengthen your vocabulary. Use these pages and add cues and summaries by applying the Cornell Notetaking style.

Write the definition for each word or term at the right. To check your work, fold the paper back along the dotted line to see the correct answers.

_______________________________________ biased question

_______________________________________ population

_______________________________________ mean absolute deviation (MAD)

_______________________________________ inference

_______________________________________ random sample

Vocabulary and Study Skills

Name ______________________ Class ______________ Date ______________

8E: Vocabulary Check (continued)

For use after Lesson 8-4

Write the vocabulary word or term for each definition. To check your work, fold the paper forward along the dotted line to see the correct answers.

a question that makes an unjustified assumption or makes one answer appear better than the other ______________________

a group of objects or people ______________________

measures the average distance between the mean and the data values ______________________

predictions or conclusions based on data or reasoning ______________________

a sample where each member of the population has an equal chance of being selected ______________________

Name ______________________ Class ______________ Date ______________

8F: Vocabulary Review

For use with the Chapter Review

Study Skill Take notes while you study. Use a highlighter to emphasize important material in your notes.

Circle the term that correctly completes each sentence.

1. The first number in an ordered pair is the (x, y) coordinate.
2. Lines in a coordinate plane that are parallel to the y-axis are (*horizontal, vertical*).
3. A (*line plot, frequency table*) uses a number line with "x" marks to represent each data item.
4. You can use a (*bar, circle*) graph to easily compare amounts.
5. The (*mean, median*) is the middle number in a data set when the values are written in order from least to greatest.
6. The (*mode, range*) of a data set is the difference between the greatest and least data values.
7. A (*line graph, box plot*) can be used to investigate the variability in a set of data.
8. A sequence is (*arithmetic, geometric*) if each term is found by adding the same number to the previous term.
9. (*Principal, Interest*) is the amount of money borrowed or deposited.
10. The (*area, surface area*) of a prism is the sum of the areas of the faces.
11. (*Circumference, Area*) is the distance around a circle.
12. The opposite of squaring a number is finding its (*square root, perfect square*).
13. The (*slope, bisector*) of a line segment is a line, segment, or ray, that goes through the midpoint of the segment.

Name ____________________ Class ____________ Date ____________

Practice 9-1

Probability

You spin a spinner numbered 1 through 10. Each outcome is equally likely. Find the probabilities below as a fraction, decimal, and percent.

1. *P*(9) ________
2. *P*(even) ________
3. *P*(number greater than 0) ________
4. *P*(multiple of 4) ________

There are eight blue marbles, nine orange marbles, and six yellow marbles in a bag. You draw one marble at random. Find each probability.

5. *P*(blue marble) ________
6. *P*(yellow marble) ________
7. What marble could you add or remove so that the probability of drawing a blue marble is $\frac{1}{3}$?

____

A box contains 12 slips of paper as shown. Each slip of paper is equally likely to be drawn. Find each probability.

red	blue	yellow	blue
yellow	red	blue	red
red	red	red	yellow

8. *P*(red) ________
9. *P*(blue) ________
10. *P*(yellow) ________
11. *P*(red or blue) ________
12. *P*(red or yellow) ________
13. *P*(blue or yellow) ________
14. *P*(not red) ________
15. *P*(not blue) ________
16. *P*(not yellow) ________

You select a letter randomly from a bag containing the letters S, P, I, N, N, E, and R. Find the odds in favor of each outcome.

17. selecting an N ________
18. selecting an S ________

Name ______________________ Class ______________ Date ____________

9-1 • Guided Problem Solving

GPS Student Page 345, Exercise 30:

a. Suppose $P(E) = 0.3$. Find $P(\text{not } E)$.
b. Suppose $P(\text{not } E) = 65\%$. Find $P(E)$.

Understand

1. What is the relationship between E and not E?

____

2. What is the sum of the probability of an event and the probability of the event's complement? ______________

3. What is the difference between part (a) and part (b)?

____

____

Plan and Carry Out

4. Write an equation for part (a) using the definition of a complement.

____

5. Solve the equation for $P(\text{not } E)$. ______________

6. Write 65% as a decimal. ______________

7. Write an equation for part (b) using the definition of a complement.

____

8. Solve the equation for $P(E)$. ______________

Check

9. How could you use a sum to check your answers?

____

____

Solve Another Problem

10. Suppose $P(E) = \frac{4}{5}$. Find $P(\text{not } E)$.

____

Name ______________________ Class ______________ Date ______________

Practice 9-2

Experimental Probability

Suppose you observe the color of socks worn by students in your class: 12 have white, 4 have black, 3 have blue, and 1 has red. Find each experimental probability as a fraction in simplest form.

1. *P*(white) ________ **2.** *P*(red) ________ **3.** *P*(blue) ________

4. *P*(black) ________ **5.** *P*(yellow) ________ **6.** *P*(black or red) ________

Use the data in the table at the right for Exercises 7–12. Find each experimental probability as a percent.

Favorite Snack Survey Results

Snack	Number of Students
Fruit	8
Granola	2
Pretzels	3
Chips	7
Carrots	5

7. *P*(fruit) ________ **8.** *P*(granola) ________

9. *P*(pretzels) ________ **10.** *P*(carrots) ________

11. *P*(not fruit) ________ **12.** *P*(granola or chips) ________

13. Do an experiment to find the probability that a word chosen randomly in a book is the word *the*. How many words did you look at to find *P*(the)? What is *P*(the)?

____

14. Suppose the following is the result of tossing a coin 5 times:

heads, tails, heads, tails, heads

What is the experimental probability for heads?

____

Solve.

15. The probability that a twelve-year-old has a brother or sister is 25%. Suppose you survey 300 twelve-year-olds. About how many do you think will have a brother or sister? ________

16. a. A quality control inspector found flaws in 13 out of 150 sweaters. Find the probability that a sweater has a flaw. Round to the nearest tenth of a percent. ________

b. Suppose the company produces 500 sweaters a day. How many will not have flaws? ________

c. Suppose the company produces 600 sweaters a day. How many will have flaws? ________

Name ______________________ Class ______________ Date ____________

9-2 • Guided Problem Solving

GPS Student Page 349, Exercise 14:

a. Science The probability that a male human is colorblind is 8%. Suppose you interview 1,000 males. About how many would you expect to be colorblind?

b. Reasoning Will you always get the same number? Explain.

Understand

1. What does it mean to be colorblind?

____

2. What are you being asked to do in part (a)?

____

____

Plan and Carry Out

3. Find 8% of 1,000. ____________________________

4. How many males out of 1,000 would you expect to be colorblind?

____

5. Will you always get exactly this number? Explain.

____

____

____

Check

6. How could you find the answer another way?

____

Solve Another Problem

7. The probability of a person being left-handed is about 11%. Suppose you interview 500 people. About how many would you expect to be left-handed?

____

Name ________________ Class ________ Date ________

Practice 9-3

Sample Spaces

Make a table to show the sample space and find the number of outcomes. Then find the probability.

1. A theater uses a letter to show which row a seat is in, and a number to show the column. If there are eight rows and ten columns, what is the probability that you select a seat at random that is in column 1? ________

Make a tree diagram. Then find the probability.

2. A coin is tossed three times.
   a. Make a tree diagram that shows all the possible outcomes of how the coin will land.
   b. Find the probability that the coin will land heads up all three times or tails up all three times. ________

Use the counting principle.

3. A pizza company makes pizza in three different sizes: small, medium, and large. There are four possible toppings: pepperoni, sausage, green pepper, and mushroom. How many different kinds of pizza with one topping are available? ________
4. You can choose from three types of sandwiches for lunch and three types of juice. How many possible lunch combinations of sandwich and juice can you have? ________

Susan has red, blue, and yellow sweaters. Joanne has green, red, and white sweaters. Diane's sweaters are red, blue, and mauve. Each girl has only one sweater of each color and will pick a sweater to wear at random. Find each probability.

5. *P*(each girl chooses a different color) ________
6. *P*(each girl chooses the same color) ________
7. *P*(two girls choose the same color, and the third chooses a different color) ________
8. *P*(each girl chooses a red sweater) ________

Name ______________________ Class ______________ Date ______________

9-3 • Guided Problem Solving

GPS Student Page 357, Exercise 23:

a. Clothes Ardell has four suit jackets (white, blue, green, and tan) and four dress shirts in the same colors. How many different jacket/shirt outfits does Ardell have?

b. Suppose he grabs a suit jacket and a dress shirt without looking. What is the probability that they will *not* be the same color?

Understand

1. Circle the information you will need to solve.
2. How do you find probability?

____

____

Plan and Carry Out

3. How many different suit jackets are there? __________
4. How many different dress shirts are there? __________
5. Using the counting principle, how many different jacket/shirt outfits does Ardell have? __________
6. How many same color jacket/shirt outfits does Ardell have? __________
7. How many different color jacket/shirt outfits does Ardell have? __________
8. What is the probability that they will *not* be the same color? __________

Check

9. How else could you find the total number of jacket/shirt outfits?

____

Solve Another Problem

10. **a.** Joseph has three pairs of shoes (white, brown, and black) and four pairs of socks (white, brown, black, and blue). How many sock/shoe pairs are there? __________

    b. If Joseph selects a pair of shoes and a pair of socks without looking, what is the probability they will be the same color?

____

Name ______________________ Class ______________ Date ______________

Practice 9-4

Compound Events

Each letter in the word MASSACHUSETTS is written on a card. The cards are placed in a basket. Find each probability.

1. What is the probability of selecting two S's if the first card is replaced before selecting the second card?

   ____

2. What is the probability of selecting two S's if the first card is not replaced before selecting the second card?

   ____

You roll a fair number cube. Find each probability.

3. P(3, then 5)

   ____

4. P(2, then 2)

   ____

5. P(5, then 4, then 6)

   ____

6. P(6, then 0)

   ____

Four girls and eight boys are running for president or vice president of the Student Council. Find each probability.

7. Find the probability that two boys are elected.

   ____

8. Find the probability that two girls are elected.

   ____

9. Find the probability that the president is a boy and the vice president is a girl.

   ____

10. Find the probability that the president is a girl and the vice president is a boy.

    ____

A box contains ten balls, numbered 1 through 10. Marisha draws a ball. She records its number and then returns it to the bag. Then Penney draws a ball. Find each probability.

9
8 5
3 10 4
6 7 1 2

11. P(9, then 3)

    ____

12. P(even, then odd)

    ____

13. P(odd, then 2)

    ____

14. P(the sum of the numbers is 25)

    ____

15. P(prime, then composite)

    ____

16. P(a factor of 8, then a multiple of 2)

    ____

Name ______________________ Class ______________ Date ______________

9-4 • Guided Problem Solving

GPS Student Page 364, Exercise 26:

Events with no outcomes in common are called *disjoint events* or *mutually exclusive events*. To find the probability of mutually exclusive events, add the probabilities of the individual events. Suppose you select a number from 21 to 30 at random. What is the probability of selecting a number that is even or prime?

Understand

1. What are disjoint or mutually exclusive events?

____

2. What are you being asked to do?

____

____

3. Why are selecting an even and selecting a prime number between 21 and 30 disjoint events?

____

Plan and Carry Out

4. How many numbers are there from 21 to 30? (Remember to include 21 and 30.) ____________
5. List all the even numbers between 21 and 30. How many are there? ____________
6. What is the probability of choosing an even number between 21 and 30? ____________
7. List all the prime numbers between 21 and 30. How many are there? ____________
8. What is the probability of choosing a prime number between 21 and 30? ____________
9. What is the probability of choosing an even or prime number between 21 and 30? ____________

Check

10. Write your answer as a fraction, decimal, and percent. ____________

Solve Another Problem

11. Suppose you roll a number cube. What is the probability that you roll a number less than 3 or a number greater than or equal to 5?

____

Name ______________________ Class ______________ Date ____________

Practice 9-5

Simulating Compound Events

1. The table shows the fraction of different types of pencils in Eva's pencil box.

Type	Fraction
Plain	$\frac{1}{5}$
Glitter	$\frac{2}{5}$
Message	$\frac{2}{5}$

a. Design a simulation that can be used to estimate the probability that Eva will need to pick more than 3 randomly chosen glitter pencils from the pencil box before getting a plain pencil.

____

____

____

____

____

b. Perform 20 trials of the simulation. Then estimate the probability.

____

2. A grocery store includes one token with every purchase. Half of the tokens are for free merchandise, and the other half are for prizes.

a. Design a simulation that can be used to estimate the probability that a customer will need to make at least 2 purchases to receive a token for a prize.

____

____

____

____

b. Perform 20 trials of the simulation. Then estimate the probability.

____

In a satisfaction survey, 11% of a tour guide's customers said that the tour was too short. However, 48% said the tour was great. Estimate the probability that the guide will have to read at least 5 surveys to find one that said the tour was too short. Then estimate the probability that the guide will have to read at least 5 surveys to find one saying the tour was great.

Tour Guide Surveys			
02	19	24	61
32	43	30	17
18	68	55	11
08	90	72	03
49	63	80	52
12	27	34	70
20	49	03	66
52	78	83	54
60	48	52	77
13	61	27	91

3. Probability of reading at least 5 surveys to find one that said the tour was too short: ______________

4. Probability of reading at least 5 surveys to find one that said the tour was great: ______________

Name ______________________ Class ______________ Date ____________

9-5 • Guided Problem Solving

GPS Student Page 372, Exercise 9:

Consumer Math A restaurant gives out a scratch-off ticket with each purchase of a $5 meal deal. Two thirds of the tickets are winners. Design a simulation and perform 20 trials to estimate the probability that a customer will need to spend at least $15 to get a winning ticket.

Understand

1. What are you being asked to do?

____

____

2. What will you use to find the answer?

____

____

Plan and Carry Out

3. What fraction shows the amount of tickets that win? ________
4. What simulation tool would work best with this fraction? ________________
5. How many meals will $15 buy? ________
6. Let 1 and 2 represent winning tickets. Perform 20 trials. Complete the frequency table.
7. What is the probability that a customer will need to spend at least $15 to get a winning ticket?

____

Meals Bought to Get Winning Ticket	Frequency
1	
2	
3 or more	

Check

8. How can you check your answer?

____

Solve Another Problem

9. A sporting goods store holds a drawing for new merchandise. Each purchase of $20 or more gives a customer one entry into the drawing. Three fourths of the entries win a prize. Design a simulation and perform 20 trials to estimate the probability that a customer will need to spend at least $60 to win a prize.

____

____

Name ______________________ Class ______________ Date ____________

9A: Graphic Organizer

For use before Lesson 9-1

Study Skill Try to read new lessons before your teacher presents them in class. Important information is sometimes printed in **boldface** type or highlighted inside a box or with color. Pay special attention to this information.

Write your answers.

1. What is the chapter title? ______________________
2. How many lessons are there in this chapter? ______________________
3. What is the topic of the Test-Taking Strategies page? ______________________
4. Complete the graphic organizer below as you work through the chapter.
   - In the center, write the title of the chapter.
   - When you begin a lesson, write the lesson name in a rectangle.
   - When you complete a lesson, write a skill or key concept in a circle linked to that lesson block.
   - When you complete the chapter, use this graphic organizer to help you review.

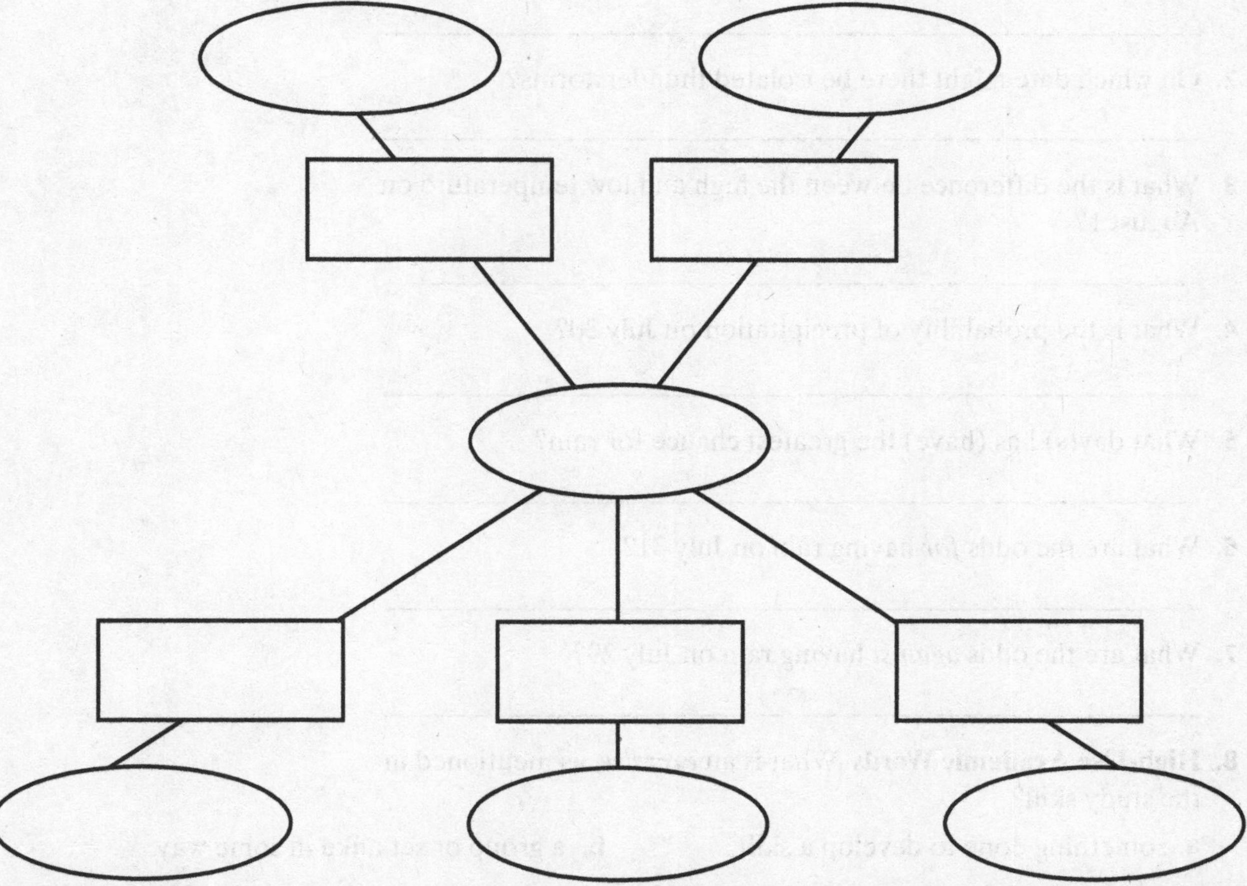

Vocabulary and Study Skills

Name ______________________ Class ______________ Date ______________

9B: Reading Comprehension

For use after Lesson 9-2

Study Skill When you complete a math exercise, always make sure your answer makes sense.

Below is an 8-day forecast of weather conditions. Use the table to answer the questions.

Date	Weather Prediction	High/Low Temp °F	% Chance of Precipitation
July 26 evening	Isolated T-Storms	67°	30%
July 27	PM T-Storms	87° / 71°	40%
July 28	Partly Cloudy	91° / 71°	20%
July 29	Scattered T-Storms	90° / 64°	40%
July 30	Partly Cloudy	87° / 65°	20%
July 31	Partly Cloudy	87° / 60°	20%
Aug 01	Partly Cloudy	83° / 59°	20%
Aug 02	Partly Cloudy	87° / 60°	0%

1. For what dates does the table give weather forecasts?

   ____

2. On which date might there be isolated thunderstorms?

   ____

3. What is the difference between the high and low temperature on August 1?

   ____

4. What is the probability of precipitation on July 30?

   ____

5. What day(s) has (have) the greatest chance for rain?

   ____

6. What are the odds *for* having rain on July 31?

   ____

7. What are the odds *against* having rain on July 29?

   ____

8. **High-Use Academic Words** What is an *exercise,* as mentioned in the study skill?

   a. something done to develop a skill

   b. a group or set alike in some way

Name ______________________ Class ______________ Date ____________

9C: Reading/Writing Math Symbols

For use after Lesson 9-5

Study Skill Write assignments down; do not rely only on your memory.

Vocabulary and Study Skills

Write the meaning of each mathematical expression.

1. $P(A)$

____

2. $P(\text{not } A)$

____

3. $P(A, \text{ then } B)$

____

Write each statement using appropriate mathematical symbols.

4. the probability of event C occurring

____

5. the probability of rolling an odd number on a number cube

____

6. the probability of event D, and then event E occurring

____

A bag contains 6 red, 2 blue, and 4 green marbles. Find each probability.

7. P(blue)

____

8. P(not red)

____

9. P(red, then blue when red is replaced)

____

10. P(red, then blue when red is not replaced)

____

Name ______________________ Class ______________ Date ______________

9D: Visual Vocabulary Practice

For use after Lesson 9-5

High-Use Academic Words

Study Skill Mathematics is like learning a foreign language. You have to know the vocabulary before you can speak the language correctly.

Concept List

counting principle	complement	independent events
compound events	simulation	dependent events
outcome	experimental probability	sample space

Write the concept that best describes each exercise. Choose from the concept list above.

1. A model used to estimate the probability of an event. ______________	**2.** A hat contains 6 names. You select 2 names without replacing the first name. ______________	**3.** There are 5 marbles, 3 green and 2 red. You draw a marble, then replace it before drawing the next marble. ______________
4. Two or more events ______________	**5.** If you flip a coin, then flipping heads is an example of this. ______________	**6.** Pedro draws a card from a standard 52-card deck. He then rolls a six-sided number cube. The total number of possible outcomes is $52 \times 6 = 312$. ______________
7. A B C In the set above, this is represented by {A, B, C}. ______________	**8.** Probability that is based on observation. ______________	**9.** Renee rolls a six-sided number cube. If an event represents rolling an even number, then this is represented by the set {1, 3, 5}. ______________

Name ______________________ Class ______________ Date ______________

9E: Vocabulary Check

For use after Lesson 9-5

Study Skill Strengthen your vocabulary. Use these pages and add cues and summaries by applying the Cornell Notetaking style.

Write the definition for each word or term at the right. To check your work, fold the paper back along the dotted line to see the correct answers.

______________________	independent event
______________________	sample space
______________________	event
______________________	theoretical probability
______________________	experimental probability

Name ______________________ Class ______________ Date ______________

9E: Vocabulary Check (continued)

For use after Lesson 9-5

Write the vocabulary word or term for each definition. To check your work, fold the paper forward along the dotted line to see the correct answers.

the occurrence of one event does not affect the probability of the occurrence of the other event ______________________

the set of all possible outcomes of a probability experiment ______________________

a collection of possible outcomes ______________________

the ratio of the number of favorable outcomes to the number of possible outcomes ______________________

the ratio of the number of times an event occurs to the total number of trials ______________________

Name ____________________ Class ______________ Date ______________

9F: Vocabulary Review

For use with the Chapter Review

Study Skill When using a word bank, read the words first. Then answer the questions.

Complete the crossword puzzle. Use the words from the following list.

parallelogram	conjecture	decagon	equation	mode
complement	symmetry	variable	discount	prime
independent	probability	dependent	outcome	slope

ACROSS

2. Events are ____________ if the occurrence of one event affects the probability of the occurrence of another event.
4. A figure has __________ if one side of the figure is the mirror image of the other side.
6. four-sided figure with two sets of parallel lines
8. possible result of an action
11. Events are ___________ if the occurrence of one event does not affect the probability of the occurrence of another event.

DOWN

1. prediction that suggests what you expect will happen
2. difference between the original price and the sale price
3. letter that stands for a number
5. ratio that describes the steepness of a line
6. used to express how likely an event is
7. number that occurs most often in a data set
9. collection of outcomes not contained in the event
10. mathematical statement with an equal sign
12. polygon with ten sides
13. whole number with only two factors, itself and the number one

Name ____________________ Class ____________ Date ____________

Practice 10-1

Angle Measures

Solve.

1. If $m\angle A = 23°$, what is the measure of its complement?

____

2. If $m\angle T = 163°$, what is the measure of its supplement?

____

3. If a 76° angle is complementary to $\angle Q$, what is the measure of $\angle Q$?

____

Find the measures of the complement and supplement of each angle.

4. $m\angle A = 41°$ ______________

5. $m\angle C = 38.1°$ ______________

6. $m\angle S = 87.3°$ ______________

7. $m\angle F = 19°$ ______________

8. $m\angle R = 76°$ ______________

9. $m\angle B = 24.9°$ ______________

10. $m\angle N = 62°$ ______________

11. In the diagram, $m\angle 1$ is 46°. Find the measures of $\angle 2$, $\angle 3$, and $\angle 4$.

____

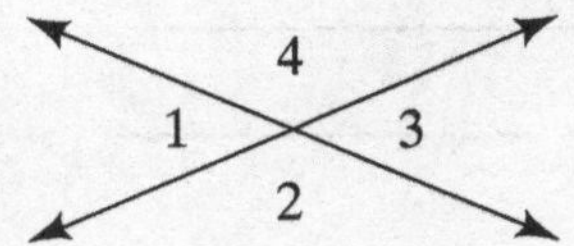

Name ______________________ Class ______________ Date ______________

10-1 • Guided Problem Solving

GPS Student Page 385, Exercise 17:

Writing in Math Can an angle ever have the same measure as its complement? Explain.

Understand

1. What are you being asked to do?

____

____

2. What do you have to do to explain your answer?

____

____

____

Plan and Carry Out

3. What is the definition of complementary angles?

____

4. If an angle and its complement have the same measure, explain the relationship between the angle and 90°.

____

5. Determine the measure of the angle. ______________

6. Can an angle ever have the same measure as its complement? ______________

Check

7. Explain your answer.

____

____

Solve Another Problem

8. Can an angle ever have the same measure as its supplement? Explain.

____

____

Name ______________ Class ______________ Date ______________

Practice 10-2

Area of a Parallelogram

Find the area of each parallelogram.

1. 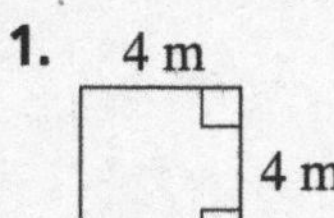

____

2. 5 cm
23 cm

____

3. 5 in.
4 in.
8 in.

____

4. 8 mm
10 mm
10 mm

____

Find the area of each parallelogram with base b and height h.

5. $b = 16$ mm, $h = 12$ mm

____

6. $b = 23$ km, $h = 14$ km

____

7. $b = 65$ mi, $h = 48$ mi

____

8. $b = 19$ in., $h = 15$ in.

____

Solve.

9. The area of a parallelogram is 6 square units. Both the height and the length of the base are whole numbers. What are the possible lengths and heights?

____

10. The perimeter of a rectangle is 72 m. The width of the rectangle is 16 m. What is the area of the rectangle?

____

11. The area of a certain rectangle is 288 yd^2. The perimeter is 68 yd. If you double the length and width, what will be the area and perimeter of the new rectangle?

____

12. If you have 36 ft of fencing, what are the areas of the different rectangles you could enclose with the fencing? Consider only whole-number dimensions.

____

____

Name ______________________ Class ______________ Date ____________

10-2 • Guided Problem Solving

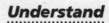

GPS Student Page 392, Exercise 22:

Geography The shape of the state of Tennessee is similar to a parallelogram. Estimate the area of Tennessee.

110 mi
Nashville
Knoxville
TENNESSEE
Memphis
380 mi

Understand

1. What are you being asked to do?

____

____

2. What shape is Tennessee similar to?

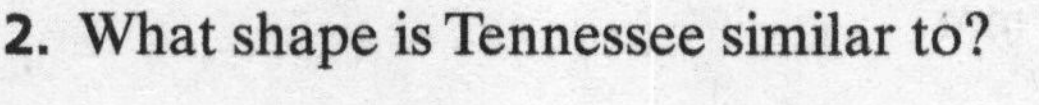

____

____

3. How do you find the area of a parallelogram?

____

____

Plan and Carry Out

4. What is the height of Tennessee? ______________

5. What is the length of the base of Tennessee? ______________

6. Substitute the values into the formula $A = bh$. ______________

7. What is the approximate area of Tennessee? ______________

Check

8. Is this estimate more or less than the actual area of Tennessee? Explain.

____

____

____

Solve Another Problem

9. Tamika's yard is similar to the shape of a parallelogram. Estimate the area of Tamika's yard.

____

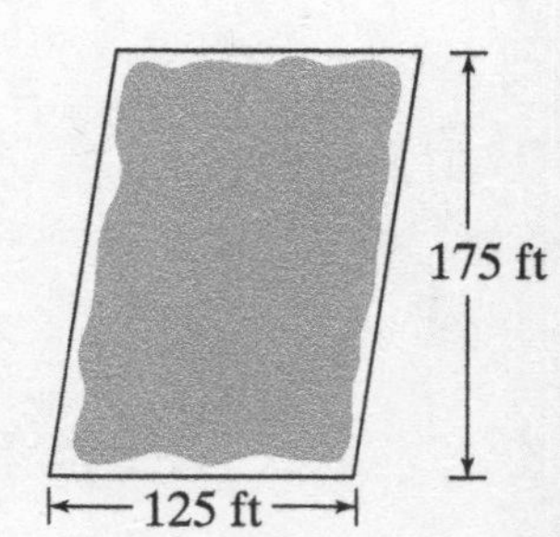

Name ______________________ Class ______________ Date ______________

Practice 10-3

Area of a Triangle

Find the area of each triangle.

1\.

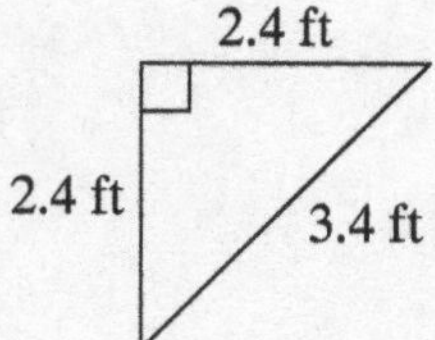

2\.

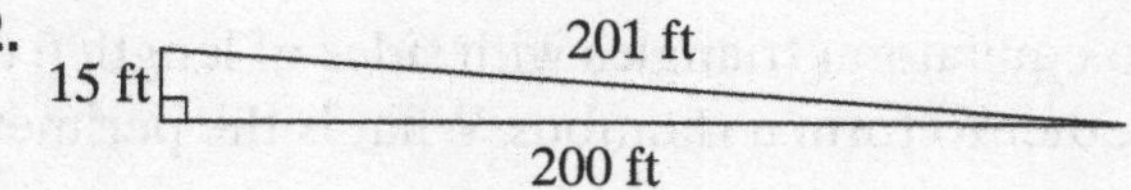

3\.

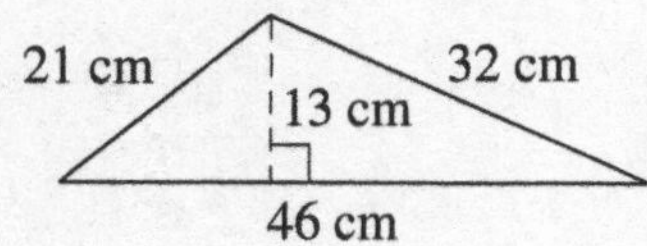

4\.

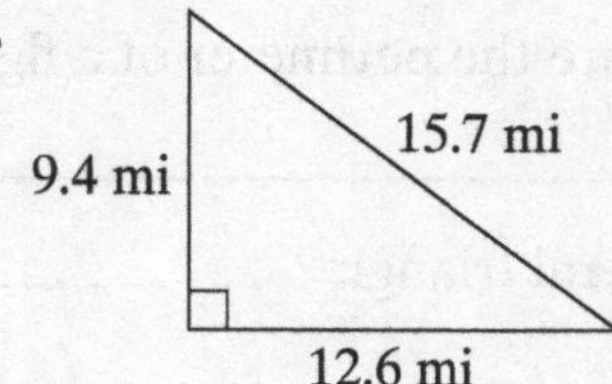

5\.

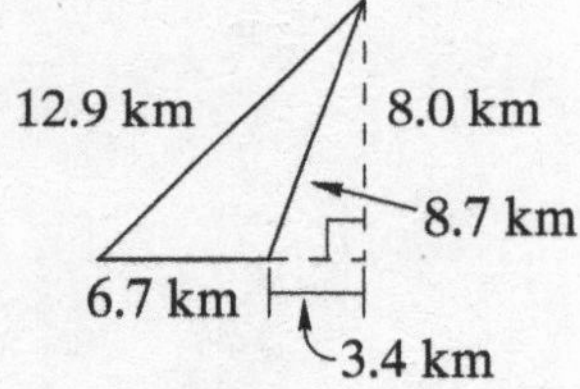

6\.

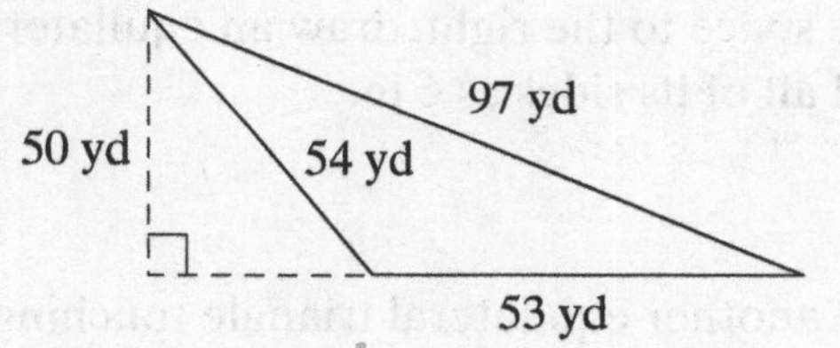

Solve.

7. A homeowner plants two flower beds around his garage. What is the total area he will have planted? Round to the nearest tenth.

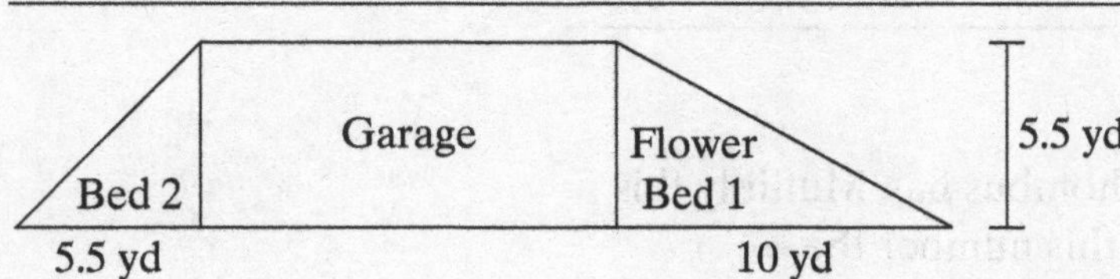

8. The side of an equilateral triangle has a length of 5.4 m. The height of the triangle is approximately 4.7 m. What is the area of this triangle? Round your answer to the nearest tenth.

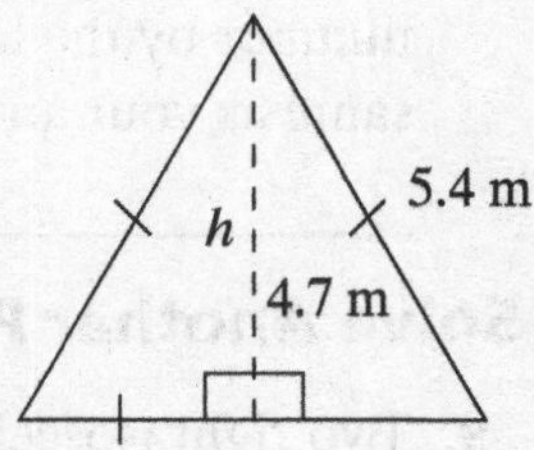

Name ______________________ Class ______________ Date ____________

10-3 • Guided Problem Solving

GPS Student Page 397, Exercise 22:

Two equilateral triangles with sides of length 6 inches are joined together to form a rhombus. What is the perimeter of the rhombus?

Understand

1. What are you being asked to do? ______________________

   ____

2. How do you measure the perimeter of a figure?

   ____

3. What is an equilateral triangle? ______________________

   ____

Plan and Carry Out

4. In the space to the right, draw an equilateral triangle. Label all of its sides as 6 in.

5. Draw another equilateral triangle touching the first equilateral triangle so that the two triangles form a rhombus.

6. Label the sides of the second triangle as 6 in.

7. Add the lengths of the sides of the rhombus to find the perimeter. ______________________

   ____

Check

8. Count the number of sides that the rhombus has. Multiply this number by the length of the sides. Is this number the same as your answer? ______________________

   ____

Solve Another Problem

9. Two right isosceles triangles with legs of 5 in. length and a hypotenuse of 7.1 in. are joined together to make a square. What is the perimeter of the square?

   ____

Name ______________________ Class ______________________ Date ______________________

Practice 10-4

Areas of Other Figures

Find the area of each trapezoid.

1.

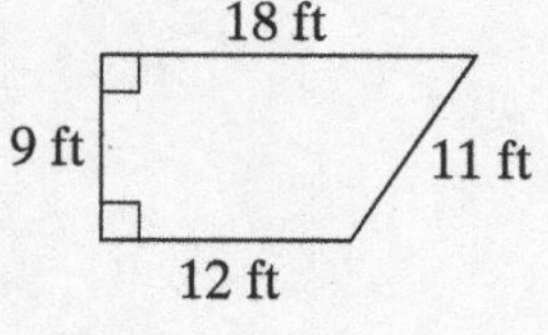

2.

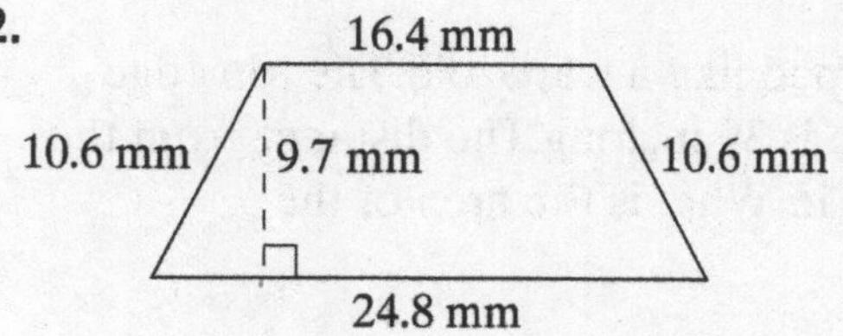

3.

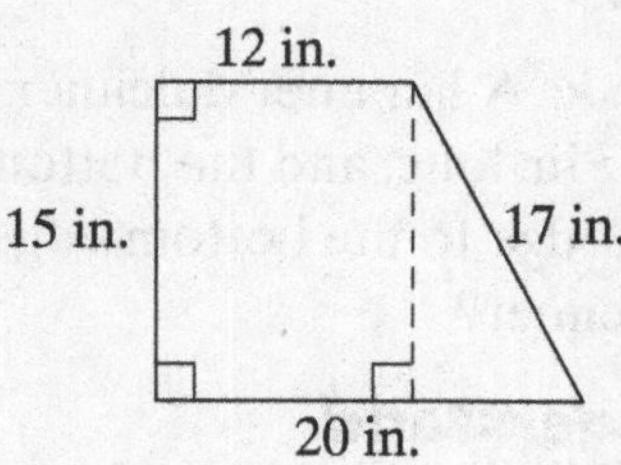

______________________ ______________________ ______________________

4.

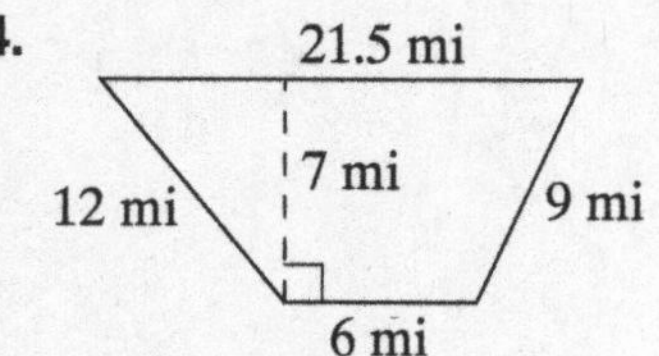

5.

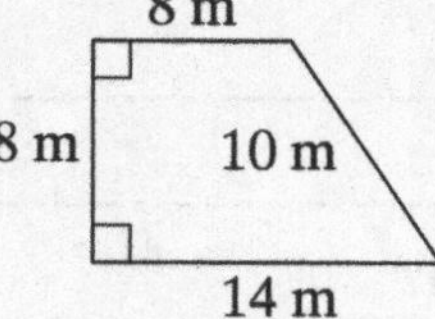

6.

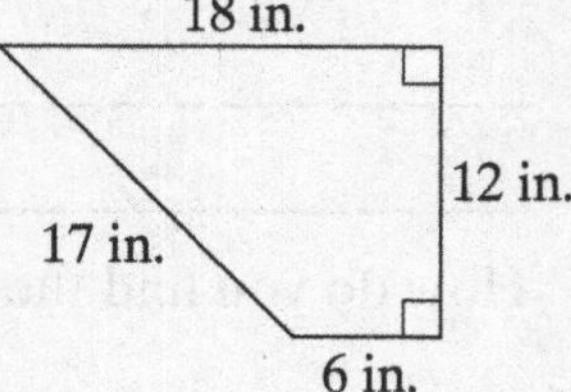

______________________ ______________________ ______________________

Find the area of each irregular figure.

7.

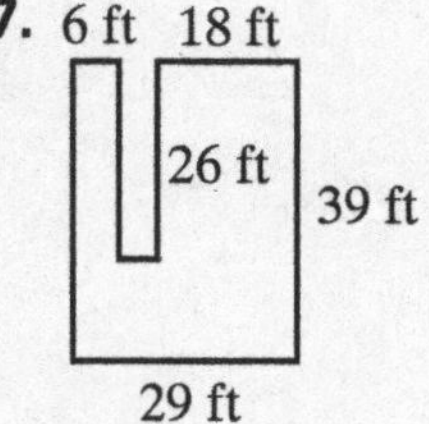

8.

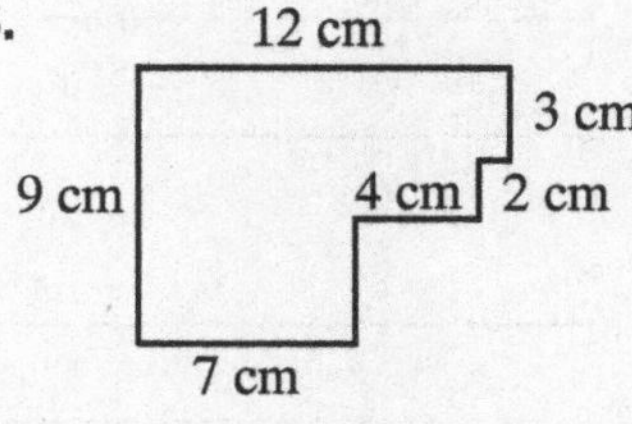

9.

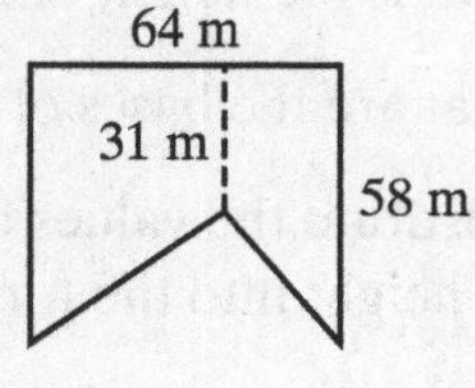

______________________ ______________________ ______________________

Solve.

10. The flag of Switzerland features a white cross on a red background.

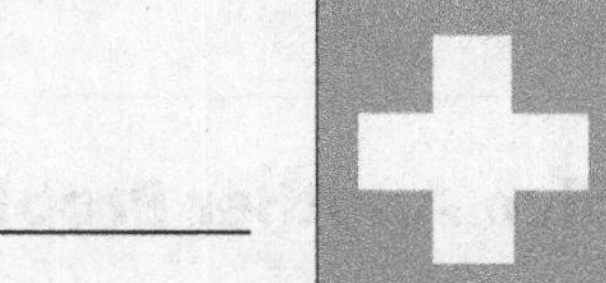

a. Each of the 12 sides of the cross has a length of 15 cm. Find the area of the white cross. ______________________

b. The flag has dimensions 60 cm by 60 cm. Find the area of the red region. ______________________

11. A trapezoid has an area of 4 square units, and a height of 1 unit. What are the possible whole-number lengths for the bases? ______________________

Name ______________________ Class ______________ Date ______________

10-4 • Guided Problem Solving

GPS Student Page 402, Exercise 17:

Music A hammer dulcimer is shaped like a trapezoid.The top edge is 17 in. long, and the bottom edge is 39 in. long.The distance from the top edge to the bottom edge is 16 in.What is the area of the dulcimer?

Understand

1. Circle the information you will need to solve the problem.
2. What are you being asked to do?

____

____

3. How do you find the area of a trapezoid?

____

____

Plan and Carry Out

4. What is the height of the dulcimer? ____________
5. What are the bases of the dulcimer? ____________
6. Substitute the values for the bases and the height into the formula for area. ____________
7. What is the area of the dulcimer? ____________

Check

8. Explain how you chose which measurements are the bases.

____

____

Solve Another Problem

9. Suppose the dulcimer had bases of 20 in. and 36 in. with the same height. What would be the area of the dulcimer? How do the areas compare? Explain.

____

____

Name ______________________ Class ______________ Date ______________

Practice 10-5

Circumference and Area of a Circle

Find the circumference and area of each circle. Round your answers to the nearest tenth.

1.

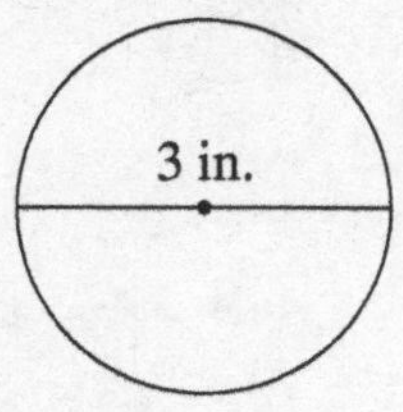

____

2.

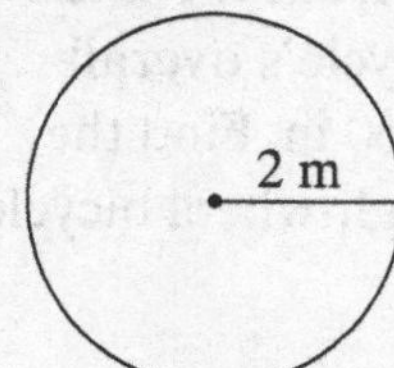

____

3.

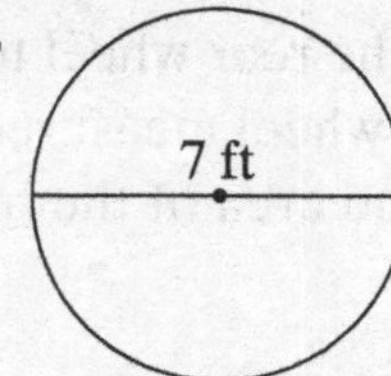

____

4.

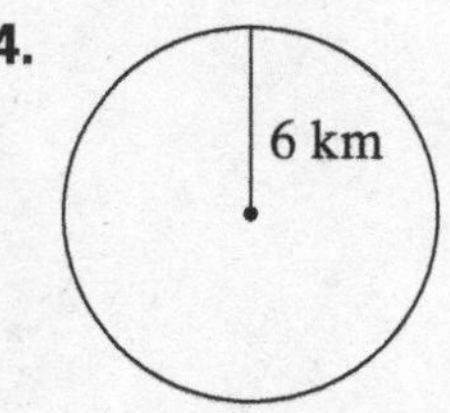

____

5.

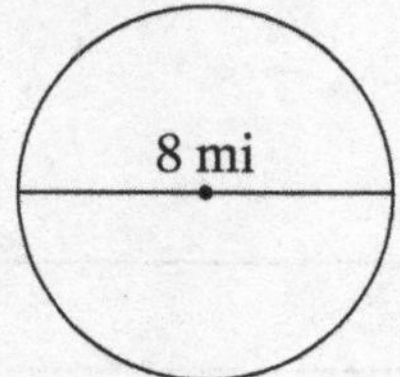

____

6.

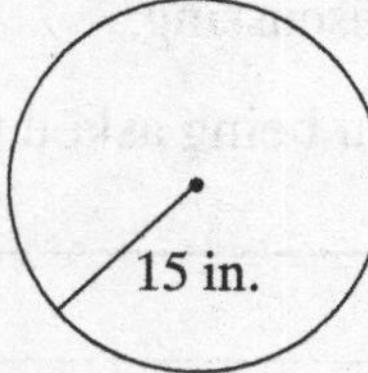

____

7.

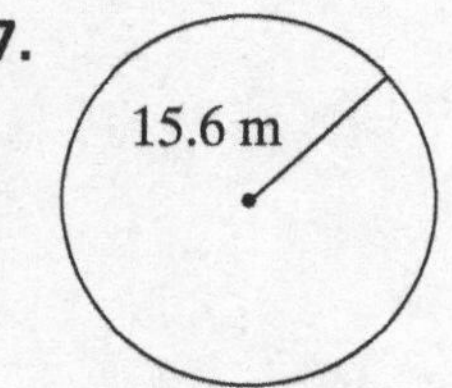

____

8.

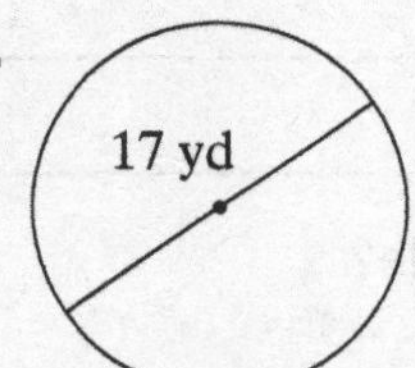

____

9.

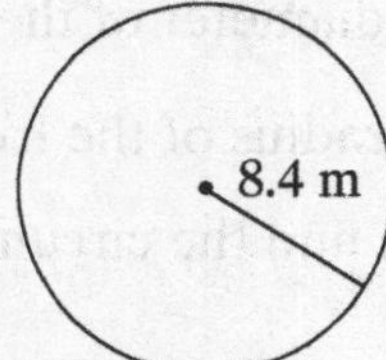

____

Estimate the radius of each circle with the given circumference. Round your answer to the nearest tenth.

10. 80 km ______________

11. 92 ft ______________

12. 420 in. ______________

13. In the diagram at the right, the radius of the large circle is 8 in. The radius of each of the smaller circles is 1 in. Find the area of the shaded region to the nearest square unit.

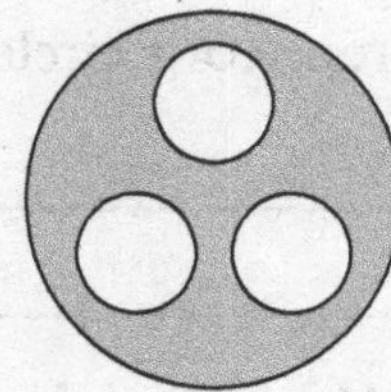

____

Name ______________________ Class ______________ Date ______________

10-5 • Guided Problem Solving

GPS Student Page 407, Exercise 29:

Bicycles The front wheel of a high-wheel bicycle from the late 1800s was larger than the rear wheel to increase the bicycle's overall speed. The front wheel measured in height up to 60 in. Find the circumference and area of the front wheel of a high-wheel bicycle.

Understand

1. Circle the information you will need to solve.
2. In the space to the right, draw a sketch of the bicycle that the problem is discussing.
3. What are you being asked to do?

____

____

Plan and Carry Out

4. What is the diameter of the front wheel? ______________
5. What is the radius of the front wheel? ______________
6. How do you find the circumference of a circle?

____

7. What is the circumference of the front wheel? ______________
8. How do you find the area of a circle?

____

9. What is the area of the front wheel? ______________

Check

10. How do you determine the radius if you know the area and circumference of a circle?

____

____

Solve Another Problem

11. The diameter of a normal front wheel on a bicycle is 24 in. Find the circumference and area of the front wheel.

____

Name ______________________ Class ______________ Date ______________

10A: Graphic Organizer

For use before Lesson 10-1

Study Skill Take notes while you study. Writing something down might help you remember it better. Go back and review your notes when you study for quizzes and tests.

Write your answers.

1. What is the chapter title? ______________________
2. How many lessons are there in this chapter? ______________________
3. What is the topic of the Test-Taking Strategies page? ______________________
4. Complete the graphic organizer below as you work through the chapter.
   - In the center, write the title of the chapter.
   - When you begin a lesson, write the lesson name in a rectangle.
   - When you complete a lesson, write a skill or key concept in a circle linked to that lesson block.
   - When you complete the chapter, use this graphic organizer to help you review.

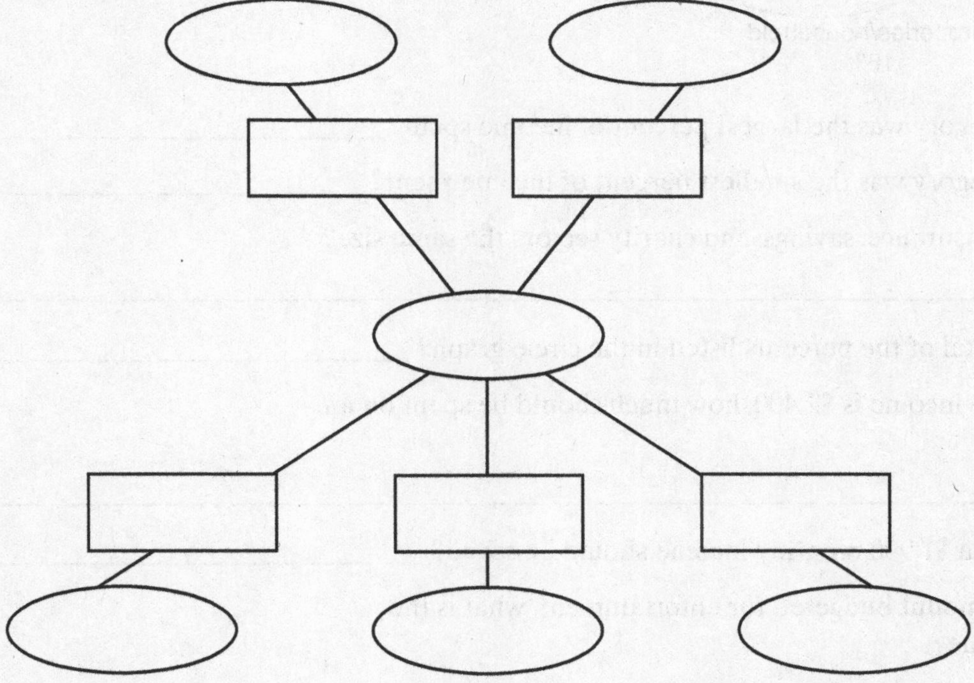

Vocabulary and Study Skills

Name ______________________ Class ______________ Date ______________

10B: Reading Comprehension

For use after Lesson 10-5

Study Skill Review notes that you have taken in class as soon as possible to clarify any points you missed. Be sure to ask questions if you need extra help.

Here is a circle graph for a monthly household budget. Use the graph to answer the questions that follow.

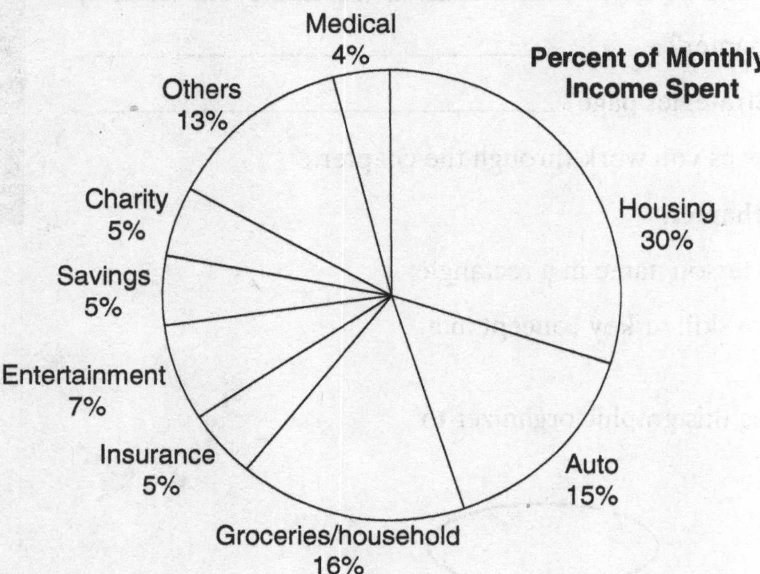

1. On which category was the largest percent of income spent? ______________
2. On which category was the smallest percent of income spent? ______________
3. Why are the insurance, savings, and charity sectors the same size?

   ____

4. What is the total of the percents listed in the circle graph? ______________
5. If the monthly income is $2,400, how much should be spent on an automobile?

   ____

6. How much of a $1,900 monthly income should be saved? ______________
7. If $60 is the amount budgeted for entertainment, what is the monthly income?

   ____

8. **High-Use Academic Words** What does it mean to *review*, as mentioned in the study skill?

   a. to put in order **b.** to study again

Name ______________________ Class ______________ Date ______________

10C: Reading/Writing Math Symbols

For use after Lesson 10-3

Study Skill When you take notes, use abbreviations and symbols such as @ (at), # (number), and w/ (with) to save time and reduce writing.

Match the symbol in Column A with its meaning in Column B.

Column A	Column B
1. $\angle ABC$	A. the measure of angle *ABC*
2. $\overline{AB}$	B. the length of segment *AB*
3. $\overleftrightarrow{AB}$	C. triangle *ABC*
4. AB	D. segment *AB*
5. $\overrightarrow{AB}$	E. ray starting at *A* and passing through *B*
6. $m\angle ABC$	F. ray starting at *B* and passing through *A*
7. $\overrightarrow{BA}$	G. line *AB*
8. $\triangle ABC$	H. angle *ABC*

Write the meaning of each of the following mathematical statements.

9. $m\angle B = 80°$

____

10. $BC = 4$

____

11. $DJ = KL$

____

12. $m\angle P = m\angle R$

____

13. $BC = \frac{1}{2}TU$

____

Find the complement and the supplement of each angle.

14. $m\angle S = 18°$

____

15. $m\angle T = 81°$

____

Name ______________________ Class ______________ Date ______________

10D: Visual Vocabulary Practice

For use after Lesson 10-5

Study Skill Use Venn Diagrams to understand the relationship between words whose meanings overlap, such as squares, rectangles, and quadrilaterals or real numbers, integers, and counting numbers.

Concept List

obtuse angle	right triangle	adjacent angles
diameter	equilateral triangle	perpendicular lines
midpoint	hexagon	pentagon

Write the concept that best describes each exercise. Choose from the concept list above.

1.

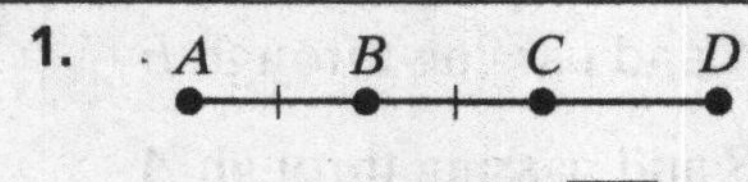

Point B on $\overline{AC}$

____

2.

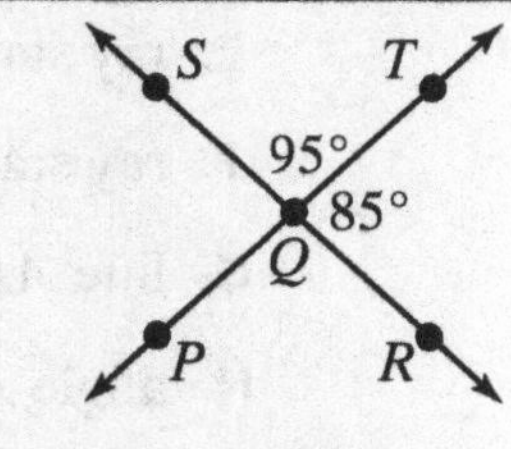

$\angle SQT$

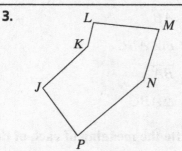

____

3.

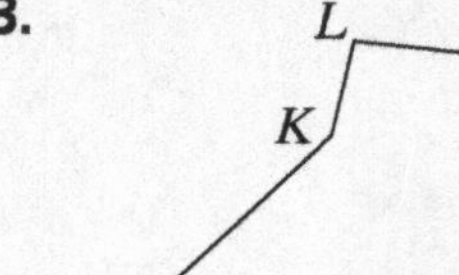

____

4.

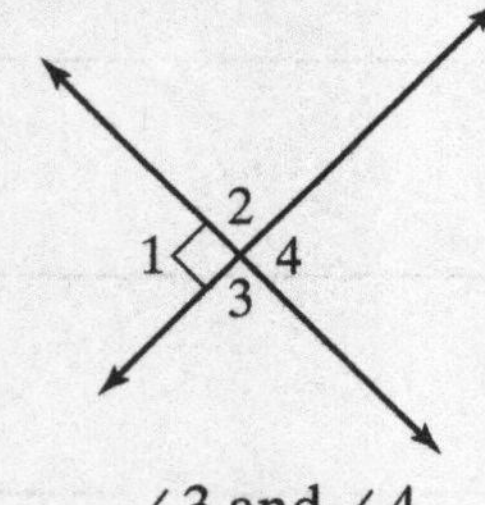

$\angle 3$ and $\angle 4$

____

5.

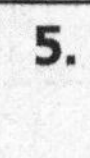

$\overline{XY}$

____

6.

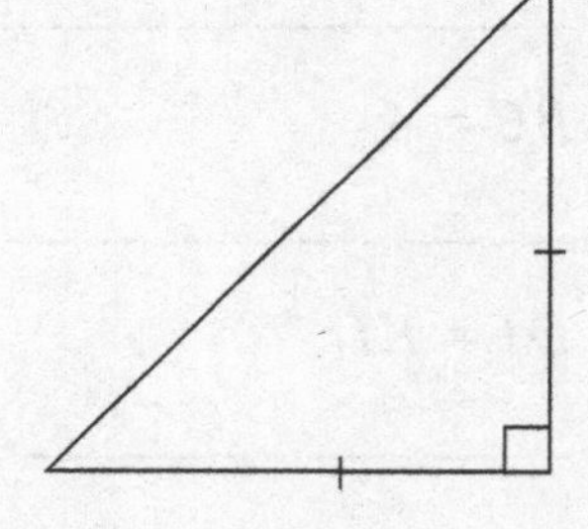

____

7.

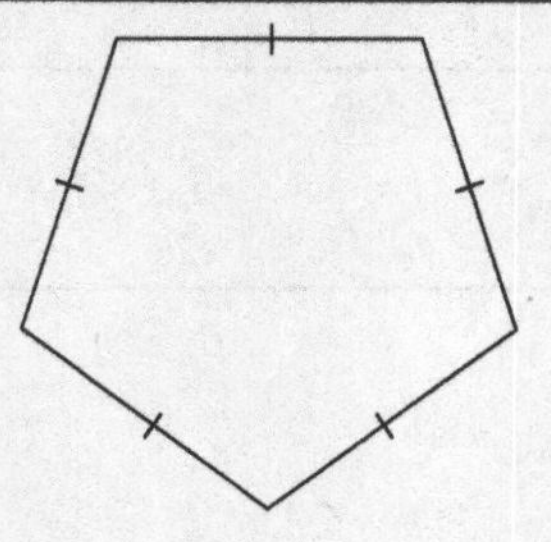

____

8.

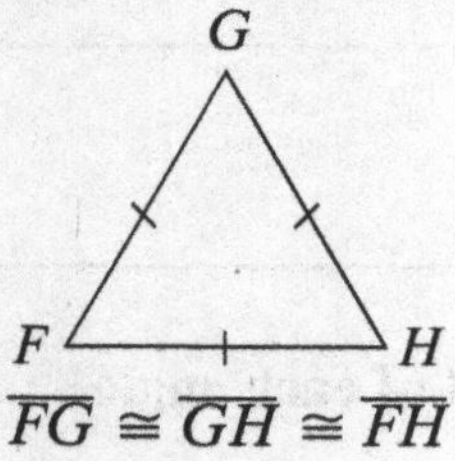

$\overline{FG} \cong \overline{GH} \cong \overline{FH}$

____

9.

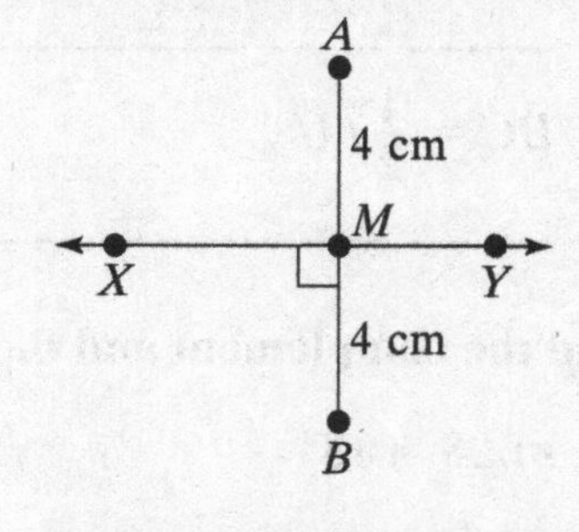

____

Name ____________________ Class ____________ Date ____________

10E: Vocabulary Check

For use after Lesson 10-5

Study Skill Strengthen your vocabulary. Use these pages and add cues and summaries by applying the Cornell Notetaking style.

Write the definition for each word or term at the right. To check your work, fold the paper back along the dotted line to see the correct answers.

polygon

parallel lines

trapezoid

acute angle

circle

Vocabulary and Study Skills

Name _______________ Class _______________ Date _______________

10E: Vocabulary Check (continued)

For use after Lesson 10-5

Write the vocabulary word or term for each definition. To check your work, fold the paper forward along the dotted line to see the correct answers.

a closed figure with sides formed by three or more line segments _______________

lines in the same plane that never intersect _______________

a quadrilateral with exactly one pair of parallel sides _______________

an angle with measure between 0 and 90 degrees _______________

the set of all points in the plane that are the same distance from a given point _______________

Name ______________________ Class ______________ Date ______________

10F: Vocabulary Review Puzzle

For use with the Chapter Review

Study Skill Write assignments down; do not rely only on your memory.

Below is a list of clues grouped by the number of letters in the answer. Identify the word each clue represents, and fit each word into the puzzle grid.

3 letters
- part of a circle

5 letters
- angle that measures between 0°and 90°
- formed by two rays with a common endpoint
- segment that has both endpoints on the circle
- flat surface that extends indefinitely in all directions

6 letters
- point of intersection of two sides on an angle or figure
- set of all points in a plane that are the same distance from a given point
- angle that measures between 90° and 180°

7 letters
- tool used to draw circles and arcs
- polygon with 10 sides
- type of triangle with no congruent sides
- polygon with all sides and angles congruent

8 letters
- point that divides a segment into two segments of equal length
- polygon with 5 sides

9 letters
- sides that have the same length
- type of triangle with at least two sides congruent
- parallelogram with four right angles
- quadrilateral with exactly one pair of parallel sides

11 letters
- triangle with three congruent sides

12 letters
- lines that have exactly one point in common

13 letters
- two angles whose sum is 180°
- two angles whose sum is 90°

Name ____________________ Class ____________________ Date ____________________

Practice 11-1

Angles and Parallel Lines

Identify each pair of angles as *vertical, adjacent, corresponding, alternate interior,* or *none of these.*

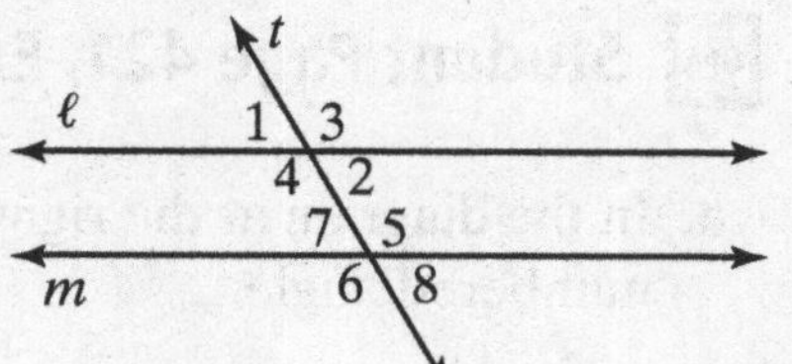

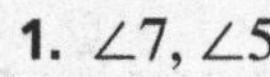

1. $\angle 7, \angle 5$ ____________________

2. $\angle 1, \angle 2$ ____________________

3. $\angle 1, \angle 7$ ____________________

4. $\angle 4, \angle 7$ ____________________

Use the diagrams at the right for Exercises 5 and 6.

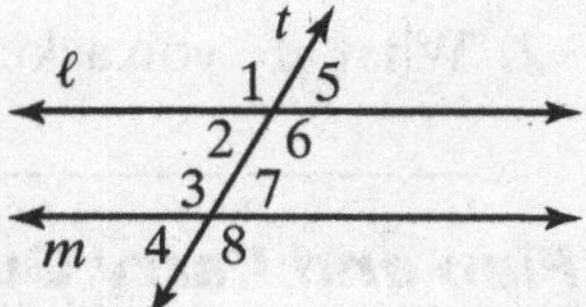

5. Name four pairs of corresponding angles.

____

6. Name two pairs of alternate interior angles

____

In each diagram below, $\ell \parallel m$. Find the measure of each numbered angle.

7.

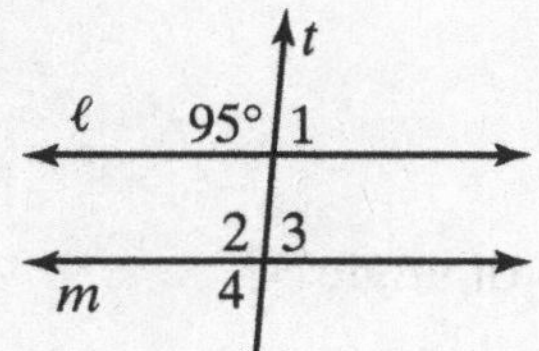

$m\angle 1 =$ __________

$m\angle 2 =$ __________

$m\angle 3 =$ __________

$m\angle 4 =$ __________

8.

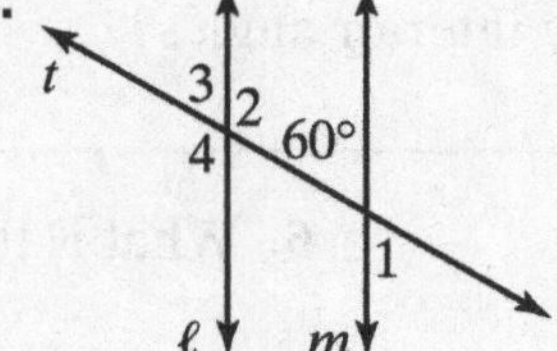
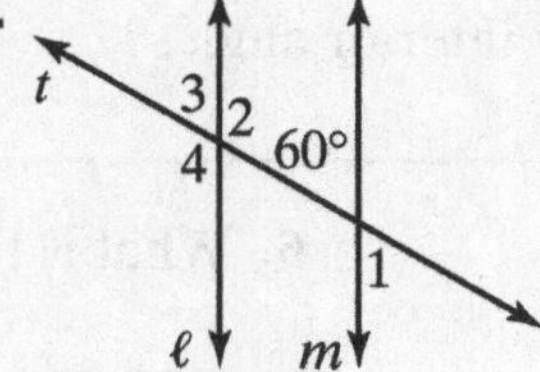

$m\angle 1 =$ __________

$m\angle 2 =$ __________

$m\angle 3 =$ __________

$m\angle 4 =$ __________

9.

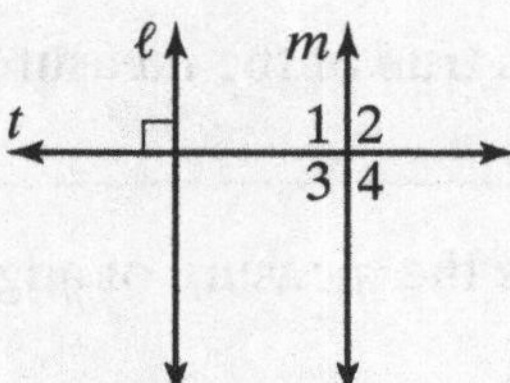

$m\angle 1 =$ __________

$m\angle 2 =$ __________

$m\angle 3 =$ __________

$m\angle 4 =$ __________

10. Use the figure at the right. Is line ℓ parallel to line m? Explain how you could use a protractor to support your conjecture.

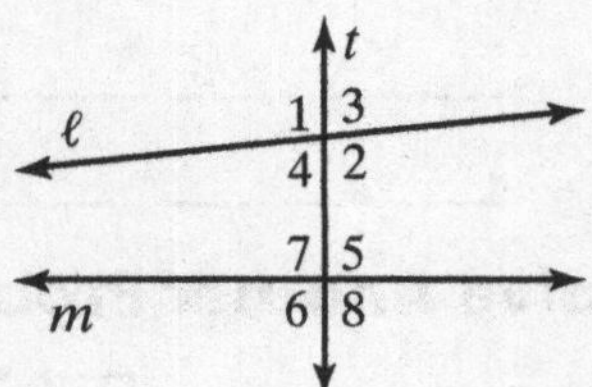

____

____

____

____

Name ____________________ Class ____________ Date ____________

11-1 • Guided Problem Solving

GPS Student Page 421, Exercise 31:

a. In the diagram at the right, $\overleftrightarrow{PQ} \parallel \overleftrightarrow{ST}$. Find the measure of each numbered angle.

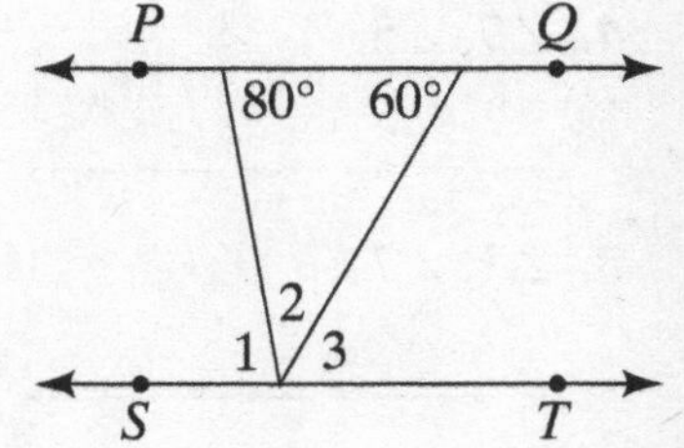

b. What is the sum of the angle measures of the triangle?

Understand

1. What are alternate interior angles?

2. What are you asked to do?

Plan and Carry Out

3. Use angle 1 and angle 3 to name two pairs of alternate interior angles.

4. What is true of the measure of alternate interior angles?

5. What is the measure of angle 1?

6. What is the measure of angle 3?

7. What type of angle do angles 1, 2 and 3 form?

8. How many degrees are in a straight angle?

9. Use the information from Steps 5 and 6 to help find the measure of angle 2.

10. What is the sum of the angle measures in the triangle?

Check

11. Explain your answer from Step 10.

Solve Another Problem

12. In the diagram, $\overleftrightarrow{AB} \parallel \overleftrightarrow{CD}$. Find the measure of each numbered angle.

Name ______________________ Class ______________ Date ______________

Practice 11-2

Congruent Figures

Determine whether each pair of triangles is congruent. Explain.

1.

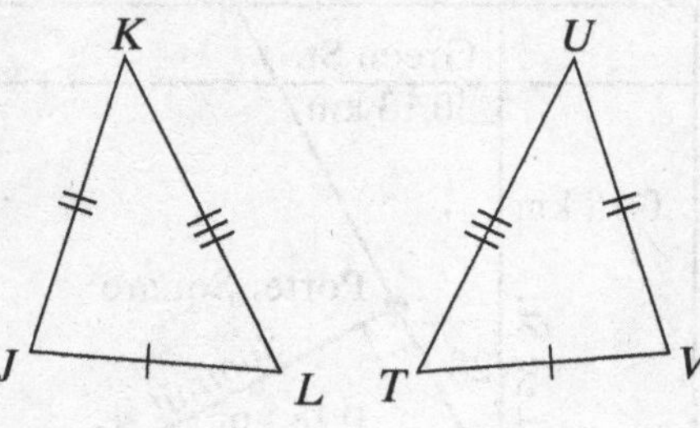

____

2.

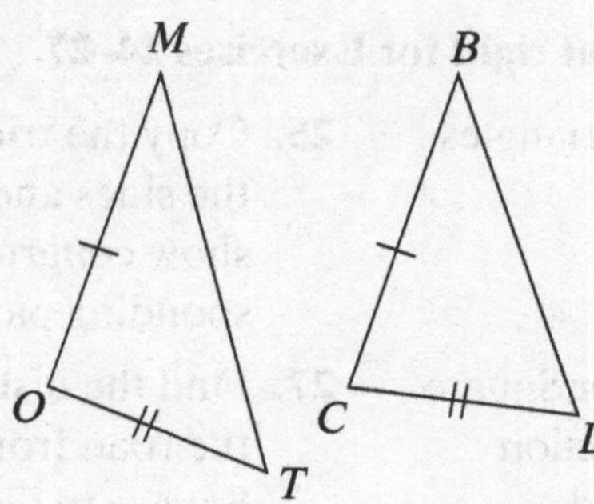

____

3.

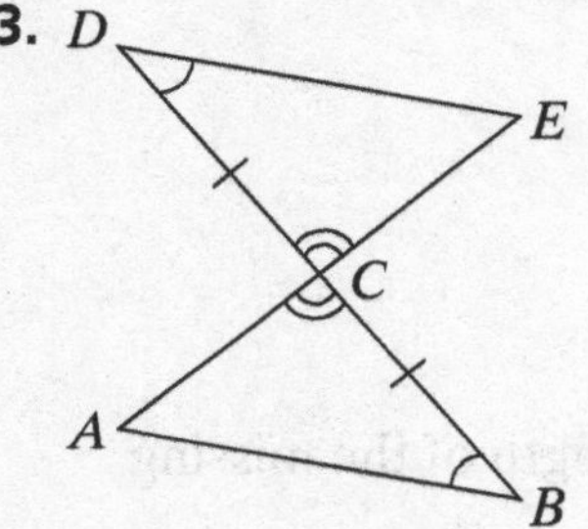

____

4.

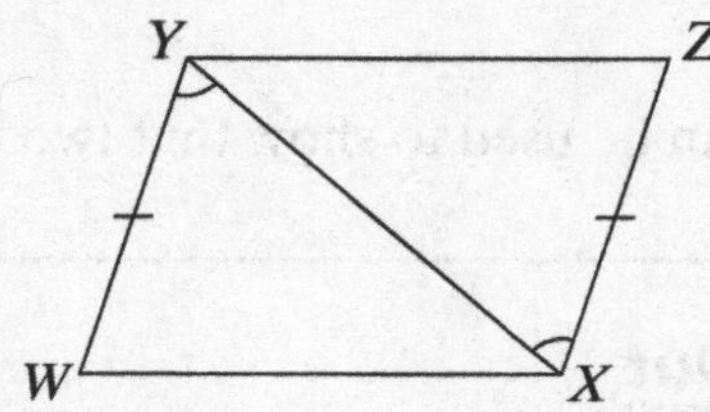

____

Determine if each triangle in Exercises 5–7 must be congruent to $\triangle XYZ$ at the right.

5.

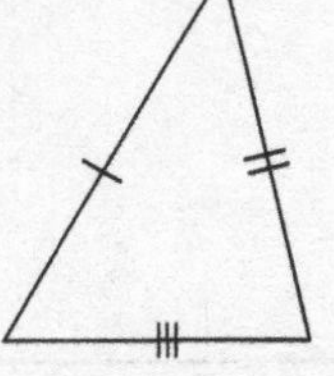

____

6.

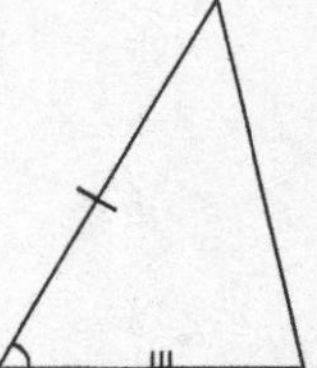

____

7.

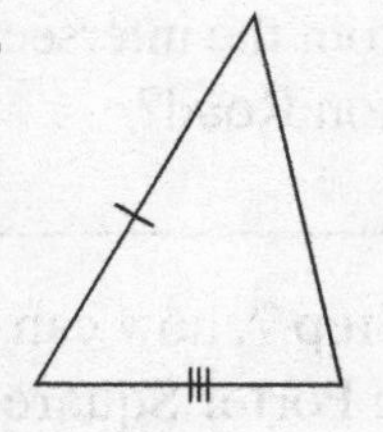

____

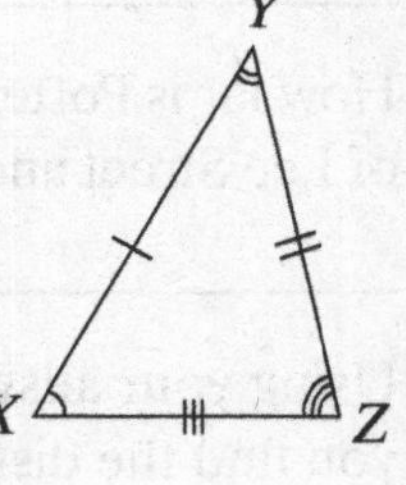

For Exercises 8–9, use the triangles at the right.

8. $\triangle XYZ \cong$ ______________ by ______________

9. Find the missing measures for $\triangle XYZ$.

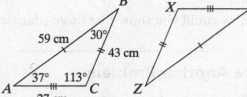

____

____

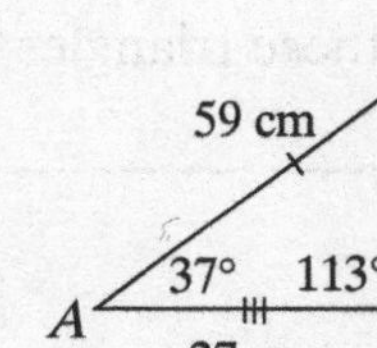

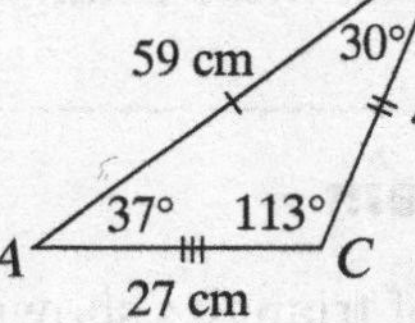

Name ______________________ Class ______________ Date ____________

11-2 • Guided Problem Solving

GPS Student Page 426, Exercises 24–27:

Maps Use the map at right for Exercises 24–27.

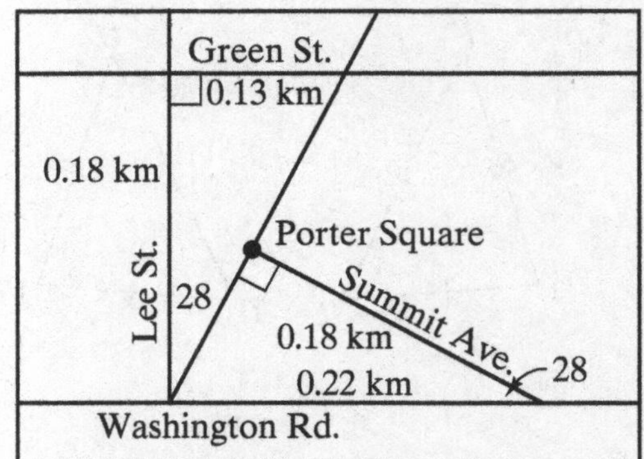

24. Show that the triangles in the map are congruent.

25. Copy the triangles. Mark the sides and angles to show congruent corresponding parts.

26. How far is Porter Square from the intersection of Lee Street and Washington Road?

27. Find the distance along the road from Porter Square to Green Street.

Understand

1. What methods can be used to show that two triangles are congruent?

____

Plan and Carry Out

2. How can you find the length of a missing side?

____

3. What is the total length of the missing hypotenuse?

____

4. Are the two triangles congruent? Why?

____

5. Sketch the two triangles. Mark their corresponding parts.

6. How far is Porter Square from the intersection of Lee Street and Washington Road?

____

____

7. What is the total length of the street from Washington to Green by the way of Porter Square? ____________

8. Using your answer from Step 7, how can you find the distance from Porter Square to Green Street?

____

Check

9. How could you show that these triangles are congruent by another method?

____

Solve Another Problem

10. Explain why the pair of triangles shown are congruent. Find the missing measures in the diagram.

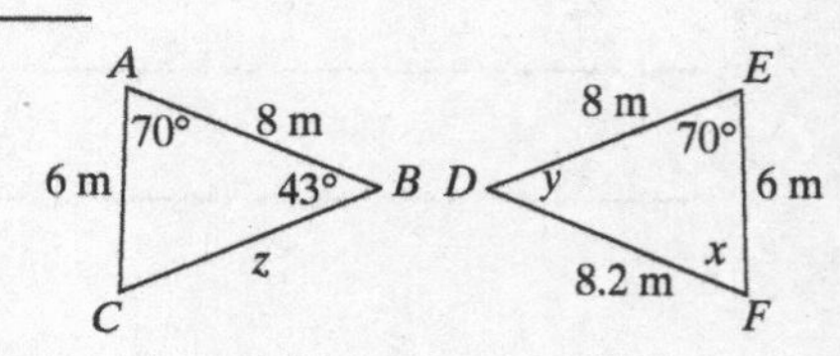

____

Name ______________________ Class ______________ Date ______________

Practice 11-3

Similar Figures

Tell whether each pair of polygons is similar. Explain why or why not.

1.
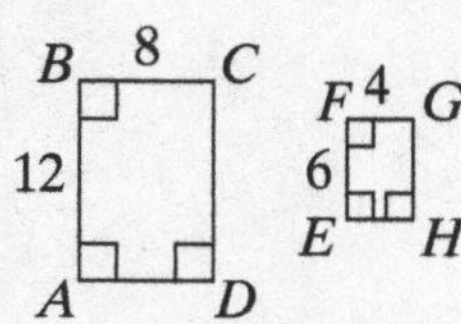

2.
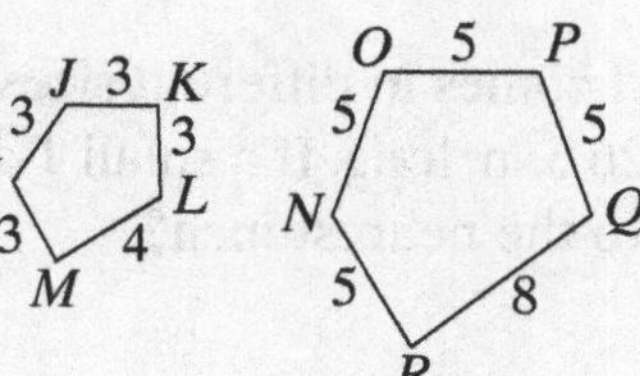

3.
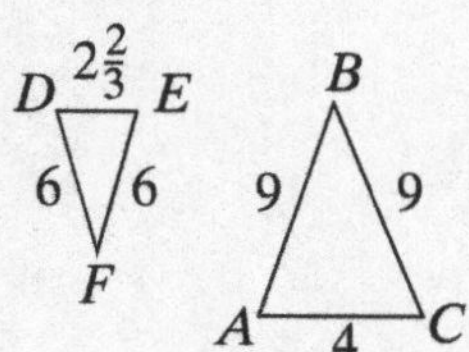

4.
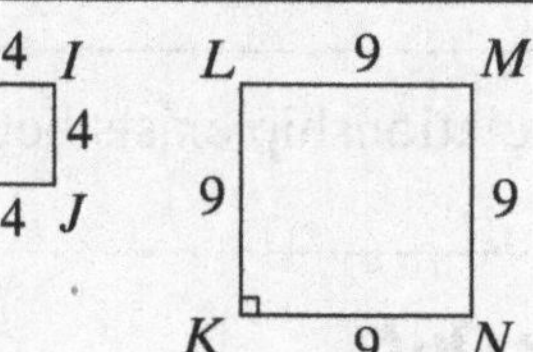

Exercises 5–12 show pairs of similar polygons. Find the unknown lengths.

5.
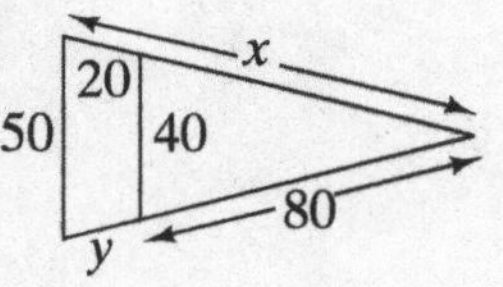

6.
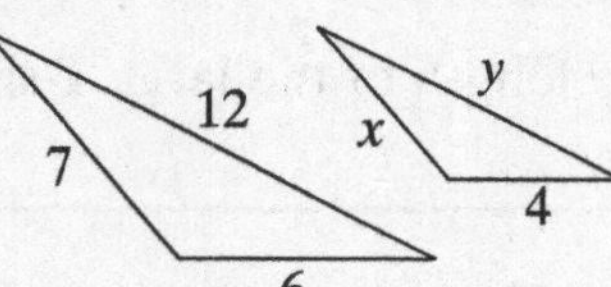

7.
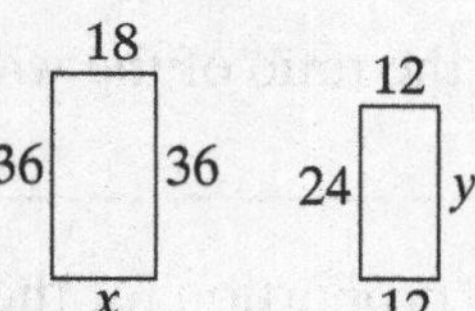

8.
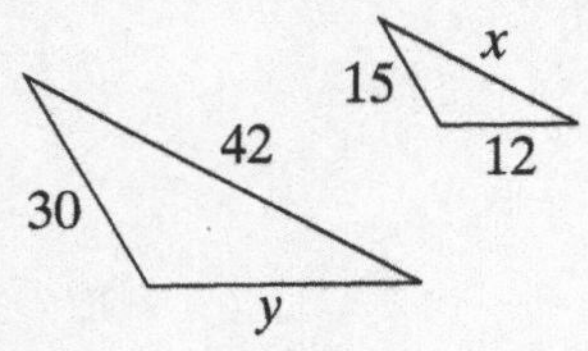

9.
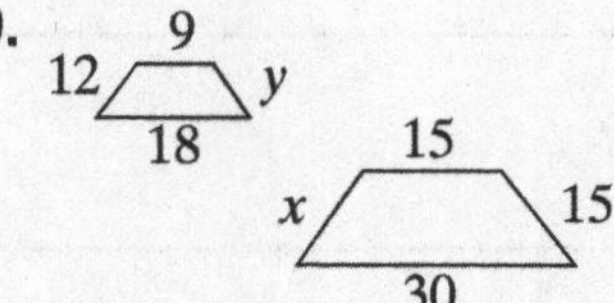

10.
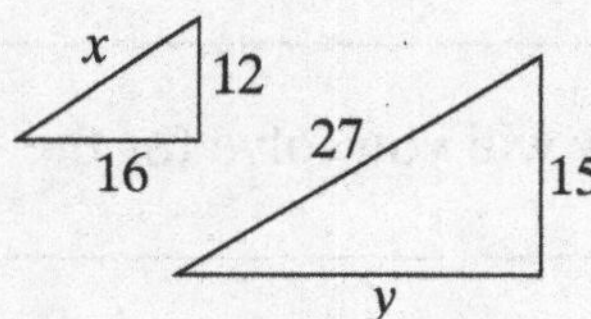

11.
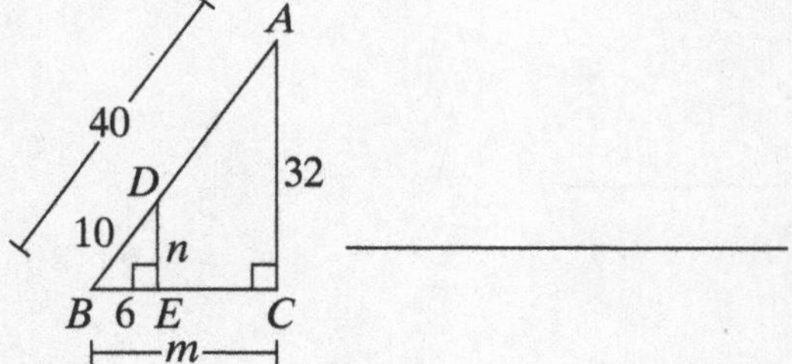

12.
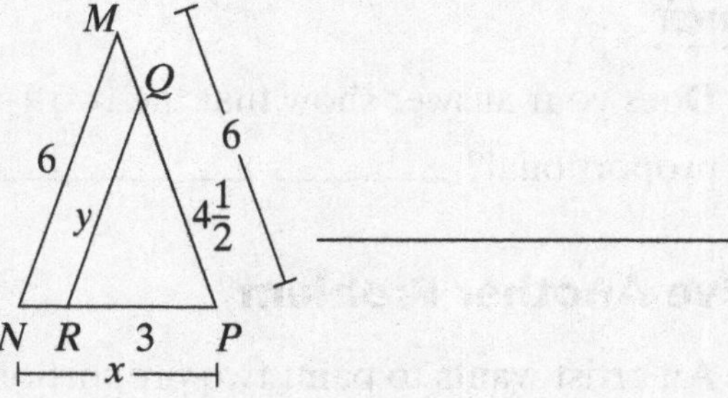

Solve.

13. A rock show is being televised. The lead singer, who is 75 inches tall, is 15 inches tall on a TV monitor. The image of the bass player is 13 inches tall on the monitor. How tall is the bass player?

14. A 42-inch-long guitar is 10.5 feet long on a stadium screen. A drum is 21 inches wide. How wide is the image on the stadium screen?

Name ______________________ Class ______________ Date ______________

11-3 • Guided Problem Solving

GPS Student Page 431, Exercise 15:

Clothing A T-shirt comes in different sizes. A large T-shirt is 21.5 in. wide and 26.5 in. long. If a small T-shirt is 15.5 in. wide, what is its length to the nearest inch?

Understand

1. What are you being asked to find? ______________________

   ____

2. What type of relationship exists between the two shirts?

   ____

Plan and Carry Out

3. What are the dimensions of the large T-shirt? ______________________

   ____

4. What is the ratio of the width to the length of the large T-shirt?

   ____

5. Set up a proportion for the situation. Let y equal the length of the small T-shirt.

   ____

6. How will you solve for the variable y?

   ____

7. What is the value of y? ______________________

Check

8. Does your answer show that the two T-shirt sizes are proportional? ______________________

Solve Another Problem

9. An artist wants to paint two proportional rectangular paintings on canvas. One painting is larger than the other. The large painting is 20 in. wide and 8 in. long. The smaller painting is 16 in. wide and 6 in. long. Are the two paintings proportional in size?

   ____

   ____

Name ______________________ Class ______________ Date ______________

Practice 11-4

Proving Triangles Similar

Determine the unknown angle measure in each triangle.

1. 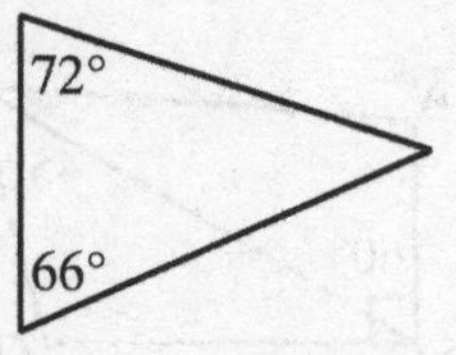

____

2. 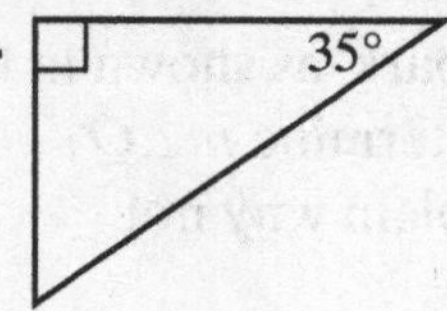

____

3. 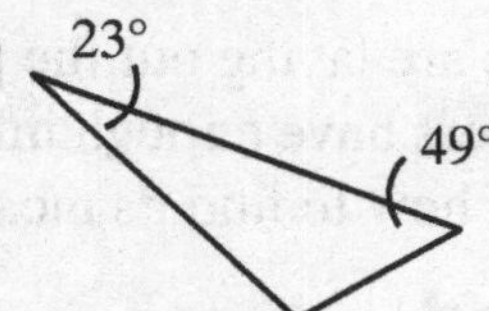

____

4. 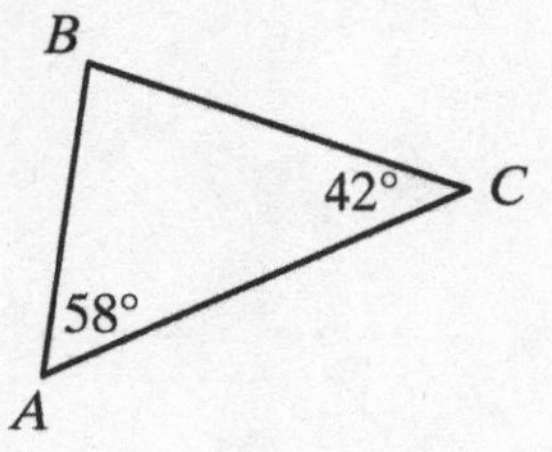

____

5. 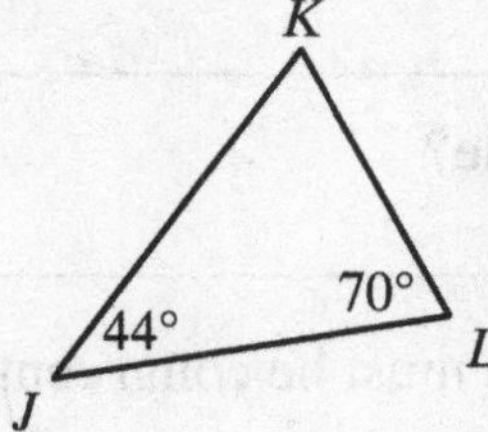

____

6. 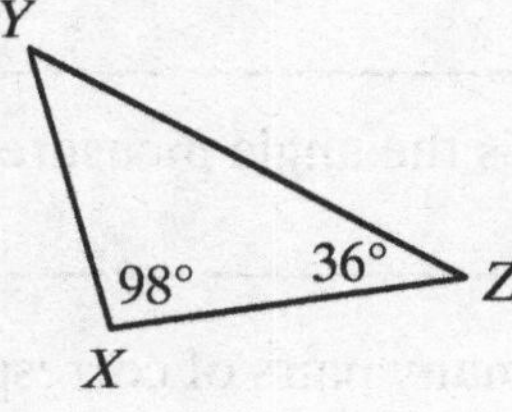

____

Show that each pair of triangles is similar.

7. 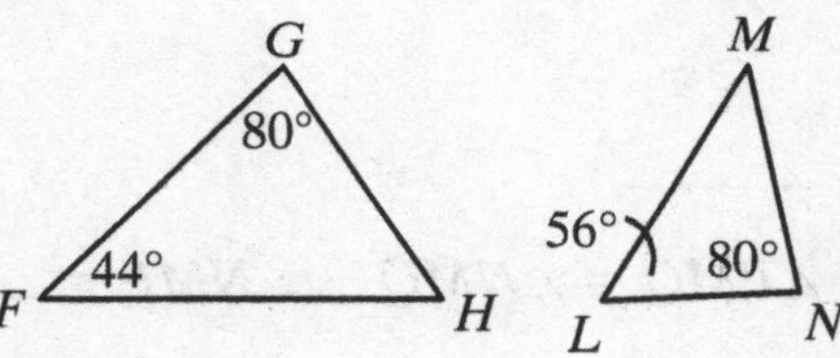

____

8. 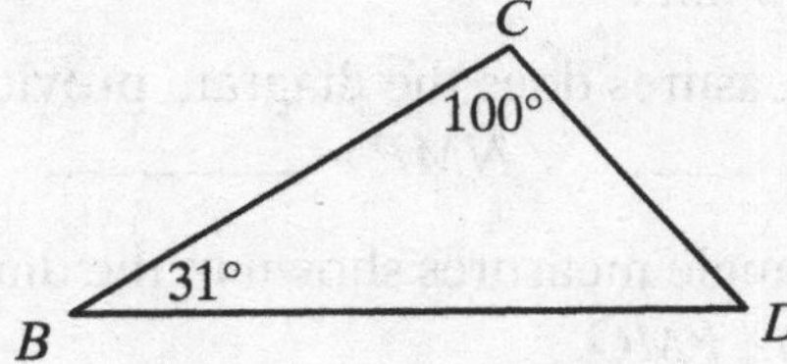

____

9. 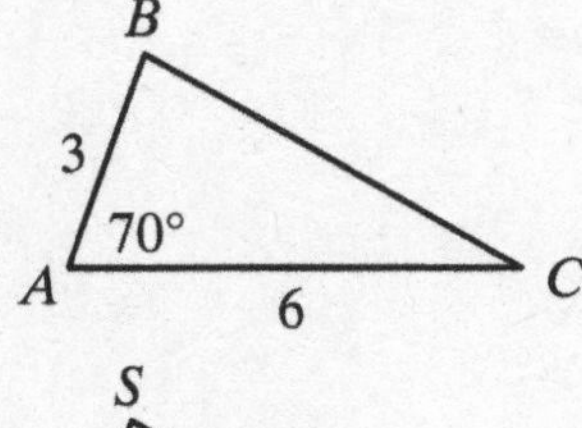

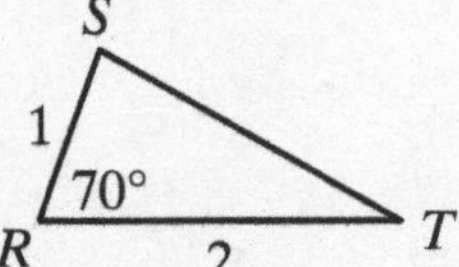

____

Solve.

10. A stained glass window has a triangular piece of purple glass with a right angle and another angle that measures 45°. What is the measure of the third angle of the purple glass? ______

Name ______________________ Class ______________________ Date ______________________

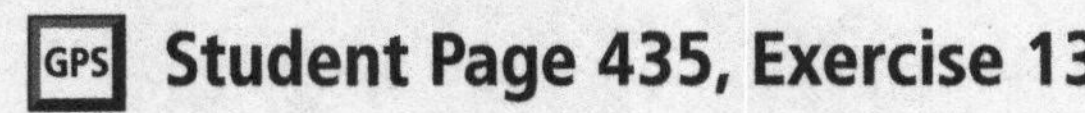

11-4 • Guided Problem Solving

Proving Triangles Similar

GPS Student Page 435, Exercise 13:

City workers are laying out the paths in a new park, as shown in the diagram. Do the workers have enough information to determine $m\angle Q$? If so, explain how to find its measure. If not, explain why not.

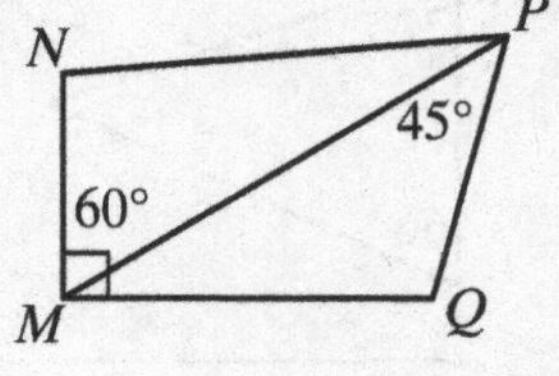

Understand

1. What are you being asked to find?

____

2. What is the angle measure of a right angle?

____

3. How many pairs of corresponding angles must be congruent in order for two triangles to be similar?

____

Plan and Carry Out

4. What angle measures does the diagram provide?
$\angle NMQ =$ ________ $\angle NMP =$ ________ $\angle MPQ =$ ________

5. Based on the angle measures shown in the diagram, you can find $m\angle PMQ$. $\angle PMQ = \angle NMQ - \angle NMP =$ ______

6. Now that you know the measure of two angles in $\triangle MQP$, use angle sum of a triangle to find $\angle Q$. $180° - (\angle PMQ + \angle MPQ) = \angle Q =$ ______

7. Is $\triangle MQP \sim \triangle PNM$? How do you know?

____

____

Check

8. Given the angle measure you found for $\angle Q$, what is the angle sum of $\triangle MQP$? Show each angle measure ______________________

Solve Another Problem

9. For part of a theater set, students are supposed to build two similar triangular wood frames. The first frame has the following side/angle/side measure: 20 cm/80°/24 cm. The second frame has a different side-angle-side measures: 15 cm/80°/18 cm. Are the frames similar triangles? Explain.

____

____

Name ______________________ Class ______________ Date ______________

Practice 11-5

Angles and Polygons

Classify each polygon by its number of sides.

1. 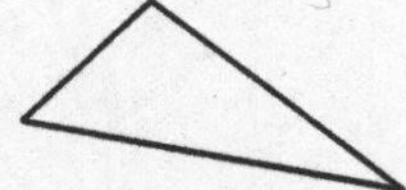

____

2. 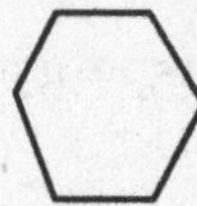

____

3. 

____

4. a polygon with 8 sides

____

5. a polygon with 10 sides

____

6. Find the measure of each angle of a regular hexagon.

____

7. The measures of four angles of a pentagon are 143°, 118°, 56°, and 97°. Find the measure of the missing angle.

____

8. Four of the angles of a hexagon measure 53°, 126°, 89°, and 117°. What is the sum of the measures of the other two angles?

____

9. Four of the angles of a heptagon measure 109°, 158°, 117°, and 89°. What is the sum of the measures of the other three angles?

____

10. Complete the chart for the total of the angle measures in each polygon. The first three have been done for you.

Polygon	Number of Sides	Sum of Angle Measures
triangle	3	180°
rectangle	4	360°
pentagon	5	540°
hexagon		
heptagon		
octagon		
nonagon		
decagon		

11. From the table you completed in Exercise 10, what pattern do you see? Explain.

____

____

Name ______________________ Class ______________ Date ______________

11-5 • Guided Problem Solving

GPS Student Page 443, Exercise 28:

The measures of six angles of a heptagon are 145°, 115°, 152°, 87°, 90°, and 150°. Find the measure of the seventh angle.

Understand

1. How many sides does a heptagon have? ______________

2. How many interior angles does a heptagon have?

3. What are you asked to find?

____

Plan and Carry Out

4. For a polygon with n sides, the sum of the measures of the interior angles is $(n - 2)180°$. Substitute what you know into the formula to find the sum of the interior angles. Show your work.

____

5. Find the total of the measures of the six interior angles given in the problem.

____

6. Subtract the total you found in Step 5 from the total number of degrees in a heptagon that you found in Step 4.

____

Check

7. Add all seven angles to verify that they total 900°.

____

Solve Another Problem

8. A decagon has interior angle measures of 156°, 178°, 124°, 132°, 138°, 142°, 116°, 178°, and 159°. Find the measure of the missing angle.

____

Name ______________________ Class ______________ Date ______________

11A: Graphic Organizer

For use before Lesson 11-1

Study Skill As your teacher presents new material in the chapter, keep a paper and pencil handy to write down notes and questions. If you miss class, borrow a classmate's notes so you don't fall behind.

Write your answers.

1. What is the chapter title? ______________
2. How many lessons are there in this chapter? ______________
3. What is the topic of the Test-Taking Strategies page? ______________
4. Complete the graphic organizer below as you work through the chapter.
   - In the center, write the title of the chapter.
   - When you begin a lesson, write the lesson name in a rectangle.
   - When you complete a lesson, write a skill or key concept in a circle linked to that lesson block.
   - When you complete the chapter, use this graphic organizer to help you review.

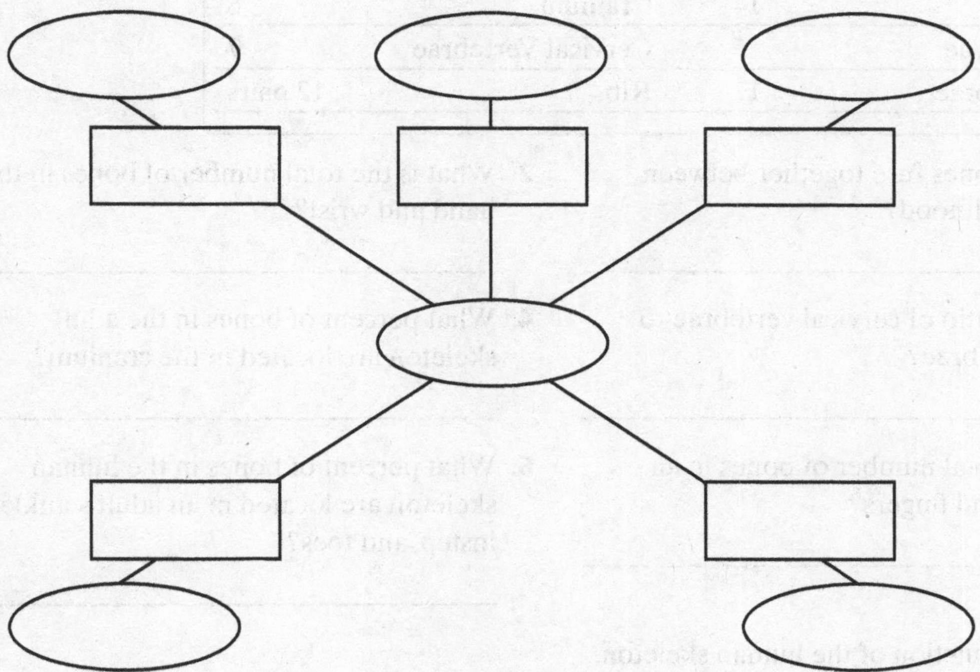

Vocabulary and Study Skills

Name ______________________ Class ______________ Date ______________

11B: Reading Comprehension

For use after Lesson 11-1

Study Skill Use tables when you need to organize complex information. The columns and rows allow you to display different types of information in a way that is easy to read. Make sure you use appropriate headings.

Read the paragraph and chart below to answer the questions.

The human skeletal system helps support the body and protects its organs from being damaged. At birth, a human skeleton is made up of 275 different bones. As the body ages, some of the bones fuse together leaving the adult skeleton with 206 bones. There are two major systems of bones in the human body; the axial skeleton which is made up of 80 bones, and the appendicular skeleton which has 126 bones. The following chart lists the types and number of bones located in various parts of the adult body.

Human Bones

Fingers (per hand)	14	Toes (per foot)	14
Each Palm	5	Instep of Each Foot	5
Each Wrist	8	Each Ankle	7
Facial Bones	14	Cranium	8
Lumbar Vertebrae	5	Cervical Vertebrae	7
Thoracic Vertebrae	12	Ribs	12 pairs

1. How many bones fuse together between birth and adulthood?

____

2. What is the total number of bones in the hand and wrist?

____

3. What is the ratio of cervical vertebrae to thoracic vertebrae?

____

4. What percent of bones in the adult skeleton are located in the cranium?

____

5. What is the total number of bones in an adult's toes and fingers?

____

6. What percent of bones in the human skeleton are located in an adult's ankle, instep, and toes?

____

7. Explain the function of the human skeleton.

____

8. **High-Use Academic Words** In question 7, what does the word *explain* mean?

   a. to display using illustrations, tables, or graphs

   b. to give facts and details that make an idea easier to understand

Name ______________________ Class ______________ Date ______________

11C: Reading/Writing Math Symbols

For use after Lesson 11-5

Study Skill Take notes while you study. Use a highlighter to emphasize important material in your notes.

Vocabulary and Study Skills

Write the following mathematical expressions or equations in words.

1. $m\angle 1 = 50°$

____

2. $\angle JKL$ ______________________________

3. $a \parallel b$ ______________________________

4. $\overline{GH} \cong \overline{LK}$

____

5. $\angle R \cong \angle T$

____

6. $\overleftrightarrow{AB} \parallel \overleftrightarrow{CD}$

____

7. $\overrightarrow{AB}$ ______________________________

8. t^5 ______________________________

9. $\overleftrightarrow{AB} \perp \overleftrightarrow{JK}$

____

Write each of the following statements using mathematical symbols.

10. Segment *AB* and segment *SR* are equal in length. ____________

11. angle *STU* ______________________________

12. Segment *BA* is parallel to segment *RK*. ____________

13. The measure of angle *JKL* is 43 degrees. ____________

14. Angle *R* is congruent to angle *Y*. ____________

15. *x* raised to the sixth power ____________

16. arc *TY* ______________________________

17. The sum of the measures of angles *ABC* and *XYZ* is 90 degrees.

____

Name ______________________ Class ______________ Date ______________

11D: Visual Vocabulary Practice

For use after Lesson 11-5

Study Skill Use Venn Diagrams to understand the relationship between words whose meanings overlap such as squares, rectangles, and quadrilaterals or real numbers, integers, and counting numbers.

Concept List

similar polygons	transversal	rhombus
supplementary	complementary	120 degrees
corresponding angles	exterior angle	alternate interior angles

Write the concept that best describes each exercise. Choose from the concept list above.

1.

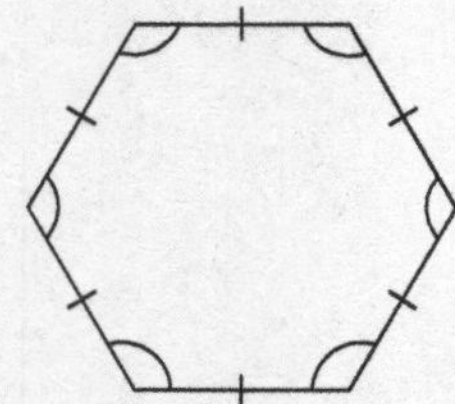

the measure of each interior angle

____

2.

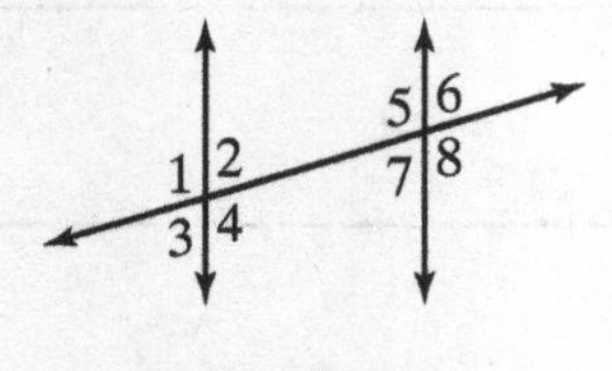

$\angle 2$ and $\angle 7$

____

3.

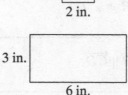

1 in.

2 in.

3 in.

6 in.

____

4.

$m\angle 1 = 30°$ and $m\angle 2 = 60°$

____

5.

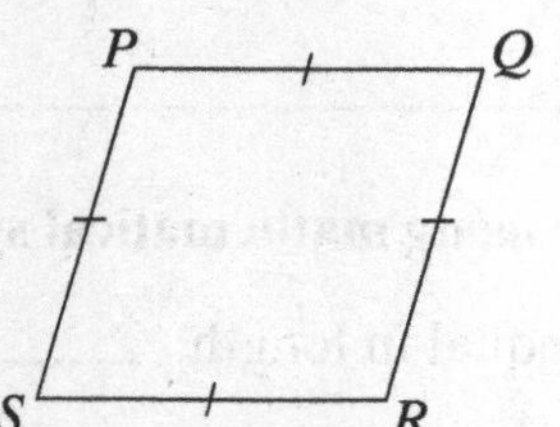

____

6.

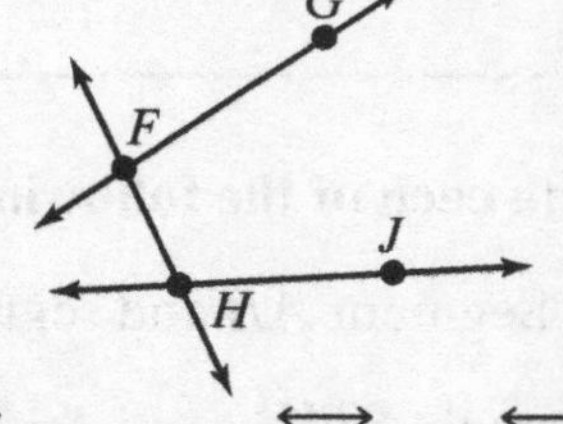

$\overleftrightarrow{FH}$ is one for $\overleftrightarrow{FG}$ and $\overleftrightarrow{HJ}$

____

7.

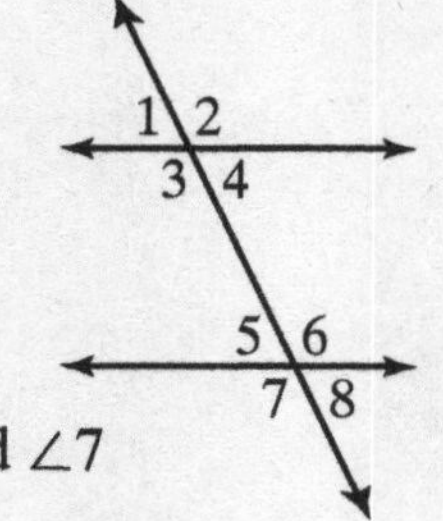

$\angle 2$ and $\angle 7$

____

8.

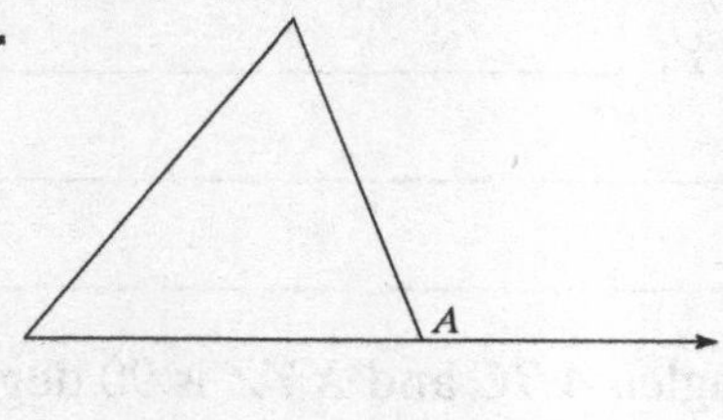

____

9.

$m\angle ABC = 24°$ and $m\angle XYZ = 156°$

____

Name ________________ Class ________________ Date ________________

11E: Vocabulary Check

For use after Lesson 11-5

Study Skill Strengthen your vocabulary. Use these pages and add cues and summaries by applying the Cornell Notetaking style.

Write the definition for each word or term at the right. To check your work, fold the paper back along the dotted line to see the correct answers.

____ vertical angles

____ adjacent angles

____ similar polygons

____ congruent polygons

____ perpendicular lines

Vocabulary and Study Skills

Name ______________________ Class ______________ Date ______________

11E: Vocabulary Check (continued)

For use after Lesson 11-5

Write the vocabulary word or term for each definition. To check your work, fold the paper forward along the dotted line to see the correct answers.

angles that are formed by intersecting lines and are opposite of each other ______________________

angles that share a common vertex and a common side ______________________

polygons that have congruent corresponding angles and corresponding sides in proportion ______________________

polygons that have the same size and shape ______________________

lines that intersect to form right angles ______________________

Name ______________________ Class ______________ Date ______________

11F: Vocabulary Review Puzzle

For use with the Chapter Review

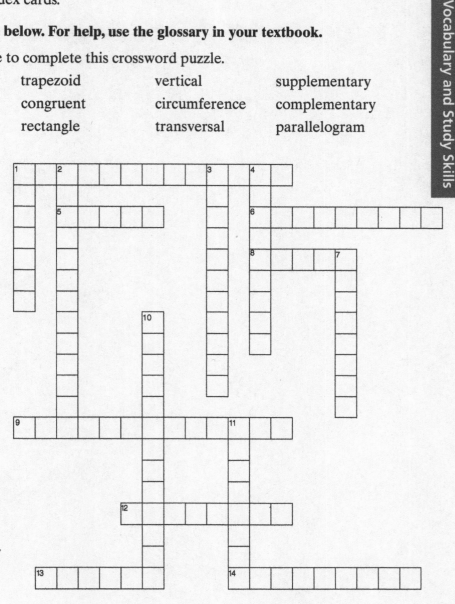

Study Skill As you read through a new lesson, write new vocabulary words and the definitions on index cards.

Complete the crossword puzzle below. For help, use the glossary in your textbook.

Here are the words you will use to complete this crossword puzzle.

right	square	trapezoid	vertical	supplementary
similar	acute	congruent	circumference	complementary
exterior angle	adjacent	rectangle	transversal	parallelogram

Vocabulary and Study Skills

ACROSS

1. two angles whose sum is 180 degrees
5. a triangle with one angle measuring 90 degrees
6. polygons that have exactly the same size and shape
8. a triangle with angles each measuring less than 90 degrees
9. two angles whose sum is 90 degrees
12. a type of angle formed by intersecting lines
13. a parallelogram with four right angles and four congruent sides
14. a quadrilateral with exactly one pair of parallel sides

DOWN

1. these figures have the same shape, but not neccessarily the same size
2. a quadrilateral with two pairs of opposite sides that are parallel
3. a line that intersects two other lines in different points
4. a parallelogram with four right angles
7. an angle of a polygon that is formed by a side and an extension of an adjacent side
10. the distance around a circle
11. two angles that share a vertex and a side but have no common interior points

Name ____________________ Class ____________ Date ____________

Practice 12-1

Three-Dimensional Figures

Describe the base and name the figure.

1. 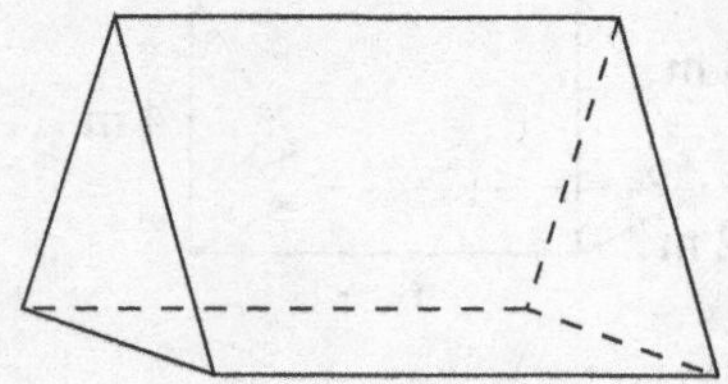

2. 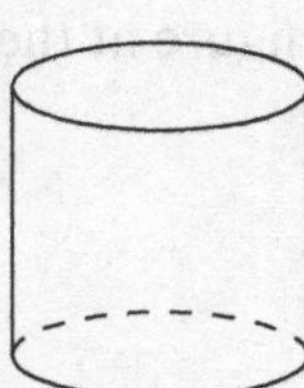

3. 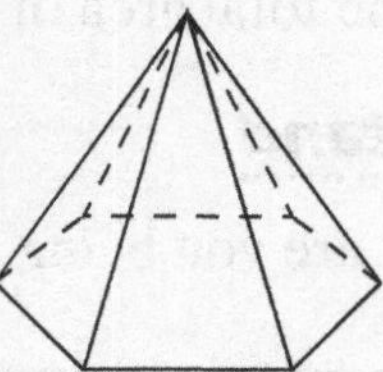

4. 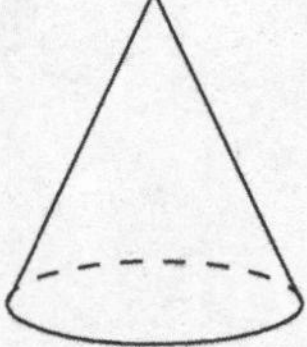

5. 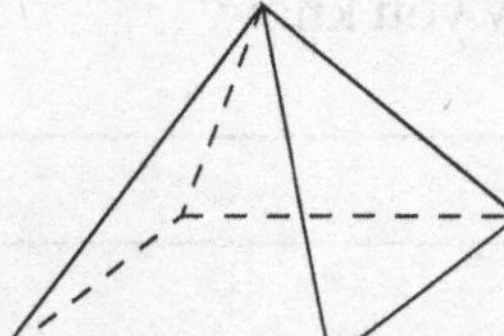

6. 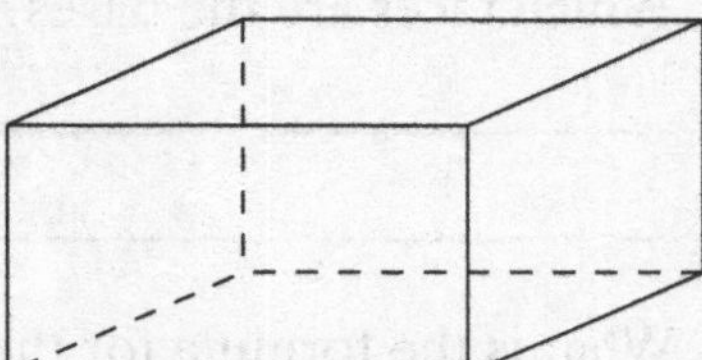

Draw each figure named.

7. a triangular pyramid

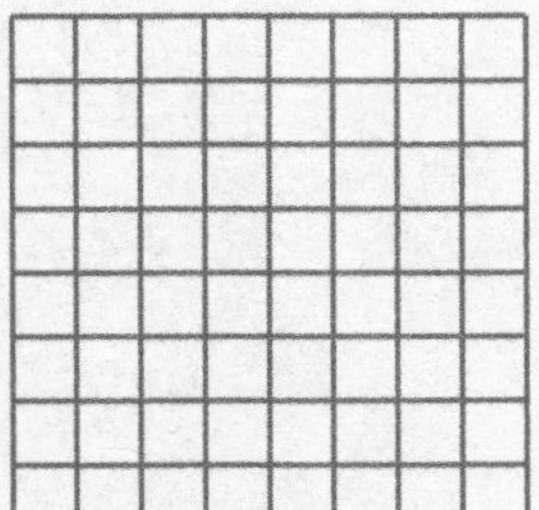

8. a square prism

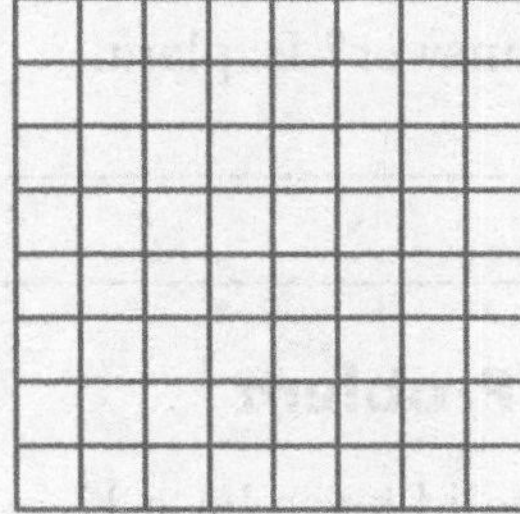

9. a cone

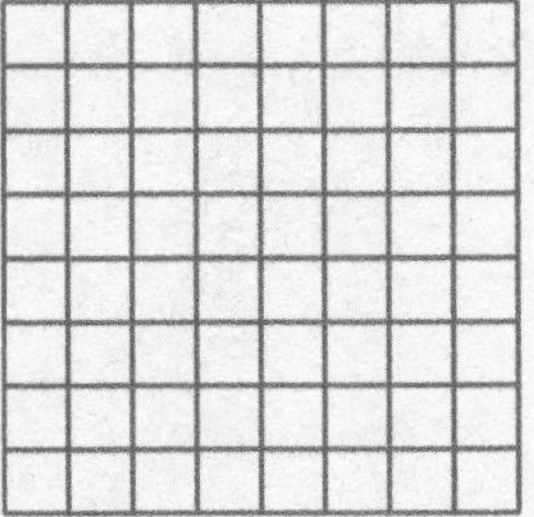

10. a pentagonal pyramid

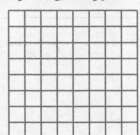

Name ______________________ Class ______________ Date ______________

12-1 • Guided Problem Solving

GPS Student Page 457, Exercise 23:

What is the total area of the two bases of the figure at the right?

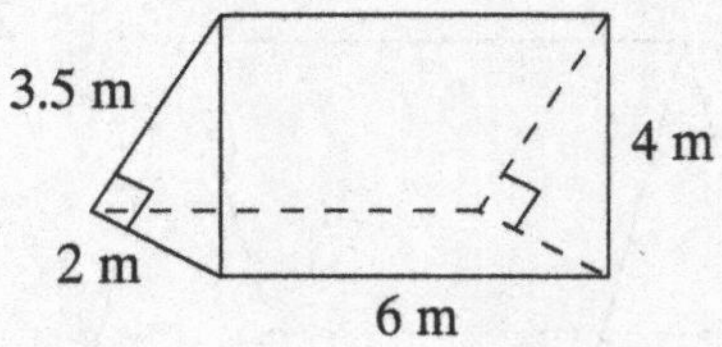

3.5 m
4 m
2 m
6 m

Understand

1. What are you being asked to do?

____

2. How many rectangular faces are there? ______________

3. How many triangular faces are there? ______________

Plan and Carry Out

4. Which faces are the bases? Explain how you know.

____

____

5. What is the formula for the area of a triangle? ______________

6. What are the dimensions of the triangular faces?

____

7. What is the area of one triangular face? ______________

8. What is the area of all the triangular faces? ______________

Check

9. Did you use the correct information from the diagram to calculate your answer? Explain.

____

____

Solve Another Problem

10. A rectangular solid has a base 11 in., height 15 in., and a length of 6 in. Find the total area of all faces.

____

____

Name ______________________ Class ______________ Date ______________

Practice 12-2

Surface Areas of Prisms and Cylinders

Find the surface area of each prism.

1.
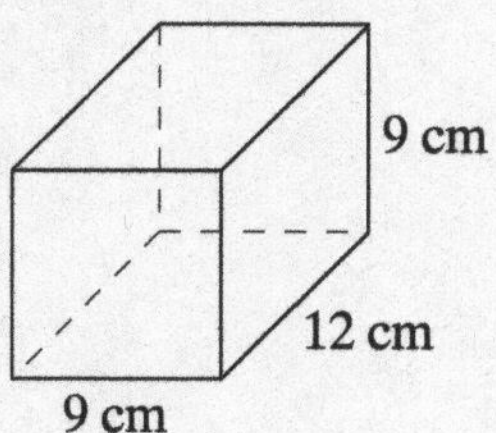

____

2.
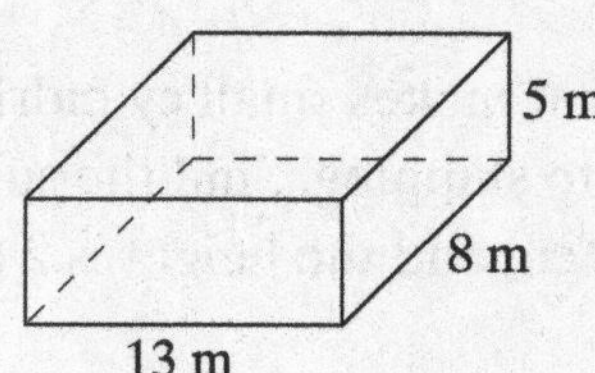

____

3.
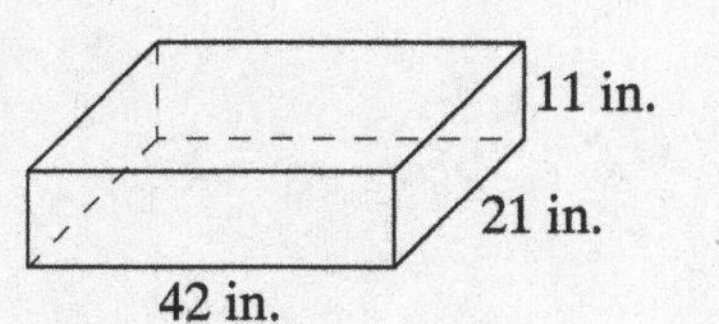

____

4.
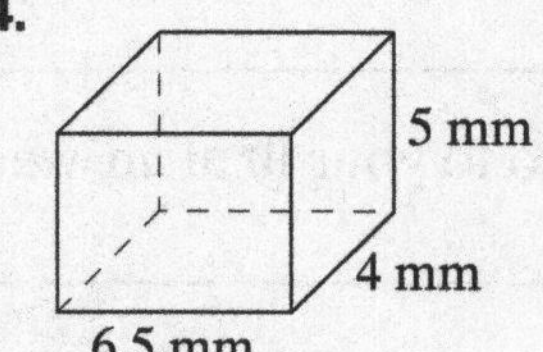

____

Find the surface area of each cylinder. Round to the nearest whole number.

5.
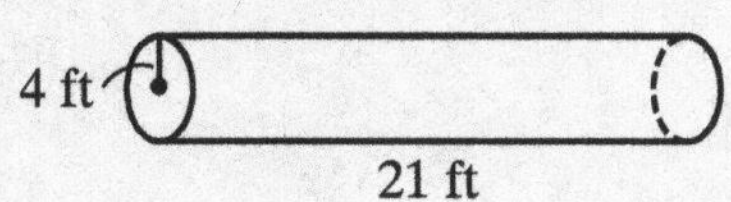

____

6.
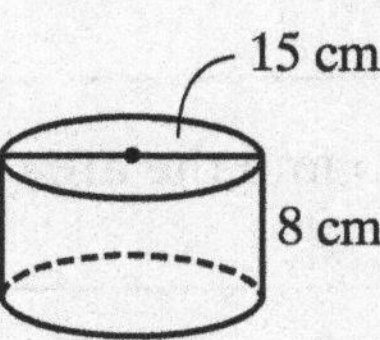

____

7.
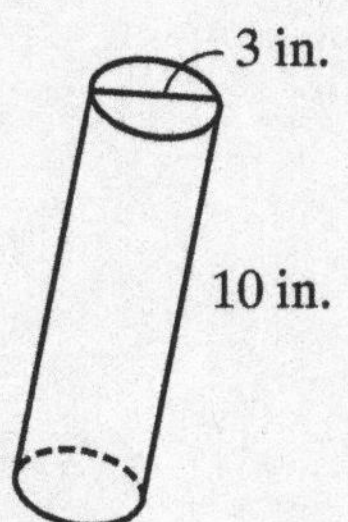

____

8.
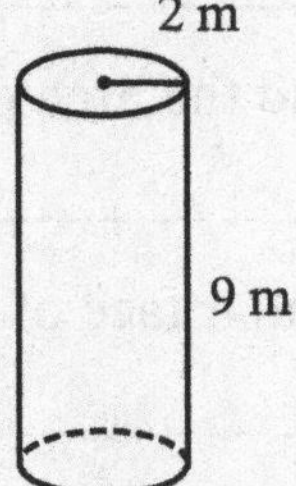

____

Draw a net for each three-dimensional figure.

9.
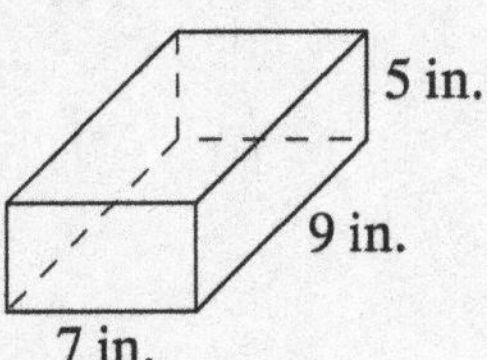

10.
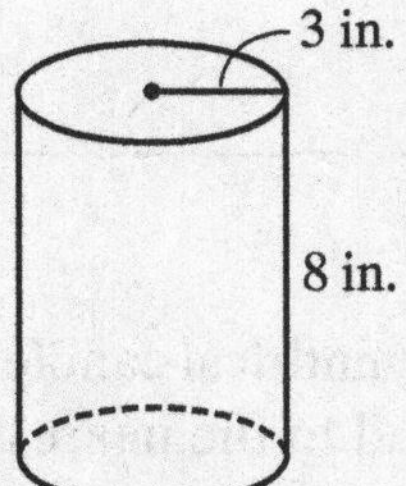

Name ______________________ Class ______________ Date ______________

12-2 • Guided Problem Solving

GPS Student Page 462, Exercise 22:

A cosmetics company that makes small cylindrical bars of soap wraps the bars in plastic prior to shipping. Find the surface area of a bar of soap if the diameter is 5 cm and the height is 2 cm. Round to the nearest tenth.

Understand

1. What are you being asked to do?

   ____

2. What do you need to do to your final answer?

   ____

Plan and Carry Out

3. How do you find the surface area of a cylinder?

   ____

   ____

4. What formula do you use to find the area of a circular face?

   ____

5. What is the total area of the circular faces of a bar of soap?

   ____

6. What formula do you use to find the area of the rectangular face?

   ____

7. What is the area of the rectangular face of a bar of soap?

   ____

8. What is the surface area of a bar of soap? ______________

Check

9. Did you find the area of all the surfaces of a bar of soap? Does your answer check?

   ____

Solve Another Problem

10. Find the surface area of a cylindrical candle if the diameter is 6 in. and the height is 8 in. Round to the nearest tenth.

    ____

Name ______________________ Class ______________ Date ______________

Practice 12-3

Volumes of Prisms and Cylinders

Find each volume. Round to the nearest cubic unit.

1. 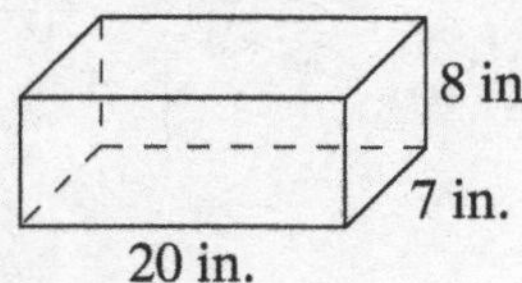

2. 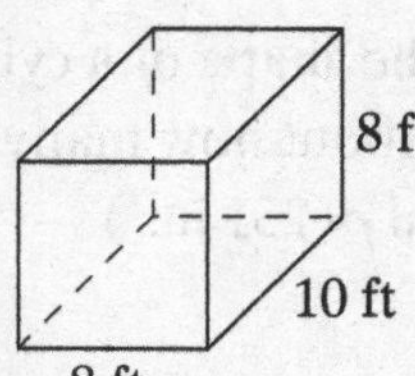

3. 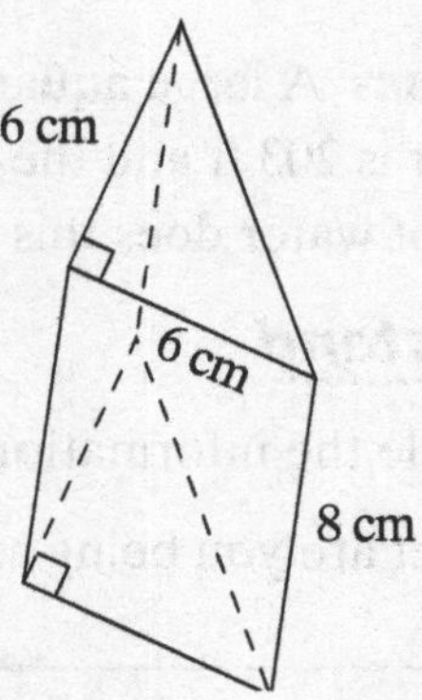

______________ ______________ ______________

4. 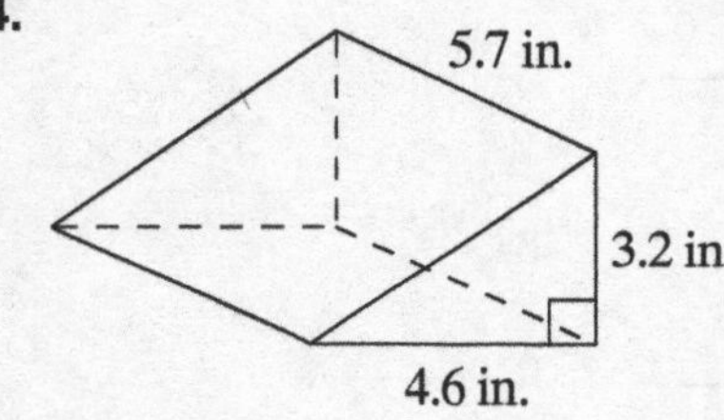

5. 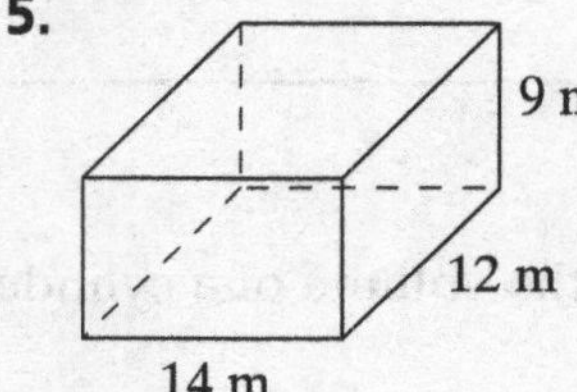

6. 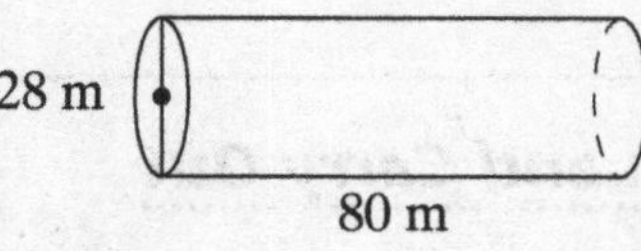

______________ ______________ ______________

7. 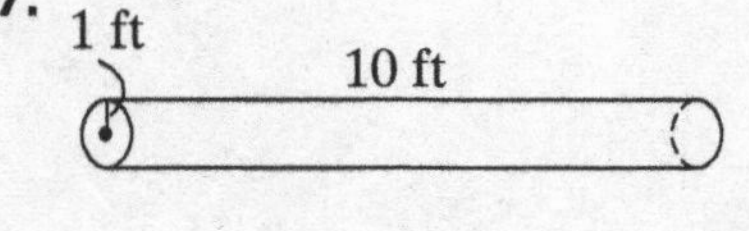

8. 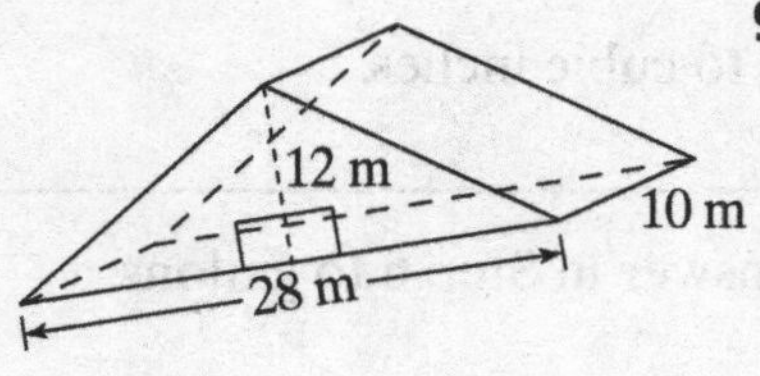

9. 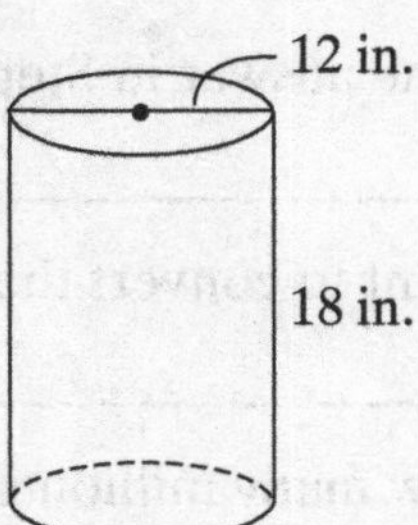

______________ ______________ ______________

Find the height of each rectangular prism given the volume, length, and width.

10. $V = 122{,}500\ \text{cm}^3$
$l = 50$ cm
$w = 35$ cm

11. $V = 22.05\ \text{ft}^3$
$l = 3.5$ ft
$w = 4.2$ ft

12. $V = 3{,}375\ \text{m}^3$
$l = 15$ m
$w = 15$ m

______________ ______________ ______________

Name ______________________ Class ______________ Date ______________

12-3 • Guided Problem Solving

GPS Student Page 469, Exercise 21:

Aquariums A large aquarium is built in the shape of a cylinder. The diameter is 203 ft and the height is 25 ft. About how many million gallons of water does this tank hold? (1 gal ≈ 231 in.^{3})

Understand

1. Circle the information you will need to solve.
2. What are you being asked to do?

   ____

   ____

3. What do you need to do to the units in your final answer?

   ____

Plan and Carry Out

4. Write the formula you use to find the volume of a cylinder.

   ____

5. Find the volume of the aquarium in cubic feet.

   ____

6. Convert the answer in Step 5 to cubic inches.

   ____

7. Use the hint to convert the answer in Step 6 to gallons.

   ____

8. About how many million gallons does the tank hold?

   ____

Check

9. Estimate the answer by using 3 for π, 200 ft for the diameter, 2000 in.^{3} ≈ 1 ft^3 and 1 gal ≈ 200 in.^{3} Does your answer make sense?

   ____

   ____

Solve Another Problem

10. The diameter of a tank is 26 cm, and the height is 58 cm. About how many liters of fuel oil can this steel tank hold? (1,000 cm^3 = 1 L)

    ____

Name ____________________ Class ____________ Date ____________

Practice 12-4

Cross Sections

Describe each cross section.

1. 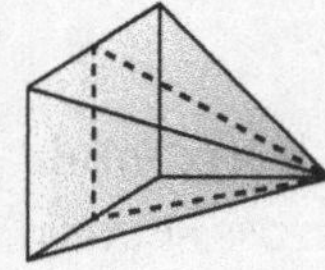

____

2. 

____

3. 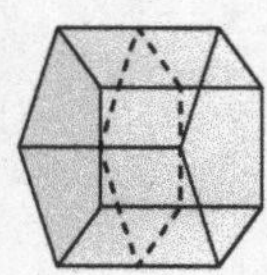

____

4. 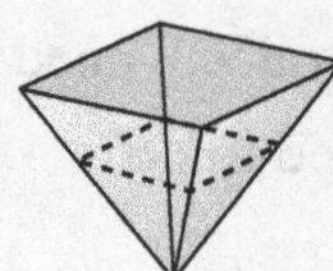

____

5. A block of cheese has the shape of a cylinder. Russell wants to cut the block vertically. Sierra wants to cut the block horizontally. Draw and describe the shape of each cross section.

   a. 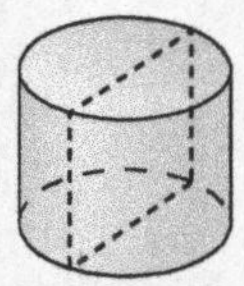

   Vertical Slice

   ____

   b. 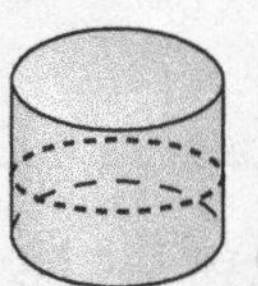

   Horizontal Slice

   ____

6. A carpenter has a block of wood in the shape of a trapezoidal prism. Draw lines on each prism to show how the carpenter should slice the wood to produce each type of cross section.

   a. **trapezoid**

   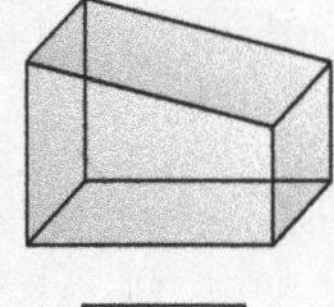 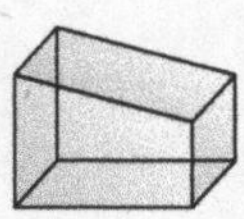

   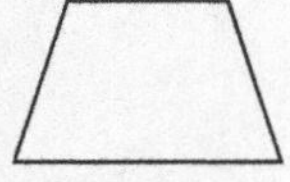

   b. **square**

   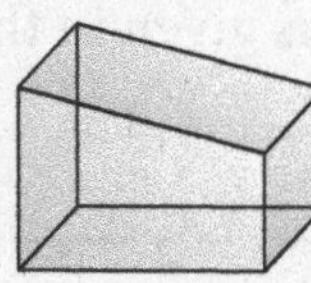 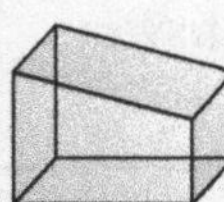

   c. **rectangle**

   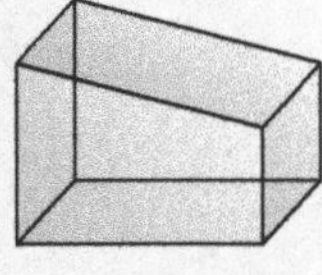 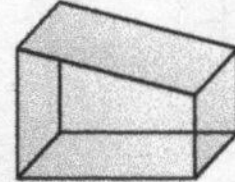

   d. **triangle**

   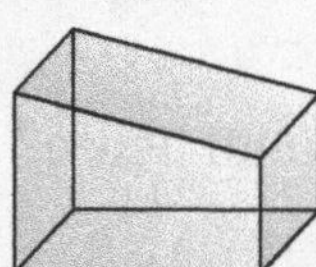 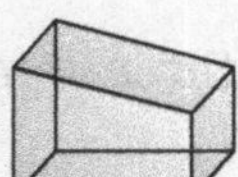

   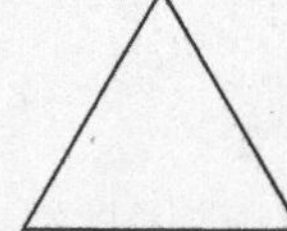

Name ______________________ Class ______________ Date ______________

12-4 • Guided Problem Solving

GPS Student Page 476, Exercise 16:

A three-dimensional figure has a rectangular vertical cross section and a horizontal cross section in the shape of a hexagon.

What is the three-dimensional figure?

vertical cross section

horizontal cross section

Understand

1. Circle the information you will need to solve this problem.
2. What are you being asked to do?

____

____

Plan and Carry Out

3. Is the three-dimensional figure you will identify going to be a prism or a pyramid?

____

4. What shape will the face(s) of the figure have?

____

5. Draw and identify the three-dimensional figure.

____

Check

6. Draw the two cross sections given in the problem on your figure to check your answer.

____

Solve Another Problem

7. A three-dimensional figure has a trapezoidal vertical cross section and a horizontal cross section in the shape of a rectangle.

   What is the three-dimensional figure?

   vertical cross section

   horizontal cross section

____

Name ____________________ Class ____________ Date ____________

Practice 12-5

Volumes of Pyramids and Cones

Find the volume of each figure to the nearest cubic unit.

1.

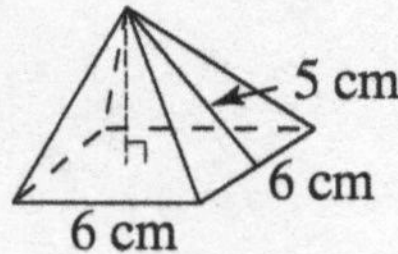

____

2.

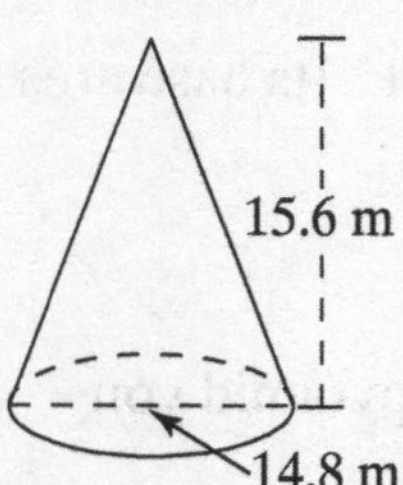

____

3.

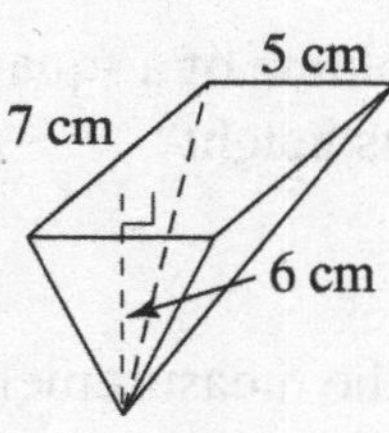

____

4.

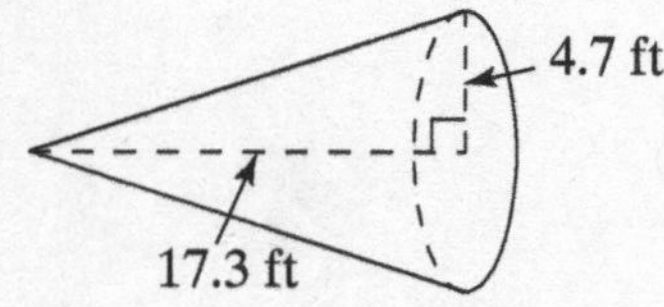

____

5.

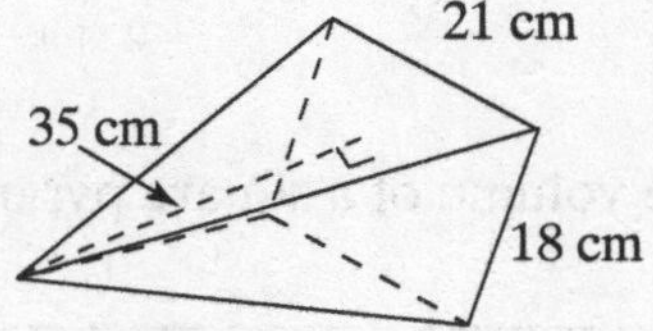

____

6.

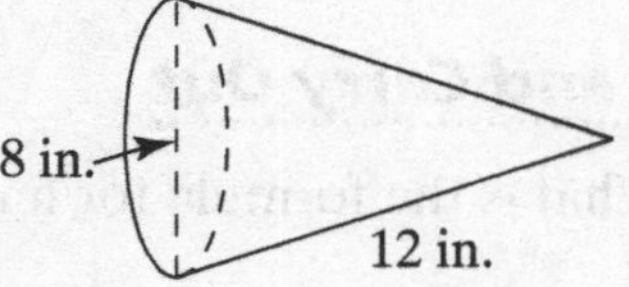

____

Find the missing dimension for each three-dimensional figure to the nearest tenth, given the volume and other dimensions.

7. rectangular pyramid, $l = 8$ m, $w = 4.6$ m, $V = 88$ m^3

____

8. cone, $r = 5$ in., $V = 487$ in.^{3}

____

9. square pyramid, $s = 14$ yd, $V = 489$ yd^3

____

10. square pyramid, $h = 8.9$ cm, $V = 56$ cm^3

____

11. Find the volume of a 4 ft by 2 ft by 3 ft rectangular prism with a cylindrical hole, radius 6 in., through the center.

____

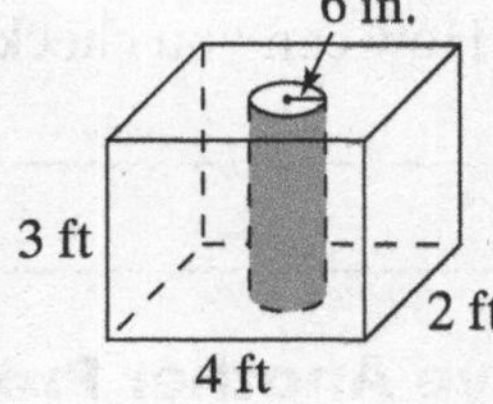

12. Margarite has a cylindrical tin of popcorn that is 18 in. tall and has a radius of 4 in. She wants to use the tin for something else and needs to empty the popcorn into a box. The box is 8 in. long, 8 in. wide, and 14 in. tall. Will the popcorn fit in the box? Explain.

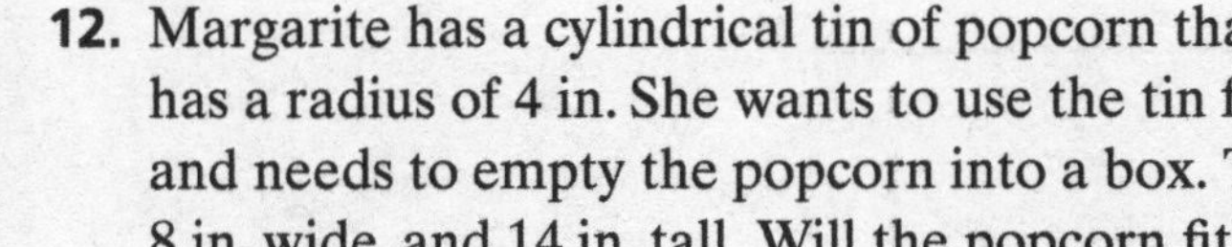

____

____

Name ______________________ Class ______________ Date ____________

12-5 • Guided Problem Solving

GPS Student Page 481, Exercise 17:

Algebra The volume of a square pyramid is 15 ft^3. Its base area is 27 ft^2. What is its height?

Understand

1. Underline the measurements of the square pyramid you are given.
2. What are you asked to find?

   ____

Plan and Carry Out

3. What is the formula for finding the volume of a square pyramid?

   ____

4. What measurements are you given?

   ____

5. Substitute what you know into the formula.

   ____

6. What variable are you solving for? ______________
7. Solve.

   ____

Check

8. How can you check your answer?

   ____

   ____

Solve Another Problem

9. The volume of a cone is 113.04 ft^3. Its base area is 28.26 ft^2. What is its height?

   ____

   ____

Name ______________________ Class ______________________ Date ______________

Practice 12-6

Spheres

Find each sphere's surface area and volume to the nearest whole number.

1. 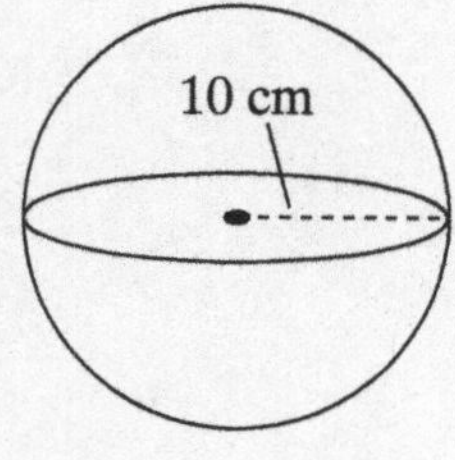

____

____

2. 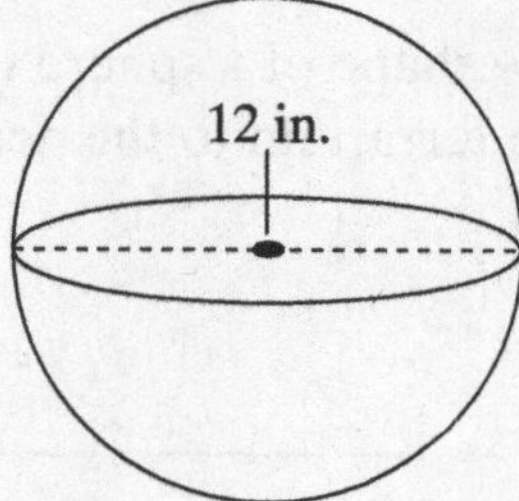

____

____

3. 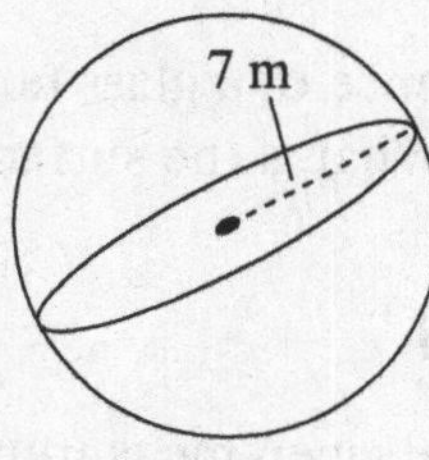

____

____

4. 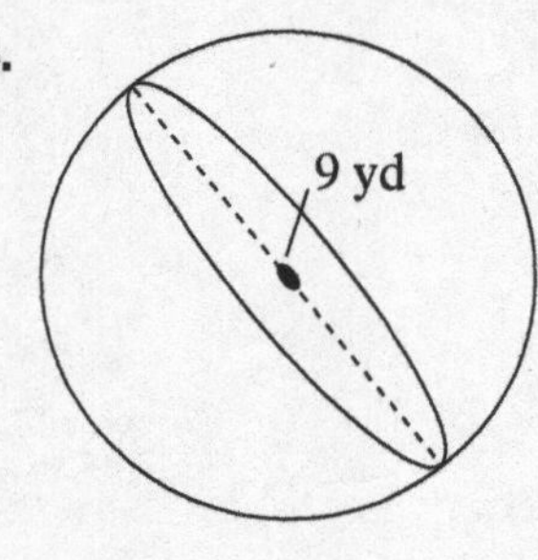

____

____

5. 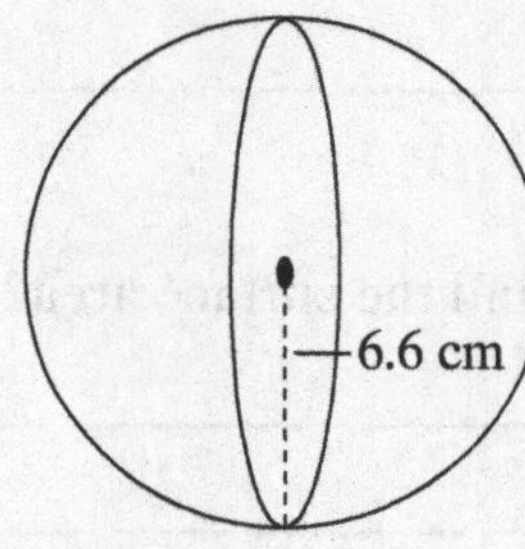

____

____

6. 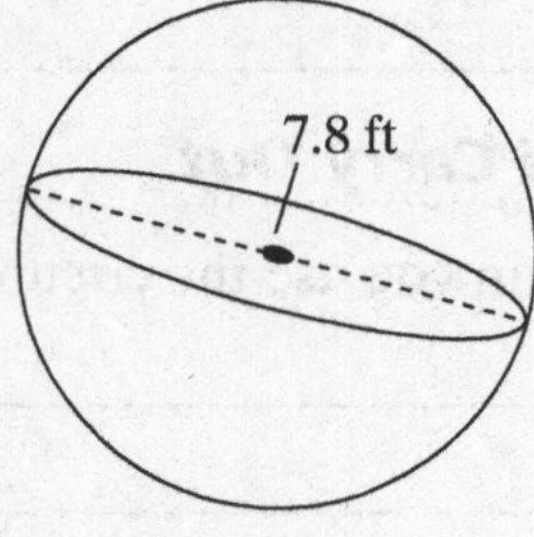

____

____

7. A sphere has a radius of 9 ft. Find its surface area to the nearest whole square unit.

____

8. A geography professor has a spherical globe with a diameter of 14 in. What is the volume of the globe?

____

9. Jenny has four marbles that are all of different sizes and colors. They have diameters of 18 mm, 19 mm, 21 mm, and 24 mm. What is the average surface area of the four marbles?

____

Name ______________________ Class ______________ Date ____________

12-6 • Guided Problem Solving

GPS Student Page 485, Exercise 16:

The circumference of a glass terrarium in the shape of a sphere is about 12.5 in. What is the surface area of the terrarium to the nearest square inch?

Understand

1. What is the given measurement? ______________________
2. What formula do you use to find circumference?

   ____
3. What are you being asked to find?

   ____

Plan and Carry Out

4. How can you use the circumference to find the surface area?

   ____

   ____
5. What is the radius of the terrarium?

   ____
6. How will you find the surface area of the terrarium?

   ____
7. What is the surface area of the terrarium to the nearest square inch?

   ____

Check

8. Does your answer check? Is your answer consistent with the circumference given in the question?

   ____

Solve Another Problem

9. The volume of a weather balloon is about 33.5 ft^3. What is the surface area of the weather balloon? Round your answer to the nearest whole square unit.

   ____

   ____

Name ______________________ Class ______________ Date ______________

12A: Graphic Organizer

For use before Lesson 12-1

Vocabulary and Study Skills

Study Skill Take a few minutes to relax before and after studying. Your mind will absorb and retain more information if you alternate studying with brief rest intervals.

Write your answers.

1. What is the chapter title? ______________________
2. How many lessons are there in this chapter? ______________________
3. What is the topic of the Test-Taking Strategies page? ______________________
4. Complete the graphic organizer below as you work through the chapter.
   - In the center, write the title of the chapter.
   - When you begin a lesson, write the lesson name in a rectangle.
   - When you complete a lesson, write a skill or key concept in a circle linked to that lesson block.
   - When you complete the chapter, use this graphic organizer to help you review.

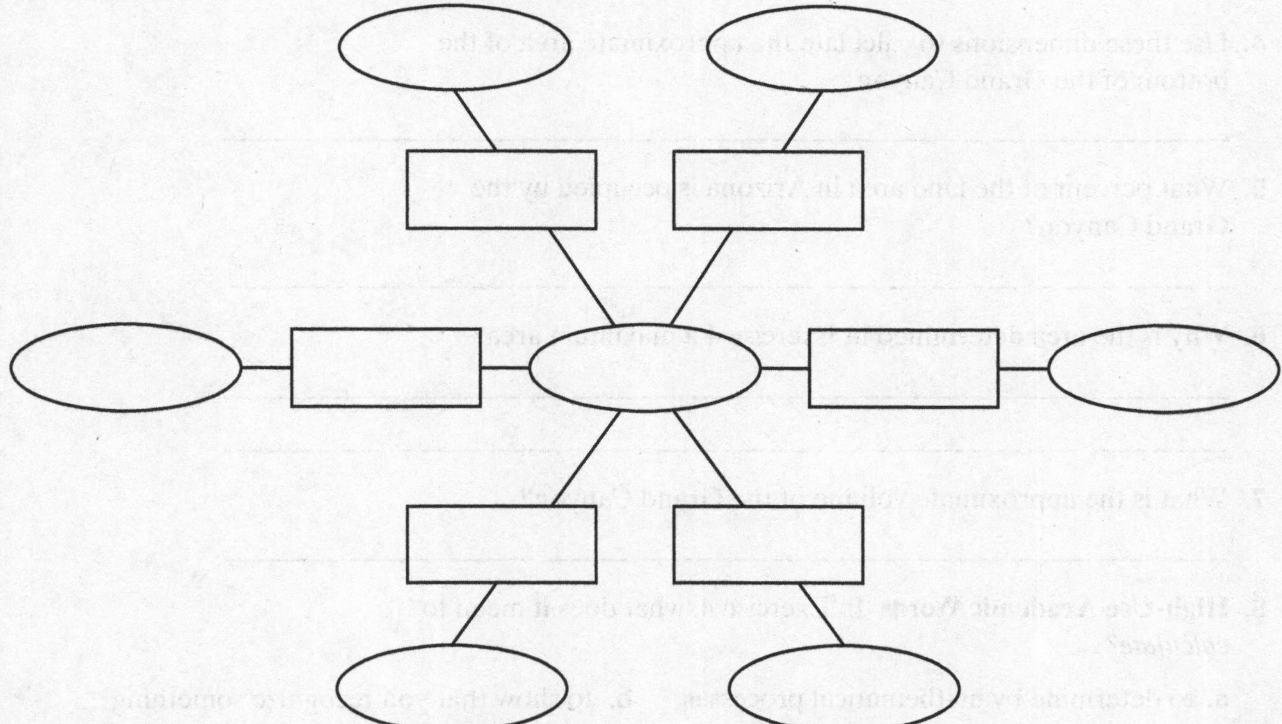

Name ______________________ Class ______________ Date ______________

12B: Reading Comprehension

For use after Lesson 12-4

Study Skill Learning to read for detail takes practice. As you read your notes, underline or highlight important information.

Read the paragraph and answer the questions.

The Grand Canyon was formed by the Colorado River in Arizona. It is estimated to be nearly 10 million years old. With a length of 277 miles, the Grand Canyon is nearly 18 miles wide at its widest point and one mile deep in some places. Arizona, called the Grand Canyon State, has a total land area of approximately 113,000 square miles.

1. What is the paragraph about?

____

2. How old is the Grand Canyon?

____

3. What dimensions are given for the Grand Canyon?

____

4. Use these dimensions to calculate the approximate area of the bottom of the Grand Canyon.

____

5. What percent of the land area in Arizona is occupied by the Grand Canyon?

____

6. Why is the area determined in Exercise 4 a maximum area?

____

____

7. What is the approximate volume of the Grand Canyon?

____

8. **High-Use Academic Words** In Exercise 4, what does it mean to *calculate?*

a. to determine by mathematical processes **b.** to show that you recognize something

Name ______________________ Class ______________ Date ______________

12C: Reading/Writing Math Symbols

For use after Lesson 12-4

Vocabulary and Study Skills

Study Skill After completing an assignment, take a break. Then, come back and check your work.

State whether each of the following units represents length, area or volume.

1. cm^2 ______________
2. in.^3 ______________
3. mi ______________
4. ft^2 ______________
5. km ______________
6. mm^3 ______________

State whether each expression can be used to calculate length, area, or volume and to what shapes they apply.

7. $\frac{1}{2}bh$ ______________
8. lwh ______________
9. bh ______________
10. πd ______________
11. πr^2 ______________
12. S^2 ______________
13. $\frac{1}{2}h(b_1 + b_2)$ ______________
14. $\pi r^2 h$ ______________
15. $2\pi r$ ______________

Name ________________________ Class ________________ Date ____________

12D: Visual Vocabulary Practice

For use after Lesson 12-4

Study Skill When interpreting an illustration, look for the most specific concept represented.

Concept List

circumference	base	cone
Pythagorean Theorem	perfect square	edges
vertices	prism	pyramid

Write the concept that best describes each exercise. Choose from the concept list above.

1. $AB^2 = 6^2 + 8^2$ $AB^2 = 36 + 64 = 100$ $AB = \sqrt{100} = 10$ 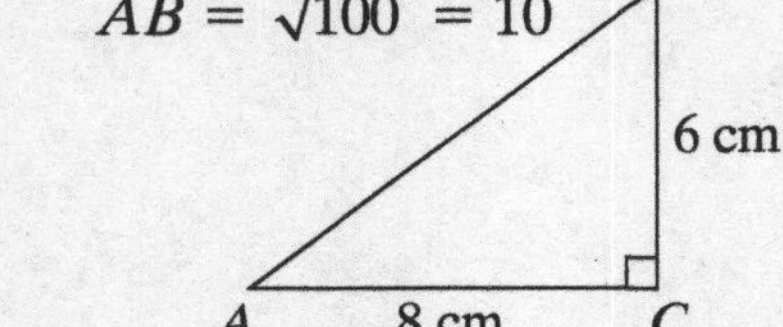 ________________	**2.** 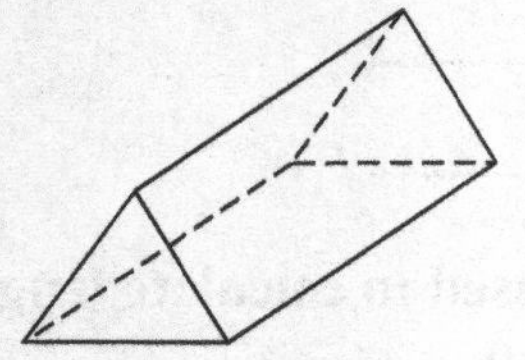 ________________	**3.** Circle P is one for this cylinder. 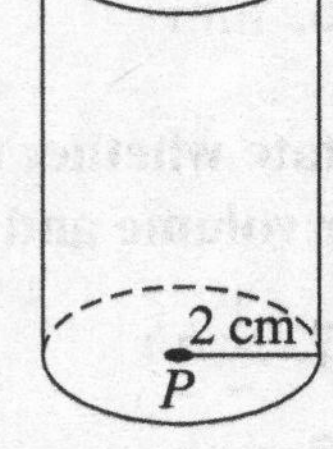 ________________
4. 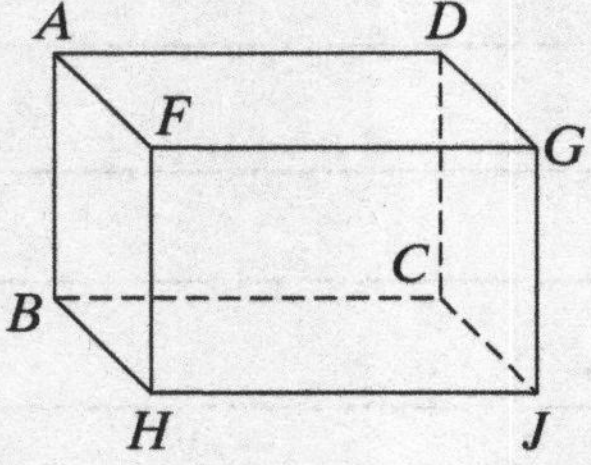 $\overline{AB}$ and $\overline{CJ}$ are examples ________________	**5.** 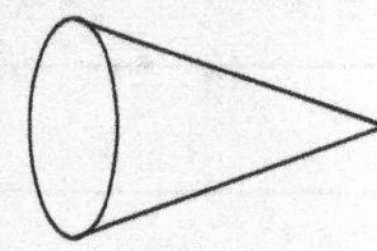 ________________	**6.** 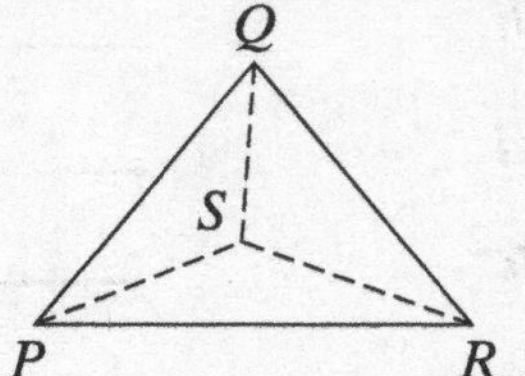 There are four of these in this three-dimensional figure. ________________
7. 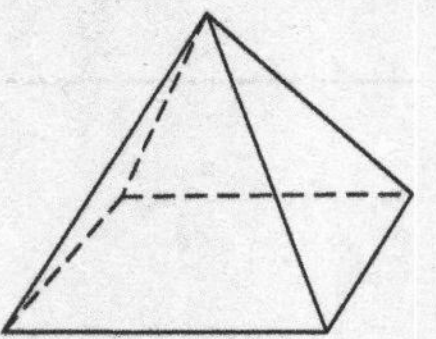 ________________	**8.** 576, since $24^2 = 576$. ________________	**9.** 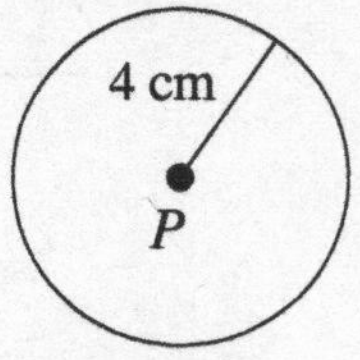 $C \approx 25.1$ cm ________________

Name ______________________ Class ______________ Date ______________

12E: Vocabulary Check

For use after Lesson 12-5

Study Skill Strengthen your vocabulary. Use these pages and add cues and summaries by applying the Cornell Notetaking style.

Write the definition for each word or term at the right. To check your work, fold the paper back along the dotted line to see the correct answers.

______________________________ cross section

______________________________ cone

______________________________ surface area

______________________________ volume

______________________________ prism

Name ____________________ Class ____________ Date ____________

12E: Vocabulary Check (continued)

For use after Lesson 12-5

Write the vocabulary word or term for each definition. To check your work, fold the paper forward along the dotted line to see the correct answers.

two-dimensional shape that is seen after slicing through a 3-dimensional object ____________________

a flat surface of a three-dimensional figure that is shaped like a polygon ____________________

sum of the areas of the faces ____________________

the number of cubic units needed to fill the space inside a three-dimensional figure ____________________

a three-dimensional figure with triangular faces that meet at one point, a vertex, and has a base that is also a triangle ____________________

Name ________________________ Class ______________ Date ______________

12F: Vocabulary Review

For use with the Chapter Review

Study Skill Participating in class discussions will help you remember new material. Do not be afraid to express your thoughts when your teacher asks for questions, answers, or discussion.

Circle the word that best completes the sentence.

1. The longest side of a right triangle is the (*leg, hypotenuse*).
2. (*Parallel, Perpendicular*) lines lie in the same plane and do not intersect.
3. A (*solution, statement*) is a value of a variable that makes an equation true.
4. Figures that are the same size and shape are (*similar, congruent*).
5. (*Complementary, Supplementary*) angles are two angles whose sum is 90°.
6. A (*circle, sphere*) is the set of all points in space that are the same distance from a center point.
7. The perimeter of a circle is the (*circumference, circumcenter*).
8. The (*area, volume*) of a figure is the number of square units it encloses.
9. A(n) (*isosceles, scalene*) triangle has no congruent sides.
10. A (*rhombus, square*) is a parallelogram with four right angles and four congruent sides.
11. A number that is the square of an integer is a (*perfect square, square root*).
12. A (*pyramid, prism*) is a three-dimensional figure with triangular faces that meet at one point.
13. A speed limit of 65 mi/h is an example of a (*ratio, rate*).
14. A (*cone, cylinder*) has two congruent parallel bases that are circles.
15. The formula for the volume of a (*cone, pyramid*) is $V = \frac{1}{3}Bh$.
16. A (*cone, pyramid*) is named for the shape of its base.

Name ____________________ Class ____________ Date ____________

Practice 13-1

Translations

Use arrow notation to write a rule that describes the translation shown on each graph.

1. 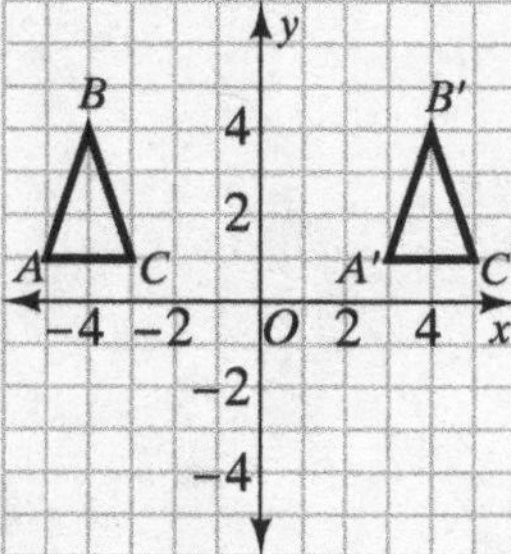

2. 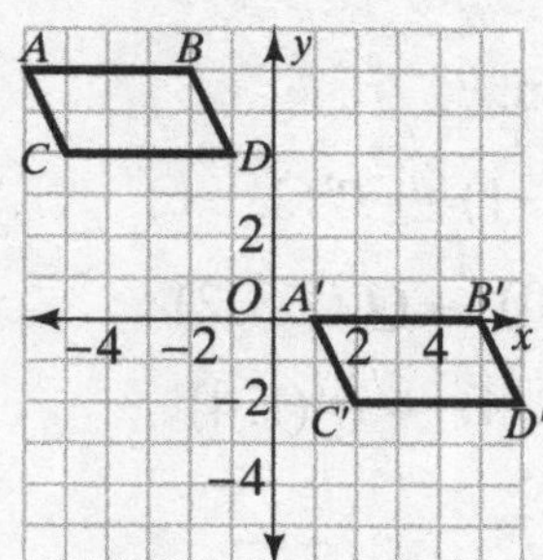

3. 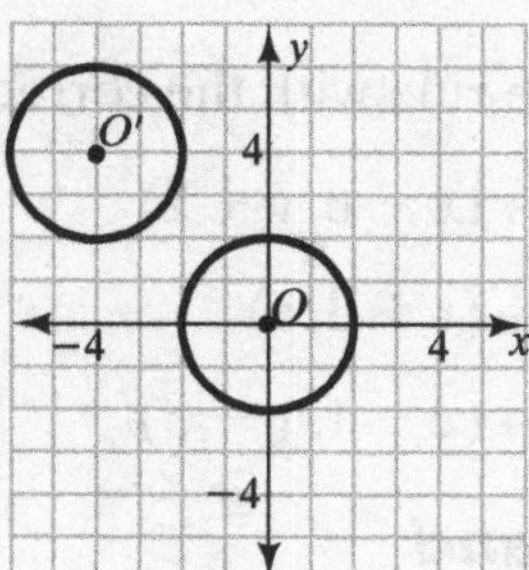

______________ ______________ ______________

Copy $\triangle MNP$. Then graph the image after each translation. List the coordinates of each image's vertices.

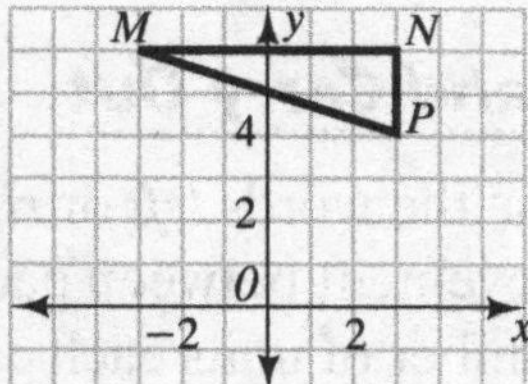

4. left 2 units, down 2 units

____

5. right 2 units, down 1 unit

____

6. left 2 units, up 3 units

____

Copy $\square RSTU$. Then graph the image after each translation. List the coordinates of each image's vertices.

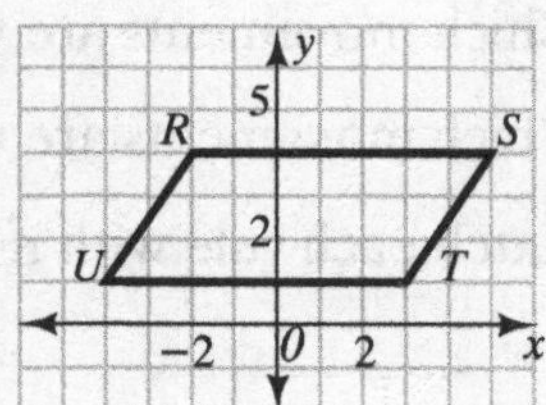

7. right 1 unit, down 2 units

____

8. left 3 units, up 0 units

____

9. right 2 units, up 4 units

____

Use the graph at the right for Exercises 10 and 11.

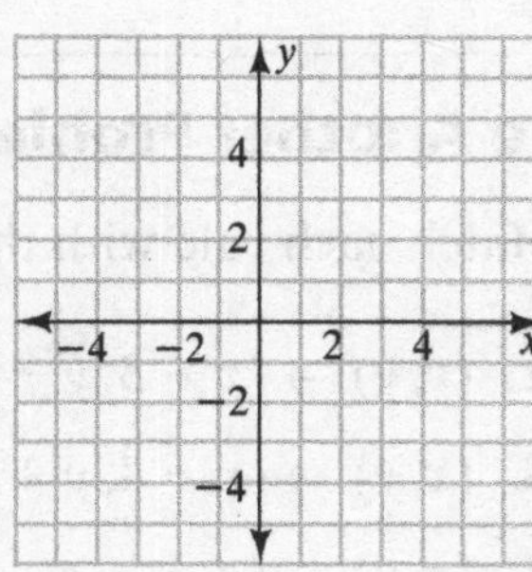

10. A rectangle has its vertices at $M(1, 1)$, $N(6, 1)$, $O(6, 5)$, and $P(1, 5)$. The rectangle is translated to the left 4 units and down 3 units. What are the coordinates of M', N', O', and P'? Graph the rectangles $MNOP$ and $M'N'O'P'$.

____

11. Use arrow notation to write a rule that describes the translation of $M'N'O'P'$ to $MNOP$.

____

Name ______________________ Class ______________ Date ______________

13-1 • Guided Problem Solving

GPS Student Page 497, Exercises 16–18:

Match each rule with the correct translation.

A. $(x, y) \to (x - 6, y + 2)$ **I.** $P(4, -1) \to P'(3, -6)$

B. $(x, y) \to (x + 3, y)$ **II.** $Q(3, 0) \to Q'(-3, 2)$

C. $(x, y) \to (x - 1, y - 5)$ **III.** $R(-2, 4) \to R'(1, 4)$

Understand

1. What are you asked to do?

____

Plan and Carry Out

2. Use the words *left* or *right* and *up* or *down* to describe the movement between each point and its image. Be sure to give the number of units each coordinate is translated.

   Point $P(4, -1)$ to $P'(3, -6)$ ______________________

   Point $Q(3, 0)$ to $Q'(-3, 2)$ ______________________

   Point $R(-2, 4)$ to $R'(1, 4)$ ______________________

3. Which movements are written as addition? ______________

4. Which movements are written as subtraction? ______________

5. Match each rule with its translation.

   A = __________ B = __________ C = __________

Check

6. How could you check your answers?

____

____

Solve Another Problem

7. Match each rule with the correct translation.

   A. $(x, y) \to (x - 3, y - 4)$ **I.** $P(5, -2) \to P'(5, -5)$

   B. $(x, y) \to (x + 4, y + 2)$ **II.** $Q(1, 6) \to Q'(5, 8)$

   C. $(x, y) \to (x, y - 3)$ **III.** $R(-4, 2) \to R'(-7, -2)$

____

Name ____________________ Class ____________________ Date ____________________

Practice 13-2

Reflections and Symmetry

How many lines of symmetry can you find for each letter?

1. W __________ 2. X __________ 3. H __________ 4. T __________

Graph the given point and its image after each reflection.
Name the coordinates of the reflected point.

5. $A(5, -4)$ over the vertical dashed line

____

6. $B(-3, 2)$ over the horizontal dashed line

____

7. $C(-5, 0)$ over the y-axis

____

8. $D(3, 4)$ over the x-axis

____

$\triangle ABC$ has vertices $A(2, 1)$, $B(3, -5)$, and $C(-2, 4)$. Graph $\triangle ABC$ and its image, $\triangle A'B'C'$, after a reflection over each line. Name the coordinates of A', B', and C'.

9. the x-axis

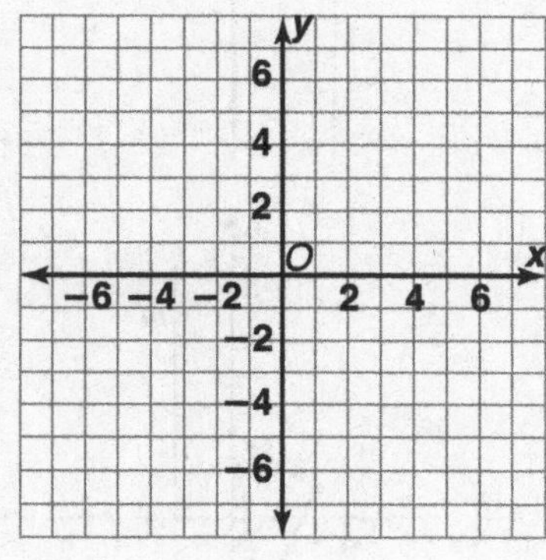

____

____

10. the line through $(-1, 2)$ and $(1, 2)$

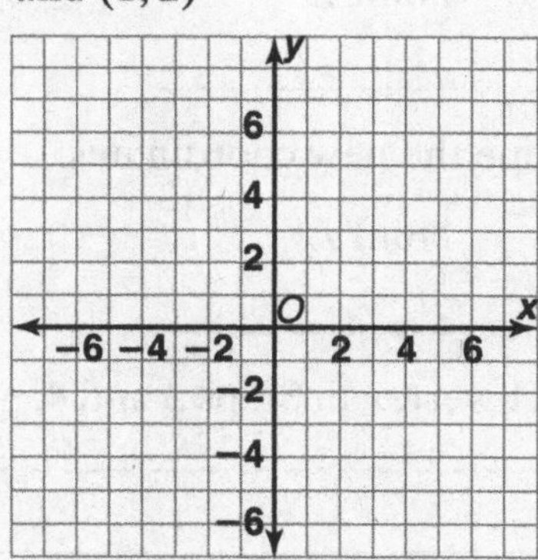

____

____

11. the y-axis

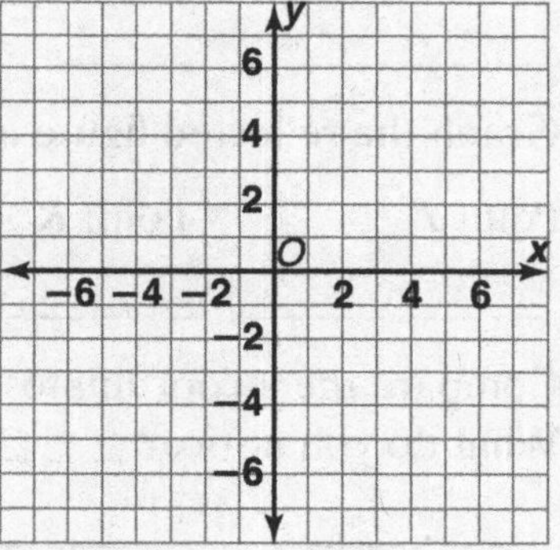

____

____

Fold your paper over each dashed line. Are the figures reflections of each other over the given line?

12.

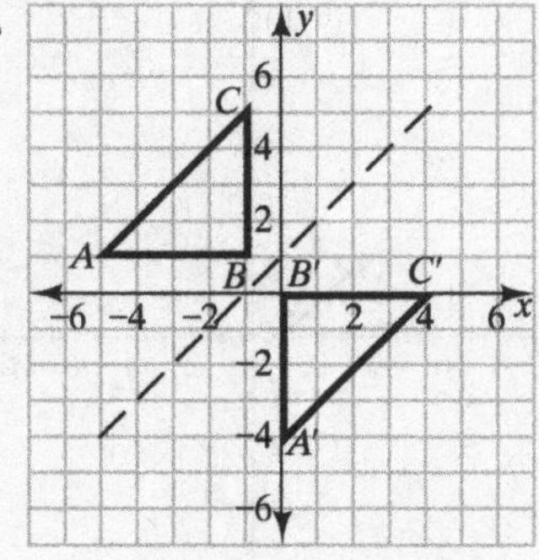

____

13.

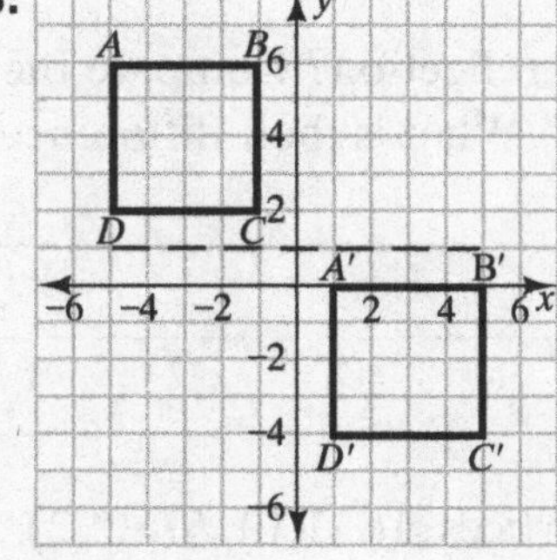

____

14.

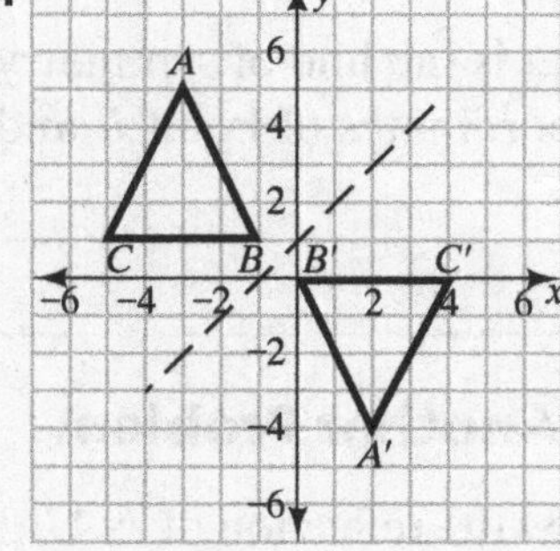

____

Name ______________________ Class ______________ Date ______________

13-2 • Guided Problem Solving

Student Page 502, Exercise 22:

a. Graph the image of $\triangle JKL$ after it is reflected over the line m. Name the coordinates of $\triangle J'K'L'$. What do you notice about the y-coordinates?

b. Translate $\triangle J'K'L'$ to the left 3 units. Name the coordinates of $\triangle J''K''L''$.

Understand

1. Across what line will you reflect $\triangle JKL$? ______________

2. How many units to the left will you translate $\triangle JKL$? ______________

Plan and Carry Out

3. Write the coordinates for each vertex of $\triangle JKL$.

Point J ______________ Point K ______________ Point L ______________

4. Graph the reflected figure and name the new coordinates.

Point J' ______________ Point K' ______________ Point L' ______________

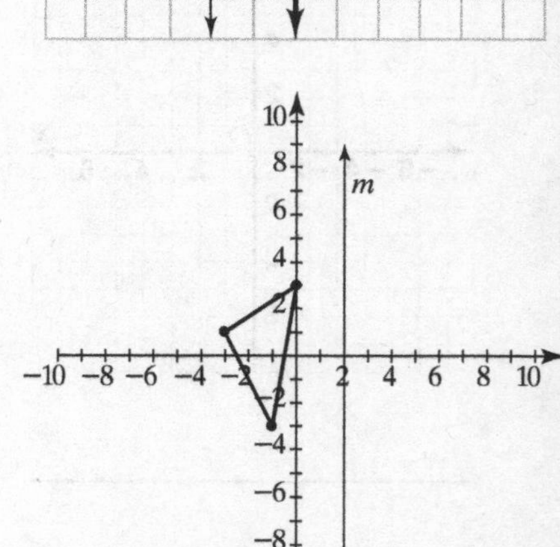

5. Compare the y-coordinates of each vertex in Steps 3 and 4. What do you notice? ______________

____

6. Translate the reflected figure 3 units to the left and name the new coordinates.

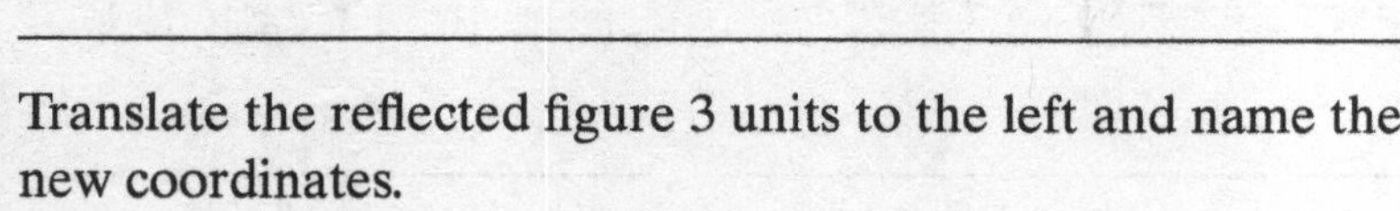

Point J'' ______________ Point K'' ______________ Point L'' ______________

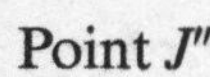

Check

7. What is the line of symmetry in your reflection? Compare the x-coordinates of Point J' and Point J''. What is their difference?

____

____

Solve Another Problem

8. Draw the reflection of $\triangle ABC$ with vertices $A(-1, 0)$, $B(-3, 2)$, and $C(-2, 3)$ across the y-axis. Give the coordinates of the reflection's vertices. ______________

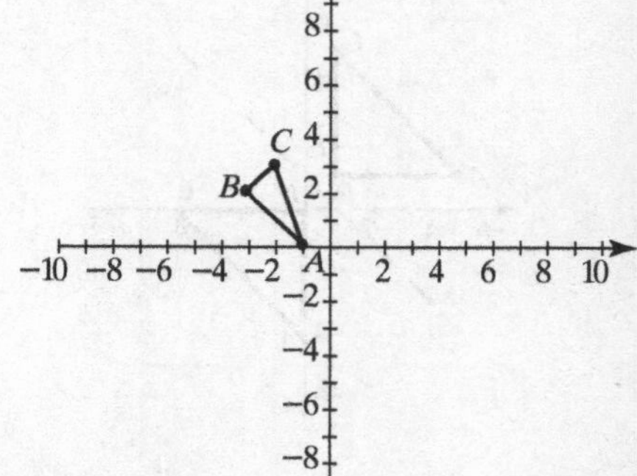

Name ______________________ Class ______________ Date ______________

Practice 13-3

Rotations

Graph each point. Then rotate it the given number of degrees about the origin. Give the coordinates of the image.

1. $V(2, -3)$; 90° ______________
2. $M(-4, 5)$; 270° ______________
3. $V(0, 5)$; 180° ______________
4. $V(3, 4)$; 360° ______________
5. Graph $\triangle RST$ with vertices $R(-1, 3)$, $S(4, -2)$, and $T(2, -5)$. Graph the image formed by rotating the triangle about the origin by each angle.

a 90°

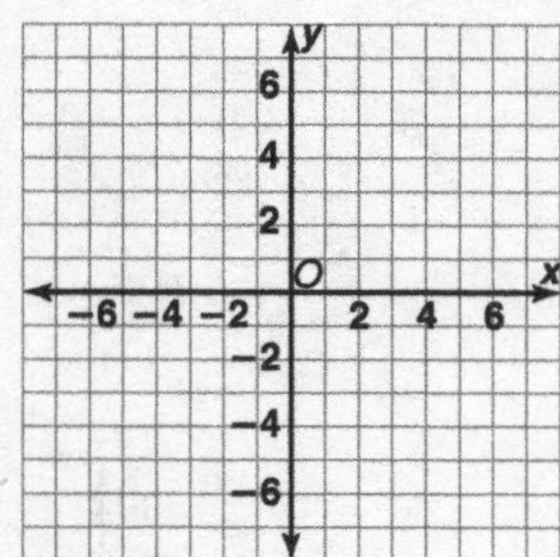

b 180°

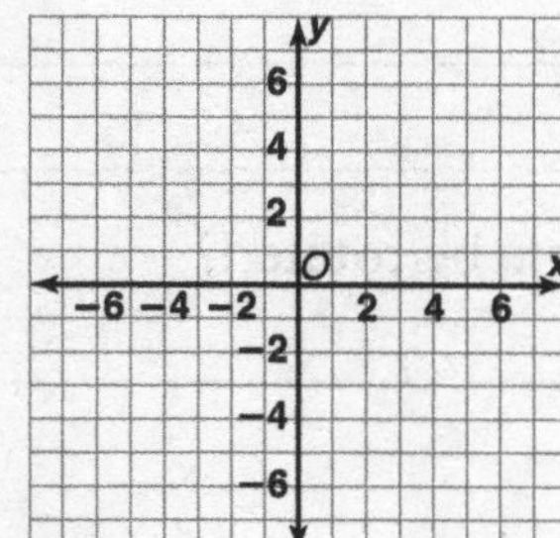

c 270°

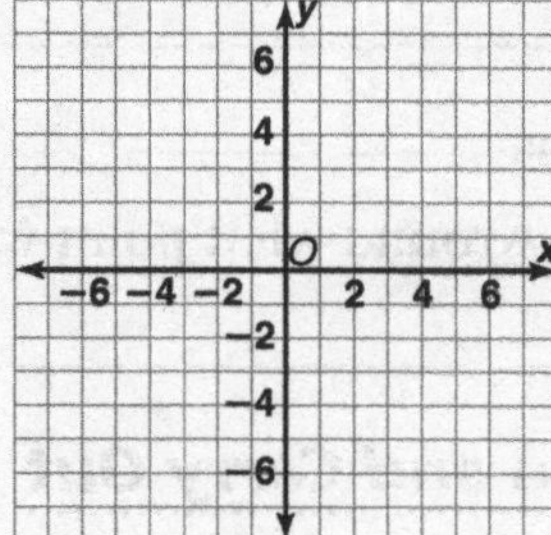

Determine if each figure could be a rotation of the figure at the right. For each figure that could be a rotation, tell what the angle of rotation appears to be.

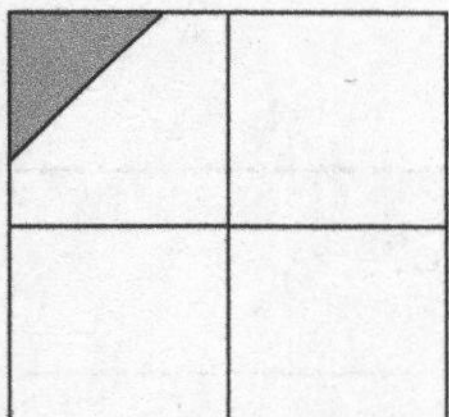

6.

7.

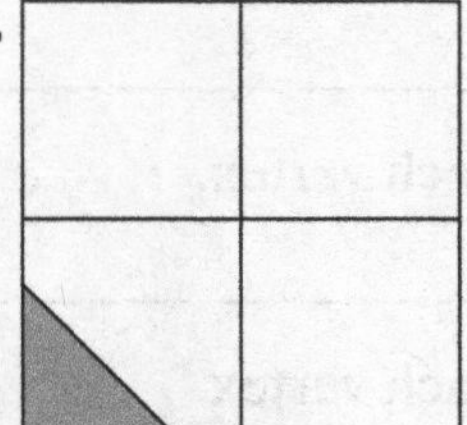

8.

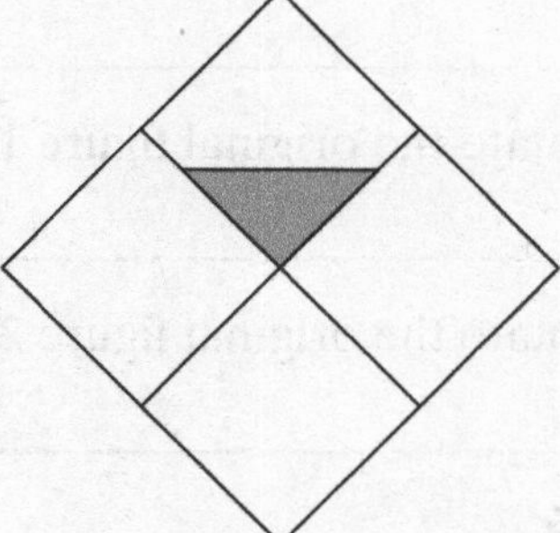

______________ ______________ ______________

9.

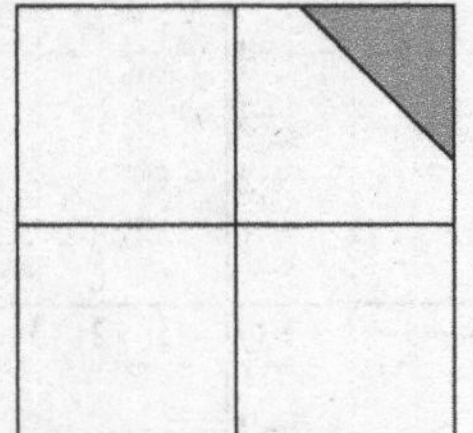

10.

11.

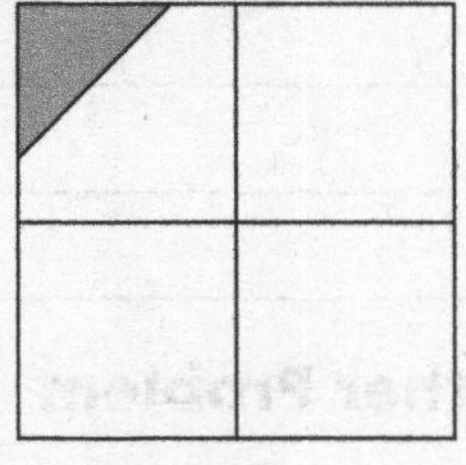

______________ ______________ ______________

Name ______________________ Class ______________________ Date ______________

13-3 • Guided Problem Solving

GPS Student Page 507, Exercise 12:

Graph $\triangle JKL$ with vertices $J(1, -3)$, $K(6, -2)$, and $L(6, -4)$. Graph the three images formed by rotating the triangle 90°, 180°, and 270° about the origin. Give the coordinates of the vertices of each image.

Understand

1. What are you asked to do?

____

____

2. Around what point will the triangle be rotated?

____

Plan and Carry Out

3. Graph the triangle. ____

4. What is a rotation?

____

5. What direction does the figure rotate?

____

6. Rotate the figure 90° and mark each vertex.

____

7. Rotate the original figure 180° and mark each vertex.

____

8. Rotate the original figure 270° and mark each vertex.

____

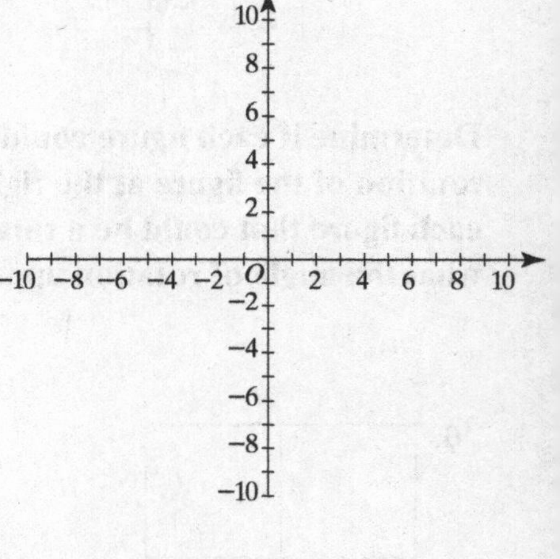

Check

9. How can you check that your figures are rotated correctly?

____

____

____

Solve Another Problem

10. a. Graph $\triangle ABC$ with vertices $A(2, 2)$, $B(1, 1)$, and $C(1, 3)$.

b. Draw the three images formed by rotating the triangle 90°, 180°, and 270° about the origin.

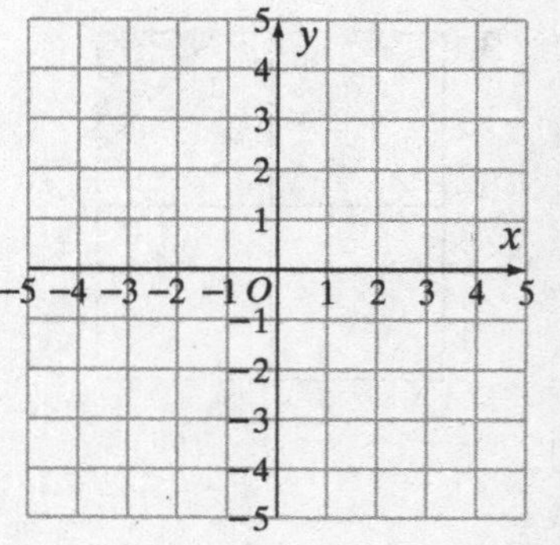

Name ____________________ Class ____________________ Date ____________________

Practice 13-4

Transformations and Congruence

The three figures in each diagram are congruent. Describe the sequence of transformations that maps the original figure onto the final image.

1.

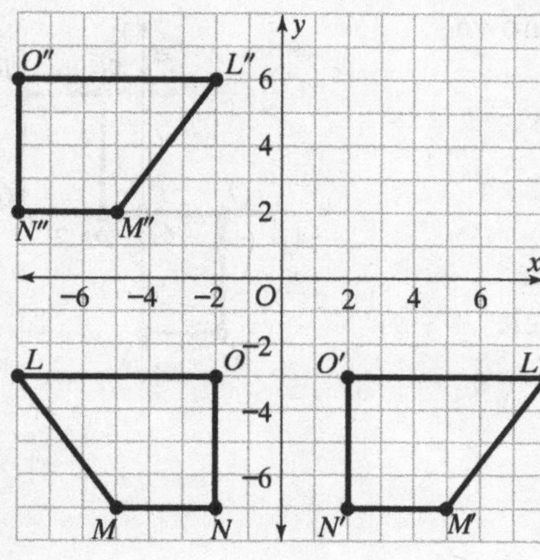

2.

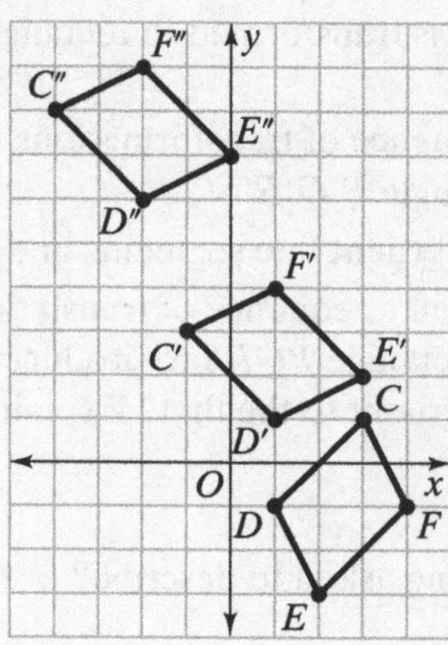

____

____

____

____

Determine whether the two figures in each diagram are congruent. If the figures are congruent, tell what sequence of transformations will map one figure onto the other. Then write a congruence statement. If they are not congruent, explain why.

3.

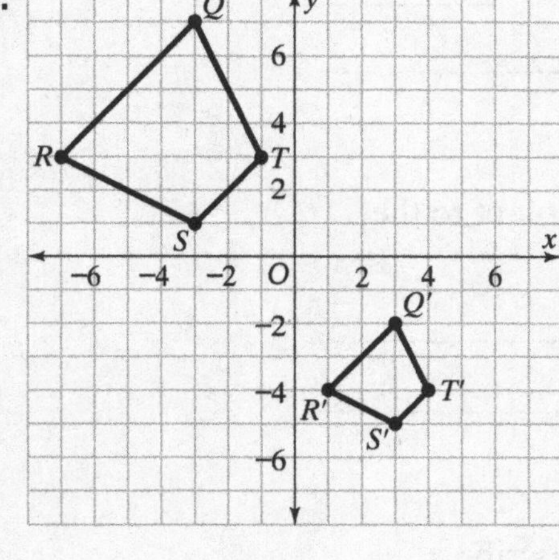

4.

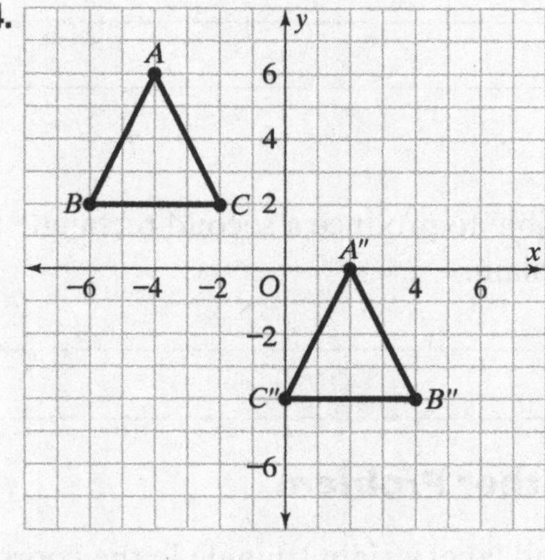

____

____

____

____

Name ______________________ Class ______________ Date ______________

13-4 • Guided Problem Solving

Transformations and Congruence

GPS Student Page 512, Exercise 10:

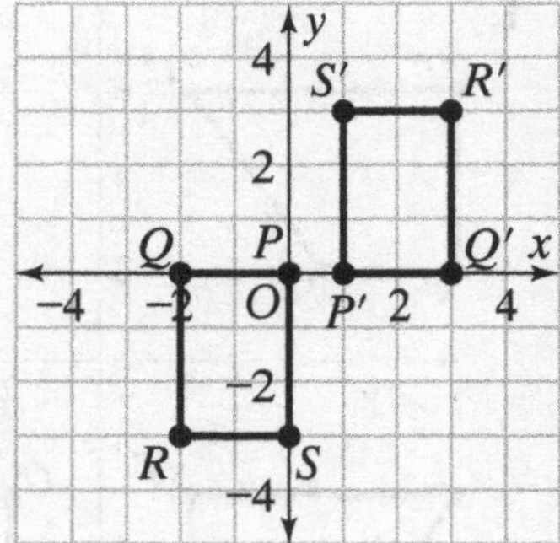

10. Rectangle *PQRS* is transformed to rectangle *P'Q'R'S'* as shown on the graph.

a. Describe a sequence of transformations to map rectangle *PQRS* to rectangle *P'Q'R'S'*.

b. Identify all congruent line segments and angles.

c. Can you perform a sequence of translations, reflections, or rotations on rectangle *PQRS* to produce a second rectangle that is *not* congruent to the first? Explain.

Understand

1. What are you being asked to describe?

____

2. What are you being asked to identify?

____

Plan and Carry Out

3. List the corresponding line segments. ______________________

4. To map rectangle *PQRS* onto rectangle *P'Q'R'S'* should you start by translating, reflecting, or rotating rectangle *PQRS*? What transformation should you perform second?

____

____

Check

5. Is it possible to produce a second rectangle that is not congruent to the first? Explain.

____

____

Solve Another Problem

6. Graph and label a right triangle in the coordinate plane. Describe a sequence of transformations. Then draw and label the final transformation image. Give the coordinates of the vertices of both the original triangle and its final transformation image.

Name ______________________ Class ______________ Date ______________

Practice 13-5

Dilations

Graph quadrilateral *ABCD* with the given vertices. Find the coordinates of the vertices of its image *A′B′C′D′* after a dilation with the given scale factor.

1. $A(2, -2), B(3, 2), C(-3, 2), D(-2, -2)$; scale factor 2

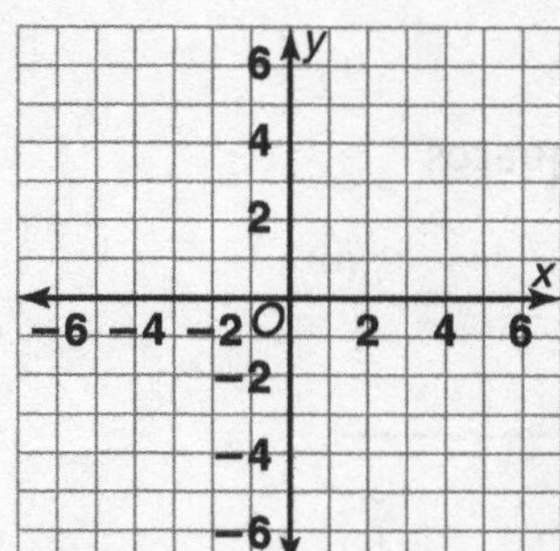

2. $A(6, 3), B(0, 6), C(-6, 2), D(-6, -5)$; scale factor $\frac{1}{2}$

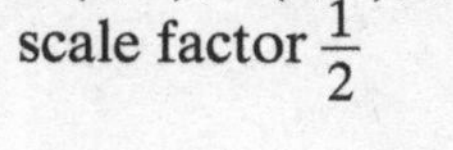

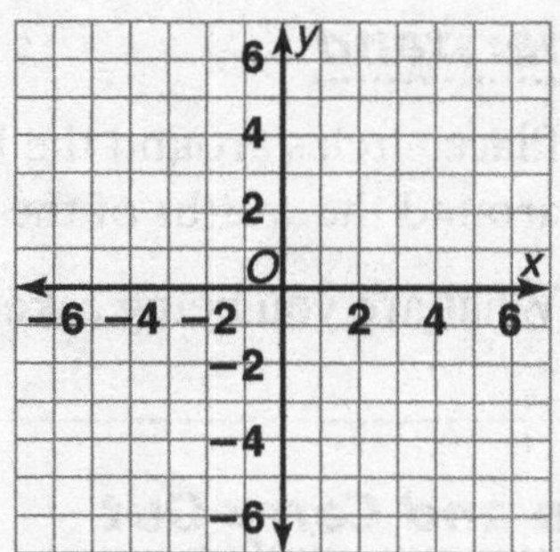

Quadrilateral *A′B′C′D′* is a dilation image of quadrilateral *ABCD*. Find the scale factor. Classify each dilation as an *enlargement* or a *reduction*.

3.

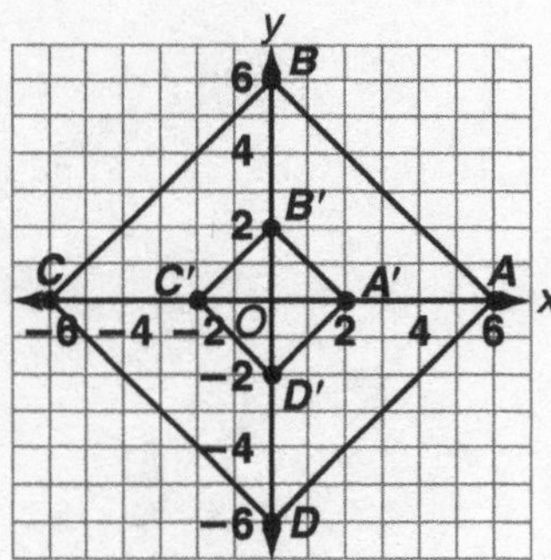

4.

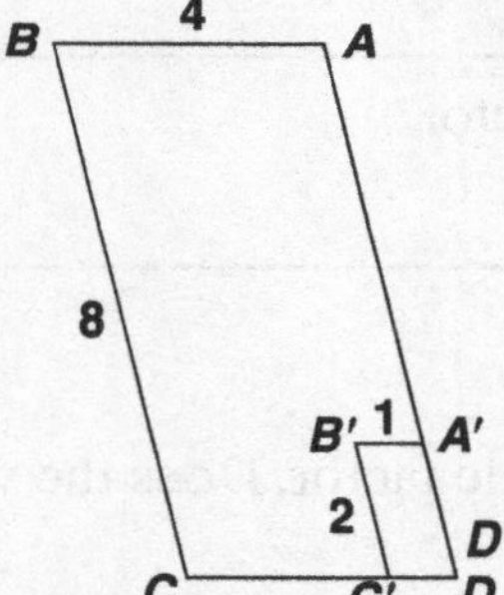

5.

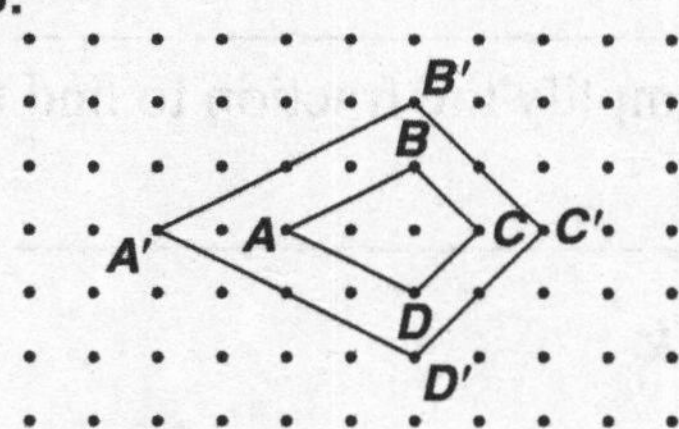

______________ ______________ ______________

6. A triangle has coordinates $A(-2, -2)$, $B(4, -2)$, and $C(1, 1)$. Graph its image $A'B'C'$ after a dilation with scale factor $\frac{3}{2}$. Give the coordinates of $A'B'C'$, and the ratio of the areas of the figures $A'B'C'$ and ABC.

____

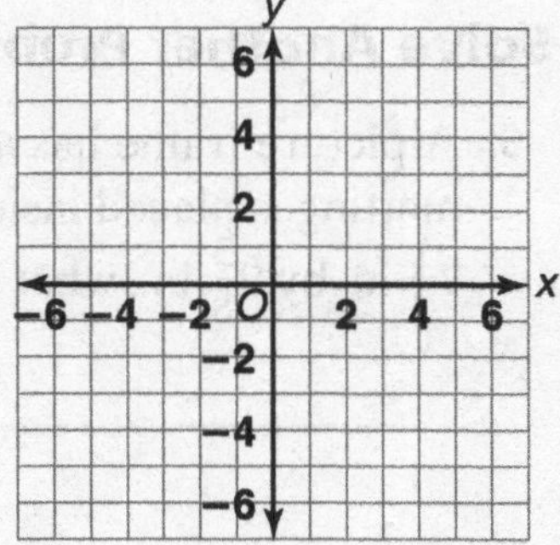

Name ____________________ Class ____________ Date ____________

13-5 • Guided Problem Solving

GPS Student Page 520, Exercise 14:

Computers A window on a computer screen is $1\frac{1}{2}$ in. high and 2 in. wide. After you click the "size reduction" button, the window is reduced to $1\frac{1}{8}$ in. high and $1\frac{1}{2}$ in. wide. What is the scale factor?

Understand

1. Place circles around the heights of the window and squares around the widths of the window.

2. What are you being asked to find?

____

Plan and Carry Out

3. Use the width dimension to find the scale factor by placing the values in the formula $\frac{\text{image}}{\text{original}}$.

____

4. Simplify the fraction to find the scale factor.

____

Check

5. Use the height dimension to find the scale factor. Does the value match your answer to Step 4?

____

Solve Another Problem

6. A picture frame has an opening that is 12 in. by 15 in. If a matting is placed inside the frame to create an opening that is $7\frac{1}{2}$ in. by $9\frac{3}{8}$ in., what is the scale factor of the reduction?

____

Name _______________ Class _______________ Date _______________

Practice 13-6

Transformations and Similarity

1. You and a friend decide to start a lawn cutting business. You use a graphics program to make a flyer advertising your business. You choose a picture for your flyer and place it on the top, left of the computer screen. The size of the picture on your screen is 12 cm wide. It looks much too large, so you reduce it to 4 cm wide. You then center the picture both horizontally and vertically on the page. Describe the sequence of transformations that maps the original picture on the flyer to the final version.

____

____

The two figures in each diagram are similar. Describe the sequence of two transformations that maps the original figure onto the final image.

2.

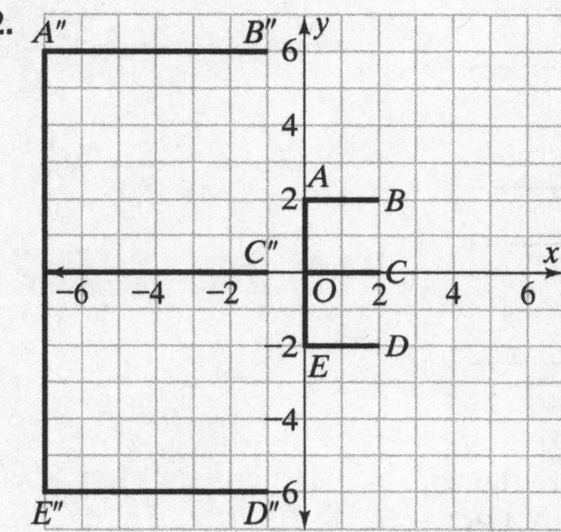

____

____

3.

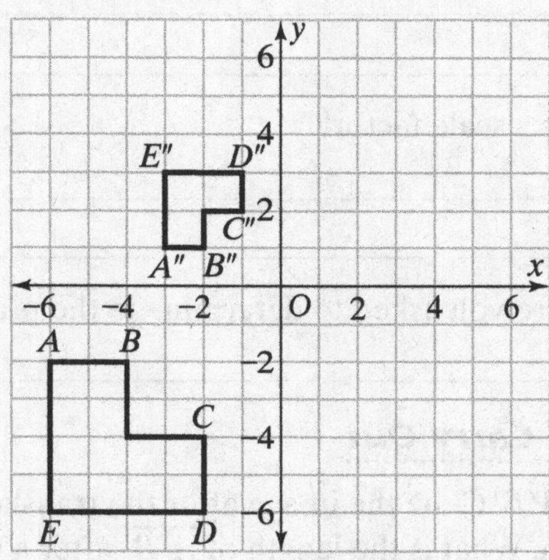

____

____

4.

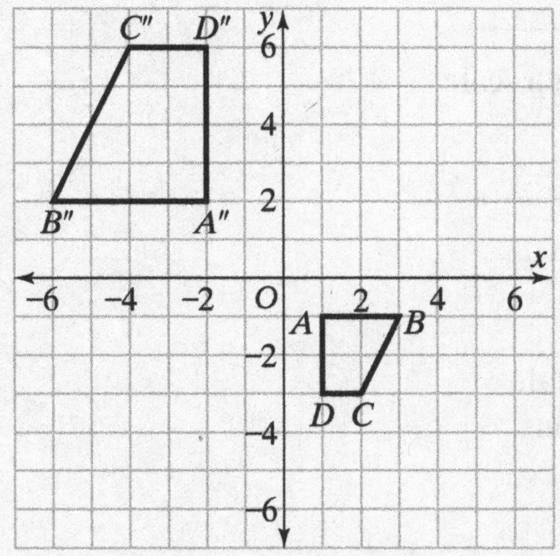

____

____

5.

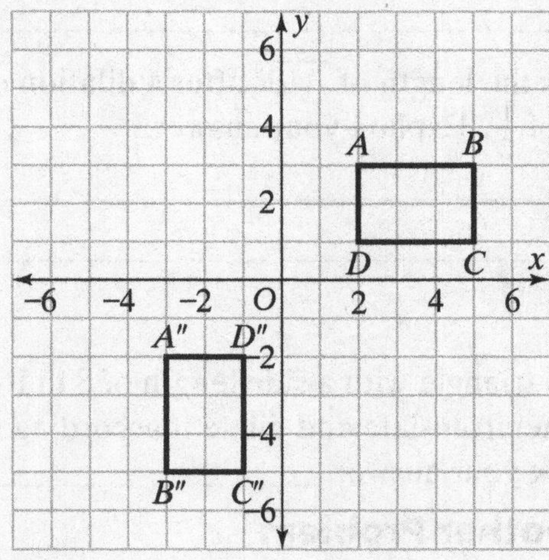

____

____

Name ______________________ Class ______________ Date ______________

13-6 • Guided Problem Solving

GPS Student Page 525, Exercise 13:

A translation 6 units down followed by a dilation with scale factor $\frac{1}{2}$ maps $\triangle ABC$ onto $\triangle A''B''C''$. If $\overline{AB} = 8$ units, what is the length of $\overline{A''B''}$?

Understand

1. What is a translation?

____

____

2. What is a dilation?

____

____

3. What is a scale factor?

____

____

4. What are you asked to determine in the problem?

____

Plan and Carry Out

5. Let $\triangle A'B'C'$ be the image after the translation but before the dilation. What is the length of $\overline{A'B'}$ after a translation of $\triangle ABC$ 6 units down? Explain your answer.

____

____

6. What is the length of $\overline{A''B''}$ after a dilation of $\triangle A'B'$ with a scale factor of $\frac{1}{2}$? Explain your answer.

____

____

Check

7. Draw a triangle with a side length of 8 units on a coordinate grid. Then translate and dilate it according to the directions to check your answer. _______________

Solve Another Problem

8. A reflection across the y-axis is followed by a dilation with scale factor $\frac{1}{3}$ maps $\triangle ABC$ onto $\triangle A''B''C''$. If $AB = 15$ units, what is the length of $\overline{A''B''}$? _______________

Name ____________________ Class ____________ Date ____________

13A: Graphic Organizer

For use before Lesson 13-1

Study Skill Many skills build on each other. Before you begin a new lesson, do a quick review of the material covered in earlier lessons. Ask for help if there are any concepts you did not understand.

Write your answers.

1. What is the chapter title? ____________________
2. How many lessons are there in this chapter? ____________________
3. What is the topic of the Test-Taking Strategies page? ____________________
4. Complete the graphic organizer below as you work through the chapter.
   - In the center, write the title of the chapter.
   - When you begin a lesson, write the lesson name in a rectangle.
   - When you complete a lesson, write a skill or key concept in a circle linked to that lesson block.
   - When you complete the chapter, use this graphic organizer to help you review.

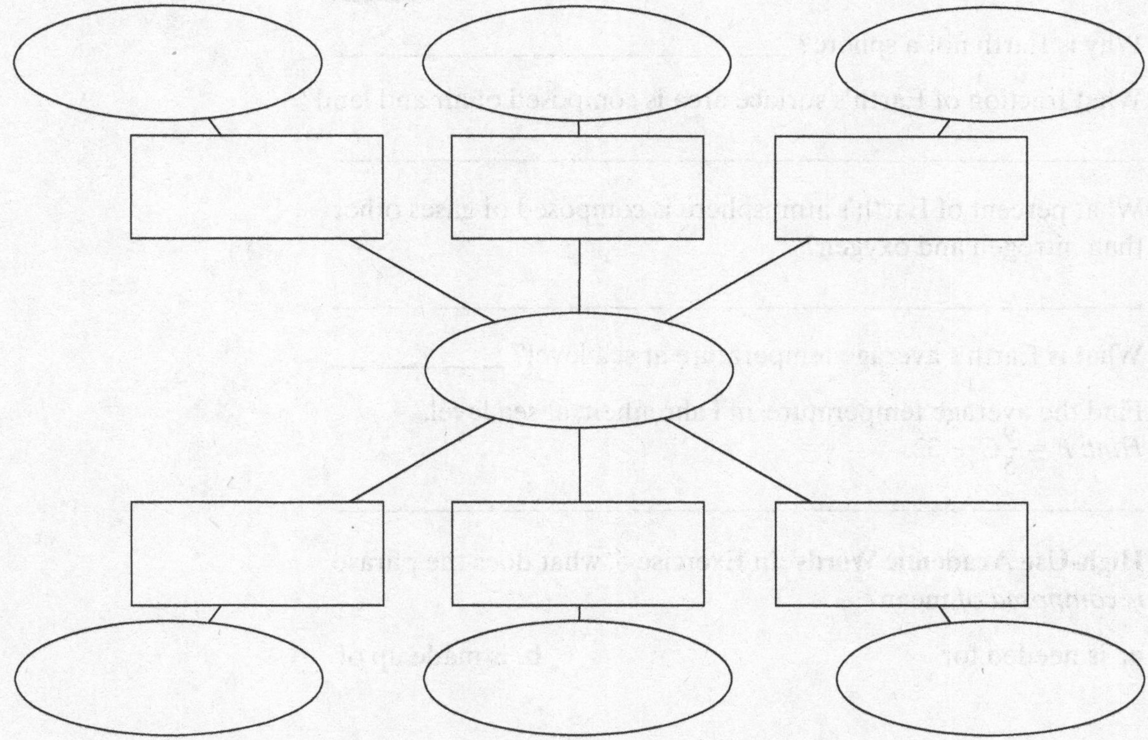

Name ____________________ Class ____________ Date ____________

13B: Reading Comprehension

For use after Lesson 13-3

Study Skill Read problems carefully. Pay special attention to units when working with measurements.

Read the paragraph below and answer the questions.

Earth has an average diameter of 7,926.2 miles. It is not a sphere, since it bulges slightly at the equator. Of the nine major planets in our solar system, Earth is the middle planet in average diameter. The composition of the Earth's surface area is 70% water and 30% air and land. The atmosphere is composed of 78% nitrogen, 21% oxygen, and a mixture of several other gases. The average temperature at sea level is 15°C. The Earth is about 93 million miles from the sun.

1. What is the paragraph about?

   ____

2. What is Earth's radius?

   ____

3. How many planets have smaller diameters than Earth? ________

4. Why is Earth not a sphere? ____________________

5. What fraction of Earth's surface area is composed of air and land?

   ____

6. What percent of Earth's atmosphere is composed of gases other than nitrogen and oxygen?

   ____

7. What is Earth's average temperature at sea level? ________

8. Find the average temperature, in Fahrenheit, at sea level. *Hint:* $F = \frac{9}{5}C + 32$.

   ____

9. **High-Use Academic Words** In Exercise 5, what does the phrase *is composed of* mean?

   a. is needed for

   b. is made up of

Name ______________________ Class ______________________ Date ______________________

13C: Reading/Writing Math Symbols

For use after Lesson 13-5

Study Skill Use a notebook or a section of a loose-leaf binder for homework assignments.

Write a mathematical statement of expression for each word description.

1. Six and six hundredths percent

____

2. Triangle XYZ is similar to triangle ABC.

____

3. Thirty-nine percent is approximately equal to four tenths.

____

4. Angle G is congruent to angle K.

____

5. One fourth equals twenty-five percent.

____

6. Five elevenths is greater than 45 percent.

____

In the diagram below, $\triangle ABC \cong \triangle A'B'C'$. Use the diagram to write the meaning of each mathematical statement.

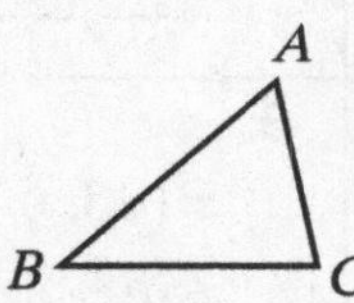

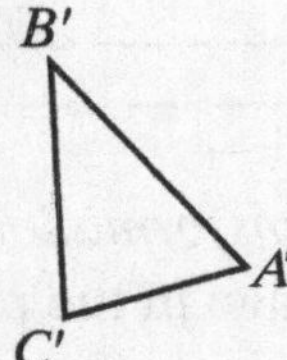

7. $\overline{AC}$ ______________________

8. $\overrightarrow{CB}$ ______________________

9. A' ______________________

10. $\angle B'$ ______________________

11. $\overline{AC} \cong \overline{A'C'}$ ______________________

Vocabulary and Study Skills

Name ______________________ Class ______________ Date ____________

13D: Visual Vocabulary Practice

For use after Lesson 13-6

High-Use Academic Words

Study Skill If a word is not in the glossary, use a dictionary to find its meaning.

Concept List

sum	table	estimate
evaluate	solve	define
order	equivalent	compare

Write the concept that best describes each exercise. Choose from the concept list above.

1.

$\frac{z}{8} = 7 - 2$

$\frac{z}{8} \times 8 = (7 - 2) \times 8$

$z = 5 \times 8$

$z = 40$

____

2.

The World's Longest Rivers

Name	Country	Length
Nile	Egypt	4,160 mi
Amazon	Brazil	4,000 mi
Yangtze	China	3,964 mi

____

3.

$7\frac{1}{6}$ and $7.1\overline{6}$

____

4.

$|-28| > 27$

____

5.

$3a + 6 + (-4.25) + (-a) + 7$

$= 2a + 8.75$

____

6.

$4n - (9 \div m)$ for $n = -3$

and $m = 7$

____

7.

$x + 29\frac{5}{8} = 42\frac{1}{9}$

$x + 30 \approx 42$

$x \approx 12$

____

8.

A *transformation* is a change in the position, shape, or size of a figure.

____

9.

$-10.1, 6.7, -10\frac{2}{3}, -4, 7.8$

$-10\frac{2}{3}, -10.1, -4, 6.7, 7.8$

____

Name ____________________ Class ____________ Date ____________

13E: Vocabulary Check

For use after Lesson 13-6

Study Skill Strengthen your vocabulary. Use these pages and add cues and summaries by applying the Cornell Notetaking style.

Write the definition for each word or term at the right. To check your work, fold the paper back along the dotted line to see the correct answers.

____________________	reflectional symmetry
____________________	rotation
____________________	transformation
____________________	translation
____________________	dilation

Vocabulary and Study Skills

Name ______________________ Class ______________ Date ____________

13E: Vocabulary Check (continued)

For use after Lesson 13-6

Write the vocabulary word or term for each definition. To check your work, fold the paper back along the dotted line to see the correct answers.

when a figure can be reflected over a line so that its image matches the original ______________________

a transformation that turns a figure about a fixed point ______________________

a change in position, shape, or size of a figure ______________________

a transformation that moves each point of a figure the same distance and in the same direction ______________________

a transformation in which the figure and its image are similar ______________________

Name ______________________ Class ______________ Date ______________

13F: Vocabulary Review

For use with the Chapter Review

Study Skill Some concepts are very difficult to grasp on your own. If you pay attention in class, you can ask questions about concepts you do not understand.

Vocabulary and Study Skills

I. Match the term in Column A with its definition in Column B.

Column A	Column B
1. angle of rotation	**A.** a figure is flipped over this
2. center of rotation	**B.** when a figure can be flipped over a line and match its original figure
3. line of reflection	**C.** when a figure can be rotated 180° or less and exactly match its original figure
4. scale factor	**D.** the number of degrees a figure rotates
5. reflectional symmetry	**E.** the ratio of a length in an image to the corresponding length in the original figure
6. rotational symmetry	**F.** a fixed point from which a figure is rotated

II. Match the term in Column A with its definition in Column B.

Column A	Column B
1. enlargement	**A.** a transformation that moves each point of a figure the same distance and in the same direction
2. transformation	**B.** a dilation with a scale factor less than 1
3. dilation	**C.** a transformation that flips a figure over a line
4. image	**D.** a dilation with a scale factor greater than 1
5. translation	**E.** the figure after a transformation
6. reduction	**F.** a transformation that turns a figure
7. rotation	**G.** a transformation in which a figure and its image are similar
8. reflection	**H.** a change in the position, shape, or size of a figure

Name ____________________ Class ____________ Date ____________

Practice A-1

The Pythagorean Theorem

Find the length of the hypotenuse of each triangle. If necessary, round to the nearest tenth.

1. 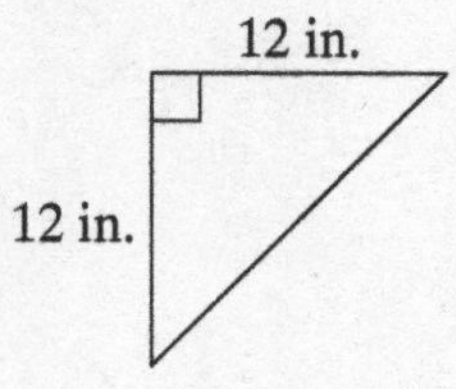

____

2. 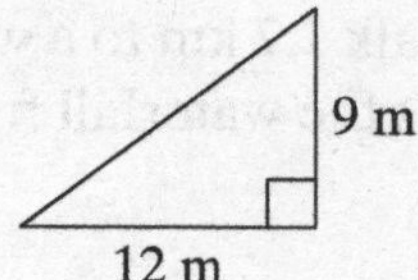

____

3. 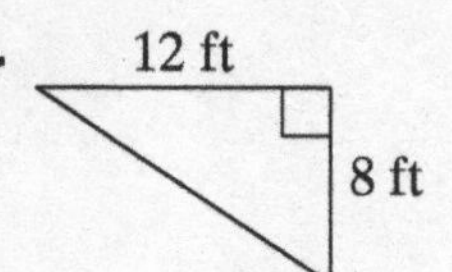

____

4. 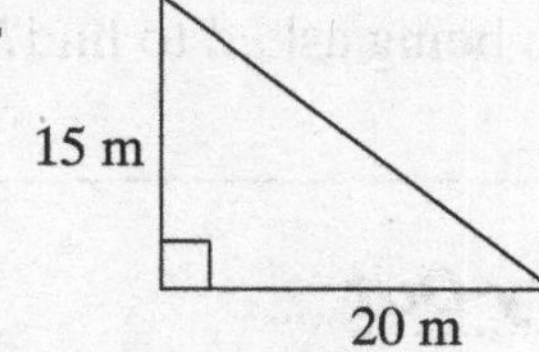

____

Let *a* and *b* represent the lengths of the legs of a right triangle. Find the length of the hypotenuse. If necessary, round to the nearest tenth.

5. $a = 14, b = 18$ ______________

6. $a = 7, b = 23$ ______________

7. $a = 15, b = 8$ ______________

Solve.

8. A circus performer walks on a tightrope 25 feet above the ground. The tightrope is supported by two beams and two support cables. If the distance between each beam and the base of its support cable is 15 feet, what is the length of the support cable? Round to the nearest foot.

____

You are given three circles, as shown. Points *A*, *B*, *C*, *D*, *E*, *F*, and *G* lie on the same line. Find each length to the nearest tenth.

9. *HD* ______________

10. *IE* ______________

11. *JD* ______________

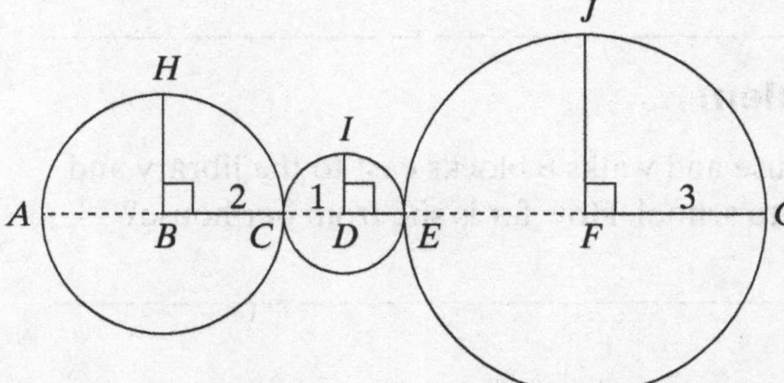

Name ______________________ Class ______________ Date ______________

A-1 • Guided Problem Solving

GPS Student Page 541, Exercise 20:

Two hikers start a trip from a camp walking 1.5 km due east. They turn due north and walk 1.7 km to a waterfall. To the nearest tenth of a kilometer, how far is the waterfall from the camp?

Understand

1. Distances are given for walking in which two directions?

____

2. What are you being asked to find?

____

Plan and Carry Out

3. Draw a picture.
4. Write the formula for the Pythagorean Theorem. ______________
5. What part of the triangle has a missing length? ______________
6. Substitute known values into the Pythagorean Theorem.

____

7. Simplify. ______________________________________
8. Add. ____
9. Find the positive square root of the hypotenuse, the missing length.

____

10. Estimate, or simplify, using a calculator. ______________
11. How far is the waterfall from the camp? ______________

Check

12. Is your answer reasonable? Use mental math to check.

____

Solve Another Problem

13. Leah starts at her house and walks 8 blocks east to the library and then 12 blocks south to school. How far is she from her house?

____

Name ______________________ Class ______________ Date ______________

Practice A-2

Using The Pythagorean Theorem

Find the missing leg length. If necessary, round the answer to the nearest tenth.

1.

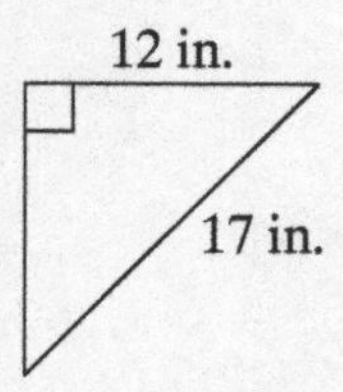

____

2.

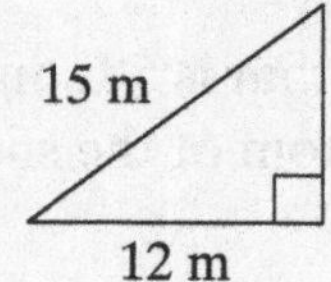

____

3.

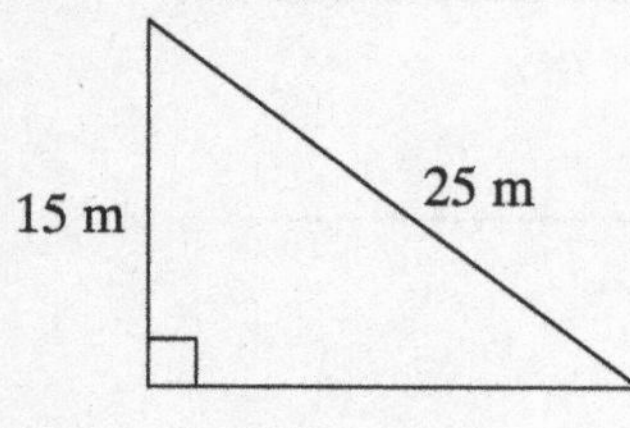

____

4.

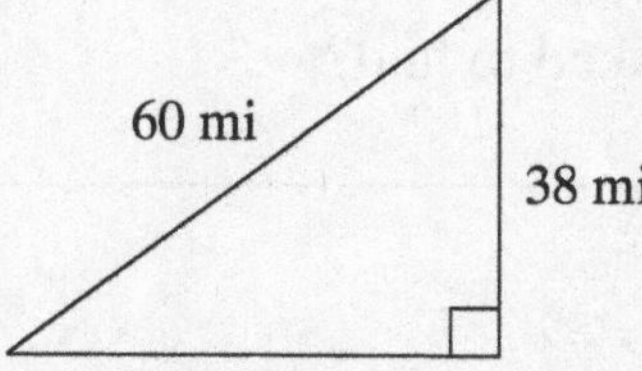

____

For Exercises 5–14, *a* and *b* represent leg lengths and *c* represents the length of the hypotenuse. Find the missing leg length. If necessary, round to the nearest tenth.

5. $a = 8$ cm, $c = 12$ cm

____

6. $b = 9$ in., $c = 15$ in.

____

7. $b = 5$ m, $c = 25$ m

____

8. $a = 36$ in., $c = 39$ in.

____

9. $a = 10$ m, $c = 20$ m

____

10. $b = 24$ mm, $c = 25$ mm

____

11. $a = 9$ yd, $c = 41$ yd

____

12. $b = 10$ cm, $c = 26$ cm

____

13. $b = 27$ yd, $c = 130$ yd

____

14. $a = 11$ mi, $c = 61$ mi

____

15. One leg of a right triangle is 4 ft long and the hypotenuse is 5 ft long. Ritchie uses $\sqrt{4^2 + 5^2}$ to find the length of the other leg. Is Ritchie correct in his approach? Why or why not?

____

____

____

Name ______________________ Class ______________________ Date ____________

A-2 • Guided Problem Solving

GPS Student Page 545, Exercise 13:

A 10-ft-long slide is attached to a deck that is 5 ft high. Find the distance from the bottom of the deck to the bottom of the slide to the nearest tenth.

Understand

1. What two lengths are given in the problem?

   ____

2. What are you being asked to find?

   ____

Plan and Carry Out

3. Draw a picture of the slide, deck, and ground.
4. What kind of a triangle is formed by the picture? ______________
5. Is the unknown length a leg or hypotenuse of the triangle? ______________
6. Write down the formula for the Pythagorean Theorem. ______________
7. Substitute values from your picture into the Pythagorean Theorem. ______________
8. Simplify. ______________
9. Use a calculator to find the square root. Round to the nearest tenth. ______________
10. What is the distance from the bottom of the deck to the bottom of the slide?

    ____

Check

11. Use the Pythagorean Theorem to check the length of the slide based on your answer, and the height of the deck. Is your answer the same as the given slide length? Why or why not?

    ____

    ____

Solve Another Problem

12. Mason is on the southwest corner of a 90° intersection. One street in the intersection is 23 ft wide. If Mason crosses diagonally to the northeast corner, he will walk 34 ft. Find the width of the other street. If necessary, round your answer to the nearest tenth.

    ____

Name ______________________ Class ______________ Date ____________

Practice A-3

Converse of the Pythagorean Theorem

Is it possible to construct a triangle with the given side lengths? Explain.

1. 2 yd, 3 yd, 7 yd
2. 4 cm, 4 cm, 8 cm
3. 12 ft, 14 ft, 15 ft

4. 5.4 m, 8.6 m, 13 m
5. $\frac{4}{5}$ in., $3\frac{2}{5}$ in., 4 in.
6. 18 mm, 25 mm, 52 mm

Determine whether the given lengths can be side lengths of a right triangle. Explain.

7. 6 ft, 10 ft, 12 ft
8. 10 in., 24 in., 26 in.
9. 20 m, 21 m, 29 m

10. 15 cm, 17 cm, 21 cm
11. 14 ft, 22.5 ft, 26.5 ft
12. 12 yd, 35 yd, 38 yd

Determine whether the triangles are right triangles. Explain.

13.

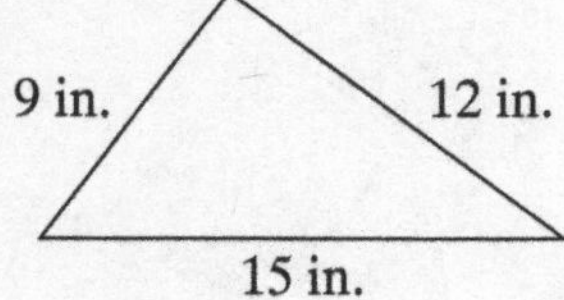

14.

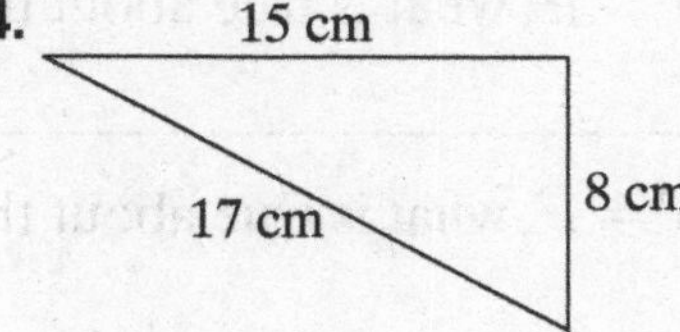

15. A company is designing a new logo in the shape of a triangle. Two of the sides each measure 2 cm. Which of the following is a possible measure for the third side: 3 cm, 4 cm, 5 cm?

16. Three nature trails intersect to form a triangle around a park. The lengths of the trails are 2.8 mi, 3.2 mi, and 4.1 mi. Do the trails form a right triangle? Explain.

17. The sides of a triangular game board are 1 ft, 1 ft, and $\sqrt{2}$ ft in length. Is the game board in the shape of a right triangle? Explain.

18. How do you know that the lengths 6 in., 8 in., and 25 in. cannot form a right triangle without using the Converse of the Pythagorean Theorem?

Name ______________________ Class ______________ Date ______________

A-3 • Converse of the Pythagorean Theorem

Student Page 550, Exercise 27:

You can use the squares of the lengths of the sides of a triangle to find whether the triangle is acute or obtuse.

If $a^2 + b^2 < c^2$, then the triangle is obtuse.
If $a^2 + b^2 > c^2$, then the triangle is acute.

In both cases, c represents the length of the longest side of the triangle. The lengths of the sides of a triangle are 5 m, 6 m, and 7 m. Is the triangle *acute*, *right*, or *obtuse*?

Understand

1. What are you being asked to do?

____

____

2. If $a^2 + b^2 < c^2$, what is true about the triangle?

____

3. If $a^2 + b^2 > c^2$, what is true about the triangle?

____

4. If $a^2 + b^2 = c^2$, what is true about the triangle?

____

Plan and Carry Out

5. Write the values for a, b, and c. ______________
6. What is the value for $a^2 + b^2$? ______________
7. What is the value for c^2? ______________
8. Compare the values for $a^2 + b^2$ and c^2. $a^2 + b^2$ ____ c^2
9. Is the triangle *acute*, *right*, or *obtuse*? ______________

Check

10. How can you check your answer? ______________

____

Solve Another Problem

11. The lengths of the sides of a triangle are 6 cm, 24 cm, and 25 cm. Is the triangle *acute*, *right*, or *obtuse*? ______________

Name ____________ Class ____________ Date ____________

Practice A-4

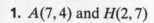

Distance in the Coordinate Plane

Find the distance between each pair of points. If necessary, round to the nearest tenth.

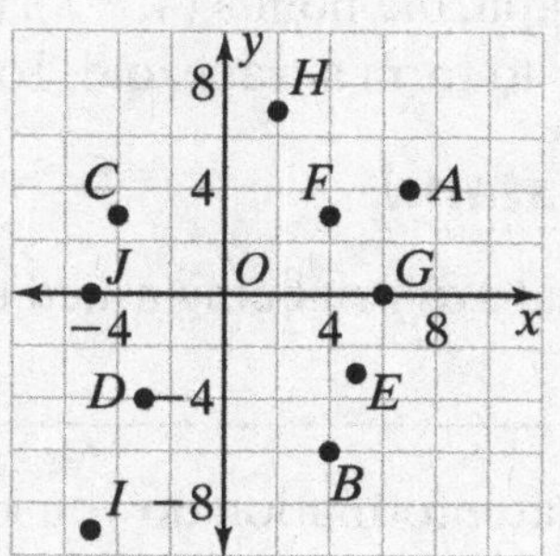

1. $A(7, 4)$ and $H(2, 7)$

____

2. $C(-4, 3)$ and $G(6, 0)$

____

3. $B(4, -6)$ and $D(-3, -4)$

____

4. $E(5, -3)$ and $C(-4, 3)$

____

5. $F(4, 3)$ and $G(6, 0)$

____

6. $A(7, 4)$ and $D(-3, -4)$

____

7. $B(4, -6)$ and $I(-5, -9)$

____

8. $E(5, -3)$ and $F(4, 3)$

____

9. Arnie plotted points on the graph on the right. He placed his pencil point at A. He can move either right or down any whole number of units until he reaches point B. In how many ways can he do this?

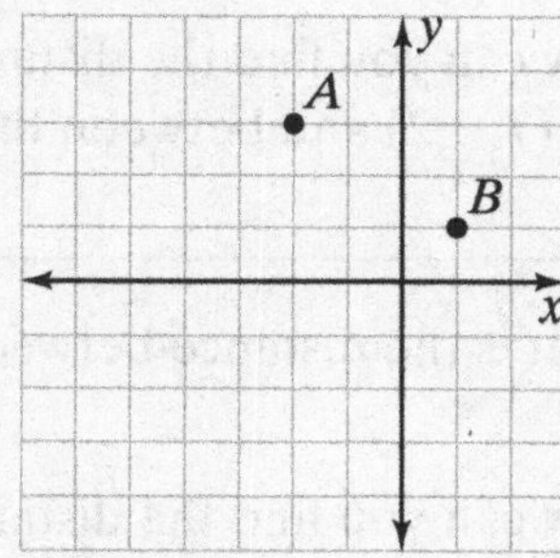

____

10. Marika had to draw ΔABC that fit several requirements.
    a. It must fit in the box shown.
    b. The endpoints of $\overline{AB}$ have coordinates $A(-2, 0)$ and $B(2, 0)$.
    c. Point C must be on the y-axis and its y-coordinate is an integer.

    Name all the points that could be point C.

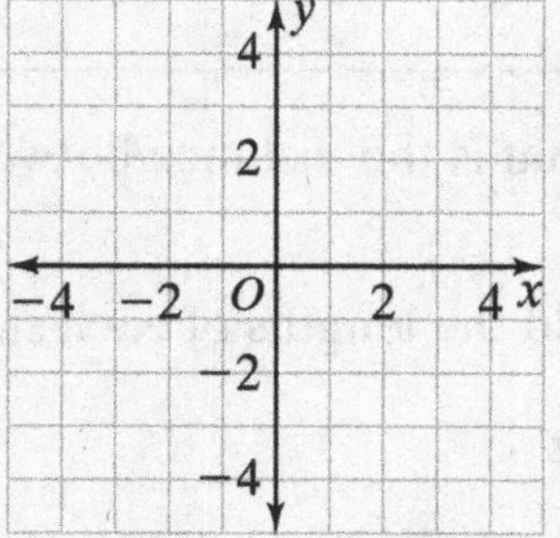

____

____

____

Name ______________________________ Class ____________________ Date ____________________

A-4 • Guided Problem Solving

GPS Student Page 555, Exercise 15:

On a graph, the points (4, −2), (7, −2), (9, −5), and (2, −5) are connected in order to form a trapezoid. To the nearest tenth, what is its perimeter?

Understand

1. What are you being asked to do?

____

2. What information do you know?

____

Plan and Carry Out

3. Plot the points on the graph.
4. How can you find the distance between points (4, −2) and (7, −2) and between the points (2, −5) and (9, −5)?

____

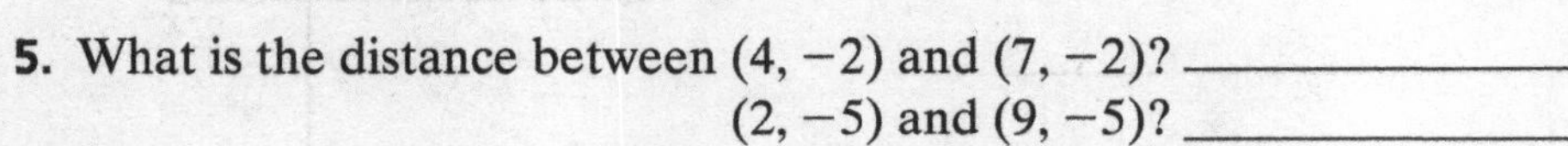

5. What is the distance between (4, −2) and (7, −2)? ____________
   (2, −5) and (9, −5)? ____________
6. How can you find the distance between points (4, −2) and (2, −5) and between the points (7, −2) and (9, −5)?

____

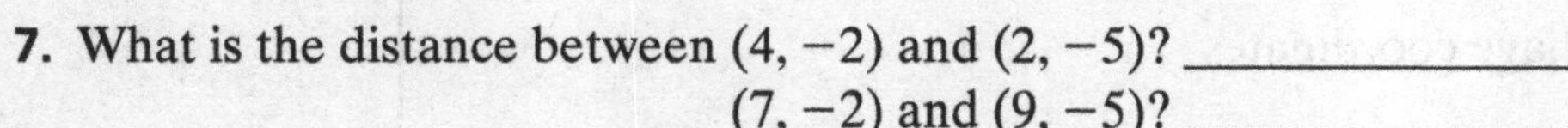

7. What is the distance between (4, −2) and (2, −5)? ____________
   (7, −2) and (9, −5)? ____________
8. Add the lengths of each side. What is the perimeter? ____________

Check

9. Is every point plotted correctly to create the figure?

____

Solve Another Problem

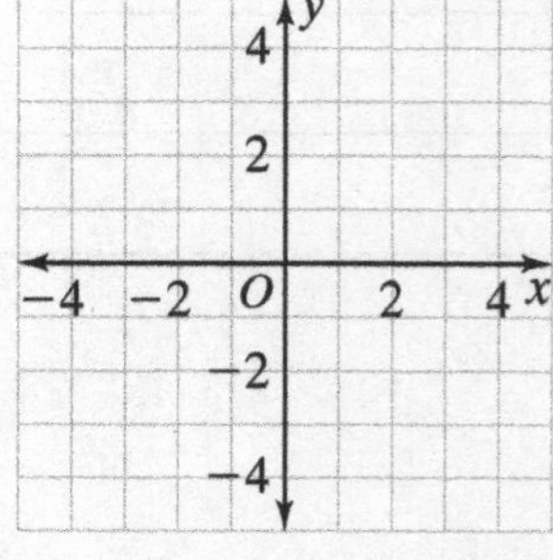

10. Plot the following points on the grid at the right. Connect the points in order, connecting the last point to the first. What is the perimeter of the shape formed? (−3, −3), (3, −3), (4, 2), (−4, 2)

____